The Scottish Gliding Union

A History

1934 - 2008

by

Ian Easson

ISBN: 978-0-9560820-0-8

Published by IKE Publishing
Printed by Dolman Scott Ltd

Acknowledgements

I would like to thank everyone who has helped in the production of this book. From those intrepid aviators who had the foresight to record their flights and experiences, to the everyday club members who encouraged and inspired me to complete this work. In particular, I would like to thank the editors, past and present, of the international gliding magazine, *Sailplane & Gliding*, who have very kindly allowed me to reprint some of the stories that had long since disappeared from our club archives. In addition I would like to thank the numerous club members who have supplied me with photographs and material, some of which were of the highest standard. I would especially like to thank Derek Piggott for agreeing to write the Foreword and, finally, I would like to thank everyone who has contributed to the club magazine, *Portmoak Press*, over the years as their stories provided the idea for this book in the first place.

Contents

FOREWORD

On the 30th August 2007, a flight of 1540 Km., nearly 1000 miles, was made by John Williams, a member of the Scottish Gliding Union, flying to and fro across Scotland, surprising everyone, perhaps even himself. This was by far the longest soaring flight ever made in the U.K. and put Portmoak, the home of the Scottish Gliding Union on the map and recognised world wide, as a premier gliding site. The flight was made possible by using wave lift and flying at 20,000 feet. By flying so high in the rarefied air, he gained almost 35% in speed and so could go further compared with flying at sea level. The flight took 10½ hrs. and he averaged about 80 knots, 90 m.p.h.

This book takes us through nearly 75 years of the SGU from 1934 to 2008 when gliding was developing from Primary gliders making hops timed in seconds, to John Williams's epic soaring flight in his Antares electric Self Launching Motor Glider in 2007. It is also packed full of interesting details of members' exploits.

The Scottish Gliding Union began in Glasgow with a few members and moved around flying from different places in their early days. They finally found Portmoak and moved there in 1957. This site had many advantages. There are two nearby hills, the Bishop and Benarty, offering ridge lift and wave conditions in several different wind directions. There is plenty of room for launches and landings and it is close to the capital, Edinburgh, and in beautiful countryside with Loch Leven adjoining the field and making a good landmark for early solo pilots. What a find – meeting all these requirements

I have happy memories of expeditions from my own club at Lasham in Hampshire as flying at Portmoak extended our soaring season into October after the summer thermals faded. We would go to explore the wave and hopefully to fly very high for International badge qualifications. Most of us didn't really take cross country flying seriously over such mountainous terrain and with the coast so close on both sides of Scotland.

However, one of our pilots, Alan Purnell, who used to lead our expeditions to Scotland, was one of the first to fly long distance cross country flights from Portmoak using wave in the 70's. The SGU pilots showed us the potential of the site for record attempts so that now our pilots go to Scotland to fly for both height and distance flights in the powerful waves over the mountains.

Often our expeditions would be fruitless because of bad weather, but once a pilot had flown in wave, they always came back for more. The magic of flying for hours in silky smooth air, without having to make more than slight movements on the controls for minutes on end, makes the experience unique and unforgettable.

It was usual to have several days of rain or low cloud before the weather became flyable and this made a special bond between all who flew there, or so I thought. Perhaps it was really the delicious Malt Whisky. Each achievement called for a celebration and everyone joined in so that we made many friends amongst the club pilots and instructors.

The Club pioneered giving glider training to several groups who would not normally have been able to glide. Members started a group known as "Walking on Air" with a two-seater glider specially fitted with an additional hand control to replace the rudder pedals so that people with physical disabilities, and normally confined to wheel chairs, can learn to fly gliders. A few years ago I flew with them in a Regional Competition at the Cambridge Club to introduce them to cross country flying. Several had already made their first solos and their enthusiasm was infectious. It was a real pleasure to fly with them and share their excitement at making their first field landings. Since that time many other British clubs have followed their lead and teach on similar gliders fitted with hand controls.

The SGU has for many years encouraged university students from both the Strathclyde and Edinburgh University to try gliding and now they have their own instructors to fly with their student members. The club also runs a Cadet scheme for younger boys and girls to enable them to learn to fly at especially low rates.

Reading some of the anecdotes in the book reminded me of being present and involved at the time and brought back very real memories.

One of the accounts that I remember vividly was Nick Goodhart's epic goal flight from Lasham to Portmoak in the 1959 National Championships in his Skylark 3. Who knows what possessed him to declare Scotland! I don't think he really believed he would get that far and none of us knew of his declaration at the time. On this flight of 360 miles, he used thermals, storm clouds, hill lift and finally wave lift to complete the flight. That day I was flying in the same competition with Nick and also Anne Burns, Phillip Wills, John Williamson and numerous other names which are now legendary.

Like Nick, I fell out of the sky and needed to take a second launch before I could get away from Lasham. I was making good progress but after about 4 hours I was forced down by the effects of a large thunderstorm near Sheffield whilst he made use of it, collecting ice on the way. My retrieve crew got me back to Lasham early the next morning but it took two days hard driving to get Nick and the glider back from Portmoak and the Championships were held up until he was back and ready to fly again.

In those days of free distance flights and no radios, there was an art in retrieving. The crews would set out in which ever direction the pilot was expected to go and had enough knowledge of the conditions to anticipate which road to take. Except for London, there were almost no airspace problems so gliders followed the weather. The retrieve crews knew which roadside telephones they could stop at with a trailer and would periodically phone back to base to find out if and where their pilot had landed. When the pilot finally landed, this method shortened the time of getting to him. After de-rigging and packing the trailer, my crew would drive back a bit, stop and brew up some food. Then I would sleep in the back of the car, arriving at Lasham at about 2 a.m. That was a good day and an efficient retrieve. Talking of distance retrieves, in one week during a competition three tasks were set into Cornwall and North Devon and I had three retrieves from there. Remember, in those days there were no decent roads and it seemed to take forever trailing a glider up and down hills along the winding roads with what would now be a vintage car.

Not long after this, free distance flights were dropped from the list of competition tasks, and out and return and closed circuit flights were encouraged to avoid the expense and exhaustion of such long retrieves.

I was also present at Lasham when SGU Director, Tom Docherty had been flying in our competition and decided to stay on afterwards. He had planned a cross channel flight with a view to covering more distance and waited for the appropriate promising conditions. He was ready when the cold front went through leaving a northerly wind and the promise of good soaring conditions. Knowing that a high cloud base was essential to glide over the channel and that there was no hope of finding any lift over the sea, to increase his distance flown, he chose to fly upwind to Cambridge first and then on to Dover in the early afternoon by which time the cloud base had risen to 5000 feet making the crossing safer. He was able to reach good soaring conditions over France and soared down to beyond Paris before landing on an airfield having covered 666 Km. He was aero towed back to Lasham the next day.

The book shows that glider pilots are a willing and co-operative breed. This is probably because gliding has always been a labour intensive sport in which the members shared the work. Just to launch a glider by winch or tow plane involves at least four or five helpers. This need for co-operation encourages a close knit community where the members all help each other and also contribute towards the running of the club. Through the National and International gliding badge awards, gliding also fosters a competitive spirit and at every stage of ability there is an incentive to achieve the next goal.

I have shown that many pilots are pioneers like Nick Goodhart, both in their flights and in the way they care about the movement. Since the early days, Philip Wills and the BGA fought to give the gliding independence from the Aviation Authorities so that we could regulate and supervise the sport ourselves. This freedom was won and, as an organisation, we are proud to have done this responsibly and successfully up until now.

Sadly, being integrated into the EASA (European Aviation Safety Agency) we have lost control and our independence. We are already being over-burdened with new and unnecessary regulations and bureaucracy. These do nothing to advance our sport and only hinder it and kill the pioneering spirit which the sport has nurtured and encouraged for so long. It will also increase the cost of all gliding and other recreational flying. However, my faith in the gliding fraternity gives me the confidence to believe that the gliding movement will continue to thrive.

This is an important book, because as well as being a record of what has happened at the club, it also focuses on the history of the sport of gliding. It will show future glider pilots what learning to glide was like as a member in the early days and how things developed over the years.

Reading this book has made me re-live my gliding years from the early 1950's to date. I have been involved in various aspects of the development of gliding, particularly developing gliding instruction, testing and ensuring that gliders coming into the U.K. were safe to fly and, of course, competition flying. I congratulate the writer and hope you will enjoy the book as much as I have.

Wishing you many happy landings.

Derek Piggott M.B.E. HonCRAeS

Introduction

When I first thought about writing this book I had been the editor of the Scottish Gliding Union club magazine *Portmoak Press* for about two years and I particularly enjoyed uncovering tales of epic flights from those far-off days. I spent many an enjoyable hour with some of those more experienced club members who were only too willing to regale stories of their epic flights.

In the main, this book is a collection of stories from those intrepid glider pilots who have soared the Scottish skies over the last seventy-five years, although the first couple tried it long before the Scottish Gliding Union was even thought of. I hope you get as much enjoyment from reading this book as I got from writing it.

I feel it is important to record historic information from various sources including, in some cases, obituaries, as these have contained factual information that would otherwise go unrecorded.

As you would expect, no history is complete without the facts and figures but I have tried to keep these to a minimum.

So, let's start at the beginning…

Early glider flights in Scotland

History books show that the first recorded 'flight' in Scotland took place in 1507. This flight was performed by an Italian, John Damian, who was the Physician of King James IV and Alchemist to the Scottish Court. He had arranged for a pair of wings to be made and, with these firmly strapped onto his arms, jumped off one of the walls of Stirling Castle – declaring he was off to France. His flight, however, turned out to be a short one. He plummeted to the fields below Castle Rock, lucky to sustain only a broken thigh. As help was being administered, he complained that the person who had made his wings had used chicken feathers instead the eagle feathers that he had specified, and everyone knows that chickens don't fly!

It wasn't until the 1890s that the next pages of Scottish gliding history were written. Born in Bath in 1867, to a Scottish mother and an English father, Percy Pilcher joined the Royal Navy at the age of thirteen. He left when he was twenty and joined the shipbuilding and engineering company of Randolf Elder (later to become Fairfields) of Govan, Glasgow, as an apprentice. In 1894, Percy became an assistant lecturer to Sir John Biles - professor of naval architecture and marine engineering at Glasgow University - as well as working as a draughtsman at what would later become John Brown's shipyard in Clydebank. Percy had developed a keen interest in aeronautics and in 1895, with the help of his sister Ella, he built his first man-carrying hang-glider in the sitting room of his lodgings in Byres

Percy Pilcher

Road, Glasgow. Before attempting to fly his own aircraft, he visited the pioneering aeronautical engineer Otto Lilienthal in Germany, and was allowed to fly Otto's glider.

Brimming with new found confidence, Percy returned to Scotland eager to try out his own design. In June 1895, Percy and Ella took their glider out to Wallacetown Farm, near Cardross in Dunbartonshire, for its test flight. His launch method was simple but effective, and very similar to the modern hang-glider launch methods – run downhill into wind, and jump. As a keen designer and draughtsman, Percy kept detailed records of his test flying and made numerous changes to improve the performance of his flying machines. His first design was the 'Bat', and there soon followed the 'Beetle', 'Gull' and finally the 'Hawk', incorporating the world's first spring under-carriage.

Percy and his sister Ella with "The Bat"

During his later test flights, he received the devastating news that Otto Lilienthal had been killed whilst flying one of his own gliders. This untimely event promoted Scotland's Percy Pilcher to the leader of world aviation. His Hawk glider, although mostly built in Glasgow, was completed and test flown in Eynsford in England when Percy moved to Kent.

Whilst he was demonstrating and test-flying his Hawk, Percy continued to develop new designs. His fifth machine was radically different from the first four inasmuch as this one would include an engine. The engine had been completed and test run and was just waiting to be coupled to the airframe, when Percy was asked, by Lord Braye, to do a demonstration flight of his Hawk at Stamford Hall. The flight took place on 30th

Percy flying his fourth aircraft – The Hawk

September 1899. The weather was very wet and windy and his aircraft became sodden. Percy didn't want to disappoint the spectators so he decided to go up in the 'Hawk'. The first attempt resulted in the parting of the towline, followed by a gentle landing. Early into the second flight, after travelling about 200ft. and gaining only about 30ft., structural failure caused his Hawk to plunge to the ground. His battered body was pulled from the wreckage but he died in hospital two days later, at the age of thirty-two. This earned him the sombre distinction of being the first Briton to be killed in a plane crash.

As part of the centenary of flight celebrations, Glasgow's Lord Provost unveiled a plaque to Percy at Glasgow airport, and a television program renewed debate about whether his plane could have flown. With TV funding, researchers built an aircraft based on Pilcher's plans - with some modifications, including a modern, lightweight engine. It flew for 1 minute and 25 seconds, 26 seconds longer than the Wright brothers managed on their historic day.

Had it not been for his untimely death, Percy Pilcher, engineering lecturer from Glasgow University, might have made the first powered flight in a heavier than air machine, rather than Orville Wright, a bicycle mechanic from Dayton, four years later in 1903.

Chapter 1

Wandering in the Wilderness 1934 – 1937

In Glasgow, in 1934, the place to be "seen in" was one of the many Tea Rooms popular at the time. These usually took four or five floors in elegant buildings in the style of the great Glasgow architect and designer Charles Rennie Mackintosh. Customers could expect to sample fine teas from across the globe, feast upon multi-tier cake stands of pancakes, scones, cake and chocolate biscuits, and were waited upon by ladies in smart black and white uniforms.

So it was, on 7th July 1934 in Miss Buick's Cranston Tea Rooms at 147 West George Street, Glasgow, a collection of gliding enthusiasts met to form the Scottish Gliding Union (SGU). Records don't show how these people were invited to this momentous event but it was obviously not by accident.

The Honourable Alan R. Boyle was elected Chairman, John (Johnny) W. Gardner the Secretary and Hugh M. Berry the Treasurer. The rest of the Board was made up of A.T.H. Tilson, E.T.H. Godfrey and W. Cameron.

During the year, the club progressed steadily along the administration route with occasional sorties into the countryside to look for suitable sites. The first site given serious consideration was Cairnoch Hill in the Campsie Fells, between Carronbridge and Denny, but the proprietor refused to negotiate. One land owner of a flat site at Grangemouth was keen, but his charge of £7 per month was deemed as too expensive [this land later became part of the refinery site at Grangemouth – probably generating considerably more than £7 per month!].

Other activities that year included fixing annual subscriptions at:

Flying Members	£3 3s 6d
Associate Members	£1 1s 0d
Entry Fee (Both)	£0 10s 6d

The Constitution of the Glasgow Gliding Club was adopted and the Board of Directors discussed the possibility of engaging Mr G.E. Collins, from the London Gliding Club, as the SGU instructor. The club also agreed to support the governing body, The British Gliding Association (BGA), in their representations to the Air Ministry over a proposed subsidy for gliding.

The club's second year, 1935, was another busy year with the highlight being the receipt of a BAC Primary Glider, donated by the Crieff Gliding Club. Most weekends were spent visiting possible sites which included: Kilsyth, Denny, Sheriffmuir, North Lethams, Wetherhill near Saline and Fairlie. At these sites ad-hoc board meetings were usually held in someone's car and were not minuted. When they could all get to Glasgow they met in Central Halls, 25 Bath Street. The Honourable Alan Boyle, still Chairman, was appointed as the SGU representative on the BGA Council.

The following year, 1936, was marred by the death of founder member Adam Houston Anderson. He died in the crash of a 'Flying Flea' at Renfrew. There seems to have been more actual gliding during the year, albeit most flights were measured in seconds. Test flights were carried out at Lurg Farm, Gartcarron, near Fintry on 23rd and 24th April in an RFD Primary:

Saturday 23rd April J.W. Gardner 29, 31 and 33 secs.
Sunday 24th April   J.W. Gardner 62 secs.
                     Mr Sinclair   33 secs.

Flying was curtailed on the Sunday when Mr Littlejohn crashed on take-off causing damage to the fuselage and completely writing off the port wing. The pilot and Mr T. Graham received minor head injuries and the aircraft was taken to the rented workshop in Stirling for repairs, estimated at around £20.

The club seemed to have been fairly ambitious in those early years and the cost of equipping it in line with their objectives was estimated at around £4000. Donations totalling £58 13s 6d had been received, including £50 from Lord Weir. Representations for changes to gliding subsidy rules were made to the Secretary of State for Air, Lord Swinton. Grant conditions were:

- Clubs to be Limited Companies.
- Clubs to hold lease of five years tenure of a soaring site.
- Clubs to be affiliated to the BGA and requiring a minimum of 25 members.
- Clubs to submit receipts for expenditure.
- Clubs to have BGA approval of site, ground engineer and flight instructor.

These conditions seemed to have spurred the club on and, on 27th July 1936, agreement was reached to register the SGU as a Limited Company. A suitable site was pursued with vigour and Gartcarron Hill near Fintry was secured for a five-year lease at £15 per annum. All was not well however. The BGA stated that the SGU did not yet merit a subsidy, as none of its members had gained their gliding certificates. A new set of conditions was negotiated, which could result in a 50% subsidy to cover machines, ground improvements, land purchases, hangars and clubhouse. These were the same conditions as before but with the SGU proving that they had the ability to meet the other 50%.

Mr E.C. Gordon was elected honorary member of the SGU and was invited to represent the club at Board level at the BGA. Founder members of the SGU were invited to take out two £1 shares and pay a first Annual Subscription of £1 1s 0d. Ordinary members were offered a single £1 share and asked to pay a £3 3s 0d subscription. Twenty five members were needed to take up the capital offer which had been registered at £200. The landlord of the club workshop in Stirling was asked to defer rental payments until June 1937.

A meeting on 25th April 1937 agreed on the appointment of Ada Dunlop as Flying Instructor and Reginald Brazier as Ground Engineer, with the flight instructor having seniority over the ground engineer. A committee, consisting of A.Aitken, T.Graham, J.Campbell and D. Campbell, K. Martin and W.R. Orme, was formed to arrange the erection of a hangar at Gartcarron Hill. A proposal was made that Johnny Gardner should attempt a demonstration soaring flight at Gartcarron Hill using the Campbell brothers' "Hols der Teufel" sailplane.

At around this time, another band of gliding enthusiasts was looking to quench its thirst. On Monday 12th July, at 7:30 p.m., the inaugural meeting of the Fifeshire Gliding Club (FGC) took place in the Rialto Tea Room in Kirkcaldy. By the 24th September the FGC had been established with Andrew J. Thorburn, Henry W. Thorburn, Alex M. Aitken, R.S. Miller, Andrew B. Rutherford and William Neith holding office. Their early training flights had been attempted in a field near Kirkcaldy but operations were soon moved to West Feal Farm on the Lomond Hills. The owners, Mr and Mrs Nicol, were very enthusiastic and supportive even going as far as allowing their farmhouse to be used for meetings and meals.

Towards the end of the year, office bearers from the SGU and the FGC met in Central Hall in Glasgow and agreed to consider the merger of these two clubs as part of the Limited Company. Following the resignation of Johnny Gardner as Secretary, a provisional Board of Directors was elected. Although administrative activities had been going on during the previous years, it was this merging of these two clubs, and particularly, as we shall see later, the flying leadership of Andrew Thorburn that was to be seen as the true beginning of the SGU in the early months of 1938.

Chapter 2

The Club Takes Off 1938 – 1941

Easter weekend 1938 saw Andrew Thorburn eager to take to the air in his Falcon. As this would involve flying an unfamiliar machine from untried sites, he wisely invited his friend John Wordsworth, an instructor at Sutton Bank, to come and assist him. As is customary for gliding expeditions, the weather was not exactly what had been hoped for and, instead of a nice steady westerly, they had to make do with a somewhat fitful northerly. This necessitated a launch point on the north face of the Lomond Hills, at a point known as Laird's Faulds (O/S ref. NO 217 072), about one kilometre north west of the car park on the A912 Leslie - Falkland road.

An early bungee launch off Bishop Hill

Launched by bungee, John Wordsworth managed a flight of about 20 minutes late on Saturday 16th April, and an hour on the following day. Landings were made in a field next to Kilgour farm, at the foot of the ridge (O/S ref. NO 222 082) . There is no record of what, if any, flying was done by Andrew himself, and it is possible that he failed to soar due to the tricky conditions. We know nowadays that this ridge does not work too well that far east, and it is even possible that there may have been some wave interference from time to time.

I'm sure many of today's glider pilots who have visited the SGU's present site at Portmoak are familiar with the 'Bowl' on Bishop Hill, but I wonder if they know that the first soaring flight from the Bowl was made away back in June 1938!

Having visited the SGU site at Gartcarron Hill, and not thinking much of it, Andrew Thorburn invited some of their members to come and inspect the possibilities of the Lomonds, and when they came on Sunday 5th June, he was at last fortunate to have a good westerly wind. Launched from White Craigs (O/S ref. NO 840 034), at the south end of the bowl on Bishop Hill at 17.05, he flew for 1 hour 16 minutes and reached a reported height of 3000 ft., although it is not clear whether this was above sea level or above the 1100ft launch point. He finally landed about a mile further east in a field adjacent to West Feal farm (O/S ref. NO 201 034), which he had already selected as the training site for the Fife club.

The visitors from the SGU were impressed — so much so that they were back the following weekend, training with the Fife club at West Feal. Things moved pretty quickly thereafter. Gartcarron Hill was abandoned, and the amalgamation between the SGU and the Fifeshire GC was finalised. Also included in the merger was the Dumbarton Gliding Club, whose instigators, John and Donald Campbell, had previously become impatient with the lack of progress made by the SGU. The new organisation was incorporated as The Scottish Gliding Union Limited on 15th July 1938, with the liability of each member limited by guarantee to one shilling.

The first Board of Directors of the new SGU Ltd. were:

President and Chairman	Alan R. Boyle
Vice Chairman	W.R. Orme
Secretary	R.B. Rogerson
Treasurer	A.T.H. Tilson
Chief Flying Instructor	Andrew J. Thorburn
Ground Engineer	T.P. Graham
Public Relations Officer	John .W. Gardner

Joint operations started at West Feal late in the year with around 20 FGC members and 15 SGU members taking part. Word had spread around gliding circles that the SGU site held many possibilities and distinguished guests soon turned up to sample the delights of Scottish soaring. Visitors included Ann Edmonds (later Welch) with a Grunau Baby and the then holder of the World Two-seater gliding record, W. Bentley-Murray with a Falcon 3 two-seater. J. Davie of the Cambridge Gliding Club also visited with his Hutter H.17. These visits coincided with the club's most recent acquisition, its first winch, from the defunct Hartlepool club. This consisted of a large Studebaker saloon car which would be jacked up and have one rear wheel replaced by a drum of cable. It is not clear if there was even any form of pay-on gear, but the device seems to have been effective enough to launch gliders into the lift from the top of the hill.

Saturday 20th and Sunday 21st August saw several soaring flights, including club members, and members of the public, in Slingsby's Falcon 3 demonstrator. By this time, the club had two primary trainers in operation, one of which was fitted with a nacelle cockpit and used for soaring flights when the occasion arose. Most of the instruction was carried out by Andrew Thorburn with Johnny Gardner deputising from time to time. Soon, members were starting to qualify for their "A" certificates, awarded for a straight glide of over 30 seconds. These were only just achievable by "hops" and "slides" and were usually launched by tow-car. The "B" certificate required a flight of one minute duration and had to include two turns. These were bungee launched from higher up the slopes above West Feal.

Flying operations ceased for the year on the 25th of September, but a lot of work took place on the ground over the following winter. The club was now outgrowing the facilities which could be provided by the Nichols at West Feal, so they obtained the use of a disused shepherd's cottage a mile further east, at East Feal. This was made habitable by Gardner and Rogerson over the winter, and a hangar was also erected. This may have been the building previously erected at Gartcarron Hill, but unfortunately no photographs exist of the exterior.

The remote location of the site, together with the fact that several of the members had to travel from the west of Scotland, meant that there was an urgent requirement for overnight accommodation. The solution was the erection of a dormitory hut, some 40 x 17 ft in size, and capable of sleeping twenty [male] members. [Females were quartered safely a mile away, with the Nichols at West Feal!]. As we shall see, this building was destined to serve the club in many different capacities over the years, and would easily become the club's longest serving asset, still in use in 2008.

Several notable events occurred in 1939. The club fleet was strengthened by the arrival of a new Tutor from Slingsby's, at a cost of £130. The first 'home grown' C certificate was flown by Alex Aitken in the nacelled primary, and the first Scottish wave flight was made by Andrew Thorburn in his Falcon 1, when he used smooth lift to gain a height of 5,500ft over Scotlandwell and Portmoak Farm.

The club's first residential courses were held in July and August, with seven trainees attending at a cost of 6 guineas for 14 days, including food and accommodation. The club at last qualified for a share of the Air Ministry subsidy, and was awarded the sum of £150. This award was probably the reason for a visit by the Secretary of State for Air, Lord Trenchard, on July 1st, following his opening of the new Central Scotland Airport at Grangemouth.

After four years of stagnation, the SGU had made great strides forward during its first year of operation at Bishop Hill, but progress was brought to an abrupt halt with the outbreak of war in September. Although it had been assumed that all gliding in the U.K. ceased immediately, it would appear that the SGU were still flying up to the end of the year, although this may have been limited to ground slides and low hops. Despite many key members, such as Andrew Thorburn, having departed to join the forces, an attempt was made by the secretary, R.B. Rogerson, to keep operating as a social club for the duration of hostilities, with activities such as Christmas parties and Burns Suppers. These efforts were brought to a halt in early 1941 when the landlords of East Feal, who were Kirkcaldy town council, served an eviction notice on the SGU, due to Department of Health regulations which prohibited gatherings of people in reservoir catchment areas. Despite a vigorous campaign of objections and representations to Members of Parliament, the club was unable to prevail, and was forced to cease all operations.

All assets were sold or became requisitioned by the forces. The three club gliders, the dormitory hut and the hangar went to the Air Training Corps, who were just commencing gliding training at the time. The Studebaker winch became an ambulance, and was subsequently destroyed during an air raid, while beds, bedding and cooking utensils were donated to hospitals. However, the club was able to pay off all of its debts, and was left with the grand sum of £17 12s 6d in its bank account.

For the remainder of the war, the club was kept going by arranging the AGMs to coincide with the home leave of a quorum of members, many of whom were now gaining skills and experience in the service of the Crown which would subsequently prove to be invaluable in gliding club operations.

During my research, I discovered the following article, written by Andrew Thorburn, and summarising those early years:

> The spike-like grass on the hill top stirred, the gentle breeze took on a new texture as surge after surge of the west wind rolled up the hillside. The promised westerly blustered and pushed, warm but powerful. Rising from the small group of supporters clustered around the Falcon I, it took only a few steps to reach the edge of Bishop Hill and look down the steep slopes to Kinnesswood and Scotlandwell nestling a thousand feet below, and ahead to the expanse of Loch Leven with

Benarty, Cleish and the Ochils and even the Campsies visible on the horizon. The scurrying clouds two thousand feet above cast moving shadows which added to the chequered pattern of the fields below.

At last, after years of investigation, learning and construction, things could be said to be – all set for go! All that now remained to be done, was to test out the natural resources of lift which the airs around Bishop Hill offered.

Turning back to the glider with a call of "Ready to go", the gossip and speculation was silenced as everyone moved to their allotted task. After sliding into the open cockpit and settling comfortably into the seat below the swept-back wing, safety harness adjusted, freedom of movement of the control surfaces checked, there came a pause for final instructions to the ground crew. Then, when the wing-tip and tail holders had rotated the nose of the glider into the wind, the two launch teams firmly grasping the twin lengths of elastic launch cord were lined up ahead on each side of the glider. The large diameter ring which connected at the centre – both sides of the V-shaped cord, was placed in the open hook on the nose of the glider and it stayed there – only by friction. Final instructions to the anchor man who tightly grasped the tail-skid as he lay prone, on the grass, and then the launch commands were barked out.

"Walk!" The teams moved – the ropes began to stretch and the tail holder held the glider stationary. The launch team disappeared over the crest of the hill.

"Run!" and as they moved fast down the slope, the elastic reached maximum tension.

"Release!" and the tail holder relaxed his grasp.

The Falcon lurched forward with alarming acceleration and immediately becoming airborne in the strong wind, dropped the rope on the sprawling group of launchers who rolled over on their backs to observe the progress of this – the first soaring flight of any worthwhile duration in Scotland.

The quality of the lift was soon very apparent from here, the engine-less aircraft was gaining height rapidly at what was proved afterwards to be a vertical speed of about twenty feet per second. Pilot's weight – 168lbs, plus 380lbs for the Falcon I, making 548lbs in full being wafted aloft with the greatest of ease.

A gentle turn to starboard, took us northwards along and above the hill slope, to Carlin Maggie – a large out-crop of rock, then an about-turn to port brought her back along the hill to Scotlandwell. Several beats in this rising airflow took the Falcon to 2,500ft above the villages, and at last, Scotland had found and used its own soaring facilities.

The lift on that day was smooth, powerful and widespread on a far more generous scale than that experienced on other sites.

Fascinated by the beauty of our local landscape, seen for the first time from this new vantage point, it was some time 'till I settled down to make comparative checks of the various areas which promised soaring lift. The section of the hill between Scotlandwell and Kinnesswood, gave the best results as it funnelled the west wind high into the sky. Though not so good, the lower slopes north of Kinnesswood stretching to Glen Vale and the West Lomond were better than any I had used south of the border. Flying westward into the wind, the lift proved to be operational right out to the shore of Loch Leven, and we now know that on occasions it goes much further than that.

Reassured by the simplicity of the effort required to stay airborne, memories came to mind of the trials of the past four years devoted to the search for this form of inexpensive flying. This was 1938 and soaring could be had on our own doorstep, so to speak.

In 1933, a search of the numerous gliding clubs started in Scotland. Disappointing news of dismal failure as clubs closed down following several years of heavy damage to gliders brought on by a combination of the wrong choice of site, and lack of knowledge about the fundamentals of Gliding. Edinburgh, Glasgow, Falkirk, Stirling, Perth and Dundee – all met the same fate, after numerous crashes interspersed with weeks of rebuilding and flights of only up to 35 seconds, and 100ft in height.

In 1934, a few of the more persistent members of these declining clubs formed a study group which met for four years, first in Cranston's Tea Rooms in Glasgow and later on a hillside near Fintry. Investigation by this group in 1935 did not offer any possibility of a short cut to soaring flight.

Fortunately, information about a small group of enthusiasts who operated at Sutton Bank near Thirsk in Yorkshire filtered through. Most interesting was the fact that they were already soaring, and had become Yorkshire Gliding Club. The group included some who were well known in aviation circles, such as Amy Johnson – the Atlantic Flyer, Fred Slingsby – who eventually became the best glider manufacturer in the U.K.

A quick trip South one weekend in July 1935 brought the satisfaction of joining that group and several years of learning about soaring from that source had its rewards. By the end of 1936, an advert in the Kirkcaldy press soon brought twenty Fifers together who wanted to learn to fly gliders. The Fife Gliding Club was formed, and elementary gliding started in a field at Chapel Level, Kirkcaldy. Instructing beginners is one thing – soaring another. In 1937, Fred Slingsby offered a second-hand Falcon I for £60 – so after some trouble with the

Customs authorities at Kirkcaldy harbour (the machine came as deck cargo in a box, from Hull and they thought all gliders were German made), I at last was the proud owner of my own sailplane.

Having flown this machine before in Yorkshire, all that was necessary was to get it established in a mobile trailer in some sheltered spot on Bishop Hill. The usual practice in pre-war years was to launch into soarable upcurrents, from the top of the hill.

After a study of Ordnance Survey maps of the Lomonds, the most likely route to the top was via the Hazels towards the waterworks, then westward over the gently rising ground past East Feal and West Feal farms. Mr. and Mrs. David Nicol of West Feal befriended us and we soon had the Falcon in its trailer on the hill top sheltered from the strong winds in the Clatteringwell Quarry. And now, at last, we were airborne. After one hour and ten minutes, a landing back at the hill top was made, and the glider stored in its trailer – everybody keyed up with excitement.

From that time on, gliding moved rapidly forward on the Lomond Hills. Further soaring flights brought newspaper publicity and visitors from the Dumbarton Club, which was making "low hops" on the very field near Cardross, that had been used more than forty years earlier by Percy Pilcher. Soon, a joining of forces with the Fife Club was arranged and the collective name of Scottish Gliding Union Ltd adopted when the club became a Limited Company in 1938.

Andrew Thorburn

Chapter 3

A New Beginning 1946 – 1951

The club archives do not show what happened to many of those early gliding pioneers during the war years but a few of them did get back together in the early months of 1946. Andrew Thorburn (Flt. Lt.), Bill Lawson and Robert Parker met in the Lomond Hotel, Kinnesswood and decided to re-form the club. At that time, the Loch Leven Aero Club flew out of Balado Airfield near Kinross and it was agreed that they should approach the Aero Club with a view to sharing their facilities at Balado. Their negotiations were successful and on the 25th July, 1946, the first glider, a Kirby Cadet was winch-launched from Balado.

Later in the year, the SGU was the benefactor of some welcome publicity. This time in the form of an article in the internationally read "Sailplane & Glider", affectionately known as the "S&G". The article sang the praises of the intrepid band of aviators and enthusiasts, and included a detailed drawing of the layout of Balado with West Lomond, Bishop Hill, Loch Leven and Benarty. There is no doubt that this article put the SGU well and truly on the 'Gliding' map.

1947 saw the serious business of club activities return with the A.G.M. being held at Balado on Saturday 26th April. R.B. Rogerson retired after nine years as secretary, and was elected the first honorary life member of the club. T. Graham was elected as chairman with Andrew Thorburn as secretary, and James Adam continued as treasurer. James had been treasurer since 1940, but subsequently retired on 14th August, and Johnny Gardner had moved to London with his work as an Admiralty Armament Supply Officer. The main topic of the A.G.M. was the recruitment of new members and the retention of existing ones.

After much deliberation, it was agreed that entry fees and subscriptions would be reduced to pre-war levels. Two more gliders were added to the fleet that year, a Dagling and a Tutor. Balado proved to be a good 'wave' site when, on 21st December, Tom Davidson claimed Scotland's second wave flight. He maintained a height of 900/1000ft. over the launch point at Balado for 12 minutes. On the same day, Andrew Thorburn contacted lift at 800 ft. and climbed the Tutor to 3500ft. in semi-darkness over Kinross. His flight lasted 21 minutes.

Dorothy Lawson preparing for her first flight in the newly acquired SG38 - Balado 1948.

Although these were indeed epic flights of the day, the wave at Balado was a rare phenomenon and circuits of one or two minutes were the norm.

Andrew Thorburn's daughter, Lynn, recalls those early days at Balado:

> *I remember the large hangars at Balado and the very eerie feeling we had as kids wandering through them, and the skeletons of aircraft abandoned there after the war. Many treasures (treasures for kids) were found, including darts, photos, letters or notes – especially in the aircraft, enamel plates and mugs, shell casings - all of which were replaced by my parents with a wee baggie of sweeties. I guess this was because some of our finds were dangerous and some were headed for an aeronautical museum.*

Summer Course - 1948

Club activities increased in 1948 when an SG38 and Eon Baby were added to the fleet. The old dormitory hut was returned by the ATC on 13th March and it was decided to move it to a new site on Bishop Hill. This site was proving to be very popular. A second winch (supplied by Greig & Scott of Kirkcaldy) and a second-hand Fordson tractor were purchased for use on the hill. Summer courses were also proving to be very popular, and were always well attended. Andrew Thorburn had the honour of making the first soaring flights from Bishop Hill since the war, on June 27th. No doubt his memories returning to those epic flights a handful of years earlier. Back at Balado, on 28th August, Andrew was the test pilot for the new auto-tow launching system. The launching seemed to be good enough but unfortunately he injured his back in a heavy landing. Always keen to find better ways of getting into the air, Andrew was back at Balado for the first aero-tows in his Eon Baby on March 27th 1949. These again proved to be successful and the year saw most pilots experiencing this new form of launching, albeit from behind Loch Leven Aero Club machines. By the end of the year, the club fleet had reduced to one Dagling, two SG38s, two Cadets and a Tutor, with the Eon Baby being crashed and written off in November 1949.

Andrew Thorburn signalling to start the launch.

A decision was made at a meeting in early 1950 to replace the Eon Baby with a T21b – partly funded by Kemsley Trust (set up by Lord Kemsley to assist aviation clubs purchase gliders and aircraft). The meeting also agreed to employ Hamish McAskill as the club's full-time ground engineer. The T21b duly arrived and the first flight took place on April 23rd. At this time, the club was auto towing using 0.098" dia. solid wire of 110tons/sq.in. tensile strength. Although reasonably priced at ten shillings per 1000ft, and a life expectancy of around 250 launches, the big disadvantage was the high petrol consumption of the tow-car. On non-flying days, volunteers were keen to develop the soaring site on Bishop Hill, but progress was slow due to poor access. The arrival of the T21b enabled five seven-day courses to be completed during July and August. By the end of August 1950, Balado had seen over 3000 launches. Twenty eight pilots had gained their "A" certificates and seven had their "B" certificates. Despite poor access to Bishop Hill, eight pilots gained their "C" certificates whilst soaring from the hill site.

1950 also saw the introduction of the club newsletter *Uplift.* This was typed up on single sided foolscap paper and was advertised as 'The Organ of the Scottish Gliding Union'. Cover price is shown as 3d per issue with an annual subscription of 4 shillings. Those who remember the old pounds, shillings and pence will immediately work out that 12 monthly issues at 3d per copy would only cost 36d or 3 shillings – records do not show

The "Wild Winch" - Ex balloon winch converted for glider launching with Lt Stevenson with the signalling bat, David Hendry "driving" the winch and Maurice Berry listening to the launch instructions.

why people would be asked to pay 4 shillings for the year. The following is a reprint of the March 1950 issue of *Uplift* and it gives an insight to the goings on at Balado at that time:

Saturday flying seems to have waned in popularity; perhaps it is a hang-over effect from the days when to go up on a Saturday was to invite the utter frustration of only getting a total of half a dozen launches – if you were lucky. Now, the sure-fire combination of Alex Fyffe, Hamish McAskill and a Duty Pilot has made Saturday flying a pleasure. February 18th was typical of the modern variety, when, with only seven people present to face up to the cold and blustery conditions, and with two pauses due to hail and heavy rain, twenty six launches were obtained. On Sundays, by comparison, with many more members present, and with two or three machines in use, the average is somewhere between 30 and 40 launches, giving the satisfactory total of over 60 launches for the weekend. That, at any rate, has been the situation recently. Two reasons have been suggested for the relatively better Saturday performance; that the smaller number of people makes for greater collective efficiency, and that the absence of a lunch-break on the Saturday compensates for the later start. The latter point does provide a case for an amendment to the present lunch arrangement. A snack meal served on the field at lunchtime, with the hot meal served after flying had finished would save anything up to an hour and a half of flying time. Alternatively, the lunch hour could be staggered, and the risk accepted of bedevilling the catering organisation.

Last week-end, the Olympia made one of its brief, butterfly like appearances, but its pilot was able to make no better use of the conditions than those who flew the Tutor. Perhaps the Olympia syndicate's views are summarised by Manclark who has so far achieved the club's greatest distinction with this machine. Interviewed by our chief reporter on a Fifeshire-bound ferry, as to when we could next expect him at Balado, Manclark sniffed at the North East wind and concluded that we would have to wait until the weather was a great deal warmer. When it was suggested to him that the Olympia should take part in the next National competition in July as the representative of the SGU, he gave a cordial response. This is a suggestion that should be followed up with enthusiasm.

Blow Hot, Blow Cold

Last month it was reported that the Directors, assailed by a mood of pessimism and an unnatural humility, had shelved the idea of purchasing a two-seater. This decision has now been reversed and the aircraft has been ordered in the high hopes that it will be delivered in time for the seven summer courses. These courses can give an immense fillip to our membership, now creeping steadily upwards towards our target figure of 120. But all members should do their best to inveigle their friends into the financial ruin of first having a course, then joining the club.

First of all we need more instructors, and we feel that one of our correspondents has hit the nail on the head when he says;

"At present, only Andrew Thorburn and Tom Davidson carry out primary instruction. At various times, possible new instructors have been suggested; several of these have agreed to become instructors, but in spite of this the situation remains unaltered. On inspection of the Balado log book, flying seems to have taken place on 43 Sundays in 1949. On 38 of these, Tom Davidson was present. It is proposed to hold courses this summer but who are to be the instructors? In addition, new members must be constantly recruited if the club is to continue as a live concern, and these must be instructed from scratch in probably at least 90% of cases. Again, who

are to be the instructors? What about some members taking an interest in instructing without being chased into it!"

<u>High Finance</u>

The launch rate in February has shown a welcome return to a reasonably high average. But, even so, this is only covering the present expenditure of something in the region of £12 per week, omitting any question of capital depreciation. With the present membership, an extra thirty launches a week will be necessary to sustain the cost of the two-seater when it is delivered. On the other hand, this machine should cause a considerable interest in our membership. The situation is that the club is committed to a policy of steady expansion, because it is only by a greatly increased turnover that the present expenditure can be justified. On this basis, the next logical move would be to purchase a Tiger Moth, which in all probability, would easily cover its costs.

The financial position is relatively satisfactory. In "Gliding and Advanced Soaring", the authors deal with the question of costs in the following manner:

"The usual entrance fee and subscription to any of the main British Gliding clubs in 1939 averaged £1 1s entrance and £2 2s to £3 3s per annum for full flying membership. These have unfortunately doubled themselves under immediate post-war conditions, due to the considerably increased cost of club equipment… Dual instruction at present costs about 15s to £1 per hour, and circuits about 3s 6d. Solo flying on medium performance single seaters may cost 10s to 15s per hour and half a crown (2s 6d) per circuit. Launch for private owners will also cost about half a crown. These figures are based upon the estimated cost of a club of about 200 members operating without subsidy….Obviously a smaller club would find it difficult

to cover itself charging the above rates" The kick is in the last sentence!

Medals of the Month

We are unaware of Sproule's politics, but we suggest that he is essentially a true-blue. His lofty dismissal of the instrument panel in the Tutor was subtly conveyed in the statement he made immediately after one of this month's flights. "I know I was flying too fast because my hat started to blow off". He also gets a medal for having the month's longest flights of 17 minutes, which was obtained from a wave which developed in the evening of a sunny day, when all the previous launches had drawn a dismal blank.

A high award should also go to Bob Gairns for dismantling and reassembling the carburettor of the Chevrolet in brilliant fashion by torch-light. We gloss over the fact that the carburettor was in perfect condition before and even after this feat.

The Black Mark goes to a practice rather than a person. Although any effort to increase the number of flying hours is welcomed, the latest vogue of night flying is under the suspicion of being too much of a good thing. On several occasions recently, the "fly home" has been made with the aid of car headlight signals, in the most nocturnal of visibility. This can never be worth the risk, and when, on one occasion, the pilot suggested that he should pay only half his launching fee because he only obtained 500ft of height because of the poor visibility, the situation becomes farcical. Our insurance rates are already high enough!

Tom Davidson, the CFI (Chief Flying Instructor) summed up the year:

Undoubtedly the acquisition of the T21b has been the most outstanding event of the year. Since its delivery to Balado in April it has been in constant use. Although dual flying has thus become possible, solo primary training has not by any means been dropped. Six courses of which primary solo training was the basis have been successfully

Tom Davidson and Ruth Lapage in the Cadet

carried out during the past summer. Judging by articles in "Sailplane and Glider" and "Gliding" on dual versus solo training, I would appear to be behind the times, but I am not yet convinced that purely dual primary training is the best. If a tyro starts with "ground slides" and then progresses to "wire" and then to "high hops" he learns to rely on himself. Nor is he so likely to be surprised later if things should not go exactly to plan when he has no instructor in the glider with him. At this stage, his flying may not be polished, but he is accustomed to taking the glider off the ground, release, glide and land it, relying on himself. He progresses then to the T21b and is taught to fly a "circuit", make correct turns and so on. When he progresses another stage and returns to solo training he does so, I am sure, with more confidence than if his previous training had been dual only.

In 1950, 3974 launches were carried out at Balado as compared with 2207 in 1949. There have, I think, been two reasons for this increase. The first and by far the most effective, being the development of auto-tow launching in conjunction with winch launching, which is now used mostly for primary training. Thus two launching lines have usually been in use at once. The second reason, especially in the earlier months of the year, has been the increase of flying on Saturday afternoons.

Notable flights at Balado have included one, by Duncan Aitchison, of 15 minutes in the cadet. He climbed, I believe, to 1700 ft and only came down to give someone else a chance. The first notable flight in the T21b was one of 33 minutes reaching a height of 2300 ft from a launch of 600 ft when David Hendry flew with his brother Jim on 31st July. On 2nd August, Bill Lawson had two consecutive flights of 30 and 36 minutes respectively, the first with a day member and the second with J. McKinstry. On 13th August, Peter Pearce with a day member as passenger climbed to 2700 ft with a duration of over 24 minutes. He could have prolonged this flight but his passenger had had enough. Much later, on 29th October, Andrew Thorburn with Tom Hendry as pupil climbed at about 3 ft per second in a thermal from 750 ft to 1800 ft, duration 30 minutes.

During the year, 42 "A" and 15 "B" certificates have been gained at Balado. Probably the most noteworthy "B" was that gained on 22nd October by Marjorie Brodie, who thus became the first Air Ranger to complete the test. At Bishop Hill, results have been rather disappointing. There have been only 45 launches during the year for a total duration of 22 ¼ hours. Nine "C" certificates were gained. There, as at Balado, a lady is to the fore; Dorothy Lawson getting her "C" on 13th August and thus becoming the first female to do so in Scotland. On the ground, the SGU has taken a distinct step forward in employing a full time ground engineer. In the club rooms too, things are much improved. We now sit on chairs at good solid tables, instead of on stools at planks balanced on oil drums. Among distinguished *visitors have been Lady Kinloch, Fred Slingsby and Jock Forbes.*

Strangely enough, the same author opened the February 1951 issue of *Uplift* with the following article:

> *The last accident that happened to CFI Tom Davidson was in 1917 when he scraped his Spad into an advanced landing field in France for a dead stick landing. Scrape being the operative word, he left his wing tips on the bushes that constituted the airfield boundary. Some time before that he had flown an Avro which had been rigged with crossed controls. This flight had terminated in the manner one associates with crossed controls , and Tom had duly walked away from the wreckage. To those who know Tom's careful approach to flying, it is no wonder that his*

Andrew Thorburn with Tom Davidson and a pupil in the Slingsby T21b two seater trainer.

> *record is so accident free, and it was something of a nine-day wonder at Balado when he tipped a frost bound potato pit with the Cadet wing. Damage to the wing was the result. But that is the shocking thing about accidents – sometimes the other chap that these things happen to turns out to be yourself.*

The club grew from strength to strength. In 1951, two launch lines became the norm at Balado. They experimented with new winch wire consisting of 700ft of solid wire with a drogue parachute at end. This lighter weight permitted higher launches, and caused less wear when crossing the intersecting runways.

The summer courses were upgraded to include accommodation and all meals in the nearby Kirklands hotel and two-seater elementary weekend courses started. Ann Douglas & Lorne Welch (later to become Mr and Mrs Welch) visited on 28th and 29th April to run and categorise an instructor's course (Lorne has been one of the RAF pilots responsible for building the famous Colditz glider). One intrepid young student attending a course that year was Ron Flockhart. Born in Edinburgh, Ron went on to become famous for driving D-Type Jaguars to win the Le Mans 24 hour races in 1956 and 1957. His driving career took him to Connaught, BRM, Lotus and finally, in his last Formula 1 outing, to a works Cooper in the US Grand Prix at Riverside in 1962. Later that year, he died in a plane crash (believed to be his privately owned Spitfire). The official report concluded that the most likely reason for the crash was pilot disorientation while flying in cloud.

Following a prolonged period of north winds, a group of intrepid explorers set off in search of a launch site on a north facing ridge, as Balado was not suitable for launching in north or south winds. The search was not successful but everyone agreed to keep vigilant on their travels around Fifeshire.

'Jimmy' the horse was a very environmentally friendly method for retrieving gliders back to the launch point.

Balado was getting busy with the Coastal Command Gliding and Soaring club moving in to share the site in the middle of 1951, and the RAF Gliding Association bringing a T31 to the site. Soon after Hamish McAskill resigned his ground engineer job to join the RAF, the winch and tow-car began to give problems. The Ford truck also proved to be too much and it was sold for scrap.

Peter Pearce managed a thermal flight of 1 hr 20 min in the Tutor, and a four-man syndicate bought a Kite 2. By far the best flight of the year was in this Kite 2 on December 9th when Alex Fyfe climbed to 10,170 ft (gain of 8350 ft). Another notable flight was Bill Adamson's wave flight of 32 minutes in a variometer-less Cadet. The year ended with a Christmas party and pantomime at the Kirklands hotel.

The following is Alex Fyfe's account of his epic flight:

> The launch, at 14:25 hours, was good and the release, which was automatic, took place at a height of 1400ft. after allowing the instruments to settle. In the last few seconds of the launch the speed jumped from 42 kt to 52 kt.
>
> The green ball of the variometer continued to indicate between 3 and 4 feet per second (fps) lift and the machine was put into right hand circles with a steady gain of height for four or five minutes. Lift ceased about a mile East South East of the airfield and course was set for the locality between the airfield and the hills to the North, in which area lift had been reported by pilots on other occasions.
>
> Lift was found there and it was the decided, from previous experience, to fly across wind. Accordingly, a northerly course was set and the machine remained in steady lift of about 4 fps. There was no drift and forward progress was slow, which agreed with former experience when wave was flown in, a few miles to the East. On that occasion, a northerly course was held without drift whilst the clouds continued to sail from West to East.
>
> Lift began to fail over the hills at between 3,000 ft and 4,000 ft, so a reverse course was set and all

agreement with previous experience collapsed. The machine scampered back towards the Aerodrome showing that the wind at this height was, as was checked on subsequent beats, within a few degrees of North. Height was lost on the downwind beat but on turning back into wind, lift was contacted in the same area as before.

Having established a pattern which worked, it was persisted in. Upwind until lift dwindled to 1 fps, then downwind to the starting point and upwind again. From the barograph, it appears that about seven such beats were made although height was not always lost on the downwind leg.

Search was made for better lift a mile or so to each side of the established marker, a rectangle of woods on the Ochil Hills below, but it was fairly uniform over the area. Generally, the forward flight was abandoned when about half way over the hills to the Earn valley, so that the entire flight was made in the lee half of the Ochils.

The valley enclosed by the Ochils on the North and the Cleish hills to the South was covered solidly with cloud but the ranges of hills were clear. One beat to the North was started just under cloud base, about 6,000 ft., and lift was such that when return was made to start the next beat at 7,000 ft., cloud top was well below. A mistake was made on this particular downwind leg in that it was continued too long and, when facing North again, lift could not be contacted. Rather than have the machine descend into cloud, a dive was made for the upwind edge of same which was cleared by the matter of 100 ft. or so.

Gold "C" height became a thought. By mental arithmetic, something like 12,000 ft. would be required to be absolutely sure; but the dominant factor was the clock – on account of the approaching darkness. The length of time necessary to regain ground level was a problem which could not be solved mentally.

It was finally decided to make 16:00 hours the latest time of landing, and to allow 30 minutes for the descent.

Accordingly, 15:30 was the deadline and gain of height was continued. A weakening of purpose set in as 15:30 approached and the flight was stretched another five minutes to ensure the ASL (above sea level) height being over 10,000 ft. The altimeter showed 9,700 ft. when the flight was abandoned, Balado airfield is 420 ft. ASL.

Return to the aerodrome was by means of a dive at 60 kt with full spoilers through a thin patch which had developed in the cloud cover a few miles west. Once below cloud base, the spoilers were closed and a quick trip at 50 kt made to the Cleish hills in the South; the East until the Great North Road was reached at just over 4,000 ft.; then North over Kinross on to Milnathort at 2,000 ft.; West to the aerodrome and a circuit to check the wind sock. Landing was effected at 15:56 hours.

From 2,000 ft. down to 1,000 ft., the air was very turbulent; conditions which did not obtain at the commencement of the flight. The barograph shows maximum height attained to be 9,750 ft., making a gain of height of 8,350 ft., and a total of 10,170 ft. ASL.

A check with the Met. Office next day secured the information that the temperature over Kinross at 10,000 ft. at 15:30 was 4 degrees Fahrenheit.

Best lift was about 12 fps, but this only occurred on three or four occasions, lasting each time for a few seconds only. Generally, it was in the order of 4 fps. The cloud strip which covered Kinross-shire stretched away to the West for what seemed like 20 miles. Eastward, it obscured most of Fifeshire although probably not stretching as far as the East Neuk. If it were a function of the wind coming over the Ochils, the possibility of soaring them from end to end on the lee side under these Met. Conditions makes interesting conjecture.

Visibility was good to the North, where the snow covered Grampians were plainly visible. A large area of the North Sea could be seen to the East. Westward was not so good whilst to the South the Pentlands were visible, although Edinburgh was standing up to its reputation of "Auld Reekie" and was completely obliterated by the smoky haze.

In retrospect, it is probably just as well that the machine was kept out of cloud because if icing conditions had existed in them, the ice could not have been got rid of for the rest of the flight.

During the climb a Jet aircraft approached from the East about 2,000 ft. below, disappearing away to the West. By some freak of sound, its noise was heard momentarily as it approached, otherwise it might have passed unnoticed being almost directly below my Kite 2.

A disturbing thought on the way up was the possibility of the ink on the barograph freezing. Fortunately the graph is complete, but a change to a non-inking type would remove anxiety on this score.

Alex J. Fyfe

Alex Fyfe in his Kite 2

Chapter 4

Latter Days at Balado 1952–1957

By the middle of 1952, the Bishop Hill site was proving to be too good to ignore. A regular team, headed by Andrew Thorburn (sometimes bringing five or six of his best behaved students) could be seen chopping trees and clearing away scrub. The welcome site of a bull-dozer on the hill soon had a 100 yard landing strip levelled, ditches filled and road foundations cut.

Back at Balado, things were not standing still. The club decided to abandon solo training and put the Dagling and both SG38s up for sale. Andrew Thorburn hatched a plan to form an eight member Sky syndicate, and the blue Olympia 2b was bought from Lasham, with the aid of the Kemsley Trust.

The Olympia came complete with trailer and all sorts of epic flights were planned. The club decided that anyone wanting to fly the Oly would have to pay £15 per year for the privilege – in addition to the normal flying & launching fees - this being to cover the cost of maintaining the machine.

Andrew Thorburn, George Whyte and Tom Davidson in front of the Blue Olympia – setting the barograph before a cross-country flight.

In April, Bill Lawson took to flying early morning weather sorties in a Tiger Moth. He would come back with details of upper wind conditions and cloud-base heights. Spurred on by this accurate form of weather forecasting a number of decent flights were had during the month.

The Oly syndicate was making good use of their new toy: Bill Lawson stayed up for 2 ½ hours in thermals and reached 3,900 ft. Andrew Thorburn, after a brave but rather humiliating cross-country attempt of 4 miles redeemed himself by thermalling to over 6,000 ft in a flight of 2 hours 20 minutes. He had his barograph with him this time and thus finally qualified for his Silver "C" height badge. Flights of more than half an hour were also put in by Tom Davidson and Roger Pears.

1952 also saw the first Scottish Silver Distance cross-country flight being made. Pip Pearce flew the Olympia the requisite 31 miles (50 km) to Carnoustie. The club newsletter *Uplift* described the flight:

That long awaited cross-country is in the bag at last. Pip Pearce was the man who did it and he deserves to be heartily congratulated on his achievement. For a first cross-country, his performance was most praiseworthy, and in addition the day was far from good.

We had hoped to persuade Pip to write up the story of his flight. Unfortunately he left for the south a few days after the flight and has not been heard of since, so details have had to be extracted from the retrieving crew.

His course to Carnoustie was more or less straight. He left Balado at 2,800 ft and lift was fairly plentiful although not very vigorous until he got to Cupar. Here he was down to 1,000 ft and beginning to look for fields before he connected with another thermal which took him up to 3,100 ft, his best climb of the flight. He crossed the Tay at 3,000 ft and, although conditions at that time seemed to be improving, he decided to land on Carnoustie beach, whence he was rescued by the retrieving crew in the nick of time, fighting with the last of his strength the hordes of holiday makers who fell upon him as soon as he landed, bent apparently on taking home pieces of the Olympia to show the kids.

His time for the flight was one hour 50 minutes, which gives an average speed for the 35 miles of 19.1 mph. Pip's landing was reported back to the club in a most efficient manner by a member of the Royal Observer Corps., who was careful, however, to reverse the charge for the call.

As 1952 progressed, Balado become more and more busy – at one point there was a danger that there were more gliding club members than Loch Leven Aero Club members. Regular visitors at the site included the RAF Gliding and Soaring Association (RAFGSA), who brought their Sky. Famous people often "dropped in", one such VIP was Tony Goodhart, who later went on to form the Royal Australian Navy Gliding Association (RANGA) in 1956. The number of summer courses were dropped to four with a maximum of eight pupils each, with serious plans being made for a one week summer camp on Bishop Hill. Camping was popular at Balado too as the Air Rangers turned up in August for their third annual camp. By now the Tutor had been fitted with a belly-hook and was attaining regular 1100 ft launches. While all this was going on, the die-hards kept thinking about the possibilities at Bishop. Jimmy Rae even converted the old Fordson tractor so that it could be used as a winch on Bishop Hill.

The 1952 annual Festival of Sport exhibition was held in Edinburgh, at Waverley Market. The BGA had procured exhibition space and asked if the SGU would be interested in attending. This triggered a frenzy of activity with many late night discussions as to how to get the best from such an event. Records of this event are scant, but a stand was manned by club members where eager tales of gliding achievements were enhanced by very impressive Trophies which were loaned by the BGA.

The Olympia continued to soar; Andrew Thorburn and Bill Lawson both flew it to over 5,000ft. Bill Lawson's epic flight was conducted inside a Cu-Nim cloud! Once again, the club mag *Uplift* relayed the story under the dramatic heading of 'Pioneer Cloud Flight':

> *The last day of the Holiday Week provided this month's big sensation – Bill Lawson's climb to Silver "C" height in a cu-nim. He had been struggling for 15 minutes in a puny thermal at 1,100 ft, when a front which had been hanging about on the Ochils arrived over Balado. Things immediately improved, and with 10 green on the variometer, he began to circle. Soon he discovered there was no need to circle, and he was able to beat back and forth along the cloud, which now stretched in a vast black wall into the distance and towered smooth and sheer almost from ground to "anvil" height. Here and there, patches of rain were falling from it, and he noticed that the lift improved as he passed through the rain. At 4,100 ft the lift began to peter out, so he flew alongside some of the rainy patches, seeking more green. During one of these sorties, he flew just a little too near the cloud, and to quote his own graphic words "It just grabbed me!".*
>
> *Once engulfed, he began to rise at great speed, and both variometers went off the scale. It was raining heavily, and he was soon very wet. Rain came through the windows which he not had time to shut, and cascaded down the instrument panel over his legs. Turbulence was not very troublesome until he got to 5,000 ft, when without warning, all the terrible things that the gliding books speak about happened at once. The Olympia kicked suddenly and heeled over into the void. The rain turned to hail and roared against the canopy. A flash of lightning sizzled blindingly across his bows, The speed was building up most alarmingly and pulling back on the stick only made things worse. Later, on the*

ground, he realised he must have been in a spiral dive, but in the pitchy darkness of the cloud with the wind shrieking in the windows and his instruments having convulsions, this blessed enlightenment was denied him. He reached for the airbrakes with a purposeful hand, and pulled.

Gradually, things settled down. The shrieking of the wind fell away to a sigh, the ASI gradually unwound and sanity returned to the Turn and Bank indicator. He was surprised to note, however, that both variometers continued to register lift, even with the brakes out, so he put them in again and with infinite caution began to circle once more in the turbulent regions above. This time he reached only 4,800 ft before he was cast down in a series of violent and uncontrollable stalls.

He had by now been in the cloud for over ten minutes and had lost all sense of direction, and much of his enthusiasm. It was with great joy therefore that he suddenly caught a glimpse of the ground, although it was at such an odd angle that at first he didn't realise where it was. He quickly sorted things out however, and discovered he was over Cowdenbeath, and so with 3,200 ft on the clock he turned towards Balado. He was foiled by only a few hundred feet and landed in a large field just behind the glass-houses. Nobody at Balado had seen him land, and when he telephoned to say where he was, David Hendry was most indignant; he had been engaged in abstruse computation with ruler and compasses, and when the phone rang had calculated that the Olympia must be at least as far as Peebles.

Bill was quite undisturbed by his flight until Monday morning, when he saw the newspaper reports of the massive storm that he had flown through and he realised with a shock what a terrible experience he'd had.

Club records show that 129 flying hours were accumulated from 2229 launches by the end of 1952.

The following year started with an expedition to the north face of the Lomond Hills. There seems to have been a lot of effort to get only two bungee launches from the top of the hill. The first launch resulted in a soaring flight to 1100ft and, suitably spurred on, the team hauled the glider back to the top and attempted another launch. This one was not so successful – a straight glide to the bottom of the hill, but a useful study of the roll clouds helped the pilots to suspect that wave interference could have caused the lack of lift on the second flight. They deduced that the updraft on the face of the hill was being cancelled out by the downdraught from the wave system. This proved to be a useful piece of information when it came to hill soaring in the future.

Ann Douglas and Lorne Welch returned in early January to 'categorise' two more instructors, although records don't show who they were. The club advertised three seven-day courses and a ten-day course, for July and August 1953, in the national 'Gliding' magazine. Costs for the courses were; Subscription £3-3-0, Entry Fee £1-1-0, Launches 3/- (15p) and Soaring 15/- (75p) per hour.

In April, the club set up a two-day trial operating out of a field at the bottom of Bishop Hill. This site was between Glenlomond Hospital and Glenvale Farm (O/S ref. NO175057). Although a number of launches took place, there were no soaring flights achieved.

Back at Balado, George Whyte's 60 h.p. Piper Cub was being worked on with a view to gaining approval for aero-towing. Tom Davidson (CFI) achieved his Silver Duration by flying for over six hours, reaching 3,700ft., in weak wave over Bishop Hill. Tom had been busy on the ground too, he designed and built a new control van – painted in yellow and white squares, to accompany the new Ford tow-truck. Douglas Fleming test flew the re-built Eon Baby which had been wrecked three years earlier, and a Cadet which had been damaged in a blow-over incident on Bishop Hill in 1950 was nearing completion.

July 1953 proved to be very good for the SGU and for David Hendry in particular. On a Thursday in the middle of the month, he attained his Silver Duration and Silver Height on a single flight over Bishop Hill. He then completed his Silver Badge with a 38 mile flight to Kirriemuir on the 25th. This was the first all-SGU Silver C badge achieved. Andrew Thorburn flew to Markinch (15 miles) and Bill Lawson claimed his Silver Duration for a five-hour, out and return flight to Bishop Hill from Balado. The newly rebuilt Cadet was taken back to permanent storage on Bishop Hill and provided six more Silver Duration flights and numerous local soaring flights.

Around about this time, Robert Parker crashed his Auster into Loch Leven. There were no injuries although his passenger, Joyce Blythe, from the Edinburgh Air Rangers thought she should re-consider her chosen leisure activity.

A new arrival at the club in October 1953 can be seen on the next page. The Zlin Krajanek (on the ground) had many admiring glances as it was, at the time, an advanced sailplane. By the end of 1953, 2984 launches and 207 hours had been recorded at the club.

The first recorded activity in 1954 was on Sunday 7th February. Ansgar Sambale and John Peterson gained Silver C legs after being bungee launched off Bishop Hill in over a foot of snow.

April saw the first use of the Tiger Moth as a tug at Balado and aero-tows were available at 15/- (75p) to 2000ft. The club fleet continued to increase, with two Cadets stored on Bishop Hill and two more Cadets, a Tutor, a T21b, the Krajanek and an Olympia 2b back at Balado. Bob Porteous climbed the recently acquired Krajanek to 5100ft in wave from a 1600ft winch launch at Balado. As well as the winch, Balado now sported two 22 h.p. Ford tow-cars and one 30 h.p. model.

The SGU continued to prove to be a popular place for visitors so the club arranged six more courses at £12-12-0 (12 guineas) including hotel accommodation. The first of these courses took place at Easter with the first thermal day of the year being recorded as 28th March. A Mr L. Marmol, the previous owner of the Krajanek, flew into Balado in his Miles Aerovan and was suitably impressed by operations at the SGU.

Records show that the first 100-launch day took place on May 9th, and that the remaining seven courses took place during July, August and the first half of September. The T21b, which arrived as an open cockpit model, was given a complete transformation during the summer with the fitting of a Campbell canopy. This meant a more comfortable, and less cold, ride for its occupants. July also saw Andrew Thorburn fly to Crail to claim his Silver Distance, and Bob Porteous flying the Krajanek to Buckhaven – although not far enough to claim his Silver Distance. Pilots attempting their five-hour duration flights were regularly launched by aero-tow to Bishop Hill. The boffins were always looking for ways to regulate the speed of the launch tow-cars and one such vehicle was fitted with an A.S.I., but records don't show how successful this proved to be. Another piece of high-tech equipment seen at the club towards the end of summer was a 16mm colour cine camera. This culminated in an excellent film of club activities and starred John Paterson and Tom Davidson.

One of the pupils on Tom Davidson's course had an exciting moment in the launching truck when John Paterson slumped unconscious over the wheel after banging his hand on one of the numerous sharp edged projections on the Monster, which were such a feature of this strong-man's car. The pupil was unable to drive, and his untutored knob-pulling had no effect. His plight was not helped by the fact that the senseless Paterson's foot was pressed firmly on the throttle, but this problem was solved for him when the door opened and Paterson fell out on the runway. The student at last got the car out of gear and went back for the body, which by this time had recovered and was miraculously still in good working order.

The 15th of January 1955 was the date of the annual Dinner Dance and Awards Ceremony. This was held at the Bridgend Hotel in Kinross, where Robert Parker presented a brand new Cross-Country Cup to Andrew Thorburn for his Silver Distance flight to Crail. It appears that the dancing turned out to be of the

Secretary D. Hendry, Chairman R. Parker presenting A.Thorburn with the Parker Trophy

highest quality, although the same might not be said about the dance floor – as one guest, no doubt demonstrating his landing ability, went straight through the floorboards!

Having checked that the floor had been repaired at the Bridgend Hotel, the SGU held its 21st Anniversary Dinner there on 29th July. Many members, past and present, enjoyed an excellent evening and Guests of Honour included Hon. Alan Boyle and Johnnie Gardiner.

Flying activities for the year so far included Silver Distances for Bob Porteous in the Krajanek, and Bob Stephen in the Oly. Not to be outdone, Andrew Thorburn flew the Oly for 60 miles to Kelso on 7th August. The same day, Maurice Berry claimed his Silver Duration on Benarty – only the second time this north facing slope had been used, the first being by a visitor in an Olympia in 1948.

Andrew Thorburn was the subject of some deft wood sculpting work in 1955. This photo shows (Major–Retd.)

Andrew Buchan putting the finishing touches to a wooden bust of Andrew at Kirkcaldy High School (Old School).

Balado airfield was proving to be a problem for the SGU as the Air Ministry announced that the club tenancy was to be discontinued, after nine years, for 'operational reasons'. Although the club had been on the lookout for alternative sites, the search now took on a new urgency. The workshops were in use most days as trailers had to be made for all aircraft and the 'Wild' winch had to be made mobile. Despite these activities, the club still achieved 339 hours flying from 5018 launches. The Christmas Party was back at the Bridgend Hotel on 17th December where awards were presented to Andrew Thorburn (Parker Trophy for his flight to Kelso) and to John Paterson (Boyle Trophy for his gain of height of 3,400ft).

Being ever aware of the meteorological knowledge needed by glider pilots, the club arranged an excellent lecture on Mountain Waves by Dr. Scorer of Edinburgh University Meteorological Dept. for early 1956. A band of extremely keen glider pilots set off home that night with their heads full of epic

Geoff Berry & the Krajanek

wave flights, determined to take advantage of their new found knowledge. The opportunity presented itself within a couple of months, on April 15th. Tom Davidson flew his Oly to Livingston (25 miles), Charlie Ross flew the Krajanek to Fintry (40 miles) following a 7000ft cloud climb. Jimmy Rae took his Oly to Fordoun (62 miles) to claim a new club record. Bill Adamson flew his Oly in wave to 7500ft, and claimed his five-hour leg, as did Ian Dodds and John Paterson flying at Bishop Hill. A party flying the Cadet from Bishop also gained five more "C" legs. Jimmy Rae flew 20 miles to Dollar and Maurice Berry flew the same distance to Kilconquhar.

Andrew Thorburn had arranged an Easter expedition to Connel, near Oban, and managed a 4000ft climb in wave over the sea-loch. His enthusiasm for the Connel expedition was infectious and a second trip was arranged for 21st – 28th July. They took five gliders, including the T21 and a Tiger Moth and completed over 30 hours of flying during the week. Andrew's daughter, Lynn, recalled the visit to Connel:

> I remember going to a club outside Oban with mum and dad and some other club members. That was how dedicated the members were – satisfied the wife and kids with a holiday but made it a gliding one. We used to fish for clams, although I recall one person scuba diving for them in the deeper water. We would sit around the open fire in the evenings and pop the newly caught clams into the boiling water. I still remember how they screamed as they were dropped into the pot! We had great fun in the evenings, singing songs and telling tales, although us kids thought that the adults were really cruel to the clams.

Sunday 21st October dawned bright and sunny at Balado with a fresh west wind full of promise for hill soaring. First away behind the Tiger was John Henry in the blue Olympia, with cockpit gaps sealed with tape against icy draughts. CFI Tom Davidson was next in the red Olympia, and after 45 minutes he returned to his duties on the airfield, having left the hill at 3,600 ft. and flown most of the way back across the loch in cloud, full of praise for the Cook Compass. Bob Stephen was next to be towed across for an hour's soaring. However, three hours later he had still been unable to gain the height for the upwind dash back to Balado, five miles away, but not wishing to delay any longer and with a mere 1,600 ft. in hand he headed for home against an estimated 35 knot head-wind. In spite of these impossible conditions, the Oly scraped over the boundary fence with nothing to spare, and a retrieve was saved.

Meanwhile, John Henry was having rough time on his five hours attempt. Low cloud continually dogged him; once he found himself in cloud while facing towards the hill. With commendable presence of mind, he applied himself to his compass and headed west, only to break cloud over the lochs behind the crest. His headway was barely perceptible and for a moment it looked as if he would have to land on the hill, but he swung off the south face and crept round the corner back into the lift. With his five hours behind him, and in the gathering dusk, he selected a field and pulled the airbrakes, closing them momentarily to float over an almost invisible telephone wire, and landed. Alistair Laird-Philip was on the spot at once and the retrieving machinery put in hand.

The very next weekend produced a healthy wave system which allowed Jimmy Rae to set a (short held) club record. He was aero-towed upwind in the red Olympia to the lee of the Ochils. He released at 2,500 ft. in 5 up and climbed in the silky smoothness at rates between 2 and 5 up. During his climb, the best lift was found farther and farther downwind of the Ochils and in front of the wave cloud. Eventually, Jimmy found himself over the Forth Rail Bridge at 11,225 ft., the greatest height ever reached from Balado. His return journey was made at 140 kt. There was, alas, a piquant note of sadness about Jimmy's flight. In his haste to get airborne he over-looked the fact that there was no barograph on board.

As 1956 drew to a close, strong winds continued to blow across Balado. As ever, the intrepid aviators experimented with launching techniques. In 2004, Geoffrey Berry recalled one particular day in November:

> We had decided to connect two lengths of the cable together to see if we could get a higher launch on a very windy day. We connected one end to the tow-car and the other to our T21. The wind was so strong that we

had people holding each wingtip and on the tail while we climbed aboard. As soon as we were strapped in we had aileron authority and asked the wing holders to let go. When they walked away and the tow-car took up the strain we discovered that we had elevator authority too and the glider started to lift off like a kite. The tow-car was still stationary but as we started to climb we pulled the car backwards! The driver gave it some more gas and started to move forwards again. By continued forward and backward motion we were able to climb this way until about 2,200ft before releasing overhead. We then entered some wave, although I suspect we were in it long before then, and climbed to 6,500ft over the airfield. The strong wind was blowing us east towards the west end of Loch Leven and even with 75 kts on the A.S.I. we only just made it back to the airfield.

The tow-car driver's normal job was to drive off down the runway with the glider in tow at the end of 1,000 ft of piano wire. When the glider released and dropped the end of the cable, the driver would release his end of the cable, turn the car around and drive back towards the launch-point. As he approached the dropped cable end with the drogue parachute he would open the door, lean out and grab the parachute and cable end and pull it onto his lap – all without stopping the car - and drop it back at the launch point.

The December 1956 edition of the club magazine *Uplift* told the story of another epic flight:

We had an idea that Sunday 4th November was going to be THE DAY, when we saw the Lawson's car streaking through the airfield gates and making straight for the red Olympia. On the drive up from Queensferry, according to our reporter, as every new wave cloud appeared over the horizon so did another 10 kt appear on the Zephyr's speedometer. David Hendry was quickly uprooted from his office chair to provide the aero-tow, and at 3,100 ft. over the Ochils, Bill released and continued to climb in smooth air to around 9,000 ft. where he hung about for some time taking magnificent pictures of the cloudscape. Forging upwind to the North-West he flew into terrific lift which took him to 12,500 ft., the greatest height ever reached from Balado. Deciding to make use of this height by converting it into his Silver "C" distance, he headed South at high speed, unable to see the ground except for the briefest glimpses through the gaps. He saw nothing at all of the ground from the Forth Bridge until he was South of Edinburgh, navigating instead by compass, ASI and watch.

When the time came for the inevitable descent through the cloud, Bill switched on his Turn and Slip indicator, set the trimmer fully forward and with a muttered prayer, plunged in. At 4,000 ft. Scotland re-appeared, but it could have been the moon, according to his description of the desolate wastes below. There was no sign of human habitation. There were no fields, and all the good books say "pick a field near a road". There were no roads. Only sheep. Sheep whose hostile stares came closer and closer until Bill, who had been earnestly searching ahead, spotted a solitary farm and made towards it. He picked a field with haystacks in the corner, reasoning that if haystacks could be got out, so could the Olympia, and landed on the Lammermuir hills, after just over three hours in the air and 49 miles from his release point.

Out of the gathering darkness, an ancient shepherd appeared over a distant hill and, after the customary conversation about not having run out of petrol and not having an engine, they made their way to the farmhouse for the phone call and tea.

The retrieve, by Jimmy Rae (last week's record holder) and Maurice and Geoff Berry seemed, in spite of their assurances to the contrary, to have been a particularly inefficient venture, for they actually stopped at the Lawson dwelling in Edinburgh for tea before continuing in darkness. They took the wrong turnings only three times, and knocked up only four people to ask the way before driving up to the farm – the wrong one as it happened and they had to reverse a hundred yards to get back to the main road. At the right farm, a tractor took the trailer up the hillside, through a water-splash to the field. The Oly was dismantled and the contingent left for Edinburgh at 11:50 p.m. arriving there at 01:20 a.m. the next morning.

Besides earning his Silver "C", Bill's flight set up a new Scottish Height Record.

News of these epic flights soon reached south of the border and a steady flow of visitors made their way north to Balado. One such visitor that year was Peter Scott, but club records don't show what he got up to.

The frenzied search for a new site had produced two possible locations; Portmoak – which was good but had a high rent, and Balgair Moor near Fintry – low rent but high development costs. The search continued.

1956 had produced 4149 launches, with 345 hour flying. The year's annual awards went to Bill Lawson (Boyle Trophy) for his 12,500ft flight and Jimmy Rae (Parker Cup) for his 63 mile flight.

Unfortunately, the year ended on a sad note. Alex Fyfe collapsed and died in Kinross on 31st December. The club magazine reported:

Alex joined the club in 1948 and became an enthusiastic member, attending on Saturdays and Sundays, looking after the maintenance of the vehicles, and taking part in the soaring expeditions to Bishop Hill in those days. In May 1951, he formed the Kite II syndicate with Hal Thorburn, Ian Sproul and Richard

Rosyski, and at the end of that year – the day after the Christmas Party in fact – he climbed to 10,000ft in wave, to establish a Scottish height record which remained unbroken until last Autumn. Failing health compelled him to give up flying and, indeed, all airfield activities, although he remained a familiar and popular figure at the club Christmas parties at Kinross.

An observant visitor to Balado at the beginning of 1957 might have cast his eyes over a yellowing piece of manuscript on which some wag had written the following 'story':

Long, long ago, when men were really men, and frequently pulled the cable back themselves when the retrieving horse got tired, there lived a man called Andra McThorburn. He was the father of Scottish Gliding and a great deal else besides. The McThorburns had always been interested in flying and in fact it was a young cousin of Andra's who, convinced that he had discovered the secret of flight, stepped smartly from the parapet of Stirling Castle, loosely attached to his invention, and broke a leg. He is important in history as being the first man to doubt the validity of Newtonian physics.

Andra himself spent all his spare time (which was considerable) toying with the splendid dream of learning to fly, and would stand for hours on the highest point of Archbishop Hill – as it was known at the time, being then much bigger – watching the seagulls sweep and soar amongst the crags. Andra envied the gulls deeply for, apart from anything else, they didn't have to pay for it.

His ideas began to develop, and he would make models to explain to his friends in the Kirk (lands hotel) how he thought a flying machine could be built. They were ignorant, loutish men, bankers, civil servants and the like, and they scoffed loudly at his wild schemes. "It stands tae reason it'll nae flee. It's ower muckle heavy!", they would say in their cloddish way, and draining their mead at a draught, burst into coarse and mocking laughter.

But far from discouraging Andra, the derision of his friends only spurred him on to bring his dreams to fulfilment, and at last he began to work on his first man-carrying machine. He called it the S.G.1. This was an abstruse mathematical reference to the predicted behaviour of the machine when immersed in Loch Leven, an essential feature of the C. of A. requirements of those days. When all his children had been put to bed – which took quite some time, because there were dozens of them – Andra would steal downstairs to work secretly far into the night. As each new dawn broke over the Och Hills, another farmer found his stock yard gate gone, and Andra's machine was another step nearer completion.

All through two long winters Andra worked ceaselessly, and the mysterious disappearance of the farmer's gates gave rise to increasing concern. The local policeman, Bow Street Runner 49, walked many miles investigating the case, damaging his bunions beyond repair. He was already sorely tried by the activities of Bonnie Prince Charlie Ross, the local bandit, who periodically came down from the hills and drove furiously through the streets of the town in his bullock cart, abducting maidens. Indeed, so numerous did his progeny in the district become, that the town became known as "Kin o' Ross, or Kinross. He painted himself with British Racing Green and wore a funny little green hat with a feather in it.

As Andra's work progressed, the case of the Disappearing Gates took a fresh turn. Fencing wire began to vanish at an alarming rate, and many a farmer woke to find his fences gone and his flocks scattered, to perish from cold and hunger on the wastes of Balado Moor.

At last Andra's machine was ready to fly. Because of all the fuss about the gates and fencing wire, he decided to make his first flight at night. Andra was never one to do things the easy way. He invited a few friends along to give him a hand, and by the time they had arrived, Andra had the machine assembled and the fencing wire laid out. Andra had been a little enthusiastic about collecting the wire, and one of the guests, a young chap called Macbeth, gasped "What! Will the line stretch out to the crack o' Deem?". Actually though, it stretched out only as far as Yetts o' Muckhart. All the young kitchen wenches from Andra's household were at the other end of the wire to pull him into the air. Andra clambered aboard and despatched a runner to order them to take up slack. The wench-driver cracked his whip, and Andra rose into the darkness.

It was unfortunate that Andra's friends, among whom were many farmers, should have been emerging from the Kirklands hotel just as Andra was making a nice landing outside. "Crivvens!" roared a farmer, "There's ma gate!", and the mob surged forward excitedly. The sight of Andra's strange machine descending from the moonlit sky made one or two of them wonder whether the drink had got them at last, and they paused uneasily. The moment's respite gave Andra time to think, and he thought fast.

"Whaur did ye get that gate?" said the farmer menacingly.

"Oh, the gate!", replied Andra airily, with a wary eye on the temper of the crowd. "I bought that from Charlie Ross last week. He said he found it in a field."

"Aye! I've nae doot he did!" Roared the farmer. "Ma field! And it's ma gate!"

"Well," said Andra easily, "you will have the honour of being my first passenger." And still talking soothingly, he persuaded them to help him pull the glider back for another launch.

There was a tricky moment when the farmers saw where all their fencing wire had been going, but Andra calmed them down again and when they had all had a flight, they forgot all about their fencing wire and went wild with excitement.

They all wanted to build themselves gliders of course, and Andra showed them how. They began by building a large number of gates, which formed the basis of Andra's design. When all the gliders had been built, they found that they had quite a number of spare gates left over, and these they used to keep their sheep out of the treacherous wastes of lonely Balado Moor. Fencing wire was, of course, in such demand for launching that there was none spare for fences.

And that's how the SGU got its start. And that's why, too, in getting in and out of the airfield nowadays, one has to open so many dammed gates!

1957 also saw the start of serious negotiations over the purchase of land at Portmoak. The club also bought

a new hangar and an old school building, which they dismantled and transported to Balado for storage. By February, the farmer who owned the land at Balado had started to plough up the airfield, thereby removing about 75%

The hangar as it stood on its original site

of the usable landing area. This latest development spurred Andrew Thorburn to greater efforts in his negotiations for Portmoak. Once again, Andrew's daughter, Lynn recalled her memories of one of those early negotiations:

> *I remember when we had to move away from Balado, driving around the countryside with dad, looking at possible sites. I particularly remember when we went to the farmer at Portmoak. Dad and Mr Bell negotiated for hours and I was given warm milk "straight from the cow" from the farmer's wife. I thought it was awful but had to drink it because I did not want to upset her in case dad didn't get to use the fields for his gliders. To this day I am a milkoholic – but only from a bottle, bag or carton, and always ice cold. But I like to believe that you lot got the site at Portmoak because I drank warm milk with straw dust floating in it! The things some people have to do!*

Summer course bookings continued to come through as early as Easter, but this caused more concern for the club as they faced the prospect of having no airfield by the summer!

The May issue of *Uplift* contained the final chapter of Balado:

> ### I am Directed
> *There are many to whom the presence of a buff-coloured, official-paid envelope from the Air Ministry among one's morning mail used to cause the spirits to fall vertically and the hair to stand up on the back of the neck. That buff-coloured official-paid envelopes from the Air Ministry should bring about such reactions is hardly surprising though, for our own recollections are that they never brought the kind of news to send one up in the air with joy. More often than not they just sent one up in the air, and eventually to some desert or other.*

Well, the SGU had a buff-coloured, official-paid envelope from the Air Ministry the other day, and the news it brought was that we must stop flying at Balado. By a special dispensation, for which we suppose we should be truly grateful, the two-seater and Cadet can continue training circuits until the end of May, then that will definitely be the end.

The contractor has already begun to assemble his plant, and since they want to use our old clubrooms for site offices, we have had to move all our furnishings to the hangar. On Easter Monday a group of members cleared the clubrooms and old workshop and made a bonfire of bits of old gliders, old blankets and papers. The fire, we are assured, didn't exactly get out of hand, but the flames could be seen for miles and a ghastly pall of smoke hung over Kinross to proclaim the ultimate fumigation of the piggery. A pair of old SG wings were burned, and the speed with which the flames consumed them would have been a nightmare-provoking sight to those people who light-heartedly smoke cigarettes in gliders.

Temporary clubrooms have been set up in the dim recesses of the hangar, and provided you don't mind walking past the Elsan in the lounge, and stumbling over a bed in the ante-room, you can reach the dining room which Percy has quickly made quite tolerable. The old ebony clock, which has only been right twice a day, is now tastefully yet somehow pathetically gracing a pile of old bricks, symbolic, we feel sure, of something or other.

Chapter 5

The Making of Portmoak 1957 – 1959

As flying came to an end in Balado, club members still flocked to the site to help prepare for the 'flitting'. It was a depressing time as all they could do was to pack up the various bits of machinery and await news of their new home. On the last day of the Balado ten year tenancy, 5th May - 1957, Charlie Ross marked the occasion by flying his Olympia 175 miles to Briarfield, near Manchester!

After frustrating delays in the negotiations between the five parties (SGU, Kinross Estates, Kemsley Trust, Mr Bell and Mr Taylor) the club moved to the final stages of purchasing some 30 acres of land in an area known as Portmoak, Scotlandwell, in May 1957. The members immediately prepared plans for ground clearing (cutting existing crops, levelling and re-seeding with grass), and a plea was put out for assistance with hangar and clubhouse erection. The plan was for everything to be operational by the spring of 1958 (less than ten months away), and they were even planning limited launching within the first few weeks of obtaining the site. In order to increase capital, the club newsletter *Uplift* asked all 100 members to consider loaning the club between £5 and £10. The June issue proudly proclaimed the official address, and explained how the name came about:

> *Of all the problems associated with the development of a new site, not the easiest is finding a name for the place. A name, we feel, as well as making it easy for strangers to find us on the map, should reflect something of the grandeur and magnificence of The Sport at its best. For this reason "Benartybog" must be rejected as hardly suitable. Inevitably, there have been several suggestions: "Kinneswood Mokeport", "Inverguilt Gliding Centre", "Wellburn Parsley Patch" and "Uplift Edge". One which we thought would find favour was*

"Bishophill Bottom". However, the choice has been made. By popular demand, our address is now: "Scottish Gliding Union, Portmoak, Scotlandwell, by Kinross." We're on the map again!

The same issue provided an update on the work at Portmoak:

The pace of progress at Portmoak increases week by week. Even the local farmers have caught our enthusiasm and arrive each Sunday with equipment of increasing complexity. Amid the clouds of dust and tractor smoke, members may be seen toiling patiently with spades and things, a pleasing contrast of ancient and modern which has surely not escaped the eye of Bill Lawson, who, between spells of furious activity, prowls about with his camera, recording our toil for the amusement of future generations of birdmen.

A visitor and potential member drove past the site three times last Sunday but didn't come in because he thought it was a display of agricultural machinery. But when he saw naked bodies grovelling in the mud, he realised it was the gliding club.

Much admiration has been lavished on the Andrew Thorburn Bridge, completed in two weekends by a great deal of hard labour. It is a sleeper bridge resting on abutments made from the stones from a nearby dyke. The ash from Eric Anderson is being dumped in the field which is destined to be the car park, and is

The Andrew Thorburn Bridge

already being spread to form the access road to the hangar.

The hangar foundations have been excavated, again by club labour, and the builder is due to start work in a couple of days. The cottage at Wellburn is in full use as temporary clubrooms now, and

Levelling the site for the hangar.

Jim Hedley has brought along a new Calor-Gas cooker and Percy is full in his praise of it.

There is still a lot to do, but this time next month we hope to report the first tentative launches.

Digging the foundations for the hangar

The 'Percy' referred to in the previous paragraph was Percy Mutum. Percy lived in Kinross and cycled to Balado with his boxes of groceries, and provided all catering facilities at the airfield. With the move to Portmoak, he turned his bike around and simply cycled in the other direction. His work at Portmoak was certainly more challenging but being ever resourceful, he set up a temporary 'kitchen' at one end of the hangar and so, the masses were fed.

As promised, the next issue of *Uplift* reported on the first flights from Portmoak:

> ### No Champagne
> In an atmosphere of no drama whatsoever, the first launch from Portmoak took place on Sunday, 23rd June 1957. The event was unheralded by any great rejoicing. Work on the ditch ceased for a moment until the cable was pulled in, then members swarmed back to work once more, and the long grind continued. It has, in fact been continuing ever since with remarkable results. The BIG DITCH, the major obstacle, has now been completely filled in. For weeks, ashes, earth, old trees, and occasionally even jeeps have been cast into the yawning chasm with little apparent result, until suddenly the thing is filled in, and we can start on another hole.
> The hangar, now that the contractors have been paid off, has gradually been pulled into something approaching its original shape, enough for work to begin on hanging the doors. The west end is almost complete and we look forward without cheer to the prospect of hoisting into place that enormous beam that the main doors are supposed to dangle from.
> Signposts, expertly painted by Maurice Berry, have sprouted to deter casual interlopers from straying too far, and to satisfy their curiosity as to what is going on, on the other side of the fence. The clubrooms are, as yet, lying where we left them in bits, and we are still

using the cottage at Wellburn, half a mile along the road. The telephone has been installed there, by the way, and the number is Scotlandwell 43.

Those first historic flights were made by Andrew Thorburn and Tom Davidson in the T21. There was no wind and the circuits lasted no more than two minutes each, but this was enough to put smiles on their faces, and they then started the preparations for the first summer course at Portmoak, due to start the following week.

The first flight from Portmoak

True to plan, that first summer course did indeed take place one week later on 1st July, 1957. The CFI (Tom Davidson) ran the course and Joe Kennedy was the winch driver. On the Monday evening there was a moderate west wind and, after the course had stopped for the day, Andrew Thorburn took various members along to Bishop Hill in five soaring trips in the T21. The lift was reached easily from mere 850 ft. launches, and when they got to the hill they found 20 ft. per second green.

The Krajanek was sold to Camphill and a brand new Slingsby Prefect was purchased as a replacement. Pilots would have to be approved by the flying committee before flying the Prefect, and they would also be required to pay an extra subscription of £5.

Hill soaring was becoming almost a weekly affair for SGU pilots. They could soar Bishop or Benarty depending on wind direction, but the increasing number of land outs at the bottom of these hills forced the club into refining their rules about hill soaring. All members were issued with a document reminding pilots about the need to obey the *Rules of the Air* and providing suitable extracts, as well as local rules for Bishop and Benarty.

September 1957 proved to be the best month so far for Portmoak. On the 16th, Bob Porteous reached 14,000 ft. in wave; On the 30th, Jack Alcock flew the Prefect 37 miles and reached 9,600 ft., and John Henry flew the Olympia 45 miles and reached 10,500 ft. Total flying, from Portmoak for 1957 was 1424 launches, 244 hours and 71 flying days (36 soaring days).

Flying continued over the festive period and the first ab-initio to fly solo from Portmoak was Jane Ross, on 5th January 1958.

By 1958, the SGU site at Portmoak was firmly on the map. So much so, that the governing body (British Gliding Association) agreed that Portmoak should host the 1958 National Gliding Week. This of course meant more frantic efforts by the band of volunteers. One of the first tasks

Levelling the airfield for aero-towing

was the levelling of the airfield by bulldozer so that aero-towing could be carried out. Although this had been part of the master plan, the timescales were now a little tighter. A temporary club room was planned for inside the new hangar, as it was thought that the permanent club rooms (still lying in pieces) would not be ready in time.

The newly levelled aero-tow strip proved to be successful and the Olympias and the Prefect were towed to the south east slope of Benarty on 16th March, where they both soared the hill. The fleet continued to grow, with Bill Lawson's Eagle arriving in April, another Tutor being purchased and a Grunau Baby, from the RNGSA at Arbroath, being based at Portmoak.

The pundits continued to make good use of Portmoak ahead of the National Gliding Week. Charlie Ross flew to Scone, Ansgar Sambale flew to Sheriff Muir and Jack Alcock took one of his pupils to 8,000 ft. in wave in the T21b. Among the entrants for the competition were Philip Wills and Geoffrey Stevenson. The week itself was a combination of good weather and tropical downpours and a not too flattering picture on the front cover of the *S&G* October 1958 showed a very wet Portmoak under the banner 'Portmoak Paddy Fields', and an article by Philip Wills entitled 'On Being a Bur-r-d' suggested that he had had a rather cold week.

The end of 1958 provided more epic flights, including one by Charlie Ross to Kilberry on the Mull of Kintyre, and a wave flight to 10,000 ft. by Tom Docherty.

Towards the end of the year a rather strange contraption could be seen scurrying

Andrew Thorburn on the tail of his Oly, daughter Lynn on the wing tip and son Brian on the nose, National Gliding Week - 1958

up and down the field between the launch point and the winch. This was the Hendry-Sambale 'Electric Hare'. An experimental device, this was a sled on an endless cable on the second drum of the winch and was used for cable retrieving. This was also the year that the famous Portmoak Ash was spread onto the field.

Although the year had shown 2779 launches, 666 hrs of gliding, 137 flying days and 81 soaring days, it was marred by the death of Jack Maclean who was killed in an accident to the Prefect on 17th August. Jack had been on aerotow behind Bill Lawson in the Tiger Moth heading over to Benarty when observers on the ground saw him getting very high behind the tug. Within a few moments, the glider had pulled the tail of the tug upwards and the anxious club members now watched in horror as both aircraft disappeared from view. They set off for the general area and saw that Bill Lawson had landed the Tiger Moth in a field at the foot of the hill. Bill explained how he had been about to release the tow rope when it auto-released from the glider. This nylon rope whipped back and wrapped itself around the tail of the Tiger Moth then got caught in the propeller and stopped the engine. Bill still had some control and was able to do a dead-stick landing into the field. They removed the nylon rope and, after a quick check that everything was OK, Bill took off again to look for the glider. He told the others to watch for him circling if he spotted the glider. Bill found the Prefect and as the others arrived, they were met by a group of distraught picnickers who had been first on the scene. The resulting post-mortem suggested that the pilot had suffered a heart attack whilst flying behind the tug and had died before the glider had crashed.

1958 had seen no issue of the club magazine *Uplift*, due, no doubt, to other pressing activities at Portmoak but by late spring in 1959, club communications were back on stream. Not, however, with the latest issue of *Uplift*, instead a brand new publication was making its first appearance, *The Portmoak Press,* issue one proclaimed:

In an attempt to bring light to the darker areas, and to spread abroad the doings of the SGU, a further episode commences in the history of the publications of the SGU. The name 'Uplift', and indeed the character, has confused many, and it is felt that the break should be made so that we do not inherit the 'Will-o-the-Wisp' appearance. To this end we have renamed our official news-sheet the 'Portmoak Press', and with this, our first issue, we trust it will begin to show some of the vigour and character of the airfield.

We are hoping to retain the star writer of 'Uplift', namely 'Donner and Blitzen' Bryce, and from time to time others who may feel disposed to add their chaff or grouse, will be heartily welcome.

At the request of many interested members, we are including the now famous account of a visiting competitor's impressions of the National Gliding Week at Portmoak last year:

(Ed's note:- In explanation, the aircraft flown by Bill Tonkyn was a Slingsby Skylark 3b [competition no. 66], his partner in this competition was Bernard Davey, the other member of the crew being Brian Gorringe. Bill Tonkyn gained first place in the final score, being awarded the BGA Tankard; read on:)

National Gliding Week – Scottish Region at Portmoak
by Bill Tonkyn

The 66 syndicate had decided to go to Portmoak for National Gliding Week. It was a nice long way from Lasham. We would all go, highly organised, and we would divide the spoils between us. However, due to one thing or another, Bernard Davey and I, with Brian Gorringe (by arrangement with Mrs Gorringe) to look after us, were the only ones to set forth in Paul's snake-proof Vanguard on the bright morning of Friday 25th July.

At the border, a seasonable Scottish mist developed and we arrived at Portmoak on Saturday afternoon in what felt more like rain to find that the rural charm of a camping site had lost its appeal. Search was therefore made for more congenial, if more expensive, accommodation until such time as tent rigging should become attractive, and an open door was found eight miles away at the Glenfarg Hotel. The landlord turned out to be an amiable rogue, to whom the merest nod was an order for two brown ales and a shandy. It was touching to see the way his face beamed as each time rain threatened, he inked in the pencil marks against rooms 9 and 16 on his list.

Sunday dawned doubtful, but with the prospect of afternoon soaring, an out-and-return race to the Lake of Menteith, 38½ miles each way, was set. Meanwhile, a conducted tour of the site seemed a useful occupation. Portmoak is a rather odd shaped field, thanks to a somewhat ungliding farmer next door, and sits on the eastern edge of Loch Leven midway between Bishop Hill and Benarty Hill, both of which can be reached by winch launches. For the mental comfort of pilots taking off on aerotow over the loch, St. Serf's Island lurks at a convenient distance offshore, and to it a winch cable can be carried by a wading man in case of need. The surface of the field, and indeed the whole club, showed evidence of much loving labour, but even so, the selection of suitable landing areas seemed to need care; in practice, however, all went well.

Shortly after 11 o'clock, patches of blue sky started appearing; at 12:45 Tonkyn had a winch launch to 800 ft. and came down again. It was so nearly soarable that the offer of an immediate second launch seemed worth accepting (after all, the ration was six) and a 20 minute struggle at 700-900 ft. ensued, with everybody else looking on. Suddenly, however, we contacted and proceeded smartly to 8,500 ft. Everybody still looked on because winching fumbles and a wind change neatly coincided with *my departure; some were still hopefully having aerotows under a sea breeze clamp when I returned three hours later after a flight which would have ended halfway but for a last moment awakening of bright shiny thermals which assured a pleasant romp home. Geoffrey Stevenson's enforced late start permitted him these conditions over most of the route, and he beat my time by an hour. Both Andrew Thorburn and Philip Wills (who started very late) turned, but failed to get back.*

On Sunday evening we rigged the tent for occupation on the morrow, and thus it was that we awoke on Monday morning to the sound of heavy rain bouncing off the windowsill on to my shirt. All day and night it rained with enthusiastic vigour, the burns swelled into raging torrents, unwary motorists ground to a steamy halt, and Portmoak receded beneath new and nameless lochs. It never really recovered.

Tuesday was Bernard's day. Bishop Hill was highly soarable, the task was free distance, and all ranks (except Bill Lawson, who was in Edinburgh counting rolls of sodden newsprint) clambered up and tried to get away. The only successful ones were Philip and Steve, who slipped off and found one genuine live cloud going to 8,000 ft. and volplaned gently down to Berwick, about 60 miles. When Bernie was sore enough and thoroughly discouraged, he handed over 66. Half an hour later, it was at the foot of Benarty Hill. A second bold plan, whereby the height obtainable on Bishop Hill (3,500 ft.) would be converted into north-easterly distance, led to an apologetic call from four miles away asking for a double retrieving crew. The field was soft, squidgy, earth but it was of interesting cross-section and the streams which ran down its steep-sided valleys formed a delta of quicksand at the bottom edge. This fact, already discovered, was later verified by Colonel Benson whilst everybody's backs were turned. Business was brisk at the Glenfarg Hotel as dusk became night.

Wednesday having passed without incident, Thursday was my day, in spite of my escapades of Tuesday, and I declared Newcastle. Off went 66, plastering mud all over her wings, to find that a Skylark 3 could only just soar in the conditions. From 500 ft., we struggled up then a side-step and away into low cloud. At 5,500 ft. things looked good. Big cumuli were building to the south, building beautifully, but they saw us coming. An hour-and-a-half later I was at 700 ft., only 15 miles out. All was not lost, however, and patience brought its reward, but even so I had only achieved 5½ crow miles in 3½ hours when the sea breeze finally deposited me in a fine hayfield at Chirnside. It was a lovely evening and seemed even better when we found out that Philip was only a mile down the road and the others still at Portmoak, the notable exception being Andrew, who had dashed from the hill to a 16 mile goal.

Friday was a day which didn't quite meet expectations. No soaring, hardly any flying, just gamesmanship. Winner probably the Gaffer, with a neat de-rigging ploy.

On Saturday the wind blew from the north and a race to Stravithie Station and back was declared, Stravithie being 23½ miles away east-north-east, near St. Andrews. In due course, Bernard joined the gang on Benarty Hill and then moved on to Lomond Hills, which are in effect a north edge of Bishop Hill. Olympias found this crossing too far from the height obtainable on Benarty, but a Skylark 3 was all right, Jack. Eventually Bernard and Geoffrey disappeared from view, the wily gaffer paid a visit to Portmoak to cross the starting line, but it did him no good at all. In fact Bernard and Geoffrey were the only finishers, and they did not have trouble-free journeys; Bernard was forced south to the coast on the way back and nearly had to land. But he didn't, his fourth cross-country was successfully completed, and we were delighted to find that his time (from take-off) was little more than Geoffrey's. We were keeping our end up. Of the others, Philip had landed soon after turning the Eagle at the turning point, and Andrew Thorburn, only four miles from Portmoak; he had arrived at St. Andrews in rain and had turned back without seeing, or being seen, by the turning point, so his achievement failed to gain the marks it deserved.

Sunday was the last flying day, as Monday produced rain and gales once more. The forecast had encouraged early rising, and an air of greater interest than had hitherto been noticeable was to be found as the task setters entered briefing. Distance on a line through Fraserburgh, on the coast 116 miles away north-north-east was announced, and activity started. Cumulus appeared, with real blue patches round them, and one by one, people got away from Bishop and set off. Meanwhile, Tonkyn sat on the ground. Having landed back after a first launch was squandered on an interesting looking cloud, only to see both winch cables disappearing together for an hour's happy entanglement (yes, that little trick happens in Scotland too) and having then recklessly gone too far out from Bishop and paid the price, I was pretty depressed at 2 o'clock as we re-rigged for an aero-tow. The clouds looked almost clapped out, but how wrong I was! Over Balado Aerodrome, former home of the SGU, the vario kicked to 5 metres and we were off. Things were good after all, the ceiling was a comfortable 7,500 ft. in cloud, and the sun shone on the beautiful hills, lochs and valleys of Scotland as the miles ticked by. It seemed best to keep inland of the line, to avoid the dreaded sea-breeze, and this was borne out by the experiences of the other contestants, all of whom scored; even Ted Stark had found the thermal he had sought all week. Further north, the lines of cloud were dwindling, but there was still a big one just in reach. If it would give even 6,000 ft., we might join Philip in Fraserburgh. But it didn't quite; neither did we.

And that was the end. We worked out the results, shared out the magnificent prizes, thanked the organisers for their tremendously hard work, and trailed home again.

Bernard, Brian and I had had a very enjoyable holiday, we had learned a lot, and we had resolved to go back to Portmoak some day soon. Thank-you SGU.

The club office bearers and directors for 1959 were:

President	-	E.V. Anderson
Chairman	-	R. Parker
Secretary	-	W.A. Shanks
Treasurer	-	W. Lawson
Asst. Treasurer	-	S. Milne
CFI	-	T. Davidson
Deputy CFI	-	W.S. Adamson
Airfield Manager	-	J. Ford
Ground Engineer	-	R. Williamson
Aircraft Ancillaries	-	A. Sambale
Aircraft Maintenance	-	R. Williamson
Vehicle Maintenance	-	J. Pinkerton
Publications	-	D. Hendry
Clubhouse Plans	-	I. Sproul
Directors of Flying	-	T. Docherty, A.J. Thorburn and J. Rae

Their tasks were wide ranging during the year, from flying activities to deciding what to do with the original Bishop Hill Hut (this was the hut that had been commandeered, then returned, by the ATC at the end of the war). In the end, it was decided to dismantle the hut and remove it from the hill, then rebuild it at Portmoak at the west end of the airfield and use it for a winch shelter, although it didn't quite work out that way.

The Hangar with toilet block at the far end and the Bishop Hill Hut bits near the far fence, awaiting assembly. Bishop Hill is in the background.

Successes during the early part of 1959 included Bill Lawson and Andrew Thorburn taking their Eagle two-seater to first place in the Easter Rally at the Long Mynd. This had been achieved with a free distance flight of 145 miles (Church Stretton to Marham near Kings Lynn), and being the longest flight of the year from the Mynd, won them the Siam

Trophy. A couple of weeks later (10th May 1959), Nick Goodhart completed a record goal flight when he landed at Portmoak, having set off from Lasham. Andrew Thorburn's daughter, Lynn, recalled his landing:

> *I remember the hangar being built and the corner being floored-off for a club area. I went outside one evening and I saw a glider landing in the dark. When I went in and told dad and the others, they checked the log, counted the aircraft and decided that I had a wild imagination! As I tried to convince them that I was not going daft, some of the other members came in with a visitor who was claiming a long distance record!*

Nick recalled his record-breaking flight for *S&G*:

> *The Bonnie Banks of Loch Leven...*
>
> *The opening day of the National Championships seemed very promising at briefing when a forecast was given which indicated the possibility of a day of thermal soaring with a strong tail wind, and a chance of thunderstorms in the evening which might add a considerable distance. The task for the day of "free distance" meant that one had no problem except to decide on the earliest time at which it would be safe to get started. The forecast had indicated that thermals of a sufficient size might develop by 10:30 or so, so I was not worried when I found myself ready for first take-off at 10:45, despite the failure of any cumulus clouds to appear.*
> *My estimate of the possibility of a very long flight had led me to make a goal declaration of Portmoak, the fine new site of the Scottish Gliding Union on the south-east corner of Loch Leven. This somewhat optimistic declaration had no significance as far as the competition went, since, in a free distance task, there are no bonus*

points for declaring one's goal. I had therefore chosen Portmoak as being the ultimate possibility, rather than with any thought of there being a reasonable likelihood of getting there.

As soon as I was airborne it became apparent that I had considerably over-estimated conditions, and in fact within half an hour I was forced to land back at Lasham. As I landed I saw Deane-Drummond slowly creeping up in a weak thermal and setting off, so immediately after landing I got a new take-off time and was towed off again. Half an hour later I was back on the ground again, with my morale at an extremely low level, as I was convinced that several others who had already left would be far ahead of me.

Finally at 13:03 I got my third and last tow (only three tows are permitted on competition day). But this time the picture was entirely different, good streets of cumulus had formed all over the sky and it was immediately apparent that the clouds had good thermals underneath them. I released a mile south-east of the airfield in 300 - 400fpm and was carried straight up to cloudbase at 3,000ft asl. There was a south-east wind of 15-18kt and a good street of cumulus led straight away on track of about 330°. Under this street, lift was so plentiful that it was virtually unnecessary to circle, with the result that 40 minutes later I found myself slightly west of Kidlington at the end of my cloud street, having averaged close to 70mph. From here on, cloud streets were less well defined and it became necessary to step from cloud to cloud. However, cloudbase was steadily rising and reached 5,000ft during the next phase of the flight, which involved flying through the Birmingham Control Zone and Amber 1. In these areas the cumulus had built up to quite considerable heights and it was tantalising indeed to have to break off the climb under several promising clouds. However, there were no serious low points and I was able to keep going, albeit at a much slower speed since I was now trying to make ground towards the east in order to ensure that I went up the east side of the Pennines.

By 16:00 I was just by Chesterfield and came to my first chance to enter cloud, getting a rather slow climb to 7,500ft. Coming out of this cloud I was immediately presented with a good growing cu-nim, but was above the base and had to enter it from the side; below me David Ince's red and white Oly 419 stood out clearly as he headed for the same cloud. Despite my entering from the side, I was soon able to find a core of lift which quickly built up to over 2,000ft a minute. This was quite the roughest cloud I have ever been in; the turbulence was such that I was convinced that I must be on the edge of the main lift area, but no amount of searching would show smooth lift but only succeeded in producing temporary interruptions in the climb.

Soon after passing 10,000ft I realised that the climb might go quite high, so fished out my oxygen mask and turned on the oxygen. Fortunately the mask is easy to put on, so even in the extreme turbulence I was soon sorted out and giving full attention to the climb; but after a quarter of an hour and at 18,000ft I could find no more lift, so straightened up on a northerly heading to come out of the cloud.

It was at this point that I received a very severe shock through both feet where they were resting against the rudder cables, although in fact I had not seen much lightning. Soon I came out of the side of the cloud and was in clear air. However the ground was quite invisible through the murk below, and a huge anvil of cloud spreading out over my head made everything seem very dark and gloomy.

When I finally got enough of the canopy clear of ice to be able to see out properly, I could see that there was a very considerable load of wing icing of a most interesting but incredibly un-aerodynamic shape, and if my instruments were right I was only getting a still-air gliding ratio of something like 1:14. One wonders under such circumstances what on earth is the best speed to fly.

Now that I could see a little bit, I realised that there was another band of cumulus 20 miles or so ahead, and I was able to enter this at just over 10,000ft and get carried back up to 15,500ft. On coming out of this cloud it was apparent that there was nothing further in the way of clouds out in front.

The ground was still hidden in a layer of misty haze and the question arose as to which way to steer. I had not bothered to get any high altitude wind forecasts for this area, and it was over an hour since I had last seen the ground. For want of a better course I headed due north and slowly, as I got lower, I began to see something through the haze.

At first I got the somewhat discouraging impression that I was over the sea, but luckily this was not so, and by the time I was down to 8,000ft I could make out that I was over moorland; and at about this height I was glad to say goodbye to the ice, which was so seriously affecting my performance. About 20ft of this ice came off the port wing and I saw it sailing away behind me. A 20ft ice spear may have come as rather a surprise to some enthusiastic moor walker.

At about 4,500ft I succeeded in identifying my position over a railway line 20 miles east of Carlisle, and at this point was surprised to find very weak lift of about 50 fpm.

This lift was clearly of wave type, and by heading just south of east I was able to keep in it and gain about 500ft. However, try as I might, I could gain no more and so was forced to set off again on what was clearly a final glide. Purely by chance, and trying to stretch my final glide to the limit, I happened into a valley which carries the Carlisle to Edinburgh railway just north of a place called Newcastleton. The ground wind was obviously strong from a point just south of east, and I was busily engaged in selecting myself a safe landing field when suddenly I found good lift on the windward facing slope, the characteristic smoothness of which clearly indicated that it was of wave type,

Quickly forgetting all thought of landing, I started working this wave lift and for a while was actually getting 1,000ft/min out of it. By continuous trial and error I kept in the area of maximum lift, and to my intense surprise in some three-quarters of an hour I managed to reach 10,000ft. Barring unforeseen circumstances, this was clearly enough to reach Portmoak, so I set off heading considerably east of north, and by taking advantage of a few minor waves I found myself crossing Edinburgh at 6,000ft.

Portmoak was obviously in the bag, but there was one major problem. I had never been there before and the site was not marked on my map. I had a reasonably strong conviction that it lay at the south-east corner of Loch Leven, but what it looked like I had no idea. I was therefore extremely glad of my excess altitude, knowing that I would have time to explore a little to find it. In the event, this problem was easily solved as the field was very obvious indeed, due to the cable retrieving tracks running the length of it and the hangar in the corner.

With 4,000ft to go, I could of course have gone on and scored more miles towards the competition. However, a quick look at low stratus already covering the hilltops made me unenthusiastic about pressing on into the Scottish hinterland, and anyway I was miserably cold and tired, so without a second thought I pulled the dive brakes and rushed down to land. The ground wind at Portmoak was strong and a touch north of east, so I might not have got so very much farther anyway. After landing I did not dare get out on account of the strong wind until help came, but of course I was soon surrounded by a cheerful crowd of Scottish Gliding Unionists, into whose wonderfully hospitable hands I was delighted to fall.

So much then for my story, but that is not the whole tale by a long chalk. There should be another complete chapter covering the marathon 36hr retrieve by Bill Swift and Sammy Sansom, but if you want that story you will have to ask one of them for it.

Statistics
Air distance	*360 miles*
Average speed	*56.4 mph*
Total road distance	*960 miles*
Petrol used	*69 gallons*
Water used	*15 buckets*

(we were having a little radiator cap trouble)

Records: British distance, British Goal, UK distance, UK goal and UK 500km speed record.

By far the biggest success of the year so far was the news that Andrew Thorburn's efforts in furthering gliding in Scotland had been recognised by the Federation Aeronautique Internationale. He was being awarded with the Paul Tissandier Diploma at the F.A.I. meeting in Moscow.

Despite the constant work going on at the airfield, the recently delivered Swallow was put to good use, albeit only by 'approved' pilots. One such pilot was Joe Kennedy. On 9th August he soared in a Lee Wave downwind of Bishop Hill. Cloud base was on the top of the hill, the wind was 15 kt easterly and Joe managed to fly in a clear patch in the downwind side of the 'hole'.

The following week, Tom Davidson flew to Fraserburgh:

The day is Saturday, the time about 10:30 and the weather, well for a working day it is not at all good. But as this could be a half day, I could probably permit myself at least one upward glance and try to assess the possibilities. Certainly not an ideal day for the garden fete along the road. Much too blustery and there is a good chance of some really heavy showers later on.

As I gazed upwards at the very healthy looking sky, already covered with 3/8th cumulus, I was certain I heard a voice say "What will I do with this barograph?" But wrenching myself from the current met. situation, I was rather disappointedly confronted by one of the workman asking "What will I do with this barrow Gaff?" and so back to bricks and things.

However, by 12 o'clock, the weather situation looked just fine and the expedition to Portmoak was organised. One quick circuit of Dundee and we were underway. I made good time to Portmoak and, having enjoyed my 50 m.p.h. snack, felt in good trim on arrival at the airfield.

I was more than disappointed, however, at seeing the hangar doors tightly shut and no sign of activity anywhere. Eventually I managed to locate a small band of "anti-gliding" folk exchanging stories in the temporary clubroom and succeeded in showing my disappointment rather well. After quite a lot of thumping around on the club-room floor, I managed to muster enough support to slide the hangar doors to one side and after a quick D.I. rolled the new Swallow to the launching point. With a lot of splendid co-operation, and the usual corny remarks about the cable dropping, the machine was whisked up through a 45 degree cross-wind to a height of 800 ft. A quick downwind dash straight to Bishop Hill and in next to no time I had climbed to 1800 ft. Conditions were much more turbulent than the previous pilot had been able to convince me was the case. Once or twice the machine was carried behind the hill and considerable height was lost in regaining the area of lift.

It was obvious that the chances of getting away would be better away from the hill. With the machine on a heading for the hangar, an area of 3 up was located, and after working this for some time, I found myself out of it at about 2,400 ft. By this time, of course, I was too far downwind to get back to Portmoak.

Thus committed, I spent the next 500 ft. searching in a downwind direction, and eventually located 2 up, 2 down and, after a little fiddling, centred onto a fairly steady 10 up. This took me quickly to cloud base at just under 5,000 ft. whereupon the lift improved nicely. Things went well in cloud and the instruments behaved themselves for the next 2,500 ft. after which minor fluctuations became a little less minor, and after a further 500 ft. in this condition, I more than welcomed a square yard of blue stuff at rather a bewildering angle.

Emerging from the cloud with 8,000 ft., I located my position over the River Tay just south of Invergowrie.

Conditions seemed well marked and looked very poor to the west, not so poor up the middle, and very good to the east. Because of the small degree of west in the wind, I favoured the not so poor up the middle and headed over the radar-masted Craigowl north of Dundee. Travelling at an I.A.S. of 55 kt, Forfar was soon below me and the height was just under 4,000 ft. At this point the cloud amount to the west seemed to be total cover. Some weak lift was encountered at the edge, but this turned out to be too patchy to be worthwhile, and it wasn't until I was down to about 3,000 ft., slightly more to the east, that the lift re-appeared.

I next located my position directly over Edzell Airfield but could see no preparation for the car races which were to take place the following day. Just north of

Edzell, I recorded a low of 1,800 ft. and it wasn't until I had cleared the hills between which I was flying, that I managed to lift the machine back to 3,500 ft. From this point, the flight was uneventful until I reached an area just south of Aberdeen where the cloud seemed to taper off into blue sky. This looked like the end of the trip and I wondered what sort of reception I would get at Dyce Airport.

However, I decided to forego the facilities at Dyce (and the landing fee) and convert my 2,900 ft. into distance towards Peterhead, and so add an extra few miles. I hadn't gone far when the green ball came back to life with a fine healthy 5-10 up. The machine seemed to be flying rather well despite my tendency to fly it too slowly. Up at 5,000 ft. and a little nearer the coast, the chances of reaching Peterhead seemed much better. Visibility was excellent by now and this was by far the most pleasant part of the trip. It was now clear that I would reach Peterhead and would probably land at the Airfield at Rattray.

Down to about 2,000 ft. and now over the coast, it seemed unlikely that I would make any more out of it, as I would have to fly dead cross-wind overland which didn't look very suitable. However, lady luck provided another stepping stone with a 5-10 up. I tried two circles in the lift and on the third the lift fell away, whereupon I headed the machine inland and soon located 10 up once more. I tried the same thing again, with the same result. The third time, I decided to fly straight along the coast, which was cross wind direction. The lift remained fairly constant, but eventually I lost the lift and decided to press on for Fraserburgh Airfield. I arrived there with 1,500 ft. in hand which gave me a few minutes flying time over the old fishing village of Inverallochy. I approached from the seaward end of the airfield, over the railway, and landed at 17:45 in a 15 knot surface

wind. The usual procedure followed and the retrieving crew arrived just before 11:00 p.m.
What of the retrieve? – Well, that was another adventure!

On the ground at Portmoak, the work continued apace. The hut that had nestled on Bishop Hill for so long had been dismantled and carried down to Portmoak. Railway sleepers were dug in to provide a foundation and the hut was erected next to the hangar. A bulldozer, complete with 'expert' driver coaxed away mountains of rubble and filled in numerous holes with topsoil.

Sadly, one of the club magazine's most prolific contributors – Dennis Bryce – died while swimming with club members in Loch Leven. His last published item was:

The Parable of the Soarer

Now there was a certain merchant, a purveyor of costly rainments and fine linens, and a man of power. And he was minded to take unto himself the wings of an eagle and ascend into the heavens. And he drew nigh unto he place that is called Portmoak. And lo, the air was filled with the heavenly host, so that he marvelled, saying "I will gird myself about with a gliding machine, and become as one with them." And he did so, and secured himself therein by strong bonds.

And the instructor appeared unto him, saying "Seest thou yonder hill?" And the merchant sayeth, "Tarry a while 'till I find my spectacles". And presently he saw the hill, and it was a ladder twixt heaven and earth, and birdmen going up and down it like yo-yos. And the instructor sayeth unto him "Harken unto my words, for they are wise. Canst thou but reach the hill, thou shalt be lifted up upon a mighty rushing wind, and if thou guidest thy craft aright, it may be that thou shalt attain zero two point five angels. But if thou heedest me not, and keepest not the hill nigh unto thyself, it is possible that thou shalt become one, though this is doubtful. And if it comes to pass that thou attainest the hill but has not an adequacy of cubits, tarry thou not, but get thee from that place and return hither. And seest that thou maintainest a sufficiency of knots, lest the ground rise up against thee and smite thee."

And a great way off, the winch driver spake, and it was the voice that crieth in the wilderness. And he sayeth "Lo, I pray thee, give me a sign". And a sign was manifested unto him, and he took up his slack and launched. And the merchant arose, and at length drew nigh upon the hill that is called Bishop, though not high enough by half.

And it came to pass that there was a great calm, and he sayeth unto himself "Lo, it is too high. I cannot attain unto it!" and he was sore afraid. And he turned his eyes unto the airfield, and it was a great way off, and his angels were not many. And he cried unto the Lord in his affliction, saying "O,Lord, who art able to keep me from falling, make thy winds to blow that I might ascend, and not be cast down." But the Lord harkened not unto him, for his ways were evil, and not in accordance with the teachings of the Cee-Effi, who knowest all things. So he was cast down from on high, and drew nigh unto the earth. And he fell upon stony ground, and brake himself upon the rocks, and great was the downfall thereof. And when he came unto himself he saw with much sorrow that the glider was brake into the bargain.

And he took himself unto a physician who sayeth "Yes, verily thou hast braked thyself upon the rocks". And he prepared for him a bed of mortar and lime of great price, and laid him upon it, saying, "Tarry thou there, and after many days shall I return unto thee and see how thou doest." And he was sick many days, but at length he arose, and girded himself about with steel, and walked.

Verily, verily, I say unto thee, "If thou art a man of power, and wouldst go up with the wings as an eagle, thou must put thy power away, and become as little children, and harken unto the words of the Prophet Cee-Effi, which are of fine gold."

Visitors continued to flock to Portmoak, and the return of founder member Donald (Doc.) Campbell was a welcome sight in September. Ron Flockhart (by now a famous racing driver), paid a flying visit by dropping in in his Auster and staying for tea.

Flying summary for 1959, in which the SGU celebrated its 25th Anniversary, included; 3543 launches, 756 hrs 29 mins flying time, 131 flying days and 69 soaring days. Certificates gained were; 14 'A's, 14 'B's, 8 'C's, 2 Silver 'C's, 10 Silver 'C' legs and 1 Gold 'C' leg.

The usual Christmas party was held in the Bridgend Hotel on 19th December. Mrs. E.V. Anderson presented the trophies to the prize winners:- R. Porteous (height), Tom Docherty (Distance), and Mrs. Dorothy Lawson was awarded a new trophy for services to the club 'The Service Salver'. This award had been donated to the club by Andrew Thorburn.

Chapter 6

The Promised Land 1960 – 1962

The sixties started quietly at Portmoak. The official club magazine reported that 'Little flying took place, but good progress had been made laying the drains!'. In line with other clubs in the UK, the SGU decided it needed a Public Relations Officer – and Andrew Thorburn stepped into the breach. Little did he know that one of his first tasks would be to write an obituary for Robert Parker who was tragically killed in a car crash in early 1960. *Portmoak Press* reported:

> *Many of our members will have heard of the passing of our friend, chairman and benefactor; Mr Robert G. Parker. It is difficult to put into words the loss experienced by his many friends, and the gap left in the organisation of the SGU.*
>
> *In checking our records, we find that Robert had been our Chairman for a period of 14 years without a break in continuity. This shows how keenly interested he was in the SGU, and the unfailing support he gave in that period is well known to our older members.*
>
> *His enthusiasm, interest and his many other attributes will be remembered.*

One member, Stan Milne, started off the year by going on a sojourn down under to experience gliding in the Southern Hemisphere:

> *Does the cable fall down, or up, down under? At the top of the launch one is not very happy about doubts on the matter – yet it was in this situation that I found myself one hot and dusty Saturday afternoon with the Adelaide Soaring Club in South Australia. The temperature was in the 90s, the launching point had no shade, the water tap too far away but survival was*

assured by the presence of a huge box of cold Coca Cola.

The Adelaide Soaring Club, founded in 1944, operates at an old war-time aerodrome built by the Americans for their Mustang fighters. The field has two splendid concrete runways arranged in the form of a cross, and launching is by two self-laying twin drum winches. The club owns two "Wallabies" – ES49 two-seater dual instruction gliders and two Grunau Babies. The club has 90 members and to ensure a flight, it is the usual system of getting up at the crack of dawn to write one's name high up on the flying list.

My introduction to the club was to a very small band of enthusiasts who were up and about on New Year's Day operating a two-seater in the heat and glare of a scorching Australian Summer. I was made welcome and assisted in the preparations and the retrieving during the day's flying. Eventually my name appeared and it was during my fourth flight in the "Wallaby" that the cable dropping episode took place. The cable would not fall as gravity would have it fall, and we did part of a circuit together before parting company. This combination gave a phenomenal rate of sink while it lasted but all this was put to rights as soon as the cable fell to the ground. The cause was due to the otfur rings being used on an obsolete release mechanism. I had many other circuits during my six week-ends with the club and managed to put in one short thermal soaring flight. On the arts of thermal soaring I was given much valuable advice but my attempts to put this into practice invariably found me circling slowly earthwards, except once when by accident I barged into a thermal and circled upwards for 18 minutes.

My hours spent at Gawler were both interesting and enjoyable. Interesting to see how other people run a gliding club, and enjoyable in being allowed to participate as a temporary member in a club that extended a friendly welcome to a visitor from Portmoak.

The AGM that year agreed that work should proceed with the design and building of a clubhouse. Work teams were encouraged to tackle the host of small jobs around the airfield. Letters were issued to all members reminding them of the need to assist with these non-flying activities. A more concerning item at the AGM related to the cost of launching and a possible increase in charges to prevent the club running at a loss. After much deliberation, the club decided that a small increase in launch fees might be acceptable, but the launch rate would need to be increased by 10 launches per week in order to break even.

A group of mathematicians - some of them keen glider pilots - from Queen's College, Dundee went on an expedition to Portmoak to survey the weather. The local paper, *The Courier,* reported these strange goings on in September 1960:

Skymen Probe Weather Secrets

On windy hillsides and shower-swept fields around the western fringe of Fife this week, a little group of volunteer "backroom boys" are trying to probe the secrets of weather behaviour.

They want to establish in some detail the pattern of winds that roll down from the Ochils and the Grampians to the headquarters of the Scottish Gliding Union at Portmoak, and if they are successful in building up a picture of the invisible forces that keep the graceful, silent "skybirds" aloft, it could lead to new gliding accomplishments in Scotland.

Mr William Shanks of Lanark, secretary of the SGU said: "A reliable stock of information of this kind could help some of our pilots to set about breaking the Scottish gliding altitude record of 16,200 ft., or establishing new endurance figures."

The Royal Meteorological Society, London, are co-operating with the SGU in the week of experiments, and six meteorologists from airports and weather stations in England are working in conjunction with six glider pilots to make the necessary observations.

Heading operations are Dr. R.P. Pearce and Mr. J.M. Rushforth, of the mathematics department of Queen's College, Dundee, who have a practical interest in both meteorology and gliding.

They have the responsibility of computing the statistics from each day's observations and their findings will eventually be published in the form of a paper, complete with charts, of the up-currents that can be anticipated for advantageous gliding at various locations around Fife and Kinross in given sets of atmospheric conditions.

Mr. Rushforth said: "It may also be possible to build up a stock of maps showing the gliding conditions to be expected in a variety of circumstances. This would be of immense help to pilots operating in this region.

"At the same time, the meteorology men up here are learning to understand better the kind of local information that glider pilots need, and the pilots are getting an insight into the meteorological methods.

"They are learning to speak each other's language and this could lead to the easier interchange of useful information in the future."

Two-man teams released hydrogen filled balloons at regular intervals from widely spaced points across fields and hillsides so that they would soar directly over the Bishop hill, towering to 1,400ft. north of Portmoak.

Observers with theodolites tracked the balloons, taking regular fixes to determine their speed.

Mr. Rushforth explained: "We can check the airflow over the hill, and in its lee and we hope to discover that there will be regions of lift over and behind the hill which will be of use in gliding.

"The other technique is to fly gliders in the same sort of regions, equipped with thermometers because the temperature structure is an important part of our investigations.

"The gliders' positions are also recorded with theodolites and the men in each aircraft take regular readings indicating the rate of rise and fall of the aircraft along its course.

"In this way we get a record of the behaviour of the glider in a given set of conditions and this can be related to information from local weather stations to give a more detailed picture of the meteorological situation."

Mr. Rushforth and Dr. Pearce, who leaves next week for a nine month spell in the mathematics department of a San Francisco university, have already published one paper on conditions around the Kinross-shire gliding centre following preliminary investigations a year ago.

On the flying front, back at Portmoak, Tom Docherty managed a 90 mile flight to RAF Acklington at Easter and the winter wave season provided some notable flights in November.

On the 6th, the first wave of the winter was set up by a north wind. Martin Seth-Smith (Skylark II) soared Benarty then contacted wave over Loch Leven, soaring to 8,700 ft., Stan Milne, back from Australia, launched in his Swallow and almost immediately contacted the same wave system to reach 5,000 ft. to claim his Silver "C" height gain. The 27th saw some more lenticulars from a north wind and John Ford was first to test it out in his Swallow. He found that it provided a max. of 5000ft and was happy to fly up and down the wave system at this height. Martin Seth-Smith quickly joined John at 5,000 ft., he then moved to Westfield and contacted the larger wave which he found good to

10,300 ft. By the end of the year, 4,000 launches had provided more than 800 hours of flying.

The clubhouse was given planning permission and it was decided that rather than the usual Christmas Party, the money would be better spent on the clubhouse – and there would be a 'club' house warming party in the New Year instead.

The notice board sported an interesting reminder of the need for fund raising:

Per Ardua – Ad Portmoak

The die is cast – The bricks gae doon,
We've signed awa fower thoosan' poon,
The work-hut's up, the clubroom's started,
An' 1960 near departed,
Gin ye wad steek the door ticht shut,
'Gainst baillie wi' a debtor's writ,
GET OOT ABOOT AN TICKETS SELL,
TAE MAK' SGU COFFERS SWELL.

Nae Mare ye'll chitter in tin bothie,
Wi' parcelled pies and tepid brothie,
But lol at ease in plat'num palace,
Enough tae mak' Dunstable jealous,
Bold Percie dolled in tall white toorie,
Removed, frae former cauld ecurie,
Regails yer gizzard wi' elan,
Frae' contents o' his frying pan.

Then, tired o' nibblin' at the stoup,
Ye hae a yen tae loop the loop,
Sae, whistlin slick atour yer shouther,
A Skylark's wings sune heist ye thither,

Tae whar the game's catch as catch can,
Wi' thermals there for every man
Twice round by Stirling and Pethheid,
An back ye glide – prood o' the Deed.
Noo comes the time the tale tae' tell,
An' Percie's there again, tae sell,
The mead that soothes the coorsest tonge
Brings burbled yarns, that glide alang,
Thro' cloudy heaven sent mighty lift,
An' down draughts fit tae soak yer shift,
At last ye totter, or ye're led,
Tae warm and cosy sleep abed.
Is this your dream – is it your yen,
That glider lads should live like men,
An' ne'er be left tae chitter there,
On Cauld, dank, dirty, widden flair,
Propped up ae time in muckle hurry,
Tae meet the needs o' contest flurry.

THEN OOT YE GET THAE TICKETS, FREE
GIFT SCHEMES BRING IN THE L.S.D.

1961 saw the completion of the clubhouse and the October issue of *S&G* sported an aerial view on the front cover with a reworked article on the history (so far) of the club, by Andrew Thorburn. With a brand new clubhouse,

The 'bothie' referred to in the poem.

the Board of Directors decided to engage Frank and Tibby Ireland as clubhouse stewards. Other decisions made by the Board included:

- Transfer the Kirkintilloch workshop to Portmoak by May 1961.
- Try to buy a second-hand tutor (making two on site).
- Visit London for the A.G.M. of the British Gliding Association (BGA).
- Apply for approval to run BGA Instructors courses at Portmoak.
- Support Rab Williamson in his efforts to be appointed 'Senior Inspector'.
- Tear the guts out of the Cunarder 'Brittannic' in order to get furniture for the new clubrooms.
- Take serious action against all pilots and winch drivers whose 'cable-antics' bring the wrath of our neighbours upon us.

This last item was expanded with the following article in the next issue of *Portmoak Press*:

Cable Damage to Fences, Crops and the dangers thereof

Would you be happy if you were working in a field under a falling glider cable? Cables have been falling far too near Portmoak Farm of late, and at the request of the Committee, Mr Bell of Portmoak Farm attended the Directors' meeting to assist them in determining the best solution to this problem.

Firstly, the Directors are re-introducing the five shilling fine for each cable dropped over the north fences; winch drivers must report these or share the fine with the offending pilots. Since discussing this, it has been noted that two weekends of SW winds have not raised the usual crop of cable offences, in fact no instances have been reported.

It is rather obvious that it is not a case of circumstances being against the pilot but simply bad pilotage in most cases. Some say "What happens when a cable breaks in a SW wind?" Again, during the two weekends mentioned, no cable breaks occurred – mainly due to the high standard of Daily Inspection and careful winch driving.

The lesson is there for us all – better airfield and flying discipline reaps benefits.

For the time being, we have agreed to a three months survey of the problem before further discussion with Mr Bell. It must be pointed out that our neighbour can take legal action to restrain us if we are causing a nuisance or danger. This would mean the cessation of flying in S or SW winds.

Even in a glider we have a countryman's responsibility to our neighbours and no farmer is going to be happy about airborne clowns unloading several hundredweight of steel wire on his head from somewhere aloft.

Please be warned.

Flying continued apace and, on the 4th July, Andrew Thorburn took three wave climbs – two in the T21 with course members and one in his Skylark 2 to 16,200 ft to claim his Gold height. The story of Andrew's 'busy' day was published in *S&G*:

<u>*On Being A YO-YO (Without oxygen)*</u>

By Monday, 3rd July, No. 5 Instruction Course had gradually slowed down to a full stop – after the usual winch frustration, and a howling wet gale that day. On Tuesday, however, the oscillation of the T-21 up and down to great heights was the stuff dreams are made of.

By mid-morning the sky developed copy-book lines of wave clouds lying across the north-west wind of about 25-30 kt, and the flight from cable-drop at 1000ft to the hill lift on Benarty, one mile across Loch Leven's storm-lashed surface, presented moments of doubt, which had to be concealed from the greatly impressed pupil. On arrival, however, the bowl supplied the usual supply of strong UP, and after half-an-hour, another simple soul was deposited back to Portmoak, firmly convinced that soaring is the Sport of the Age.

The next two pupils, both light-weights, had to be satisfied with extended circuits over the Loch and back as we just couldn't make it to the hill in strong wind. When pupil number four squeezed into the T-21, the nose bit the dust as his 15½ stone, wrapped up in 6ft 4 inches of brawn and muscle, reduced my share of the cockpit to something less than the breathing space generally allotted to a tame mouse. With a jolly quip about midgets, and an inward sigh of resignation, I prepared to float the load as gently as possible upwards on our very tender launching cables.

At 800ft (200ft less than the 1000ft usually needed for the over-loch trip to Benarty), I thankfully dropped the cable still intact, and started off on a high-speed short circuit. Over the loch, however, we still had green on the vario and it soon became apparent that our increased cruising speed, due to great weight, was not producing the plunging downward flight I had anticipated. Either we had with us a hydrogen producer plant in operation, or some unusual form of lift had come to aid us. Reaching out for the slopes of Benarty, we quickly climbed to 3000ft in the best patches of lift, and I then decided to investigate the possibilities of wave lift out over the water.

As we slowly drew away from the hill into wind, the coarse texture of the air changed to the classical silky smoothness we have become accustomed to in past flights of this kind, and with a slick grin I suggested to my companion that we might manage to transport ourselves unto ten angels. From his grunt of response, I gathered that he obviously did not believe me – so I shrivelled further into my small corner and manipulated the controls gently, as one must on such occasions. In a matter of minutes, the green ball was at the top of the scale and indicated steady unbroken lift of more than 20ft per second, so, as the altimeter hands started to chase each other rapidly around the dial, the astonishment of my passenger turned to enthusiasm. We floated up past the forming edge of the wave cloud above and behind Benarty and soon, at 8000ft looked down upon its crests.

By 10,000ft my triumph was complete and the panorama of waves was easy to see for miles beyond the Grampians and South to the Cheviots. The lift was still just under 20ft per second, and as we neared 13,000ft I asked my friend what effect he expected high altitude to have on him. He answered by saying he spent weeks at a time above 10,000ft in the Alps every year. At 14,000ft he assured me that if I passed out, he would be able to get me down. At 14,500ft I thought: this is a lark, higher than all other SGU efforts in a b....y two-seater with a ten-ton passenger! At 15,000ft I thought: Hell! - no barograph – still, it's fun – FUN? 15,200ft with NO BAROGRAPH!

The grin on my companion's face disappeared as I reached for the spoilers, pushed down the nose, and reduced climb to a mere 3ft per second. Gradually we progressed into the down-draught in the lee of the cloud ahead, and soon the red ball was jazzing around the 20 mark.

As we came back to land at Portmoak we noted that the time in the air from start to finish was 61 minutes. This will give a very clear idea of the power of the lift encountered.

Two more circuits with another pupil and then back to Benarty with a new customer. This time the lift on the hill was partly cancelled out by the down from the lee of the wave cloud just ahead, but after a struggle to 3000ft., progress ahead was made, and once more over the loch the altimeter started to wind-up.

Pleased to be able to make a fresh contact for my pupil's sake, but appalled when I thought of the Skylark and barograph down below, I suggested that 7,000ft would be enough. The look of scorn in his eyes sent me back to the best lift, and at 10,000ft I suggested that the scene would not improve with height. "But I might not get back here again" he said, so I dutifully took him higher until at 12,250ft my hand firmly clutched the spoiler lever and down we went once more. This time the trip took 1hr 12 minutes (we had dawdled quite a bit on the hill searching for the lift).

This was too much to bear – so I pleaded with the Course to release me for an hour. They did! Out came the Skylark 2 and we were off. In the meantime the Red

Oly, which had been nosing around at 2,500ft all morning with various pilots, was still in the air.

Back on the hill, I worked the lift to 3,000ft. and set off once again over the water to pick up the lower levels of the wave. Almost immediately contact was made and as I climbed rapidly in the usual 20 up, other sailplanes disappeared below.

Words cannot express the ease with which it all took place – the only effort required was to decide when to come down. At 14,000ft. the sense of well-being developed as before, and by 15,000ft deep breathing and heightened pulse rate came as a warning that old men of 51 are more susceptible to altitude than the younger members of the species.

Southwards lay wave after wave and a following wind of about 40 kt. A nice day to do a Nick Goodhart trip in reverse. What of Course No.5? Poor devils! Not another instructor available – paid cash for the week too. 15,700ft., still going up at 15-20ft per second. – 16,000ft. focusing my eyes became a distinct effort. Seems funny – better get down – sense of responsibility wins the day – or was it fear? Out came the spoilers at 16,200ft., nose down to 65 kt – into the sink area, and so rapidly back to Portmoak. – all in 65 minutes. Barograph trace is perfect, and shows a maximum of 16,200ft,; gain of height 15,000ft. at least. Gold "C" height – three times in one day! Highest solo, and highest T-21b in the SGU.

Blimey! Must ask Santa for an oxygen bottle this year.

For the eggheads
Leuchars met. Conditions on 4th July 1961 at 12:00 hrs:

Winds Feet	Direction	Knots
2,000	330	22
3,000	330	25
5,000	340	26

Winds Feet	Direction	Knots
7,000	340	29
10,000	340	36
14,000	330	44
18,000	330	49

Lapse Rate:
Dry adiabatic up to 5,500 ft. Isothermal up to 6,500 ft. Rather less than saturated adiabatic at 16,000 ft. Lower air mass: cold with a slight inversion at about 8,000ft.

Andrew Thorburn

By the end of the year, the club had purchased another Tutor, two ex-RAF winches and 12 acres at the SW corner of the field. Things were certainly looking up.

Flying, or to be exact, approaches were still causing concern for the CFI and his band of instructors though. The problem was the inability of pilots to see, or even worry about, the telephone and electricity cables strung between poles on the perimeter of the airfield. Numerous aircraft were slicing cables with their tail or, in one case, their front skid! This particular incident related to the Skylark 2 when *'enshrouded in wires, it twanged its way to a perfect deck landing in the car park. Speed of entry – 40 kt, stopping distance 50 ft – klunk!'.* Soon, bills were arriving from the telephone company, the power company and the repairers of bent gliders. These pilots were given the salubrious title of the 'Wire Pullers Club' and each of them was advised to undergo eye tests before being invited to go flying with the CFI.

In the fullness of time, Andrew Thorburn did succeed in getting these cables buried by the utility companies although, as will be seen later, pilots continued to undershoot into obstacles around the site.

Andrew had been busy in other areas too. He had set up a scheme whereby senior pupils from his Kirkcaldy High School could receive training flights at weekends, as part of the Duke of Edinburgh Award Scheme. This was followed up in 1961

with the Fife Schools Gliding Club being formed and flying on
week-day evenings from 5 p.m. 'till dusk.

By the end of the summer of 1961, three pilots seemed
determined to achieve their Silver C badges, as reported in
Portmoak Press:

> *A sudden enthusiasm seems to have struck some of
> our pilot members for obtaining their Silver C badges.
> Three pilots; Jimmy Burgess, Ian Dandie and Jim
> O'Donnell have launched a determined attack by
> completing their five hours. Jimmy Burgess achieved his
> in the Tutor after many a long wait for 'Tutorable'
> weather. The best of luck to them all.*

The above-mentioned Ian Dandie took up the post of
Convenor of the Publications Committee (for *Portmoak Press*),
with reporters Valerie Wyles, Mabel Ritchie and Christine
McLauchlan.

The annual prize-giving at the end of the year saw Andrew
Thorburn winning the club championship and the Maclay
Trophy, and, for best height, the Robert Parker trophy. Tom
Docherty won the Alan Boyle Trophy for best distance.

As in today's gliding clubs, those days in the early sixties
enjoyed youthful wit amongst the students, and the following
item appeared in the *Portmoak Press* at the end of 1961:

The Care and Feeding of Gliding Instructors

Part 1
*In learning to fly, the beginner is faced with two major
problems. First, the aircraft – second, the instructors.*

*The instructor is a special breed of glider pilot. He usually is
an instructor because he is no good as a soaring pilot. He is
easily recognised by his courage, extreme skill, low forehead
and mean little eyes.*

Because the instructor already knows how to glide, he has the student completely at a disadvantage. He is unimpressed with whatever skills the pupil might have outside the gliding world and is therefore dedicated to show the pupil how little he knows and how completely unsuitable the pupil is as glider pilot material.

Those who wish to make a success of their gliding courses are advised to refer to the few common-sense rules laid down in Part 2, when dealing with glider instructors.

Part 2

Let him know who is boss: This is done by keeping your mouth shut because he already knows that he is.

Earn his respect and admiration: Best done by saying that your father is the chairman of Lasham and could possibly loan the club a Skylark 3f and a trailer for a year or so.

Reward his efforts: It is well to bribe him with cigarettes, mints and the odd bottle of beer. In return, he might show you a little about flying a glider.

Let him know your problems: Hint that you have a smashing sister who could possibly be interested in gliding. Instructors are all girl crazy and you will get extra circuits whilst he thinks this over, and it also serves to keep his mind off your mistakes.

Show admiration for him: Let him know how impressed you are that he can fly, even though he is suffering from an acute hangover. Instructors are egotistical and will mistake this for a compliment.

Tell him your ambitions: Report for training with hair uncombed, a yellow shirt and dirty shoes. He will then begin to realise that you are potentially good gliding material and may even aspire to become an instructor yourself one day.

Demonstrate your aptitude: Fly with one wing low and slip and skid in all turns. Get plenty of bounce into your landing and ground-loop once in a while. Instructors prefer to think that all pupils are knuckleheads, so convince him that you

are indeed a lunatic. Instructors will generally send you solo when there is nothing else that can be done, and they are convinced that you are bent on committing suicide anyway. Bounce him hard a few times and he will send you solo to save slipping a disc. You can then teach yourself how to fly. Never disobey instructions: When your instructor tells you to go to hell, shout "Take up Slack.", and take off.
Don't take unnecessary risks: Fly solo whenever you can.

1962 saw the Olympia 2b being sold to a group at Doncaster. A replacement was sought and an order was placed for a new Oly 460. A new Swallow was ordered, and delivered by the summer.

The year started off with Gold Height claims from Jim Duthie, Arthur Cruikshanks and Jimmy Rae, and by the time the year was out a number of epic flights were claimed by locals and visitors alike.

The 1962 summer courses were fully subscribed in record time and a busy year was anticipated. Work started on the clearing of the 'Plantation' area of the site. For some time, depending on the wind direction, some winch launches were performed 'around the pole'. This was a large yellow ex-trolleybus pole which stood in the corner of the field. The launch cables were dog-legged around this pole on the way to the launch point, and launching pilots had the unique experience of 'twanging' at about 200ft. as the cable slid over the top of

"Bloody Mary" by Lawson, Milne, Rozyki and Benny

the pole. Launching around the pole was indeed an art that many visiting pilots to Portmoak were slightly nervous of. This pole is still in use today, albeit slightly shorter and in a new role - sporting the club windsock at the east end of the site.

Work was started on the annexe to the clubhouse – for staff accommodation and engineering work also continued apace with Messrs Lawson, Milne, Rozycki and Benny completing their new winch 'Bloody Mary'.

As the year progressed, it became obvious that Charlie Ross was aiming for the club house trophies. First up was his Gold Height, then towards the end of the year he entered the history books for the first ever glider flight from Scotland to England – although there had been at least one flight from England to Scotland. Charlie's flight was from Portmoak to Yeadon, near Leeds, and clocked up 170 miles. These flights earned him the Championship trophies for best distance and best height at the annual Dinner Dance at the Station Hotel in Kirkcaldy, on 8th December. Charlie's taste for 'Border Crossing' was to lead him to even greater journeys early the following year – as will be seen in the next chapter.

The year had seen a number of cross-countries including flights to Aberdeen (78 miles) and Fordoun (55 miles) by Oly pilots. The gliding site at Arbroath (Condor) proved a popular destination for a number of pilots and the aero-tow retrieves were common from there during the summer. The *S&G* provided yet more publicity when it listed a summary of wave flights from Portmoak in 1962:

1st Feb	9,550 ft.	V. Wyles	Swallow
8th Feb	11,850 ft.	A.J. Thorburn	Eagle
	11,500 ft.	A. Cruikshanks	Swallow
	11,400 ft.	J.E. Duthie	Swallow
	11,400 ft.	J. Rae	Skylark 3F
	7,600 ft.	W. Lawson	Eagle
20th May	5,200 ft.	J.E. Duthie	Swallow
27th May	6,600 ft.	J.E. Duthie	Swallow

24th June	6,350 ft.	J. Rae	Skylark 3F
1st July	12,550 ft.	C. Ross	Skylark 3F
	9,450 ft.	V. Wyles	Swallow
	9,350 ft.	W. Rozycki	Skylark 2
	8,850 ft.	J.R. Ford	Swallow
	8,800 ft.	J. Burgess	Swallow
	8,500 ft.	J. Rae	Skylark 3F
	5,100 ft.	D. Scott	Swallow
17th Sep	10,000 ft.	J. Rae	Skylark 3F
22nd Sep	9,800 ft.	C. Ross	Skylark 3F
7th Oct	8,750 ft.	C. Ross	Skylark 3F
	7,150 ft.	J. McLauchlin	Swallow
28th Oct	8,850 ft.	J. Rae	Skylark 3F
31st Oct	15,200 ft.	C. Ross	Skylark 3F

The usual influx of visitors at Portmoak included C. E. Wallington and Betsy Woodward as well as a group from B.E.A. at Edinburgh's Turnhouse airport.

Chapter 7

Over the Sea to Ireland 1963 – 1964

1963 saw the newly crowned club champion, Charlie Ross, off on his 'Border Crossing' sorties again. The following recollection of his flight, on the 2nd of February, was published in the *S&G* that year:

> *The morning dawned with an overcast sky, I believe, but by 8:30 James Rae was chasing about waking everyone with the cry of "Wave!". By 9:30 the Tiger and the Skylark 3 were lifting off in a flurry of disturbed snow into a light N.E. wind. After twenty minutes, I released in weak lift in front of an insipid looking flat lenticular over the Ochils, at 4,700ft. At 5,500ft the lift disappeared and I realised that I was going to have to find lift, or land short of Portmoak.*
>
> *A filmy wisp of cloud appeared ahead and I reached it at 4,800ft. and found weak lift at 1ft/sec. Not daring to leave this, I waited for something to happen, which it duly did.*
>
> *The lenticulars around formed up, lift increased to 3ft/sec. and I climbed slowly to 7,000ft. Things were changing at 8,000ft: above the lenticulars, I saw the gaps between the bars close with newly-formed cloud. No further lift forthcoming, I turned SW in order to be over lower ground before descending and flew towards a slot which was slowly widening ahead.*
>
> *This slot, by the time I reached it, was some two miles in width and stretched east/west. I flew west, along the lift edge at 50 kt, at 7,500ft., all the way to Loch Lomond. In the lee of the higher mountains I could see much shorter, steeper lenticulars where I hoped there would be stronger lift. Over the loch I found strong lift at 18ft/sec and I climbed quickly to 14,000ft, using oxygen*

from 12,000ft. Severe canopy icing occurred at 9,000ft when the temperature reached -20°C.

At 14,200ft. the lift stopped dead and through the clear vision panels there was a truly magnificent panorama of white capped mountains, blue seas dotted with islands glinting in the sunlight and, stretching away to the west, the Mull of Kintyre. What a view - what a chance – what a mess if I missed out.

Working carefully to avoid the down-draughts of the lenticulars, I soon arrived at Campbeltown at 9,000ft.

Up 'till now, we at Portmoak have all been flying along the wave clouds, and those who ventured downwind have been caught by the tremendous sink. I decided to try an idea that James and I had. Instead of increasing the speed when sink is encountered on leaving the wave bar, I flew along in the lift increasing speed to around 65 kt and then tight-turned downwind.

This worked beautifully. Instead of losing 3,000ft., I only lost 1,000ft. and then, as the vario came back to a more normal reading, I turned and angled into the lift of the next wave and slowed down to 40 kt. Very often, if the lift is approached directly, one misses the narrow, smooth band completely, but never the sink!

Now the choice lay in landing safely at Machrihanish airfield below, with its 10,000ft. runway, or going west, across the Irish Sea, and trying for 300Km. The upper wind appeared N.E. at 25 kt. The lift stopped at 9,000ft. and the lenticulars lay N.W. – S.E.

The call of 300Km won, and off along the cloud I went, maintaining around 8,500ft – 9,000ft. Opposite Portrush, on the Irish coast, I turned and flew down-wind, and as I progressed the wave system slowly collapsed, and I let down through a tiny slot into dead air. At 3,000ft. I passed over Toome airfield, and decided that, as I still required some 25 miles, it might pay to be prudent; so to facilitate retrieving by air I landed there. Only 160 miles direct line – still, look out Betsy, here we come!

Special thanks are due to the Tiger pilots who undertook the long and cold retrieve; to the airfield managers who put up with aircraft without radio; to the boys in the Ulster Flying and Gliding clubs for their magnificent aid; and to Mr Scott of Toome who fed, transported and provided storage.

This truly epic flight earned Charlie yet another entry in the history books; *'First Glider Flight from Scotland to Ireland'*. The reader might be forgiven for thinking that this was the end of the story, with a simple aero-tow retrieve. Not so! Dorothy Lawson recalled 'The Other End of the Rope', also published in the *S&G*:

The telephone rang through the tea-time clatter at Portmoak. There was a rush to answer it, for 18:00 hours on Sunday 3rd February, was the time Charlie Ross had arranged to phone again – from Ireland.

Ten hours before, snugly in bed at Portmoak, he had heard a call himself, at close range. It was from James Rae, whose motto must surely be, "See a wave, and have a go, by aero-tow."

At 14:30 Charlie phoned after landing, with discretion and consideration, at the disused airfield of Toome Bridge in Northern Ireland. An aero-tow retrieve would solve a lot of problems and the interval to 18:00 gave time to make the necessary arrangements for the next day.

James's plan was to fly to Renfrew and re-fuel before crossing the Irish Sea, but when Monday came, Renfrew had low cloud and would not accept the Tiger without a radio. Machrihanish was suggested, for there the weather was good. Good weather – yes, but 80 octane fuel, no.

Consequently, the Tiger, tanked to the brim and carrying extra fuel, flew under low cloud by way of Stirling and Loch Lomond to reach the blue sky and 3-mile runway at Machrihanish. This took one hour 35 minutes and darkness was approaching. The Tiger was picketed down and Monday night was spent in Campbeltown.

Tuesday morning brought snow, front after front of it. It lay, and then it drifted. The only thing to do was to get the Tiger into a hangar and catch the last B.E.A. flight out before the snow closed the airfield. The snow storm in Ireland was even more severe and Charlie went home by boat, and back to work until conditions improved.

On the following Sunday, the Met. had good weather to sell. A chartered Tri-pacer flew James to Machrihanish, and Charlie to Toome Bridge. The Tiger re-fuelled at Newtownards – the home of the Ulster Flying Club, before towing the Skylark to Machrihanish. There, a strong wind was blowing, far too strong for comfort, so into the hangar went the machines and off to Campbeltown for the night went the pilots.

On Monday 11th, eight days after Charlie's grand flight, the final leg of the retrieve was flown – helped, believe it or not, by an Ochil Lee Wave. From Stirling to Crook of Devon, the Tiger, though throttled back, gained 1,000ft.

This remarkable flight, with its "get you home again" service, highlights the wave flying at Portmoak. Two heights of 13,000ft. were reached by winch launch via hill lift on 9th December, and 10,000ft. and 15,000ft. from aero-tows on 16th December. These were two Sundays in one month, but if views from office windows are anything to go by, waves are active on weekdays too.

It really is not necessary to travel to California, France, Italy or New Zealand for Gold C heights. The launch point is much nearer, at Portmoak.

By Easter of 1963 the 'workers', led by Jimmy Rae, had produced the first K9 winch with a second one under construction. Members were falling into two camps: The winch brigade and the aero-tow brigade. The former wanted the club to spend more money on winches in order to maintain the 'low-cost' launch facilities. The latter maintained that potential cross-country flights were being 'missed out' by a number of pilots not taking aero-tows away from the 'hill'. To a certain extent, this situation continues right through to the present day.

Following the publicity in *S&G* at the beginning of the year, and to provide further incentive to members, the club decided to hold a number of weekend competitions with a Scottish Regional Contest being held over two weekends in June. Previous attempts at this type of competition had failed due to the lack of support over a full week, so two weekends – giving four days of competition – seemed to be the answer. Entries were received from Yorkshire, Dumfries, Lossiemouth, Arbroath and Aberdeen. The following summary, and results, were published in the *Portmoak Press* (and *S&G*) at the end of the summer:

> *A preliminary poll of would-be competitors in the Scottish area, early in 1963, proved that there was an interest in week-end competitions; the proposal that the competitions be handled in this fashion resulted from earlier attempts to organise whole week competitions in 1961 and 1962. It was suggested that crews should leave aircraft and equipment at Portmoak over a period of two weeks, thus helping travelling arrangements.*
>
> *The organisation of the events was greatly helped by the generous offers of Tigers from both Aberdeen and Yorkshire Clubs and we were able to have the fullest use of the Aberdeen Tiger with pilots Angus Macaulay and Bill Dunn, the second Tiger being our own, with the Yorkshire tug as stand-by but, in the end, not used.*

At first briefing on Saturday 8th June, it was noted that 12 teams representing Yorkshire, Dumfries, Arbroath, Lossiemouth and the SGU had entered, two being hors concours. It is best not to dwell upon the met. conditions of the 8th and 9th, as the east wind and stable sunny conditions proved to be unsuitable for contest flying, and as a result, both days were No Contest Days. The tasks were respectively Out-and-Return and Free Distance.

June 15th – This proved to be the best day of the series, as nearly all the competitors scored. At briefing, the task was declared to be Free Distance, and as forecast by the meteorologist, Peter White, the early mists cleared at 11:30 hrs and thermals started soon after. Wind strength was light and westerly. An early departure from the area was the ATC Weihe (Henshaw), this aircraft proving to be quite a consistent performer, several Skylark 2s following minutes later with Riddell's Skylark 3 in the lead. This lead was maintained by Riddell, who landed at Dyce Airport (83 miles). Four other aircraft landed within a few miles of one another; Docherty (Olympia) and Thorburn (Skylark) at Fordoun Airfield (61 miles), Rae (Skylark 3b) south of Stonehaven, and Alty (Skylark 2) north of Stonehaven (64 miles and 69 miles respectively).

June 16th – Task: Pilot-Selected Goal; wind westerly, 20 kt; convection not as good as on the previous day. Launching for this task was by winch, as the necessary starting height could be achieved by slope soaring on the Bishop Hill. After sampling this lift, some pilots returned for later starts and to dish out fresh instructions to crews.

Three pilots achieved their declared goals: J.C. Riddell (Skylark 3f), Fraserburgh (114 miles); Jim O'Donnel (Weihe), Kinnell Airfield (42 miles); J.A. Dandie (Swallow), RNAS Arbroath (38 miles), and a *fourth, A.C. Boyce (Skylark 2) over-flew his goal at Kinnell Airfield and logged an extra 25 miles.*

Final Results:

1	J.C. Riddell	Yorkshire	Skylark 3F	1800 points
2	D.G. Alty	Fulmar	Skylark 2	854
3	T.P. Docherty	SGU	Olympia 2	794
4	A.C. Boyce	Dumfries	Skylark 2	725
5	A.J. Thorburn	SGU	Skylark 2	717
	C.B. Sutherland			
6	J. Rae	SGU	Skylark 3B	700
7	T.A. Moffat	ATC	Weihe	529
	R.G Henshaw			
	J. O'Donnel			
	G. Berry			
8	J.A. Dandie	SGU	Swallow	184
	J.E. Duthie			
9	R. Stothard	Yorkshire	Eagle	18
	E. Reed			
10	G.A. Glennie	Condor	Skylark 2	0

The presence of keen, competitive, pilots at Portmoak spurred on a number of club pilots – as had been hoped, and a record number of Silver C legs were logged. Five complete Silver Cs, and a dozen Silver legs were all claimed during one competition weekend. The success rate slowed down to the normal 3 or 4 per month, with the occasional rise by visiting pilots, principally from RNGSA Fulmar whose T-31 had been very active on Bishop Hill.

Non-flying activities continued at the club. The Territorial Army arrived to level out some rough ground and build two bridges into the plantation. As this area was being cleared, some entrepreneurial club member suggested selling the (about to be) felled fir trees – just in time for Christmas. At one shilling and sixpence each (8p), and with over 300 being sold, a few well-needed pounds were added to the SGU coffers. Another item to be 'felled' that year was the infamous 'Yellow Pole' from the south side of the dogleg on the ash strip. Winch launches from that direction would now be without the dogleg and resultant 'twang'. As mentioned in an earlier chapter, the pole was shortened and re-cycled as the wind-sock pole. It still stands today at the eastern end of the airfield and has sported many a wind-sock over the years.

Summer courses, some in the new format of two instructors, two aircraft and winch driver, proved to be successful with a batch of 'A's, 'B's and complete Silver 'C's being completed.

As was becoming normal in Autumn, Portmoak saw many visitors. One being Peter Scott – in his Auster – on his way to Loch Ness for a monster hunt. The 29th of September provided one of the last 'good' days of the year with Ansgar Sambale gaining 15,000 ft. on a cross-country to Acklington (90 miles), and John Paterson reaching 12,000 ft. on his way to Berwick (63 miles) – both claiming their Silver distances and Gold heights. Ansgar recalled his flight for *Portmoak Press:*

Two Up, Both Away

Before I start, I should like to advise you to take your camera with you when you intend to embark on a similar venture. It's always good to have some sort of support for your stories, especially when you tell them to your grandchildren.

Since I am not a good story-teller, I should like you to understand that my only reason for telling this one at all is the excessive pressure I was subjected to, not by my grandchildren, but by a certain moustachioed gentleman from Kirkcaldy who is desperately short of repeatable stories for Portmoak Press.

Anyway, it was a day like any other day. It was just as windy and blustery as it was almost the whole week before and a certain gentleman from Dunblane – who had waited throughout that week for just such a day – lost his patience just when there were signs of improvement to be seen. He left in the morning with my humble consolation (poor Tom).

At lunchtime, it was obvious that conditions were very good. On the ground the wind was still very strong and from the west. Just after lunch, John Paterson and I had a quick look at the map, discussed the situation and decided that down-wind was the only chance to cover those elusive 32 miles that are known in glider circles as the "Silver Distance".

The upper wind appeared to be very much from the North, which meant crossing the Firth of Forth at a particularly wide part. The wind was decidedly too strong to explore the regions further north which looked so very much more promising. One layer of lenticular after another, as far as the eye could see! Yet, down-wind was for us as I found out for myself a little later.

Thanks to the help which was given abundantly, the Oly and I took off at 15:09. John had taken off in his Swallow five minutes before me. He had a good launch and the lift at Bishop Hill seemed as expected. I also had a good launch, though it was turbulent. A glance at the surface of the loch (Leven) revealed a great deal about the air in the neighbourhood. In the region of St. Serfs Island there were violent gusts hitting the water and spreading out in all directions. Towards Kinross the water was definitely calmer, and further north indicating strong winds slightly north of west. As I turned towards Bishop the turbulence increased. It was rather useless to try to read the variometer. Close to the hill I lost 200 ft. very rapidly. On reaching the face of the hill, I found no lift at 800 ft. Only after rounding the second knoll did I encounter any lift. This lift was very turbulent but at least the varios were in agreement. The both were stuck at their respective "up" stops! Two figures of eight in this lift made the hills fall away like some soiled sheet of paper from an office desk. John, still 2,000 ft. above me headed west, and I soon followed. The altimeter worked like a clock that had lost its wheel, winding its way in a friendly clockwise direction. At St. Serfs, only a couple of miles west of Bishop, I was above cloudbase at 4,700 ft. in silk-smooth lift. Soon I progressed over the tops of the lenticulars – still progressing towards the west. What scenery!! But I was here with some purpose in mind, so after a quick look around – checking my instruments and position – I found both varios reading three-up. Yes, only three metres up, and falling off. I saw John at a lower altitude and returning from his westerly sojourn. A careful look at my good-natured lenticular, which now stretched from the Dollar area, over Portmoak and out towards Leuchars and far into the North Sea, revealed a considerable "hump" just east of Portmoak. I headed eastwards and on reaching that area was rewarded by the varios creeping back to a more positive indication.

With this increase of height, the wind became stronger and veered further north. Lift appeared to be best right above the cloud rather than in front of it as I had expected.

With such lift, a cloud cover of about four eighths, a joy ride like that was very enjoyable. What a view to behold! 9,000 ft. and still going up faster than the lift in the Eiffel Tower. All the while, the horizon widened. There was that layer of cloud just below me with such a brilliant whiteness that it made my eyes water. Then ahead of me, an even bigger cloud. No doubt that it had some help from the Ochils. In front of that were another, and another, and another. It was like a sea of gigantic waves in the sky. The further north I looked, the bigger they seemed to be. The sun helped to accentuate the appearance by throwing long shadows into the cloud valleys. Most of the ground, which I could see through the holes in the cloud, appeared to be completely black except for the silvery lochs and rivers. However, right below Loch Leven and the surrounding countryside was bathed in brilliant sunshine. The coastline between Montrose and Berwick was clearly to be seen well within gliding distance – so I thought.

As I reached 14,500 ft. I was tempted to explore those regions to the north of me. I was just aware of the first signs of anoxia so I increased my speed to 100 mph, still in lift. As far as I could judge, my penetration was not good enough to reach the wave ahead of me. So I headed south. To my amazement, the next cloud – some eight miles downwind – offered no lift at all. 12,000 ft. and heading for the next one right over the River Forth. At that moment, and only for a few seconds, I saw John above the Forth heading north east. Although I was still at a reasonable height, and flying at 80 mph, my flight path was such that I would touch down in the middle of the river! Have you ever swallowed butterflies? No, neither have I although now know what it feels like! However, John was already half way over, and I was a little higher, so on I went. At 11,500 ft. and six miles from either shore I swung around again to soar another wave. At 14,000 ft., I inspected both bridges and found that my retrieve would not be over the road bridge as there was still a large gap between the two main construction sites at the north and south shores of the river.

Downwind again for another wave bar. It pushed me up to 15,000 ft. but, as I had no oxygen, I broke off at 2 metres up, going westward. No good this way, the wind was too strong. I next spotted a wave bar above the Lammermuir Hills to the south west of Edinburgh, and well beyond the Forth. On reaching this wave, I was rewarded with steady lift again. Seeing those enormous waves to the south west, I was sorely tempted again. High above what I took to be Carlisle, were two crisp lenticulars, perhaps more than 30,000 ft. up. Since I was sure that I had covered 32 miles, I set course west. It meant travelling over a large hole in the cloud which stretched from the Moorfoot Hills to the Cheviots. It soon proved to be impossible for the Oly to cross. After covering only about one third of the way across the hole, I turned back towards the Cheviots again. There I managed to gain no more than 500 ft. So I crossed the highest point at 6,500 ft. making for the next smooth lenticular just to the east of Alnwick. Behind this were another three bars stretching out over the North Sea. Southwest of Alnwick airfield, I climbed from 4,000 ft. to 4,700 ft. already looking for suitable landing places. Within easy reach were three aerodromes. Even Newcastle was within reach. However, there was no indication of promising lift anywhere downwind except for a lenticular way out over the sea. There was no sign of any flying activities anywhere around me and I decided to head for Acklington. From 4,500 ft., I completed a wide circuit all the time expecting to see some sort of signal from the airfield. Nothing was forthcoming, not even red, so I started my final approach. I landed and rolled out to the very end of the runway. After a few minutes, I was welcomed by Sgt. Wilkinson who took all the worries off my hands. Indeed, the end of this flight turned out to be as pleasant as the flight itself. Everything was organised for me, even my lodgings for the night.

Thanks to all those who offered me their hospitality. I can surely say that this was a day to remember. I'm sure John Paterson will agree with me. He landed somewhere near Berwick-Upon-Tweed to claim his Silver distance too.

Ansgar Sambale

Ever keen to raise funds for the club, numerous parties were planned – with associated raffle ticket sales. It seemed that any excuse for a (fund raising) party would do. Some of these included a special party for visitors from BAE, a Fancy Dress party in November and the annual Dinner Dance at the Station Hotel in Kirkcaldy on 21st December.

A special celebration dinner had taken place on 27th April. This was to recognise the awarding of the Royal Aero Club Bronze Badge to Tom Davidson. Tom, at that time CFI, was given the award:

> 'For many years of service to gliding, and flying in general. His efforts started when he flew as a fighter pilot in World War I and was commanding Officer of several units during World War II.'

1964 saw the SGU reach the ripe old age of 30. Flying and non-flying activities continued with the old winches receiving new roller-boxes and work being started on a diesel bus winch. The steady stream of visitors continued, and one of them - John Goddard of the Army Gliding Club - raised the local height record to 17,000 ft.

Tom Moffat & Val Peddie

The Fife Schools Gliding Club was formed and based their newly acquired T49 at Portmoak. The following extract is from the Kirkcaldy High School magazine in June 1964:

Several years ago, senior Kirkcaldy High School pupils aided Mr Thorburn, our principal art master, to establish the Fife Gliding Club. This has since developed into the Scottish Gliding Union, which, with Mr Thorburn as president, has its own airfield at Portmoak.

In repayment of this past assistance from pupils, Mr Thorburn has instigated the formation of a flying club for Fife schools. Recently, the Director of Education, Dr McIntosh, sampled the flying at Scotlandwell, and enthusiastically agreed to help the scheme. With funds allocated by the Fife Education Trust, a new Slingsby two-seater glider has been purchased for what is now officially the Fife Schools Gliding Club.

The main aim is to give a large number of senior pupils a little gliding experience, and to train a selected few to solo stage. It is hoped ultimately to link up with the Duke of Edinburgh's Award Scheme, whereby pupils can include a course in gliding in their pursuits and projects. Unfortunately, as the scheme has only been put into operation this term, it has not been possible to commence serious training of pupils. Nevertheless, at least 130 senior pupils (who travel to the airfield in groups of eight, each evening) have already had introductory flights, and by the time this article is in print, another 70 pupils will have experienced "the joys of motor-less flight." Mr Thorburn hopes to begin instruction early next session and to have about twenty pupils flying solo by the end of the year.

Gliding is a challenge to young persons of adventurous spirit. Besides being both appealing and character-building, it provides a practical demonstration in geography, mathematics and physics, and therefore is to be encouraged from the scholastic point of view. However, the scheme was officially supported basically as a form of enjoyment for the pupils and not as an extension of classroom work. The pleasure from gliding (or to be more accurate – soaring) is derived not merely from the actual piloting of the glider, but also from the teamwork involved, and all other aspects which combine to make a successful flight.

On the evening of my own flight, my eagerness changed gradually to trepidation on arrival at the airfield where the attractive blue and white school glider stood awaiting our arrival. Cautiously resisting the temptation to eat too many sandwiches before my flight, I joined the other pupils on the runway, and was rather surprised to find that a junior pupil at our school – a third year boy – would be responsible for controlling the winch which would tow the glider to a height of a thousand feet. I was, thankfully, not the first person to take off, and I must admit that the sight of other flights safely accomplished was most encouraging. A kindly warning that the take-off would begin with a rather rough ride along the ground, followed swiftly by a smooth but steep climb, prepared me for an experience in reality not nearly as alarming as it sounds.

Flights vary greatly according to circumstances; but whether strong up-currents of wind permit cross-country flying, or poorer conditions insist on "crabbing" along the hillside, the experience of flying is singularly wonderful. The landing, which produces the disappointment felt when all good things come to an end, certainly proved to be no anti-climax. After an apparently vertical descent, we levelled out before the seemingly inevitable crash and taxied along uneven ground to an expertly planned halt beside the other members of the party – the culmination of a most exhilarating and interesting experience.

Gliding is a sport in which I would encourage all go-ahead young people to participate. Through the Fife schools' scheme, pupils will fly at reduced rates –

merely four shillings per flight (which lasts approximately 15 minutes) plus a charge of one shilling to cover transport costs to and from the airfield.

I would like here to thank Mr Thorburn for the opportunities for pupils which he inspired, and to wish himself and his proteges every success in the future.

Edith Aitken SVI

The Fife Schools' T49 was offered for use by SGU members, as was Roger Pears' Ka7. A Vasama, recently claiming the prize for best Standard Class sailplane, and a private T49 (Manclark) were also based at the site. Two Swallows had different outcomes during 1964; one was flown by Bill Shanks to Fintry – claiming his Silver Distance, the other was written off by Rab Williamson. The summer of 1964 provided many wave flights, including Bill Lawson's Gold Height in his Olympia 463. The wave system also provided Stan Smith with his Silver Distance and Gold Height in the same flight. Other Silver Distances claimed that summer were George Elliot, Graham Smith, John McLaughlan and Tom Webb.

On the training front, John Everitt – the National Coach – held a number of courses in the BGA Capstan. At the end of his visit, he made an interesting 'observation', following an official near miss between an American Hustler fighter bomber and two SGU gliders. He said that he had become more and more aware that SGU pilots had been lulled into a false sense of security – being used to flying in a relatively quiet piece of airspace – and were not keeping a good look out. This alarming piece of information was rapidly transferred by the CFI into briefing material for immediate cascade to all pilots. Alan Cameron experienced one of John Everitt's courses, and his exploits were published in *Portmoak Press*:

Having got to the stage where a lot of pilots stick, namely – only the distance flight to be completed for

Silver "C". I felt that some advanced instruction was in order to help me over that hurdle. It was thus that with a little difficulty I arranged for a week's instruction by that pundit among pundits, John Everitt.

Monday came, as Mondays do, one of the nicest mornings I have seen for a long time. I was told to go ahead and attempt my Silver "C" distance, having been checked out for an "away" landing on the previous Saturday. The wind from the South West was very light and my first launch in the Swallow ended in a circuit. The Capstan by this time was ready and was being circulated by John and Stan Milne. They eventually went up and stayed there, so I took a second launch and managed to use a thermal to work my across to the hill. The hill was working, but only just, and after scratching around looking for thermals over Balgedie and not finding any, I landed for lunch.

Considerably fortified, I rejoined the fray and with the wind slightly stronger, made my way to the Bishop. I tracked my way along the north face as the freshening wind had veered to about WNW. Over the gully, I observed the waves on the surface of the reservoirs confirming a NW wind. In the morning, it had been my intention - with the SW wind – to move out over the loch, find a thermal that I could struggle up in, then stay with it moving downwind to Arbroath – that goal of goals. However, with the wind change, a different strategy was suggested by J.E. – namely to penetrate upwind to Perth then go across wind in the Arbroath direction, using Strathmore as a thermal source.

From the barograph, which I had actually installed and switched on, I reckoned after the flight that I must have spent about an hour and a quarter out of a flight of an hour and forty minutes fighting my way like that problematic frog in the well – two miles north and one mile south in a vain attempt to reach Perth.

I gave up the attempt to reach Perth over the Tay just upstream of its junction with the Earn river and proceed towards Errol and Dundee. Over Errol, this prospect of reaching Arbroath faded as there was no sign of any thermal activity in the direction I wanted to go. However, I estimated that from about 6,000 ft., I ought to reach the 50 km. distance with about 1,500 ft. to look for a reasonable landing field. I therefore went back into the thermal I had just used to reach 5,000 ft. and eventually got flying out at 5,900 ft. Turning out, I headed for Arbroath near the coast to be as much down wind as possible. When I approached Dundee, I was down to 2,500 ft. due to some unexpected downdraughts and I didn't fancy over-flying Dundee at that height so turned away to the north and had to come down in a newly-cut field at 6:30 p.m., about one mile due north of Tealing airfield – a flight of 28 miles, or 5 miles short of my Silver "C".

The retrieve was eventful, but that is another story.

Reflection on the flight, with analysis by J.E. showed I had been right in turning across when I did but made a mistake in going up-wind of Dundee, when a search down-wind might have kept me in the hunt.

On Tuesday, it was Stan Milne's turn to do the solo flying and I'm glad to say that he did better than I, and reached East Haven. I flew with J.E. in the Capstan, taking off after lunch and into a Northwest wind. We were soon at 3,000 ft. over Balgedie, where we contacted wave. With some careful manipulation we were soon at 7,000 ft. and going up quietly at between 4 and 6 metres per second. At about 12,500 ft., I asked "What height do you feel the effects of anoxia?" John said, "About now." Needless to say, I started to look for the down button., the lift took us up another 500 ft. before we had flown forward out of the wave. The view from 13,000 ft. is really something. Montrose to Glasgow! You should try it sometime.

I'm glad to say at this point that John went up about tea-time, by courtesy of Bill Lawson, to complete his Gold "C" with his gain of height.

After Monday and Tuesday, the rest of the week was bound to be an anti-climax, but it was very enjoyable to hear and learn from John Everitt's seemingly inexhaustible supply of gliding stories and experiences. The only day we didn't get any flying was Thursday, when we had some heavy rain showers. The weather cleared up in the late evening and with possibility of another wave flight, the Capstan course insisted that John take his wife, Chris, up in the Capstan to let her see Scotland. Although the wave was there, it was of changing wave-length and it couldn't be worked.

It may seem strange to say my only flight with John was our wave excursion but if on just that short flight a little of John's skills passed to me I consider the week's course a success and well worth being repeated annually.

Alan Cameron

1964 ended with a couple of notable flights on 20th December; Jimmy Rae flew to Prestwick and Andrew Thorburn flew an out-and-return to the Lake of Menteith.

The annual prize-giving saw the Club Championship and the Sutherland out-and-return trophy going to Charlie Ross, the Gain of Height went to John Goddard, the Best Distance was won by John McLaughlan and the Service Salver went to John Henry.

Chapter 8

Coast to Coast 1965 – 1966

Wave was evident on 1st January 1965, and many pilots took advantage to welcome the new year in true Portmoak style – from 6,000 ft. The next day brought sadness to Portmoak when Tom Johnston was involved in a fatal accident in his Swallow on Benarty. As was the norm in those days, the safety officer would issue a brief summary of accidents by way of reminding people to be vigilant. The next issue of *Portmoak Press* contained this safety item, along with an obituary:

The accident to Tom Johnston in the Swallow on Benarty.
The correct line to the hill passes to the windward side of the spur which projects towards the Northeast. This is near the east end of the main part of the hill. It would appear that probably due to the difficulty of seeing exactly where he was, owing to the very bright, low, sun he got to the leeward of this spur and thus into a downdraft. It seems probable also that he was flying too slowly and that this, along with the turbulence behind the spur, started a spin. The lessons to be learned from this are:
1. *If in any doubt, especially in rough air, increase speed.*
2. *Great care must at all times be taken to keep to windward of any hill or ridge or other obstruction to the free flow of the wind.*
3. *Keep a careful check at all times of your position in relation to the hill on which you are flying.*

Tom Johnston
On 2nd January, the Scottish Gliding Union lost one of its most popular members in a flying accident when Tom A. Johnston crashed his glider on Benarty Hill.
Tom was an industrial chemist with Scottish Oils Ltd., of West Lothian and lived in Edinburgh.

He joined the Territorial Army (Royal Artillery) in 1932, and went to war with them in 1939. He was then seconded to the R.A.F. where he became a pilot. He was dreadfully wounded and spent a year in hospital, but instead of being discharged from the Forces, he returned to the Gunners and served with them in Europe for the rest of the war. He rejoined the T.A. (City of Edinburgh Artillery Regiment) after the war. Although he retired from active service in the T.A. some years ago, he never gave up his work and filled several appointments and attended camp. His last command was that of H.A. Battery where there has never been a more popular commander.

About two years ago, Tom became interested in gliding and was an enthusiastic member at Portmoak, where he was a regular attender and was very well-liked by everyone for his cheerfulness and kindness.

It was noted on the first course that he attended how conscientious he was, and eventually he would have made a good instructor. Tom did not stand by and let others do the work and, in spite of his disability, he would always lend a helping hand.

In the first week of January, 1965, the Edinburgh University Gliding club took up residence at Portmoak. This recently formed club had reached agreement with the SGU Board that they could fly at Portmoak on Wednesdays and Fridays. As part of their funding agreement with the SGU, their winch launches cost them four shillings (20p) instead of the normal rate of seven shillings (35p). Their flying was subsidised by the University Sports Club and one of their members, Dr Cruickshanks, was an SGU instructor.

Andrew Thorburn enjoyed the January wave so much that he wrote about it for the June issue of the *S&G*:

Cut me another slice please, mother!
While soaring from time to time, peacefully, at heights above ten thousand feet, the aching emptiness of the sky above central Scotland brings home to one some of the emotions that must beset man while travelling in space.

Often, no task having been set, the aim of the flight is merely to enjoy Nature's abundant gift of aerial support found over, and in the lee of, the Scottish mountains. Adjust the trim, choose a course to maintain track along the wave of rising air, and then the mind, relieved of thoughts technical, is free to ponder over the endless infinity of space.

Far below, planes with engines shuttle to and fro as weekend pilots and fare-paying passengers are violently thrust through the lower reaches of the sky. Down, and four miles east of Portmoak, a twin-engined speck of silver suddenly ejects a flowering rash of parachutes. The Skyjumpers' club are practising over the new Glenrothes airstrip – but they too are down – and going further down – not up as we are.

The mind is drawn from the creeping things beneath by the even song of the hovering sailplane as it rides the silk-smooth waves. In all directions the surrounding landscape is concealed by the undulating clouds, leaving only the gap below through which to maintain contact with places known. Here and there some five thousand feet further up are a few soft lenticular cloud forms, awaiting the man with oxygen breathing equipment to challenge them. Without this life-preserving substance we edge gently out of the lift, when the altimeter indicates about fourteen thousand feet. And so such flights in solitude pass, leaving us happy to have claimed as our own the few hundred cubic miles of space that few can attain, or even want.

Not so, however, on Sunday, 14th February. Casting loose from the Tiger at two-and-a-half thousand over Glenfarg, a quick search through the canopy of the 460 revealed Ian Dandie flying the Skylark 2b which had been towed up just before me. He could be seen poised in front of the wave cloud overhead. Settling down head-into-wind, showing airspeed 45 kt, the vario confirmed the wave area by indicating a climb of 5 kt, and before long the cloud was sinking astern.

Soon we were flying in formation at the pre-arranged rendezvous eight thousand feet over Newburgh. Poised alongside each other, cameras busily clicking, there was time to reflect upon the pleasures of companionship in such an empty void. Moving eastwards in formation along the river Tay and at 12,000ft above it one could at least claim half of the sky on this occasion – or could one? What was that speck high and ahead? A jet? No – a Skylark4 – must be Roger Mann, cuddling his oxygen bottle and on what turned out to be a successful quest for a Diamond height at 19,000ft. And now, down below, the front of the wave cloud began to erupt gliders with monotonous regularity as they cast off from aero-tow and climbed up into the sunshine.

Number four on the scene was the swallow flown by Gordon Downes, who landed south of Dunbar, some fifty miles away. Then Bill Lawson in his 460 came up to join us and the Fife Schools' T-49 piloted by Jim O'Donnell moved rapidly across the clear space below at about 10,000ft. The Ka-7, wingtips reaching forward, wafted upwards and moved off into the west. The club Olympia 2b with seventeen-year-old Douglas Mackay – one of the Fife School pupils – floated up among the others and he later landed at Crail for his Silver.

The Moonrakers, who had chosen the right time to visit us on a wave safari, bobbed their glider with the R.A.F. roundels up and down among the rest. A new touch of colour came into view as the Vasama, in tones of sky blue, streaked about at high speed, its pilot, Tom Paterson, eventually landing at Lanark for his Silver badge.

The Weihe and the Skylark 3b, both with several pilots taking turns, were employed in this yo-yo act and before long the sky north of Portmoak, between ten and fourteen thousand feet up, supported what looked like a swat of flies just after a spring hatching.

By now the formatting 460 and Skylark 2b were at thirteen thousand, just entering a layer of haze in front of a higher lenticular. The canopy of my glider completely coated over with ice crystals, so that keeping the Skylark in view through the clear-vision window was quite a task. The sub-zero temperature soon turned pleasure into pain, and so with a wobble of the wings to the other glider I dived away down to the ten thousand feet level, where things were a good deal more comfortable.

I reached this altitude and spotted the Forth road and rail bridges some twenty miles south of the overcrowded scene I had just left. From here it seemed that an out-and-return trip of about 150km would be an interesting thing to do, so, settling down with 80 kt on the clock and half-a-knot on the vario, I worked along the uplift side of a wave cloud below me, which as it turned out took me all the way across central Scotland to Loch Lomond and back.

En route, various points of interest were photographed – Kincardine Bridge, Alloa breweries, the windings of the river Forth at Stirling, Charlie Ross's caravan site at Fintry, the south end of Loch Lomond, Dunblane, where we have a new winch under construction, and so on.

On the homeward flight over Charlie's caravans, I met the man himself in the Skylark 3b. We were both steaming along at 80 kt, and our closing speed must have been in the region of 200 m.p.h. He was doing the same out and return trip.

Fifteen miles from home the airbrakes and downdraughts were used to get down to a more civilised level just below cloud, and when I landed back at Portmoak – a human icicle – I had been airborne for about two-and-a-half hours. The trip to Loch Lomond and back, however, took only a little over half of that time – making a speed of around 75 m.p.h. for the 150 km out and return.

I keep hearing about some French place called Fayence and another site in Italy that has flying conditions along a valley only fit for Hell's Angels – but what is wrong with spending a holiday high up the Scottish "burds" – O ye men from south of the Border? This is the place to chase "polars" – we have the climate here!

As for me, next time I intend to snuggle an oxygen bottle with me and stack myself at an even higher level – the middle reaches between ten and fourteen thousand are becoming overcrowded.

That first month also saw Eric Higgins fly the Weihe to Balloch, and Valerie Wyles to Wemyss Bay to claim their Silver distances. Valerie recalled her flight for *Portmoak Press:*

Coast to Coast

There was almost complete cloud cover on the afternoon. I went to Portmoak intending to have a short hill trip. However, on arrival I noticed they were aero-towing – even to the hill (Benarty). I watched a couple of tows go off and then Bill Lawson demanded to know why I was not attempting a cross-country. There were several good reasons – or so I thought – but these were all waved to one side.

The Oly was D.I.'d and a barograph smoked in record time. The Tiger landed and, while it was being refuelled, Charlie Ross came over and explained where the wave was working best and how to make a distance flight using it. OK, it sounded simple. He would drop me at 3,000 ft. over Glenfarg.

Off we went. Glenfarg came and went, at 4,000 ft., but no sign of lift. Now we were scraping along in fuzzy bits of black cloud – and he'd said that we wouldn't need to go into cloud! Then severe sink was registered, even on the tow. We were back down to 2,900 ft. in double-quick time – the whole combination sinking like a stone in rather rough air. By now I was concentrating fiercely on keeping station. Before I could realise what was happening, we were climbing smoothly, the tug was rocking his wings and the vario was showing five meters up – the needle firmly on the stop, and we were over Newburgh. Little did I know how fortunate this was at the time.

Here, over the Tay valley, there was a wide gap in the cloud and it was easy to climb to 9,000 ft in front of, and above, a perfect lenticular. To the east, the humps of cloud were perfectly formed but what was the point of going east? To the west, it didn't look nearly so impressive. The cloud was flatter, and greyer, and had fewer gaps. But this was where I must go. I travelled along my lenticular until it ended. Where now? Downwind, Charlie has said, so downwind it was.

Before long, I got my first landmark. The power station at Kincardine, 6,000 ft. below. Along this wave to 7,000 ft. and Alloa. Now where? Downwind was asking for trouble this time – Control Zone! Upwind looked better, but the Oly just wouldn't go. It didn't seem to want to cross-wind either. I cruised backwards and forwards trying to decide what to do.

Go home? I'd never live it down. Go west. The Oly travels quite nicely at 80. I sailed along, resigned now to a land out.

But what was that below? Moors, hilltops, patches of snow, bog – most unfriendly. I became rather unhappy, but steamed on. At last more lift and, with it, a glimpse of the Lake of Mentieth – a ray of hope – I might just make it. Back to 7,000 ft., but now the sun had set to the south west of me. The clouds were grey and flat, and most unpromising. Perhaps if I make a dirty dive south westwards, I might just make the Clyde coast. Sixty, eighty, one hundred on the clock, but the altimeter was unwinding towards 5,000 ft. There was Loch Lomond and, joy, lift over it. I climbed back to 6,500 ft. The cloud was thinning now, thank goodness. There was Helensburgh, and the Gareloch, Loch Long, the Holy Loch with 'Hunley' sitting in the middle of the floating dock. It was getting dark, I must think about landing. Now that I wanted to descend, I found it difficult! There was the Clyde coast, let's have a look. But where were all the big fields I'd heard about? I picked one. Oops! That one was almost vertical. Try again. That looks better. A road, telephone wires and a few cottages. Down we go. The sheep ran in a bunch, the Oly rolled to a halt, and I climbed out.

Almost immediately, two people were waving. 'Where's the nearest phone?' They didn't know, they'd just arrived from Burntisland! They took a photo of the Oly and vanished. I waved at several passing cars. They waved back and drove on! Ah, help at last. The Police. They had heard of a fatal air crash. I was all right! Oh, good. They drove off! Eventually, I reached a telephone and before long the retrieve crew was on its way. The Oly was derigged and loaded in brilliant moonlight with one or two lenticulars being illuminated above us.

It was two o'clock in the morning before we got home, but considering I didn't take off until after three in the afternoon, I reckon it wasn't so bad. My thanks to the efficient retrieve crew of Ansgar, Bill and Dorothy.

The distance flight was the bare minimum – 116 km from 3,200 ft. Thank goodness the wave had moved over to Newburgh.

Following intense lobbying by the BGA and the Air Ministry, the RAF and the Americans re-aligned their low flying zones away from Portmoak, and all other gliding sites in the UK. This had been a long and laborious task and the outcome was almost reversed when, within a few weeks of reaching the agreement, one unfortunate SGU pilot landed his glider within a mile of the runways at Prestwick. The Air Ministry wrath was brought firmly down upon the club and a stern reminder was issued by the CFI to the effect that there was no excuse to get low near a known military zone. The *Portmoak Press* included an article with big black bold wording *"NO FLYING BY AN UNAUTHORISED AIRCRAFT IS PERMISSIBLE WITHIN A RADIUS OF FIVE MILES FROM THE PERIMETER OF ONE OF THESE 'DROMES".*

Percy Mutum finally decided to hang up his overalls and take some well-earned retirement. Dorothy Lawson reminded everyone of how much effort he had put in to serve the club:

Our first experience of Percy was when the SGU invaded the Loch Leven Aero Club in around 1948. There was evidently more business to be had by feeding the 'gliding people', rather than the occasional cuppa for the power brigade, so he provided lunch and tea every Sunday for around thirty of us. This, remember, was when food was rationed, all water had to be carried from the other side of the airfield and the kitchen equipment was primeval. This underpaid and overworked task went on with cheerfulness and good humour for the years until we moved to Portmoak. Then, for a time, the kitchen quarters moved to Wellburn and guess what, not only did Percy help us with the flitting, but he appeared on his bicycle each Sunday to cook for us as before! The next move the kitchen made was to a partitioned-off portion of the hangar where, again under dreadful conditions, Percy was the head cook and bottle washer. This phase was probably the worst, but it was to lead to better days when, in the newly built club rooms, he came back to help the resident staff. Then, wearing his white coat and apron as before, but working with up to date equipment, he was able to execute the order – which used to be a big joke – for 'One roast beef please Percy'.

We shall miss our faithful friend Percy, but do appreciate that now and then he must long to put his feet up and rest a bit on a Sunday. Now that we are properly established, this is exactly what he is going to do, and we thank him and wish him well.

The 'Resident Staff' referred to above, were Frank and Tibby. They looked after all catering in the new clubhouse, as well as room bookings for visitors. By the end of 1966, Tibby had handed over the reins to her second in command, Betty Barr.

Building and engineering work continued apace throughout 1965. The ash strip had its dog-leg reduced by the judicious use of a large bulldozer, a new bridge into the site entrance was completed, as was the concrete floor of the hangar. Ansgar Sambale, not content with simply driving the winch, completed his new Daimler cable-laying bus-winch and began experimenting with nylon sheathed winch cables. And as if that wasn't enough, the new hangar for the Tiger tug was also completed that year.

Andrew Thorburn could "turn his hand to anything" as reported in the *Portmoak Press:*

Searching around for some new gimmick to entertain the club members on a Saturday evening, the Chairman decided to bring along a potter's wheel and some clay from his school art department. The response was fantastic. Instead of the few regulars who can be expected to be seen propping up the bar on Saturdays, a fair gathering of members turned up and, before long, many of them disclosed their innermost souls, in the frantic effort to "make pots".

As one after the other they donned the all protective artist's smock and spun the clay through eager fingers, it became obvious that deep down under the rugged contours of every glider pilot, there lies a potential Bernard Leach. After a short demonstration by the Chairman, various well-known characters created forms which are to be fired, glazed and passed down to posterity.

1965 saw a particularly large amount of visitors arriving at Portmoak in search of 'The Wave'. The publicity received by the club that year was almost uncontrollable. On one day alone, 15 visiting pilots were all to be seen overhead the airfield soaring in wave over 10,000 ft – the highest being 17,500 ft. As each week passed, news of epic flights was being spread to almost every gliding club in the UK. Adding to this 'wave frenzy' was the RAF Moonrakers club, from Upavon. Their widely-read newsletter, entitled 'Scottish Wave Project' was published in the *S&G* and this sparked off many RAF sorties to Portmoak over the coming years.

Not to be outdone by these visitors, SGU pilots set off on various cross-countries at the end of June and at the beginning of July: While the treasure hunters were enjoying themselves, Frank Reilly took the open-cockpit T21, with a passenger, to 13,500 ft. Later in the day, with another passenger, he set off on a cross-country flight but only got as far as Scotlandwell – one mile away. The following weekend saw more ambitious declarations but the early starters were forced back to Portmoak by heavy rain squalls. Frank Reilly set off again at 12:30 and got as far as the Dumfries gliding club where he soared around for some time until the locals got their gliders out of the hangar and launched to join him. That was enough, he landed. The next day, Andrew Thorburn declared Doncaster, crossed the Forth to Edinburgh, didn't like the prospects of a long thermal flight, so turned back across the river to land at Donibristle – all of ten miles away. It really was a wave day, and Jimmy Rae proved it by taking an aerotow to 4,000 ft. He contacted the wave and completed the 'milk run' to Loch Lomond and back. Later in July, Andrew Thorburn sampled ridge, thermal and sea-breeze to get his Oly 463 as far as Fyvie (101 miles), Gordon Glennie claimed an O/R to Arbroath. Ansgar Sambale took a pupil to 11,000 ft. in the open-cockpit T21, but both pilots broke off the climb after suffering the effects of anoxia.

The April '65 issue of *Portmoak Press* included an interesting article from a semi-anonymous member called "Andra":

The One That Got Away

Sunday morning at Portmoak on 26th April dawned clear and sunny. The hangar bashers had the doors open, gliders parked outside and the tractors running by 08:30 a.m. All this accompanied by the usual loud banter and furtive moves to get names on the Flying List before the undeserving who were still asleep.

This performance, as usual, had awakened me in my little wooden hut and I found myself awaiting the moment when a runaway tractor would appear through the walls – but as memory of the weather forecast, and the fact that Ian Dandie would be along soon for a trip in the 460, penetrated the gloom, I decided to forestall him in order to live up to the name of "hog" in the group.

By the time breakfast was over, and the 460 rigged, the Tiger was warming and Jimmy Rae was doing his "gingering up" act with the prospective Silver distance aspirants lining

*up the Olympia, Swallow and Vasama. I put the 460 to
number four in the line.*

*Cloud streets had been forming along Cleish and Benarty
since 09:30 a.m. so it was decided to tow the gliders upwind
along the street to a point beyond Kelty – to allow a down
wind run of 35 miles to Crail for the beginners.*

*The Oly went off with John Goudie, who promptly climbed
to cloud base and seemed well away on his first fifteen
miles. The Swallow next was dropped among the thermals
about seven miles upwind, then the Vasama and next myself
in the 460.*

*Immediately on take-off it became obvious that this would
be a good day if it were taken before the arrival of the warm
front – predicted for about teatime – so on the way up
through the thermals I marked the locality of the best one
(over Ballingry) and waited to see if the others upwind were
as good. After jazzing behind the Tiger through two or three
more, I cast adrift at 1800 ft. just beyond Kelty and did a few
turns in weak stuff then back to my "best spot". As expected,
we wound up to a 2500 ft. cloud base and at 4000 ft.
emerged through the usual cotton wool cloudscape of
streets running to the north east. By the time it was
necessary to find another thermal, we were over Cupar and
it was most likely that John Goudie would have been able to
glide it out to Crail from there. I could see no sign of him
and, as the other two gliders had landed just as I took off, it
seemed that a profitable idea would be to forge off slightly
crosswind with a view to visiting the Aberdeen club at Turriff.
This was a trip of 100 miles but the day was young and there
was a reasonable prospect of getting to the north east
before the sea breeze clamp moved inland there.*

*Having settled upon this, the journey north across the Tay
to Coupar Angus followed the usual routine. Thermals were
contacted in streets – the cloud shadows on the ground
ahead indicating where some were growing and others
decaying. Selection was easy and it became only necessary*

to fly along just under the cloud base which was now about 3,400 ft. Below 2,500 ft. the thermals were narrow and tight turning was necessary but above that level everything spread out. Before long, the usual landmarks drifted by. Kirriemuir, Forfar, Brechin and Edzell. But, there above the Yankee installation, it was possible to see ahead the unwanted layer of low lying haze from the sea already well inland and covering the northeast corner of Aberdeenshire – from Stonehaven to Lossiemouth. To the west, over the Grampians, the clouds were all stuffed with mountains and the valleys studded with boulders – a most uninviting prospect. At this point, I had two options – (a) carry on through the stable layer, trying to slope soar every gully, or (b) turn at Banchory and beat the warm front from the south in a race back to Portmoak. I decided to visit Gordon Whitehead at Turriff or bust!

The next two hours were, for me, a most enlightening experience. We have heard how the pundits manage to do cross-countries in stable air – well this was it! Leaving my last thermal at Cairn o' Mount, on a course due north, the sea breeze front gave broken lift for eight miles over the mountains and then the deadly smooth air over Banchory told its own story. Gradually slumping to 1,200 ft. I pushed a lone gull aside to nibble at the feeble lift off the village and eventually got to the south east facing slope of Hill of Fare. This offered gentle lift which, after thirty minutes, could get me no higher than 1,600 ft. I decided that hill-hopping was the only answer. Nine miles further on I could see another little knob of granite but how to get there from 1,600 ft. and still be airborne was the problem. About four miles in that direction I could see what looked like a heath fire at a place called Milltown and, glory be, the smoke was rising!

Having picked likely landing places on the way, I held my breath and made a northward dash through the down in the lee of the hill and arrived at the rising smoke with 1000 ft. on the clock. This was no smoke, it was agricultural lime dust –

why it was rising I cannot tell, but at least it got me to the other hill face above Monymusk. This was a sweaty business, easing back and forward in the tiny bit of slope wind watching the farmer's bairns waving up from below. After fifteen minutes of this, I found myself back up to 1,600 ft. again I flew four miles to Bennachie where it was possible to skim over some burnt out tree stumps and granite boulders on a short beat to recover the 1,600 ft. level. Try as I could, the clock would not read one inch higher. There was still a tantalising sixteen miles between me and Turriff. I peered through the haze for signs of gliders ahead and hovered over this legendary peak for nearly twenty minutes calculating the best track over the undulating landscape in the hope that I could glide it out from that height. Landing fields were plentiful so, committing myself for the last glide, I set off on the shortest route via the windward sides of the sloping fields. Halfway there I thought I would make it, but at the ten mile mark a sudden down settled my hash, and the glider, on a fine grass field – only six miles from my target and 101 miles from Kelty.

After the usual attention to the glider, I contacted Gordon and Portmoak. At the Aberdeen site I had a two-seater view of the airfield "so that you will get there next time" and after the most wonderful hospitality in Aberdeen from Morag and Gordon, we were back at Portmoak about 01:30 a.m. next day.

Thanks are due to Brian and Ian Sproule for making the long retrieve trip – no expenses spared (mine, of course).

P.S. Get some slope soaring practice in – 24 miles from the windward sides of boulders can be mighty useful.

Andra

The year ended on a sad note when Eric Higgins was killed in a launch accident to the Vasama. Alex Dickson wrote the obituary for *Portmoak Press*:

Eric
Is there a way to express sorrow in words? Eric Higgins is dead. All of us know of the tragic accident which claimed his life at Portmoak recently. How or why it happened is unimportant alongside the realisation that he is gone and we are the poorer. His death is a personal blow for all of us; the club, its members, everyone who knew him. We remember, and we are stunned. Perhaps most of us need no further reminder, no words, about 'The Wee Man'. Eric was 24, an instrument fitter with the Flying Division of Ferranti's in Edinburgh. He soloed at 16, as an ATC cadet. Travelling from his Paisley home to 661 Gliding School at Turnhouse, he became a staff cadet and then a junior instructor. He joined the SGU. When Turnhouse closed for gliding, and Abbotsinch followed, Eric spent his Sundays at Portmoak. He was on the Technical Committee and he gained his Silver C here, and his

The wrecked Vasama

logbook shows more than 60 hours gliding time. A married man, Eric and his family had recently moved into their first home earlier this year. Our sincere sympathies go to his widow, Mrs Catherine Higgins and her children, Gregory, aged two, and three-months old Claire

On Sunday 21st November, another tragedy was narrowly averted. The Tiger (tug) landed on some wet sticky mud. This rapidly slowed it down, and as it came to an abrupt halt, it nosed over onto its back. The Pilot, Bill McLaren, smartly switched off the fuel and ignition. A quick pull at the safety harness and he landed on his head, then crawled clear, luckily unhurt.

At the end of the year, Bill Shanks stood down as secretary and was replaced by Ray Grieve, and Ian Dandie became CFI, replacing Tom Davidson.

When Ann Welch visited to attend one of the many parties at Portmoak, she produced a magnificent pottery eagle – donated by the Hungarian team to the BGA at the end of the World Championships at South Cerney. Ann said it was her wish to present this trophy to Tom Davidson as a token of the BGA's appreciation for his contribution to gliding.

The statistics for 1965 showed that it had been the best year so far; 240 flying days, 143 soaring days, 5988 launches, and 2034 hours flown.

The annual prize-giving took place in the Station Hotel in Kirkcaldy. Andrew Thorburn picked up the Championship trophy and the Parker Cross Country trophy, Roger Mann won the Boyle Altitude trophy (for his 19,000 ft. flight in January), and Mrs McPherson received the Service Salver.

Hon Treasurer Mrs Eric Verden Anderson presenting the 1965 Club Championship trophy to Andrew Thorburn. Looking on are Provost Eric Verden Anderson and club secretary William Shanks.

1966 saw a large issue of *Portmoak Press* (26 pages) declaring that the club mag was 'under new management'. It contained, amongst other things, an item giving notice that all visiting 'wave' pilots would have to book their 'places' at Portmoak in advance. This followed a discussion by the Board agreeing that the club was in danger of becoming a victim of its own success, with so many visitors arriving unannounced and literally jamming up the airfield. Another article explained that a new high intensity light on the clubhouse roof was to be used as a signal to 'call down' pilots before nightfall.

The Tiger tug had been sent to Strathallan Air Services, near Crieff, to be repaired following its roll-over and returned to full service before the summer season. Portmoak Farm, and a large chunk of ground, had been offered for sale at a reduced price of £14,000. The club had secured a grant to cover half of the cost and set about funding the balance.

The stand-by winch was converted to double up as a cable-laying winch. This cunning device enabled the winch to drive to the launch-point, attach the cable-ends to the anchor points then drive back to the other end of the strip to continue the launch, and significantly reduced cable-wear.

Bruce Marshall completed an interesting Silver Distance; he recalled his flight for *Portmoak Press:*

> *Thunderball*
> *Saturday, 18th June, was not my idea of the perfect cross-country day, with only a light south wind, early over-convection, and a low cloud-base. Rain was already falling in places when I was put in the Oly and told to GO. I was by no means even confident of staying up. However, the aero-tow took me to the west end of Benarty, and I was waved off in lift at 2,000 ft. The thermal appeared quite innocent, not very strong, and I circled up in light rain to cloudbase at 3,000 ft. This seemed rather low for setting course in these conditions, and as I had been into cloud a couple of days earlier – with no dire results, I switched on the Turn & Slip, assumed a philosophical state of mind, and went in.*
> *Keep the speed between 35 and 50, rate of turn no greater than two; don't try to hold the needles on specific figures, as long as they are within a safe range. That*

seemed to be the secret. No further attempt was made to centre in the lift – it was quite unnecessary. Rate of climb had improved to 3-4 metres by 4,000 ft., and was off the top of the scale at times afterwards. It was all quite smooth, till near the top of the climb, when the brakes were used when the speed exceeded 60. At 8,000 ft., I reckoned that I had enough height to glide out my Silver distance, and attempted to set course to the north-east.

Soon afterwards, I found myself in clear air, but with dark, tumbled masses of cloud all around. A small hole showed some hilltops far below. Were these the Ochils, Sidlaws or Grampians? At least it wasn't the sea! Loneliness is being above cloud with no idea of your position. At this moment, I would have much preferred to have been sipping coffee back at Portmoak. In cloud once more, I found that I could not hold a steady compass course, and was rapidly losing height, although I was not entirely sorry to see it go. In fact, I used the brakes to drop out of the bottom of the stuff. I found that I was just to the south of Perth – the river Tay showed up well through the murk. I must have been wandering in circles during the descent. Perth was crossed at 4,000 ft., heading for the sunlight which I could see to the north-east, beyond a dark curtain of cloud.

About this time, the first flashes of lightning added some urgency to the proceedings. Slipping under the edge of the cloud, I found that the sun had gone, leaving an overcast and completely dead looking sky. I felt tempted to land at Scone, as I no longer had the height to reach the line, but could think of no excuse for landing so soon after being so high, and so I pressed on. Shortly afterwards, at about 3,000 ft., I found a patch of no sink – a weak thermal from someone's bonfire. I started to circle, to be rewarded with the sight of a huge black wall of cloud behind me. At that very moment, a brilliant flash of lightning shot out of the cloud and struck the ground, not two miles away. Clearly, this was not the time or place to linger. I turned again to the east.

Down to 2,000ft. over Coupar Angus, I was beginning to look for likely fields when I once more struck lift – a good, steady, 1-3 metres up. This proved to be something rather exotic. A thunderstorm often pushes out a wedge of cold air at low level in front of it. This prises up the environmental air like a miniature cold front. I could actually see this happening when I turned crosswind to work the lift, as cloud was being formed and pushed upwards on my left, almost like a wave cloud. I gained 1,500 ft. in three minutes, the tendrils of cloud started to grope for the Oly, and I set course once more. From this height, the 50 km line was within reach, though whether the 1% rule could be beaten remained to be seen. The final glide was made through dark, smooth, lifeless air. The cockpit now became littered with maps and computers, as I tried to keep track of my whereabouts. The Loch of Lintrathen, up in the foothills of the Grampians, opposite the magic line gradually slid past. I headed as near to the high land as possible, to increase the distance from my release point.

An enormous field turned up in just the right place – two miles north-west of Kirriemuir, and the approach and landing presented no problems. I picketed the Oly under a darkening sky, listening to the approaching storm. The distance from the release point was 60.5 km which, with a loss of height of 1,850 ft., gave me 5 km in hand.

Thanks are due to everyone who was involved in sending me off, against my better judgement, and to my very efficient retrieve crew. Apologies to all those who sat, biting their fingernails, while the storm raged over Portmoak; anyway, it's nice to know you cared.

By the end of 1966, after much discussion as to the pros and cons, radios were installed in various ground vehicles, and Portmoak Base went 'On Air'. On the flying front, Roger Neaves claimed a gain of height of 19,500 ft., Alistair Dick completed an out and return (O/R) to Arbroath and Andrew Thorburn did an O/R to Stonehaven. Silver distances were completed by George Peddie, Alistair Dick, John Goodwin and Jack Melrose.

Chapter 9

The Unknown Winch Driver 1967 – 1969

1967 saw Andrew Thorburn stand down from his Chairman and Director roles on the SGU Board, although he continued with his Publicity and Development Officer duties. Office bearers were: Chairman – Tom Docherty, Secretary & Treasurer – Bruce Marshall, Hon. Secretary & Airfield Manager – Bill Shanks, Social Secretary & Publications – Miss M. Ritchie, Hon. Treasurer – A. Dick, Chief Flying Instructor – J.A. Dandie, Tugmaster – J. Rae, Records Officer – Tom Davidson, Safety Officer – Jim O'Donnell, Chairman (Club Committee) – Mrs D.S. Lawson.

Anyone who has visited Portmoak since 1967 might have noticed a rusting crankshaft 'growing' out of the grass in front of the briefing hut – with a simple plaque declaring 'To the Unknown Winch Driver', they might even have assumed that the crankshaft was the relic of some major engine seizure with one of the many Portmoak winches. Not so, *Portmoak Press* provided the answer, read on.

The object itself arrived one Saturday evening, when two members of the Action Group (SGU members who were involved in many manual tasks around the airfield), during a pause from their ditch-digging labours, decided upon a quick run up Bishop Hill to Carlin Maggie, just to keep in trim. They set out, taking along a lady pundit member to set the pace. On the way back down, in the

gathering dusk, they came upon the remains of the wreckage of a Hawker Hart which had crashed on Bishop before the war. One of the few recognisable pieces was the crankshaft of the Rolls-Royce Kestrel engine and, as it seemed a shame to leave it lying there, our two stalwart lads picked it up and took it with them. I shall not enlarge on the horrors of that journey, but the party finally staggered triumphantly into the clubhouse, proclaiming that the winch had finally fallen to bits. On telling their tale, one venerable member (a wild lad in Balado days 'tis said) remarked 'You must have been daft! There's hope for this club yet!' Chairman Tom made bids of up to six bob [30p] for the crankshaft, but these were rejected after a quick costing of the high-grade man-hours spent on the project. It was instead decided to mount it outside the clubhouse, where it now stands, looking much better than many pieces of modern sculpture. Mrs Lawson intends to train honeysuckle up it, and a short service in memory of the Unknown Winch Driver is to be held every 31st April.

The early part of 1967 provided 12 Gold and 7 Diamond height claims, many of which were recorded by visitors. One local was Charlie Ross, who claimed his Diamond Height by a gain of height of 21,000 ft. Ian Dandie completed his PPL and progressed on to become a tug pilot, and this spurred on Alan R. Milne to do the same. Another local pilot, Douglas MacKay, who had learned to fly – and gain his Silver C - at Portmoak during his school years completed his commercial pilot's training at Scone and went on to fly with B.U.A. out of Lydd. Bill Lang attended one of the summer courses that year and he recalled his first solo for *Portmoak Press:*

On the second course, Ansgar had me doing all the flying from the first day. Generally, he only touched the controls for demonstration purposes. Stalls and spins became a regular feature. Then, when he kept 'pulling the plug' on me on the launch, while I looked for 'non-existent flying objects' or some other pointed distraction, I knew that the big moment was near.

There was little apprehension in the thought, reactions to cable-breaks were now swift and automatic, I was thoroughly enjoying my flying and looking forward to every launch.

Late that afternoon, the quiet easterly wind dropped almost to a flat calm. Ansgar gave me four circuits instead of the usual three. 'This is it!', and the adrenaline started to pump gently; however… anticlimax – no solo!

After tea, Andrew took over. When we arrived at the launch point, he looked round at me and said 'When's your turn?'. I looked at my watch and the setting sun, did a rapid calculation and lied whitely, 'Third, I think!'.

Our record keeper for the day, Vera (bless her) motioned me over and whispered, 'Actually, you're sixth on the list, but the others have agreed to stand down and let you in'. How she managed such a swift agreement without consultation – I'll never know.

The three circuits before my turn took an age. Then, suddenly, I was sitting quietly and quite composed in familiar old T21b (No.2), with cockpit checks completed and 'taking up slack'.

The open cockpit T21b

Andrew sat back, hands and feet fully clear of the controls. The cable tightened, 'All out', and No.2 was pitching easily on her wheel – steadying, then lifting off gently and easing up into the full climb, everything going nicely, 40 kt with the altimeter winding up to 800 ft. Our good old winch driver, Alan Milne, eased the speed. The cable released and so we dropped nicely to normal flying attitude as if No.2 – having done it all before – knew the importance of this flight.

A gentle turn into a left-hand circuit. Then quietly from Andrew, 'Turn 360° left'. For once, the pitot head swept round the horizon as if it was on rails, speed constant.

From Andrew, 'Good, very good!' and no further comment, into the down-wind leg, cross-wind and approach, spoilers open, round out gently, hold off, and we were down.

Andrew undid his straps, looked at me 'You're doing the next one yourself!'.

The ballast weight went in, and I was off. In spite of me, No.2 behaved like a perfect lady. I suspect Alan was virtually flying her from the winch.

On release, she seemed to want to fly a shade slower than before and had to be held down to normal flying speed. Then there we were, sailing through the quiet evening air with no qualms whatsoever.

Final turn, spoilers open and we're floating gently into the airfield to a fair landing.

Two more circuits and Andrew and the boys were offering congratulations. The first big hurdle was over. Now to the Capstan and, with luck and practice, the Swallow and so very much to learn.

1967 saw the Tiger Moth tug (G-ANPC) written off in a crash on Bishop Hill while aero towing. Tom Docherty fortunately escaped uninjured.

The club held an open day during May 1967 but, due to heavy rain, no flying took place. Instead, the many visitors were given guided tours of the hangars and workshops and seemed content with being allowed to sit in gliders without the fear of actually flying in them. Despite the lack of flying, the bring and buy sale realised £35 for clubhouse funds. Not to be put off by this lack of flying, Charlie Ross managed ten wave flights on ten consecutive weekends.

A large pile of pre-cast concrete slabs appeared outside the hangar and members were reminded that these were for the flooring of the hangar and to make sure that children were kept away. Work started at the end of the year and was completed the following year. A second bus winch was brought into service and an SHK arrived on site, this being the property of Messrs Ross, Rae & Reilly. Another aircraft seen at Portmoak towards the end of the year was an Auster belonging to Donald Campbell's brother John. This aircraft would be flown to Aboyne one weekend every month, being ferried there and back by an Aboyne member. The tug pilots were in awe of this luxurious (draught-free) tow plane.

A Caravelle accident, in England, in November killed an old SGU gliding stalwart, Donald Campbell. Andrew Thorburn wrote his obituary for *Portmoak Press:*

Donald Campbell took up gliding in 1936. He soon found out that the only way to get into the air in those days was to be prepared, and able, to build and repair his own machine.

Along with his two brothers, who were equally enthusiastic, he helped to form the Dumbarton Gliding Club which operated from a local field previously used by the famous Percy Pilcher. In 1938, the Dumbarton Club became part of the SGU at Bishop Hill, and Donald and his brothers were soon familiar figures there with their privately owned Prufling and Hols.

During these formative years, a visit to the Campbell workshops near Dumbarton was quite an experience. This was a large brick cow-shed, with practically every stall occupied by a partly constructed glider, or Flying Flea.

Like most of the others associated with gliding in that area at the time, Donald worked for the Blackburn aircraft firm. During the war years, he built an H.57 glider in his home. An active member of the SGU after the war, he decided to give up his job, and get into glider repair work on a professional basis. Starting first with a year as a ground engineer at the Midland Gliding Club, and later he got going as a self-employed Glider Inspector – advertising under the title of 'The Gliding Doctor'. His mobility and qualifications were much appreciated in the early post-war years, when growing clubs could not afford a full time repair man of their own.

Always on the lookout for something new and exciting in the light aircraft world, he became the UK agent for the Benson Gyrocopter, and his workshops at Hungerford were, for some time, entirely devoted to the construction of these novel craft.

His enthusiasm for the kind of projects with which his working day was made up, was completely matched by that of Nan, his second wife. They were an ideal business couple, and well-liked wherever they went. We could always expect to have a visit from them every Christmas at Portmoak.

Their loss, in the Caravelle accident, has deprived gliding of two very happy and worthwhile personalities.

Towards the end of 1967, the country was hit by an outbreak of Foot and Mouth disease. The SGU voluntarily agreed to suspend cross country flying. Not to be outdone, Z Goudie stayed within range of Portmoak and claimed his Diamond height on Christmas Day.

The annual Trophies were awarded to Charlie Ross, Club Champion for Best height and O/R flights, Tom Docherty got Best Distance and the Silver Salver went to Valerie Peddy.

Z. Goudie's flight on Christmas day spurred on the die-hards and the 1st January 1968 saw a number of gliders take to the air over Portmoak. All staying within range of the site, due to the cross country ban, but looking for height claims. First up was Ian Ronald who launched at 10:07 and gained his Silver Height. He was not followed, the pundits were waiting for 'tomorrow' (it's always better tomorrow). The 2nd January was indeed 'better'; four Gold C Height claims, and one flight to 15,000 ft., as well as a T49 flight to 13,000ft with G. Smith and K. Buckton. January 3rd produced only one claim for Gold Height but M. Clement recorded 12,000 ft, Bruce Marshall got to 10,000 ft., as did Joe Kennedy.

The Foot and Mouth restrictions were finally relaxed on 1st February 1968 and the SGU got down to the serious business of flying, and preparing for the summer season. By May, Portmoak Farm, with its 130 acres, was in the possession of the SGU. Plans to remove fencing and prepare the land were put in place, with an estimated completion by November that year – with the firm promise that the 'bigger' Portmoak would be fully open for business in 1969. These plans were ambitious, and included extra accommodation, a door at the back of the hangar to allow aircraft to be taken out from either end, workshops to be moved to the farm buildings, and a new area for caravans and tents. The club proudly announced that *'one part of the airfield reaches out halfway to Bishop Hill, so that in marginal soaring conditions, away landings at the bottom of the hill need no longer be a problem, as Portmoak will be within 200 ft. of the hill slopes.'*

On a more serious note, the Safety Officer deemed it necessary to highlight three incidents that could have been disastrous:

More History Lessons

Recently, a Ka6 was lined up for an aero-tow. At the 'All Out', the Ka6 over-ran the cable. The glider pilot promptly pulled the release knob. However, the glider was not left behind. The pilot released again, and again, but still he was dragged along. The combination was accelerating all the time. The tow-rope had wrapped itself around the wheel. Now the pilot of the Ka6 had to act quickly, and he did. He applied full rudder, dug one wingtip into the grass and proceeded to travel sideways behind the tug. Then the tug stopped!

Thanks to the prompt and correct action of the pilots, no serious damage occurred.

I am sure the seriousness of this incident is obvious to all of us.

The conclusion is this: There should always be a 'bat man' well forward of the tug on the same side as the wingtip holder of the glider. If the glider pilot shouts stop, the man at the wingtip will be able to relay this message via the 'bat man' to the tug pilot.

Another Incident

In the evening of a day of east wind, the Swallow had its last launch to fly back to the hangar. It had a good launch and completed the circuit by over-flying the launch point at about 400 ft. At the same time, a friend had taken the pilot's Jaguar from the launch point to drive it back to the clubhouse. Both the glider and the car proceeded along the runway. Neither could see the other. The jaguar was accelerating and catching up with the Swallow. When the height between them was hardly ten feet, the pilot noticed some movement (shadow) on the runway. He had enough speed and sense to act promptly. The driver was not aware of anything unusual.

Again, your imagination will not be overstrained to recognise the danger.

The conclusion: No cars on the airfield itself at any time. Use the tractor for retrieving. Its top speed without load is 12 MPH, and you have all round vision.

And Yet Another One

Andrew Thorburn was about ready to be launched in his Oly 463. The cable was already attached. He was checking something in the cockpit, his head was bent right down inside. A fly (or flea) caused an itch on his right cheek. The man on the lamp saw one finger up as Andrew tried to rid himself of that itch. Flashes for 'Take Up Slack' followed immediately, and for some peculiar reason the winch driver reacted promptly. Andrew, with his head still down inside the cockpit became aware of movement. As he looked up, his face showed signs of amazement and bewilderment. He then waved his hand and shouted No-no-no. The man at the lamp reacted quickly with an 'All Out'

Andrew was launched in spite of his protesting No-no-no. It all happened to be no more than an amusing incident.

However, consider this: Had he not been an experienced pilot and in his panic operated the brake instead of the release, what could have happened then? Perhaps a wingtip on the ground, the glider cart-wheeling and decapitating a few bystanders? Or does this assumption overtax your imagination?

The 1968 awards went to Charlie Ross (club champion and best height), Jimmy Rae (best distance), Alistair Milne (out & return) and Betty Barr received the Silver Salver. Mrs Mac received a special award on her retirement from the office, after 20 years.

As part of the steady climb in the stature of the SGU, it was agreed that the BGA would host an instructor's course at Portmoak in early 1969. The National Coach, Bill Scull, conducted the course and a number of 'new' SGU instructors were produced at the end. This was just as well, as the Easter courses were fully subscribed and the summer bookings were almost at capacity too – instructors would be in demand during 1969. Reg Curwen became the CFI and Airfield Manager, with Jim O'Donnell as his deputy CFI. Ansgar Sambale remained the Resident Instructor and Assistant CFI.

In addition to SGU members, and the ever-increasing numbers of visitors, three more 'groups' took up residency at Portmoak. These were the Universities of Glasgow & Strathclyde GC, Edinburgh University GC, and the Tipsy Nipper syndicate.

Tom Docherty's Super Cub arrived on site just after Easter but Tom still made good use of his soaring skills. On 19th May he wrote himself into the record books by flying the SHK to Rotherham and claiming the first Gold Distance from Portmoak.

August saw an intrepid bunch of 'Portmoakians' head off to Booker for the Regionals, *Portmoak Press* reported their progress:

The club Olympia 460 (128) headed south for the 1969 Regional Competitions held at Wycombe Air Park. The pilots involved were Alan Milne and Z Goudie. The only other crew member was Gerry Purcell's 'dead third man' borrowed from the 441 syndicate. Supernumerary for a few days, however, were 'Tiny' Irving and Eric Andron. Their expedition nearly got no further than Kelty when an over-enthusiastic Goudie tried to do a flick-roll with the car trailer combination (those radial tyres have gone to his head) but, nevertheless, twelve hours saw them more or less safely to their journey's end at Wycombe.

Next day (Friday) saw them engaged in some preliminary flying, ready for the contest proper – due to start on the Saturday. In the event, however, the clag rendered it a no-contest day and it was not until Sunday that serious flying began (and nearly ended).

The task was a 'Cat's Cradle' with turning points at Booker, Moreton-in-the-Marsh, Grove (near Wantage) and Stockbridge. Z was pilot for the day and landed at Didcot in Berkshire. The field was good and empty, and was still empty when Z returned some time later to check that the glider was OK, but when they eventually arrived to de-rig, some twenty or thirty cows had made their way through a series of rather informal hedges to taste this delicate bird. Resultant damage was nine ribs out of the trailing edge on one wing, a foot through the aileron on the other and the fibreglass fairing in the tail was cracked. On return to Booker, help came quickly to hand in the shape of Arthur Doughty (who inspected) and Ralph Jones (of Southern Sailplanes) who arranged for repairs to be carried out in his premises at Thruxton. Our heroes dashed off there next day and by 2 a.m. the following morning, 128 was airworthy again.

Their bad luck had cost them a contest day which also brought the SGU some ill fortune – Tom Docherty was put out of the game with a collapsed undercarriage on the syndicate SHK (444). Hard lines indeed, as he had been doing well until this happened.

The weather rendered both Tuesday and Wednesday no-contest, and Alan had to wait until Thursday before he could tackle a contest task. This time, an out-and-return to Nympsfield (207k) was set with the option of an out-and-return to Tewkesbury. He got away well, to beyond Cirencester, but 'damp' set in from the west. A dash into this 'dead' area was called for to reach the turning point and return but, in the event, Alan emerged from cloud at Gloucester, having overshot Nympsfield – eventually landing in the playing fields of the Hoffman Ball Bearing Company, who gave him a very hospitable welcome.

The weather on Friday was again pretty dubious but a 'free distance' task was set. Z headed south-west and landed in a field next to the house of none other than Philip Wills! The gremlins were at it again, however, as his wingtip hit a knobbly bit of flint on landing, and another 3 a.m. finish was necessitated. Friday was eventually declared a non-competition day as insufficient distances had been covered to qualify it for one.

The task on Saturday with Alan back in the 'hot' seat was a triangle of about 150k – Blenheim Palace, South Marsden, Booker. Alan made it to the first turn-point and almost to the second, landing just short of South Marsden. The principal difficulty of this flight, as with others, was in map-reading. Poor visibility left only a narrow cone of unfamiliar countryside and Eric Andren made much of Alan's radio position reports of 'two miles south of last position'. A landing was eventually made in a field called 'Big Maid's

Knee' or something which sounded like that and Alan didn't leave until he had signed the farmer's visitors book, sampled his beer and met his daughter. Saturday ended with a barbecue at Booker where they roasted a whole pig.

Sunday was again a no-go day but Z and Eric did a little local soaring and camp was struck on Monday, the return journey taking a mere ten hours.

The outright winner of the Competition was Ralph Jones (Cirrus), second was Alf Warminger (Phoebus). Competing in addition to a host of Ka 6Es were 2 Diamants, another Phoebus, 2 Fokas, Skylark 384s, an ex-world championship Dart 15, Tom's SHK and Ray Stafford-Allen's T49. Five Supercubs and a Tiger were used as Tugs – 30 aircraft to 2000ft. in 40 minutes was typical!

Back at Portmoak, the fences had been removed from around the farm to open up the new field, Roger Constable had replaced Reg Curwen as CFI and a new K13 syndicate had arrived on site.

Chapter 10
1970 – 1974
Those Portmoak Waves Again

The swinging sixties had ended and the SGU looked forward to the 'Soaring Seventies'. Due to other commitments by the *Portmoak Press* editor at the time, there had been no issue of the club mag during 1970.

Flying was, however, more successful with a plethora of badge claims during February and March – 4 Diamond heights, 15 Gold heights, 1 Silver height and 4 Silver durations. Tom Docherty attempted and O/R to Turriff and Tony Shelton managed a flight to Newcastle. Ian Dandie replaced Roger Constable as CFI and Robin Shaw replaced Alistair Milne as Safety Officer.

The Fife Schools Gliding Club now included Braehead School from Buckhaven in Fife, and many pupils enjoyed the facilities at Portmoak during 1970. The following article is taken from "*State School*", written by the then Headmaster, R.F.Mackenzie.

We sent our pupils for one day a week gliding in the months when the gliding station wasn't that busy. Some of the pupils had included

Pupils from Braehead School being shown the T49.

this study in the work they were doing for the Duke of Edinburgh Award. For our youngsters, aiming at the Bronze Award, this meant proficiency in ground handling of gliders, launching procedures, signalling, the pre-flight cockpit check, and instrument reading and setting. It meant also five instructional flights, a knowledge of the rules of the air, and making a model glider and using it to demonstrate normal flight, the stall and the effect of trim changes.

Being under sixteen, our pupils were not permitted to go solo. On each visit to the airfield they got one flight. But they were kept busy throughout the day driving the tractor and assisting in the routine of launching. They took a responsible part in this drill, realising that safety was involved and that the more efficiently the drill was carried out, the more the flights that would be launched. Pupils labelled 'difficult' in school (which sometimes means that they are not so docile as their fellows), pupils who resisted attempts to teach them quadratic equations or the exports of the Philippines and who, strangely enough, took no interest in the marital adventures of Henry VIII, sprang into lively activity when faced with the launching drill. Their instructors, members of the school staff (able glider pilots with a background of service experience, and not easily pleased), were delighted with the reactions of the pupils.

Flying was the thing. Then, when the delighted and fearful shock and thrill of the first flight was broadening into a relaxed understanding of the requirements of successful gliding, the instructors introduced the classroom work. But flying came first.

We asked the pupils to write down how they felt on their first flight. Nearly all of them were, before the trip, 'sort of nervous' or had 'butterflies in my stomach', and had the feeling of having their stomachs coming out of their mouths as they were being launched into the air. They all enjoyed the smoothness when the cable was released and they were airborne and independent of ground ties. One boy wrote, 'It was the most exciting thing I have done. The first thing you feel when you climb into the cockpit is of being scared but when you have been reassured that it

Signalling to the winch.

will be all right, it is better. The instructor tells you how to manoeuvre the glider and then you are hauled up. Once you have released the cable it is quite a feeling to be dependent on yourself. When the glider dives you get a funny feeling but it was a very good day.'

As an English teacher I was interested to see if the pupils would be able to put vividly on paper a new a memorable experience. Most Scottish primary schools are absorbed in teaching pupils the rules of writing and they damp down or indeed quench a youngster's delight in the bright ring of words. I have often thought about the contrast between the wooden, lifeless and timid way in which they handle written words and the confidence and enjoyment with which they handle print. I had put the contrast down to the fact that primary schools do so little art that pupils come to the secondary school without any prejudice against a paint brush. I had thought that if teachers in the primary school wearied pupils with art as much as they now do with English, then their painting would be as dull as their writing. But a distinguished Scottish poet told me that using words is quite different from using paint and, if I understood him right, that you can't hope to use words vividly until you have served an apprenticeship in the feel and relationship and value of words, in the craft of writing. This is a question to which I hope we shall be one day able to give a clearer answer. In the meantime here is part of an account written by one of the boys:

'After the signal was given to the winch, the glider started to move. Then it left the ground and soared into the air. The glider rose steadily, until it reached the length of the cable, the cable was released and the glider rose gracefully like a huge bird over Loch Leven. There was a wonderful view of a few islands sticking out of the mist. You thought the plane was hardly moving. It turned gently sideways towards the hill. It flew over the airfield, turned, and landed smoothly. Each of us handled the controls, and flew the glider. It was great.'

As a contrast, here are extracts from what the girls wrote. One of them, who, the instructor said, had what seemed like a natural gift for flying and handled the controls with relaxed understanding, wrote this:

'What I found very extraordinary was how long the wire stretched which pulls the glider into the air. I never would have believed it but when I was in the air I didn't want to go back down again.'

Another girl wrote:

'The views were lovely. We saw swans flying overhead and also boys bringing in turnips in the fields below us.'

Back in school, the pupils learn something of the theory of flight. It is no longer a remote, academic question, how a body which is heavier than air can stay in the air for so long. The study of weather becomes relevant. If it's your day for gliding, the approach of depressions, warm or cold fronts, the forecasting of the weather, is something intimately intertwined with your happiness. If you want to become a good glider pilot, you have to try to learn about thermals, from a few short lessons, as much as a seagull gets out of a life's experience. And experience of gliding gives the pupils the ability to envisage the third dimension when he looks at a map. When he looks down on Fife from a thousand ft and sees Loch Leven and Kinross, roads and a railway and cars and farms and woods and a river, and the Lomond Hills strangely flat-looking from that height, he may begin to take a new, lively interest in maps, seeing them not as diagrams but as a kind of bird's-eye view (or glider's-eye view) of the earth beneath. And it is a wonderful experience for a fourteen-year old pupil to see a large part of his home county not as a series of snapshots taken from a bus run or a cycle run, diminishing in clarity the farther it gets from the main road, but as a whole, and to realise that this is the part *of the earth's wrinkled surface on which he has his being.*

Coleridge said that it was one of the functions of poetry to let people see things freshly and with a sense of wonder. He could have said the same of education. We have to use everything that lies to our hand to tell our pupils of the earth's wonders. Our pupils, playing with the computer, had discovered what was for them a new truth, that multiplication is merely repeated addition. Gliding has a similar effect, and after even one trip, they return to school seeing life with a new freshness. And I think that getting their heads into the clouds once in a while has helped them to put their ft more firmly on the ground.

The year was tinged with sadness as news of Dorothy Lawson's death was received (see chapter 3 for a photo of Dorothy preparing for her first flight). Also that year, another SGU Stalwart passed away – this time, it was Tom Davidson, at the age of 79.

1971 started with some excellent wave conditions and Tom Bradbury put pen to paper for the benefit of *S&G* readers:

Those Portmoak Waves Again

This is a brief account of two consecutive wave days at Portmoak, March 9th and 10th, 1971. On both days, the waves were soarable above the 5km level and several people went high, the best height being about 27,500ft on the 9th; this was achieved by Arthur Doughty in a Skylark 4.

The surface charts for midday on 9th and 10th both showed high pressure west of Ireland with a north or north-westerly airflow across Scotland. On the 9th, a cold front moved south across Portmoak soon after midday. The front trailed back towards south west Iceland, and *next day a small warm front wave developed and ran down over the western end of Scotland during the afternoon. Satellite photos showed a considerable width of cloud associated with these fronts each day, but the Scottish highlands bore the brunt of the weather and to the lee of the Grampians there was always some sort of slot for people to descend through. At first glance, the charts hardly suggested two such good wave days, but the front did not in fact change the essential character of the air, except in the lowest 5,000ft. On both days the winds and temperatures aloft were fairly similar. The upper winds were from the sector 330 to 300 degrees, with speeds increasing upwards from about 35 kt at 10,000ft to 50 kt at 30,000ft.*

These speeds are for the undisturbed flow upwind of the mountains. Once the wave flow developed, the wind speed altered considerably in different parts of the wave, and the effect was surprising. More of this later.

On Tuesday the 9th, the best waves were found in the morning before the cold front came through. Most of the climbs were started from above the old airfield at Balado. Earlier that morning an unknown pilot announced on the radio that he was in snow, and that it was blowing at 70 kt. Since it was evidently fine for miles around Portmoak, we supposed the call came from the wilder parts of the Highlands, and were not perturbed. However, it was disconcerting to hear Portmoak radio at 13:30 saying that cloud was on the Ochils and snow showers were reducing visibility. Luckily this did not last, but at least one pilot had an interesting ride home. The listeners heard how his descent below cloud had brought him out over some unidentified town. This was followed by a rather prolonged and ultimately triumphant scrape home along a lesser range of hills. It was at times hard to be sure of one's exact position when the only identifiable landmark was the Firth of Clyde 30 miles away.

On Wednesday 10th, there was much more space between the clouds until late in the afternoon. The cloud pattern was unhelpful and the waves were weak in the morning. The surface wind was back to WSW, nearly at right angles to the upper winds. Later on, both waves and clouds developed spectacularly. The interesting feature which persisted all day was that the waves had a quite definite tilt forward with height. From the scruffy little bar of cloud marking the wave to the lee of the Ochils near Milnathort, to the top of a very slow climb, we had to move three miles upwind for a gain of only 6,000ft. It was only after checking the photographs that I realised just how far forward the wave sloped.

This tilt to the wave front was so marked that above 20,000ft the lift just ahead of one big lenticular actually overlapped the low cloud marking the next upwind wave abeam Crieff. From bottom to top, the area of lift sloped forward a good seven miles. No wonder we find these high lenticulars misleading when trying to work the wave low down.

These tilted waves seem to be markedly symmetric. The lift on the upwind side may be greater than the sink on the lee side, but if so the effect is balanced by the much greater width of sink.

Going into wind between West Lomond and Bridge of Earn, the distance between waves was about seven miles. For six minutes, the rate of sink was fairly constant and averaged 8.3 kt. Assuming that a Skylark 4 sinks at about 5 kt at a true airspeed of 80 kt, the air was descending at 3.3 kt. Arriving over the bar of cloud, it was disheartening to find no lift. As before, the lift was well forward of the low cloud, the best of it being nearly a mile upwind of the cloud top. Here there was a relatively narrow band of air rising at 6 kt. After checking the in-flight notes with the barograph trace I have the impression that the slope of the wave was steeper on the windward side than on the lee side.

I can imagine that going downwind at a ground speed of something like 120 kt, one might well miss the narrow band of lift, especially if it occurred unexpectedly far from the bar of cloud.

Most people are familiar with the way the wind varies as it flows through the wave pattern, with the strongest winds usually over the wave crest and sometimes down over the lee slopes of the hills as well. If one draws the wave tilted, as it seemed to be that day, then it may be that the band of strong winds will extend much further downwind from the crest of the wave than if the flow was perfectly symmetrical. I think I ran into this near Loch Lomond when trying to push forward into wind at a height of 19,000ft. It took a little while to appreciate that I wasn't getting anywhere at an IAS of 80 kt, and increasing the speed to 110, which should have meant about 140 true, did not improve matters. One doesn't expect to see much progress over the ground, but when one isn't gaining on the clouds either it becomes disheartening. Both clear-vision panels were open because the canopy was frosted over, and the only result of 7,000ft of noisy descent was to disperse about two square ft of frost. Forward progress seemed negligible, the cloud top was about 12,000ft and the control zone not far downwind, so it seemed wise to crab across wind to the wave I had left so light-heartedly a few minutes earlier.

Even this wave wasn't up to much at first, but became magnificent further east. More than one pilot made good speed along it, with 4 kt up at an IAS of 80 kt in places. Even including the fumble at Loch Lomond it still only took 45 minutes to cover the 105 Km to Leuchars where the wave seemed to be blocked off by a different line of cloud.

Pilots' Reports – March 9th

<u>John Ellis</u>. *ASW15, time not recorded. Initial climb in secondary wave from hill-soaring Bishop Hill; transferred to primary at about 10,000ft. Reached 23,650ft. Climb timed at 1,000 fpm between 16,000ft and 19,000ft.*

<u>PD Boyer</u>. *K8B, 10:45 to 14:45. Picked up from two puffs of cloud in likely wave location. Tracking ahead of this, reached sink and turned to find large black cloud formed behind. Thermalled up under the centre of this over Balado airfield, with all the usual indications of a strong thermal. Reached cloudbase and tracked to leading edge. Climbed in secondary wave towards Falkirk from Ochils to 5,000ft at 4 kt, then at 6 kt to 7,000ft, in weak lift to 9,000ft, and finally at 12 kt to 14,000ft, after which it fell away to half a knot. Rain squalls closed the airfield below, and the gap closed in. After making for a landing at Falkirk, picked up wave again, and soared from Cleish to Portmoak using wave, thermal and hill lift.*

<u>RJ Buckels</u>. *Olympia 460, 15:45 to 17:45. Released in weak wave at 4,000ft over Milnathort and climbed slowly to 6,000ft around the cloud. Lift increased to 5 kt above cloud and went to 10,300f. This appeared to be the limit, so initiated a move forward to the next bar, which was reached at 5,300ft at Dunning about five miles SW of Perth. This bar appeared to be just upwind of the edge of the Ochils, and was assumed to be the primary wave, the previous one having been the secondary. Stronger lift (5-6 kt) was worked to 12,000ft. As this appeared to be the top, a move WSW along the wave was initiated, speed being adjusted to give zero sink as lift was encountered. At a position about two miles WSW of Auchterarder, the bar tended to turn NW, almost at right angles, for about four miles before lying once more NE-*

SW about five miles WSW of Crieff. Moved along this bar in a SW direction until over the largest strato-cu beneath, slowed from 85 kt and climbed at 7-8 kt from 11,000ft to 14,800ft before leaving wave (no oxygen), which had deteriorated to 5 kt.

Bernard Kirby. Olympia 460. 09:45 to 12:20. Left Bishop Hill at 2,000ft and flew towards bonfire four-five miles upwind of Loch Leven. Zero sink at 1,800ft. Contacted rotor just north of this; lift gradually increased to 10 kt at 10,000ft, then died. Moved towards Dollar, contacted 8 kt and climbed to 13,250ft before breaking away from 5 kt lift (no oxygen).

Ian Hobday. Std Cirrus, 18:00 to 19:15. Three wavelengths investigated, best lift 2-4 kt, wind northerly, absolute altitude 8,800ft.

David W Evans. Olympia 463, 09:45 to 15:00. Contacted from creep-out from Bishop Hill, one or two miles SW of Balado airfield, after hearing report from Steve White. Six to eight kt lift at its best. Maximum altitude, 22,170ft.

Arthur Doughty. Skylark 4, 10:30 to 13:45. Entered wave about 12:20, discovered on exploratory probe from the west end of Benarty Hill. Average strength 4-6 kt with short spell at 6-8 kt. One wave system only used; explored to SW of Kincardine Bridge. Climb abandoned at about 27,500ft, when slot started to close in, although still climbing at 3 kt.

Steve White. Std Cirrus, 10:00 to 13:30. The wave was contacted upwind of Bishop Hill near Balado at 3,000ft asl, with lift very weak and broken until 6,000ft. There was a steady 4 kt going up to 8 kt between 10-20,000ft. After discontinuing the climb, three other upwind wave systems were used. Wavelength about six miles. Wind relatively light even at height.

Pilots' Reports – March 10th

David W Evans. Olympia 463, time not recorded. Wave contacted over Glenfarg from end of cloud street, breaking off at 12,350ft because I had no oxygen. There was even stronger wave lift between Dollar and Kinross, but had to leave it at 13,000ft.

John Ellis. ASW-15, time not recorded. Weak wave contacted north of Bishop Hill almost direct from hill lift. Taken to 5,000ft in the Balado area, then transferred north across the hills to another system running from seven miles south of Crieff to Perth. Not particularly strong lift – max 2 kt. Best height was 8,500ft.

Ian Hobday. Std Cirrus, 10:00 to 15:00. Wave marked by smoke from field fire forming a wedge in the valley over Kinross. Wave system used from Dollar to Perth, and climbed to 13,800ft.

Arthur Doughty. Skylark 4, 14:30 to 18:10. Discovered from exploratory probes from Benarty Hill. Lift variable, mainly about 4-6 kt, but a short spell with needles on the stops. Best height, 16,500ft.

Steve White. Std Cirrus. 14:30 to 16:30. Together with an Olympia 460, the north face of Bishop was left at 2,000ft in zero sink, eventually arriving over the river Tay. Wave cloud was forming all around over the Ochils and a climb to 10,000ft was made where sight of the Oly was lost. Continuing to 15,000ft, one could see wave extending from south of Dundee in the east to Loch Lomond and beyond in the west. Trading climb for speed flying along the edge of the wave, at times at max permitted, without losing height, Loch Lomond was reached after 40 minutes, an average of 150 Km/h. The wave extended further now in a SW direction to Machrihanish and on to Ireland. However, turning south the return leg was flown along the wave to Portmoak which was reached at 9,000ft.

On approaching Loch Leven, the wave suddenly collapsed within minutes and a hurried descent with full airbrakes had to be made before the gap closed in.

The wave systems continued beyond the so-called 'season' at Portmoak with wave flights taking place right into the height of summer. On 15th July, A.R. Milne and G. Polkinghorne set off in the Capstan (286) equipped with oxygen, barograph etc. to have a crack at the British two-seater altitude, which in 1971 stood at 19,000ft. At 12,500ft., 286 refused to climb any further, and the record was left 'unharmed'. A couple of days later, Frank Reilly entered the record books with Portmoak's first 500Km., flying to Haddenham in Buckinghamshire. Frank recalled his flight for *Portmoak Press*:

> *The Friday evening weather forecast for Saturday, 17th July, looked good so I decided to have a go for 500Km. Leuchars Met. Office confirmed in detail the previous night's TV intimation. Wind was to be 25 kt or so in the north, tapering off further south. Thermal strengths would also die off on the way south.*
>
> *By about 10 a.m. on Saturday, the weather was looking good, and I intended to set off at about 10:30 and cross the Forth. I declared Compton Abbas as goal, safely over the record. Tom Docherty and Kenny Jamieson agreed to retrieve.*
>
> *The first launch, just before 11:00 a.m. confirmed thermal strengths to be 4 to 6 kt, right up to 5,000ft. over the site. Conditions looked good over the Forth – then I had to land to give Tom the car keys!*
>
> *Next launch was at 11:40, behind Tom in the Super Cub. I pulled off at 1,800ft. and proceeded to 5,000ft. in 6 to 8 up. 11:50 and I was on my way – via Kincardine this time, as the other side of the Forth now looked as if the sea breeze had started already.*
>
> *The river being crossed at 4,000ft. which, with the cloudbase at 5,000ft. was legal. Minimum thermal strengths of 4 kt seemed to be the order of the day. Wind was NW but no more than 15 kt.*

From Kincardine I flew south, passing near Whitburn, with the speed to fly ring set for a two knot average – which was conservative, as I did not stay in any thermals which did not average 4 kt in the first turn. Course was now changed to SE now that I was well clear of the Edinburgh Control Zone. Speed was about 60-70 kt between thermals.

Thermals were still good, the wind having died off noticeably, and near Peebles I found the best one of the day – 8 to 10 kt. Once clear of the controlled air space, if less than 500ft. from cloud I did not circle but pulled the speed off in the lift and sometimes disappeared a couple of hundred ft into cloud but still on course. Below 500ft. from cloud, I used thermals which were over 4 kt. Apart from a patch between Selkirk and Jedburgh, thermals were plentiful and Carter Bar on the A68 was quickly passed. The visibility at this point was such that the Firth of Forth was easily observed, as was the south east Fife coast.

Cruising height was mainly 4-5,000ft. occasionally to 5,500ft. and down to 3,000ft near Consett. Sea breeze was in evidence now and had closed in as a wedge towards Darlington. I kept about ten miles to the west of this and headed for my next landfall at Scotch Corner on the A1, the Leeming then Dishforth airfields. Only 4 knot thermals were accepted, but they were becoming few and far between. At about 4:00 p.m., the 300K mark was passed just east of Leeds.

Industrial and atmospheric haze was now becoming more prominent but navigation from 5,000ft. was no problem – M1 from Leeds and Sheffield over to the west. My southerly course would now have the M1 in sight until the M45 junction south of Rugby. My exact course was now being determined by the best bits of sky but speed flying was maintained until about Rugby, where I was down to about 1,500ft. when the gaps between the good thermals were becoming quite big. I changed my speed settings and accepted anything that was going up! This worked and, by the time I was over the radio masts south of Coventry, I was back at 5,000ft. Time was now about 6:40 p.m.

A dead sky to the west now forced abandonment of my goal and the only bits of cloud were towards the south east. The wind was now north east and was no longer of any assistance. I got my last thermal back to 4,000ft. near Brackley and commenced a glide out for Booker, now knowing that I would be comfortably over 500km. No more thermals, and the cross wind, meant that I was down to 800ft. at Haddenham with a good newly-cut field available, so I flew a good circuit and landed. The time was 7:50 p.m. and the distance covered was 527km.

Meanwhile, back on the M1, at unmentionable speeds, one long Sunblest bread van proceeded south on borrowed cash to arrive within radio range about midnight, a valiant effort. The local police kindly directed the combination to the exact spot.

We were on our way by about 1:00 a.m., stopped for a bite on the M1 north of Birmingham, and at a shop to redeem Tom's watch from Pawn – Tom and Kenny having left without money, believe it or not. We arrived back at Portmoak at 10:00 a.m. tired but satisfied – with the first Diamond distance from Portmoak. Thanks to Kenny and Tom for an excellent retrieve.

As 1971 continued, the new North/South runway was brought into use, making Portmoak useable from almost any point of the compass. Newcomers to the fleet included a syndicate Falke and a second Olympia 463, replacing the club's Olympia 2b.

January 16th, 1972, was a sad day indeed. Colin MacDougal crashed the Swallow on Bishop Hill, and was killed.

Winter dragged on that year and there was not much flying until late February. Kenny Jamieson caused a bit of a stir when he took a pupil up in the recently refurbished T49. Taking off to the west, towards Loch Leven, after a below average winch launch, they got into difficulties and decided to land straight ahead, over the frozen edges of the loch and on to St Serf's Island. Although completely unharmed, their adventure had only just started. Boat owners had to be found, and permission to be obtained before anyone could get out to them. After making landfall on the island, the next problem was how to get the T49 back! After considerable discussion and negotiation, a cunning plan was hatched whereby a raft would be built and the various

The fuselage of the T49 being ferried to its trailer.

bits of the de-rigged T49 would be ferried back.

Easter saw an improvement in the weather and the badge claims for March & April of 1972 included 3 Diamond Heights, 11 Gold, 7 Silver durations and 3 Silver distances. The club Tiger Moth was sold and replaced by a hired Condor, and a club owned Falke (G-AZOK) was delivered.

Just as the summer was about to start, Jim O'Donnell took over as CFI. One of his first jobs was to prepare for an open day on 25th June. This event was a big success with over 85 hours flown on the single day. So successful was this particular open day that the Board decided to organise another one for September of the same year. Unfortunately, a persistent batch of sea fog or as the locals call it – haar, refused to burn off and the open day was curtailed with no flying having taken place at all.

The club agreed to purchase Tom Docherty's Super Cub in order to set up a regular aero-towing operation. At the A.G.M., Tom stood down from his Chairman's role and Jimmy Hempseed gave up his Secretary post.

October 20th saw Tony Shelton set off on the first declared 300 km triangle by an SGU member. His two turn-points were Balmaha and Edzell but due to a distance miscalculation, he could not claim his Gold badge.

In 1972, Ray Hill found himself working in Zambia. Some years later, he recalled his experiences at the Copperbelt Gliding Club for *Portmoak Press:*

It was suggested that it might be interesting, particularly for those SGU members who have only flown at Portmoak, to write a bit about my first gliding club, in the Copperbelt Province of Zambia. This was a small weekend-only set up with none of the professional support we take so much for granted here at Portmoak.

In the earlier days of the Central African Federation, with a big South African influence, gliding had been very strong in Zambia; there being plenty well-off members who apparently imported the latest hot-ships with monotonous regularity, and the whole movement well administered by the Central African Soaring Association (CASA) in Salisbury. After independence, the affluent background slowly disintegrated and things became more spartan.

In the early 70's, there were two clubs running on a shoe-string basis; Lusaka with three aircraft, and Copperbelt with four gliders and a tug. The dominant figure was Vic Brierly, who was twice Rhodesian Champion, 18 years as CFI and the Senior Inspector. In 1961 he climbed to 35,700 ft in a Grunau Baby in a Cu-Nim.

When I went out in 1972, the tug, a Piper cub and a Grunau Baby had just been written off in a combined crash and we had to revert to winching. It took two weeks to find the winch and quite a time to get the hang of operating it. During my time there I never had a simulated cable break – quite unnecessary. To my surprise, I soon found myself secretary of the National Aero Club of Zambia which had replaced the CASA as the BGA equivalent. This meant that I had to look after glider registrations, C of A, and FAI certificates. Some of the negotiations with the Zambia Department of Civil Aviation were hilarious.

The hilarity ceased after a few months when, just before I was about to go solo, all private flying was banned as a security risk – the ban lasting for almost 12 months. At last we had a chance to catch up on maintenance which, of course, under Vic's direction we had to do ourselves. Importing spares was always a problem. During this time, we got hold of a Piper Tripacer and somehow got it airworthy and approved for towing.

We flew at Mufulira airfield, government owned, maintained by a copper mine, with a lateral strip 5,000 ft. long. The surrounding country was hostile to outlandings – bush and twenty ft high ant hills. Silver Cs were only attempted when the thermals were good enough to make getting to the nearest airfield reasonably sure, and only after the pilot had his 5 hours duration leg completed. The clubhouse belonged to the Mufulira Flying Club, who were degenerating into a drinking club – they had to sell their only Cessna 150 to pay for repairs to the engine! We, and a skydiving club, managed to keep things going. While the clubhouse was a bit tatty, the bar was super and evening meals were magnificent – a feast consisting of steak, lamb chop and bierwurst done on a charcoal grill. The beer was the best in the world and we had a swimming pool, paddling pool, and a children's play-ground.

The weather was wonderful – dry season May until October, wet season November to April, but still plenty of sun all year round. Huge thermals were common with cloudbase sometimes as high as 13,000 ft. It was always dark by 7 p.m. so the bar profits benefited accordingly.

Lusaka folded up through lack of support in 1973 and we acquired two of their aircraft – bringing our fleet up to a T49, a K4, a Bergfalke II, an Olympia 2b, a Sagitta (Dutch aerobatic single-seater) and a syndicate Standard Austria.

When things went well, it was superb. Spending Saturday night sleeping on the clubhouse steps waking at 06:30 in blazing sunshine, and frying up the bacon and sausages on the lawn – what a great way to start the day. When we got too hot, a swim was the order of the day.

During the following years the T49, Bergefalke and the K4 were badly damaged, the security ban came on again as the Rhodesian troubles developed and people started to drift away from the club. One night a Zambian with sten gun removed the till contents and half the stock. Eventually the club folded with the remaining aircraft either being wrecked or sent down to South Africa. The clubhouse is derelict. I'd hate to go back.

1973 was a quiet year, albeit involuntarily. Due to the international oil crisis, a ban on all Sunday flying activities was enforced. Despite the Sunday ban, some good flights were completed during the week-days. On one really good day in October, 22 pilots climbed to between 7,000ft and 16,000ft. The main concern for the CFI was to ensure currency of those pilots who only flew on Sundays, and a tight training plan was drawn up.

Tony Shelton planned another 300Km triangle, and this time convinced the St Serf's Island pilot, Kenny Jamieson, to join him in the K13. This time they were successful and Tony recalled the flight for *Portmoak Press*:

> *On Monday, November 5th, 1973, according to the BBC weatherman and Ansgar Sambale (resident instructor at the SGU), the next day was going to be superb. Our own aircraft not being available, we obtained authorisation to fly the Glasgow & West of Scotland's K-13.*
>
> *From previous experience, Kenny knew that the main ingredient for a successful two-seater trip is to establish, before take-off, who will be making the necessary decisions regarding utilising the aircraft and conditions to the best advantage, and the obvious choice was Tony.*
>
> *We took off at 10:46 and released above the clubhouse at 3,000ft, having declared a 300km triangle with Killearn and Fordoun as turning points.*
>
> *We flew straight towards the Ochils, arriving at 2,500ft. The nearest wave cloud was not stationary and slowly advanced towards Perth. We flew diagonally along the wave in weak lift, eventually reaching 5,000ft near Alva where we were faced with cloud. Here we turned clear of the high ground and the low cloud. At 3,000ft we got established in weak wave, which rapidly developed into strong lift taking us to 10,000ft. We then cruised at 80kt along the wave bar towards Killearn.*
>
> *It was at this point in the flight that we began to feel the adverse effects due to the missing seal on the aerotow nose hook, from which we were subjected to a strong blast of exceedingly cold air.*
>
> *We flew slightly south of Killearn along a strong wave. Killearn was situated between our wave bar and the one to the north. We climbed to 11,000ft and flew directly overhead Killearn from one wave band to another, taking two photographs of Killearn Church, quickly*

becoming established in a strong wave. We increased the speed of the K-13 to 100kts and were still achieving lift of one knot. We raced to the west along the wave at speeds from 100kts to 120kts.

By this time we were both experiencing considerable discomfort due to the intense cold, but by mutual agreement, decided to press on.

On this leg of the flight we had been cruising between 8,000ft and 11,000ft and had a speed usually in excess of 100kts, this being made possible by a strong and clearly defined wave cloud. However, as we approached the north of Perth the wave system was less clear, so we climbed to 14,000ft and dived on a course towards Fordoun. The strong lift had tapered off and we reached Drumtochty Castle in the foothills west of Stonehaven, beyond our turning point. Fordoun was completely clamped with cloud and there was no indication of lift anywhere.

We turned and decided to try to land near Edzell. The visibility was extremely poor and we did not get clear air until parallel with the Montrose Basin. We slowly worked our way towards Arbroath and then decided to land at Riverside, Dundee. Our height was now down to 3,000ft. As we approached the Tay Bridges there was a small ragged wave cloud, which developed in a remarkably short time into a strong lift of 1000ft/min. We reached 11,500ft, pointed the K-13 at Loch Leven and gained Portmoak Airfield as quickly as possible. Time from take-off to landing – 4hrs 13mins.

As the people in the clubhouse can verify, two extremely frozen figures hobbled in, both without feeling in the ft and elsewhere. As well as the great enjoyment that we both had, it really proves that high performance is not the sole key to long flights in wave.

The first week of February 1974 was officially declared an excellent day. As well as several Gold height climbs, SGU members claimed two Silver heights and one Silver distance. Alan Milne, chairman, and erstwhile tug hangar door builder left Scotland for a new job south of the border, so the club was on the look out for a new Chairman.

Frank Reilly eagerly stepped into the breach, but not before he climbed in wave to 20,000ft in SHK to complete his three Diamonds. One of his first jobs as Chairman was to help organise "Operation Farglide", established for attempts at distance records from Portmoak to the continent.

The club fleet was increased by a second Pirat and a Bocian, although it was reduced when the club Falke was written off in a crash on Benarty.

Improvement work continued at Portmoak throughout the summer of 1974. Jimmy Rae organised the widening and paving of the bridge and club entrance. The earth bank was removed from the east end of the grass strip and a second wind-sock was erected.

Another day to be declared as 'excellent' was Saturday 5th October. Forty five pilots climbed to over 10,000ft, Frank Reilly getting to 26,000ft. In addition, 14 Gold and 8 Diamond claims were made, as well as triangles of 247 km, 310 km and 390 km.

Tony Shelton, spurred on by his two earlier cross country flights, set another 300 km triangle around Balloch Pier and Edzell. This time, on December 11th, he completed the task and went into the history books as being the first pilot to complete his Gold badge legs solely in Scotland.

Chapter 11
1975 - 1979
Lochs & Castles

The start of 1975 found the SGU looking for a new resident instructor when Ansgar Sambale retired, and for a new ground engineer following the retirement of Frank Ireland.

Another Frank, Frank Smith, a well respected instructor at Portmoak during the 1990s and 2000s, recalled one of his flights in 1975 for *Portmoak Press*:

> *This is a true story of my quest for Silver "C" distance during the year 1975. In those far off days I lived about 15 minutes drive from Lasham Airfield. A great convenience if, like me you were a confirmed gliding pilot. Even more convenient was the fact that our syndicated Oly 463 was kept rigged in the hangar just waiting to be rolled out and flown.*
>
> *Lasham is based on an old wartime airfield and is probably the largest gliding centre, in the world. It's where I started gliding and in those days Derek Piggott was the CFI. It was he who sent me solo in the December of 1971.*
>
> *The Oly 463 is a lovely wooden aircraft built by Elliot's of Newbury, who also used to make furniture. It has a roomy cockpit with a one-piece canopy affording exceptional lookout. The raked back seating makes for a very comfortable ride. One of its greatest attributes is that it can milk even the weakest of thermals - staying airborne when all others have failed to remain aloft. Our particular Oly carried the number 364, which I always thought was rather special. Though not a speedy machine - it has a best L/D of 32 - the 463 is a delight to fly.*

For all of you who have never flown a wooden ship, try and do so at some time in your gliding career, they are a lot of fun.

Anyway I digress, on to the main story. By the early part of 1975 I was in possession of the Bronze C badge with all the necessary navigation bits and pieces completed and couldn't wait to have- a go at my first cross-country. All I needed was the weather.

Something else I should mention here. My boss at work was a very understanding sort of bloke, he would even ask why I wasn't away gliding on sunny days. Other colleagues at work would go around with their arms outstretched as soon as they saw me. Digression again.

So with the scene set all one had to do was wait for "The Day". Now, all pilots will know that the surest way of ensuring a terrific day ahead is to arrange to visit relatives, go shopping with the missus, baby-sit or whatever on that particular day. The weather during the early part of May had been pretty mediocre and carried on that way into the latter half of the month. So when a friend of mine living nearby suggested making up the numbers on a sea fishing trip the next weekend I agreed.

Saturday the 31st of May 1975 has probably gone down in the annuls of gliding history as "The Classic Soaring Day" of the twentieth century - at least in the south of England. As soon as I had drawn back the curtains on that historic day I knew I had blundered. Our fishing trip was booked on a Littlehampton boat which meant leaving early for the south coast. On the drive, down I consoled myself with the belief that it would all overdevelop and rain by mid-day.

So there I sat, fishing-rod in hand, somewhere in the English Channel staring at the shoreline and watching the most magnificent sky I have ever seen develop and embrace the whole of southern England. I remember telling somebody on board of my predicament, he said "Never mind perhaps you'll catch some flying fish." The sky didn't overdevelop, if anything it got better, cloud base rose in the afternoon to some ridiculous figure and the agony continued. I was finally let off the hook - I can joke about it now - when the boat weighed anchor about five o'clock and we chugged back in.

I really shouldn't have gone to the club the next day. It was a Sunday and folk clutching barographs were still frantically looking for official observers to ratify their claims and the talk was all about yesterday. They'd just about run the pot dry for superlatives to describe the conditions. Then some bright spark spotted me and asked where I had been. I just couldn't bear to say I'd been fishing. To make matters worse, all through that perfect day our Oly had been the only glider to remain in the hangar. I felt sick - how could I have missed out - somebody said there's always tomorrow, I went home.

The Sailplane and Gliding magazine for July/August 1975 carried a report of the Nationals, which were being held at Husbands Bosworth. In it is recorded that 21 out of 23 competing in the Open Class beat the UK speed record round a 500 km triangle on Saturday the 31st of May. Enough said.

It was a bank holiday on the Monday. Back to the airfield, the weather didn't look too bad, maybe, just maybe, it might be on. After three attempts at even staying up I went back home again. I gave Tuesday a miss, Wednesday was promising though the weather to the Northwest looked rather strange. However, I wanted to go south-easterly, so there should be no problem. The Silver C milk run from Lasham in those days was down to Shoreham Airfield. All they needed was a prior phone call to say you might he dropping in.

I remember taking off and quickly climbing to 4000ft and tentatively flying off downwind. South of Alton I stopped - I could still get back - the umbilical cord was still in place. However, the weather came to my aid in the form of a large thunderous looking cloud, which proceeded to dump tonnes of water on the ground between the airfield and me.

So, no choice but to go for it, down past Petersfield and Midhurst. Low and unsure of position I landed out near a small village called Bepton. Roy, my syndicate partner, and his girlfriend came for me. They brought a picnic hamper and there we sat quaffing tea and cakes in some far-flung field.

I remember being pleased at accomplishing my first out landing without incident but disappointed I'd failed to make the distance.

After this the weather deteriorated, with July not really producing anything suitable. From being primed and waiting for the right conditions for days I started to take the foot off the pedal. That is 'till the 25th of August. The pundits at Lasham were starting to talk about the Wednesday coming with some degree of optimism. That was good enough for me. With a day's holiday booked at work, I waited expectantly. Sure, enough the weather forecast on the Tuesday bode well.

I woke very early on the Wednesday to the sound of the dawn chorus in full swing. It looked promising and by full light and with the sun climbing into the heavens it looked even better. Suddenly I had this terrible thought, what if one of the other three syndicate members turned up before me. This thought grew and festered. Only one thing to do motor up to Lasham and put a large notice on the seat of 364 saying that I was trying for Silver distance, and that's what I did at some ridiculous hour. I know that's selfish but I was getting desperate.

The story moves on. Late morning - two failed attempts to stay up - the sky is booming and everyone is soaring - except me. Remember, Lasham is a flat site and if you don't catch a thermal early on the likelihood is that you will need another cable. So third attempt and we're off, a good climb to 4000 ft and a run down to Old Sarum, out to the Southwest of Lasham and North of Salisbury. The flight was uneventful really, Sarum was reached with plenty of height and I remember watching an old T21 being winch launched as I pulled out the brakes of the Oly and slowly spiralled down. The young air scouts on the ground helped to push the glider off the grass strip and then wanted to know where I'd come from. It was with great satisfaction that I was able to say Lasham Airfield, and that at long last Silver C was in the bag.

Back at Portmoak, Phil Lever completed his 300 km triangle in his Kestrel and Tom Docherty (Kestrel 19) flew in company with George Green (Std Libelle) to cover 393km before the pair landed at East Leake near Nottingham.

The usual band of stalwarts continued to work away as 1976 progressed. The caravan site was nearing completion, two diesel busses were under conversion to become reborn as Portmoak winches and an Open Day was planned for May 23rd. Although planning permission had been received for an extension to the clubhouse, it was not proceeded with. As if all of this activity was not enough, the club was host to a Regional competition from 3rd to 11th July. Four days were deemed as contest days and the eventual winners were J Howlett and J Meyer in their shared Ka6CR.

By the end of summer, no less than 22 Gold heights and 2 Diamond heights had been claimed from Portmoak – further fuelling the annual visitor "Gold Rush". One band of visitors, however, turned up with no interest whatsoever in flying. A small band of men turned up to start work on the north field aero-tow strip under the Manpower Services Job Creation Scheme.

One SGU member went off to fly in the World Gliding Championships in Finland. George Lee, who also flew as an RAF pilot out of Leuchars competed brilliantly and won the Open Class World Title.

Back at Portmoak, Tom Docherty also completed an historic flight, by claiming UK distance record for his 633 km flight to Sussex. *Portmoak Press* reported this epic flight.

Although I had been attempting a flight to the south for a number of days prior to 31st July, a layer of stratus cloud confined to our immediate area prevented a start. However, the forecast for 31st seemed, on the face of it more promising. This was confirmed by 'phone call from Justin Wills who had been in touch with Bracknell Meteorological Office. Justin's plan was to start from Doncaster or Dishforth simply because time would not allow him to travel as far north as Portmoak for a start. Conditions looked good early morning, with a forecast wind of some 330°. There were signs of early convection just after 9 a.m. coinciding with my arrival at the club for breakfast.

Alistair Murray, who was also having breakfast, must have sensed the degree of urgency in my planning and I told him what I had in mind; in fact, I had two plans depending on how things went. One was for a formal declaration of North Hill, a gliding site run by Devon and Somerset Gliding Club, which is situated near Dunkeswell, not far from Taunton, around the turning point/junction of the M1/M45 near Daventry, south of Husbands Bosworth. The second plan was to take advantage of above average conditions and a fast time to follow track from Doncaster to Cambridge, skirting London TMA to Folkestone and, hopefully making the Channel crossing. My equipment included the passport and French maps just in case. Immediately after a hurried breakfast, I rigged and ballasted just outside the clubhouse.

Then my thoughts turned to the availability of a tug and tug pilot. I had phoned Graeme Smith late the previous evening, and with the promise of his help, things looked set for an early start. However, I located Graeme fast asleep and after three attempts to rouse him he surfaced. He soon had things organised and I was launched at 10:15 pulling off at less than 3000ft ASL. I had a quick glance at Benarty to see how Alistair Murray was faring, having been launched by winch a little earlier.

I was, however, unable to locate him and immediately ran into convection, 2 kt becoming 4 kt. This took me to cloud base which was something a little less than 4000ft ASL although Edinburgh, when I contacted them, were giving an actual cloud base of something like 2500ft which seemed difficult to understand. However, the answer was to become apparent quite soon. Edinburgh Control responded immediately to my request to transit the zone at cloud base, having stated my intention of a distance flight to the south.

I have found it most helpful to be as brief as possible, identifying the aircraft and competition number, stating the intention of the flight, and asking for precisely what you want as a glider pilot to make your transition of the zone and the area as easy as possible. Inevitably with an early morning start, cloud base is likely to be low, and to remain VMC well below cloud base would almost certainly prove impracticable. Hence my request for a special clearance to transit at cloud base which was readily granted. In the zone at the northern end of the bridges, I circled in 2 kt of lift, which gave me a good opportunity to size up the picture immediately to the south. Clearly the reason for the low cloud base report from Edinburgh Control was caused by an area of scraggy cloud drooping down over the airport to the west of Edinburgh. – I decided to skirt this by over-flying Edinburgh at 4000ft ASL. It was however, impossible to see what lay beyond Edinburgh on track because of this curtain of cloud. It was only when I was south of the Pentland Hills that I was able to see more clearly the weather on track to the south. It is important to establish with Edinburgh their QNH and to set this on your altimeter so that any question from Edinburgh as to your height can be given accurately and quickly. So it was that Edinburgh enquired about my height as I over-flew the city, asking me to let them know as soon as I dropped below 4000ft - which brought an immediate response from me that I was in fact sinking. A quick response from them asking me to let them know when I dropped below 3500 – which happened all too quickly, and the same for check height of 3000 as I sank steadily south of Edinburgh. The reason for him monitoring my height closely, became apparent when without any fuss he slotted in an in-bound Trident at 3000ft just to the east of me, having us both in visual contact. I must have been down to about 2500ft ASL before I was re-established in lift again. It looked to the south as if we were having some wave interference, and with that in mind, I specifically asked Edinburgh if he would allow a 20 min. cloud climb to give me that extra bit of height. I received a quick affirmative from the controller, with the request that I call out my height at 500ft intervals. I do think it is better to be specific in the amount of time you require to be in cloud, rather than leave it open-ended as this will almost certainly bring a refusal. As it happened, the time in cloud was less than the time requested, leaving the cloud at something a little less than 5000 ASL. Edinburgh had asked me to confirm my route, which I explained was a straight line from the

Edinburgh zone to Catcleugh Reservoir just clear of the Otterburn danger area. Conditions improved steadily and the crossing of the Cheviot Hills presented no difficulty. My map showed a change in course at Catcleugh Reservoir, which is an excellent landmark, southwards towards Doncaster.

Conditions were definitely better slightly west of track, which was as had been suggested by the forecast the night before.

Between Barnard Castle and Darlington I was still able to talk to Zed Goudie in 363 who was very helpful in organising Graeme Smith to set out on retrieve.

Justin Wills who was still on the ground at Dishforth gave me a quick call having overheard my conversation with Zed. I was surprised to hear he was still on the ground. He explained that an area of claggy weather had prevented an earlier start, and that this had drifted downwind south of the Doncaster area, moving probably at about 16 kt. Dishforth, Ripon and Harrogate slipped by to the east of my track and it was clear that conditions were changing dramatically. Tracking just to the east of the Leeds-Bradford SRZ. I had obviously caught up with the poorer weather, which had prevented Justin's early start. It looked as though we were suffering from almost total cover.

Lift was still to be found, although I had to spend more time in assessing the situation and prospect of the next lift. This slowed me considerably.

A fairly fast time had been made to Dishforth. If I remember correctly the time was about 1 o'clock. Eventually we reached Nottingham having changed to a southerly heading at Doncaster. The Nottingham Water Sports Centre stands out quite clearly from the air.

The city of Leicester was on track to the south, conveniently leading on to the M1, flying further south slightly to the west of Husbands Bosworth – being careful not to mistake the M6 junction with the M1 for the M45 junction turning point.

South of Leicester, I was listening to pilots from Booker having a difficult time on their task, some reporting bad conditions near my turning point, with landings to the south west at Gaydon and elsewhere. I photographed the turning point but with the adverse comments from other pilots, and poor outlook towards the south west, I decided after some 20 mins on the new track to change my plan. This was becoming more urgent anyway because of the loss of height. At this point I picked up a bit of weak lift and worked this while I made up my mind what was the best prospect as to direction. Landing at this point would have made the 500Km distance touch and go so it was important to make the most of what height I had left. Just then, in fairly poor looking conditions, a Swallow glider joined overhead. This must have come from a nearby gliding site to the south, possibly Weston-on-the-Green. This bolstered me up somewhat and I had a look to the south to see where the Swallow could possibly have gained the additional height. I flew to that area, and sure enough located 3 kt. This brought me back up to a reasonable height, and pretty well made up my mind to pursue a track to the south. Eventually Bicester came into view – Oxford – a reasonable bit of lift at Benson which made the prospect of a glide-out to Lasham feasible. Conditions in the Lasham area seemed to be slightly brighter although no lift was experienced until I was south of Alton, which lies south of Lasham.

With this final bit of lift it was clear that I could make the coastline and encouraged me to call up Lasham. After three calls on 130.4, I changed to 130.1, which brought an immediate response from a single airborne glider (Lasham had not been flying very much that day because conditions had not been too inspiring). Mike

Cockburn answered my call from his Kestrel. With the help of people on the ground, it was suggested that I land at a site like Ford which had recently become a registered airfield, thereby allowing an aero-tow retrieve back to Lasham. Accommodation was organised for crew and myself at Lasham. The flight ended at Ford with something in excess of 2000ft. No one was available at the airfield – although Joe Cox, the airfield manager, eventually turned up and proved most helpful. Meantime the Lasham tug, with Chris Day at the controls, was on its way. The retrieve was uneventful and a party of well-kent faces abandoned their pint pots to welcome me on landing at Lasham. The hospitality of everyone at Lasham was in evidence throughout my stay.

As most glider pilots know, epic flights sometimes result in epic retrieves, and Tom's retrieve was no exception. Part one was an aero-tow back to Lasham to await Graeme Smith (Tweetie Pie) with the trailer. Again, *Portmoak Press* took up the story…

Wing Nuts & Glider Pilots – G.K.Smith

Is it possible to tell the difference? Perhaps not until the wing nut becomes associated with a "pinch bolt", and therein lies a tale. No doubt all glider pilots, sufficiently keen to obtain the necessary equipment, learn how to use it. Anyone who undertakes a flight such as Tom Docherty did to break that 17 year old record goal flight (H.C.N. "Nick" Goodhart 360 miles Skylark 3, 10th May 1959), must feel the pinch at times, and also must be "nutty" about gliding.

Yes Tom, Saturday morning 31st July 1976 was not too easy. We had said fond farewells to an excellent summer course until half past something or other on Friday evening. Saturday turned out to be quite a day. I dashed around trying to get my Pye Bantam serviceable, until Roy Surtees pointed out that there was a radio set in the car. Unfortunately, it had also caught a summer cold. Having received Tom's radio message that the trailer should follow, I went out to connect things up. Cy Black (Arbroath) kindly offered to help, and I made arrangements for telephone contacts with Betty etc. Returning to the vehicle, all connections, hitch, lights and car controls were checked, and then away to an unknown destination. On the M9, I debated whether to take the East or West route South. Had we been in good radio communication I would have taken the Lanark-Abington road on hearing that Tom was making good progress to the Midlands. As it was, I had to allow for a retrieve from Yorkshire, which dictated the more tedious Peebles-Newcastle road. Outside Newcastle, Betty was able to tell me that Tom had been heard near Husbands Bosworth, so there was some motoring to do to catch him up. I filled up with petrol, checked connections and set off down the motorway again. The combination rode well at 55/60 mph. I did feel one kick, which I put down to a side-wind passing through a bridge on the A1(M), and the Daimler fairly purred along. Driving through Yorkshire I was receiving some garbled glider transmissions, and tried to get a message relayed on all channels, to no avail. Thirty gallons of petrol later, I pulled into a service area; Betty was now able to tell me that Tom had landed at Ford aerodrome, and would be aero-towed back to Lasham. The record looked as if it was in the bag, and all now would be plain sailing.

I was 50 miles or so off friends in Oxfordshire, where I decided to head for, to take a break before the final 1½ hours down the Abingdon by-pass to Newbury and Basingstoke. I pressed on round the Oxford by-passes, at about 11 p.m. Half way down the Abingdon bypass, probably at no more than 45/50 mph, there was just a slight clonk at the rear-end. I was reducing speed gradually, with a view to investigating if necessary, when a frightening white apparition appeared on my starboard side. Gradually widening its angle to the car, travelling at an apparently alarming rate, with a bow wave of sparks, this apparition careered across the two carriageways (no central reservation). Mounting a slight bank, it kicked its backside up in the air before finally disappearing from view. My heart sank into my size 7's; but there was work to be done. Pulling over to the side, I checked the rear end of the car. The ball hitch and the front half of the tow bar, albeit with the electric cables pulled out of the terminal box, and a broken length of the brake cable were still attached. Crossing the road, I was amazed to find the trailer had run down a 45-degree incline into a 4ft high by 6ft wide gully running parallel with the road. The trailer was standing upright parallel with the road. A giant hand could very well have picked it up and placed it there. What a relief to find that there did not appear to be any damage. Some nice soft squashy grey clay had cushioned under and round the trailer, acting as a first class buffer. I debated whether to get a breakdown outfit out immediately, but as it was a pitch-black night, and being in an area where I have plenty of contacts, prudence suggested a delay until the morning. So, back to friends for the night, knocking them up well after midnight.

On Sunday morning, in conference with my very able friend Mr "Bob" Sommerscales (he is the chairman of the Upward Bound Gliding Trust at Haddenham), we viewed the job with a clued-up member of his staff. The trailer had in fact survived its wild passage in the night. The rounded nose helped and the robust construction had survived – a wooden trailer would most certainly have been damaged. A call to Tom with the good news and the bad news (he elected to hear the bad news first), then off to work we went.

A gentleman crippled with arthritis was prevailed upon to drive his Bedford flat truck, with Hiab loader, out to the spot some 15 miles. Three of us then worked with fireman's hoses, chains, wire, ropes and hooks. After about one and a half hours we finally recovered the trailer to road level, without even denting a mudguard. I am sure the only alternative would have been a crane, which would have cost the earth. There are some very decent folk about when you get into trouble, Bob gave up his Sunday and provided the equipment needed and charged the princely sum of £6.00 for his efforts. To avoid any damage to the Daimler, Bob tied the trailer to his Triumph and drove slowly back to his garage where a temporary repair was carried out.

On the Southbound carriageway, Bob found the offending pin that caused this incident. It is a fairly large diameter pinch bolt, which holds two halves of the trailer tow bar together, locking two circular serrations into mesh. The locknut is just a simple bar, which can be tightened with one hand. The "nut" was still in situ on the bolt, which had sheared at the weld in the trailer half of the tow bar. The nut was still tightish on its threads, due to the thread wear during its life. The bolt gave the appearance of having fretted for some considerable time before the failure occurred, maybe many months. As Tom pointed out subsequently, you cannot beat that intimate knowledge of combination behaviour acquired by the owner – he listens to every little squeak and knows where it is.

If you decide to use this sort of towing system, it is better to tap and thread the material taking the pinch bolt, and place the nut on the outside end of the pinch bolt, locking it up properly – do not rely on a weld only. If you have an expanding/retracting arm on your trailer, allowing the tow hitch to be lowered to the ground for tilting the trailer, make sure that the wing nut and pinch bolt threads are not being damaged. The wing nut loses its feel and you cannot tell if it is tightened or not. The next time you see that non-mechanically minded partner amble over and give the wing nut and extra 20lbs/ft tweak, explain that they could be doing more harm than good. Better still, make it foolproof. Then there is the awkward question of "chaining" trailers or not. Provided you are in full control of the combination, and your faculties, precisely at the time of breakaway, there is probably a good chance that you will be able to keep the combination in line. There are a lot of variables working against this; speed, loading, wind, degree of braking, none of which the chain has any control over. Food for thought.

Congrats Tom on a very good flight. Your excellent write up of the Edinburgh control crossing makes very interesting reading. Can we have a repeat and a channel crossing next year? As for that chap Justin, somehow he will have to be nobbled in '77 – fancy not even letting your barograph dry before he was up and having a go!

Club records for 1977 show that Jim O'Donnell resigned after four years as CFI and was replaced by Roy Surtees. The old workshop hut was converted into offices and a briefing hut (this had been the original club house situated atop Bishop Hill). The caravan site became operational in time for summer and steady progress was made by Tony Shelton and Alistair Murray on the ever-growing Portmoak winch fleet.

In the air, George Peddie was proving that luck was certainly on his side. He recorded one particular flight for *Portmoak Press:*

A Day of Small Miracles, or "Jammy Side Up"

Sunday 5th June started off bright and breezy with a strong north wind. A very casual declaration was made (this was to give me some days of worry in case the NGA would not accept it) of Edzell Radio Mast, Balloch and return. After a poor launch in rain, I eventually got another good launch to 1000 ft. and made my way over to the north face of Benarty.

Forty minutes of frustration followed as I tried in vain to thermal up into the wave. At last a visiting Ka6E and a Skylark marked a good thermal and we were soon clear of the hill. At 4,000 ft. I left the other two and headed towards Westfield opencast mine where a clearly defined wave cloud had formed. The lift in front of this was very strong, up to 20 kts. at times! This took me quickly to 11,000 ft. which was just high enough to clear the top of the cloud in front. I made my first jump upwind to West Lomond. The lift here was also very strong and, in flying along it to the east, I climbed to 12,500 ft.

From a point west of Dundee I flew north to Blairgowrie using another three wave bars. Here, there seemed to be a change in the general wave pattern – the clouds were joining across the gaps, leaving only very small holes for navigation. Eventually I realised that the setup was as for a north easterly wind and we were off again.

Going via Alyth and Forfar, using another three waves, I soon found myself looking down at Brechin from the south west.

The outlook from here was literally gloomy with an apparent total cloud cover above the turning point. I considered moving along the wave towards Montrose to see what the view was like from there, when up came miracle No.1. I could see the Edzell area dimly under the wave up-wind. Suddenly it became much brighter and *clearer, as if the sun was shining through. When I made the move forward I found that this the case and through the newly formed gap was my first turn point.*

Two very hurried photos were taken in 10 kts. of sink and I was now committed to go to have a look at Loch Lomond.

From Edzell I went south towards Arbroath where there was less cloud. At Friockheim I turned west and passed Dundee to the north.

Travelling more or less downwind I was able to use the most direct route without too much worry about sink. My target was a very strong looking wave cloud over the Earn valley, just south of Perth. With the clouds looking tall and thick to the west I climbed to 10,000 ft. before going on.

South of Auchterarder I saw a most curious cloud formation – a perfectly formed arch. I was tempted to fly through it but as strange clouds are usually formed by equally strange, possibly violent, currents I detoured round the phenomenon.

This meant flying through cloud to the north west. When I broke clear after a few minutes I was astonished to find that the sky to the west was almost clear of cloud. High level clouds moving in from the west made me think that a new weather pattern was causing the wave system to collapse. However, it was still going full blast in my vicinity north of Dunblane, as I got another 20 kt climb to 10,500 ft.

There were still sufficient wisps of cloud to mark the wave as I set off across the Trossachs towards the middle of Loch Lomond. As I progressed I planned my route into the turn point sector.

Obviously I was not going to have any trouble in seeing the pier. Having just experienced how easy it is to go downwind in wave, I decided this was the best way to approach the turning point.

Minor miracle No.2. As I came into a position south east of Ben Lomond, a healthy looking cloud started to form. Better still, it indicated that the wave here ran in a south west direction, which was exactly where I wanted to go!

Although I was still at a comfortable 8,000 ft., I took another 2,000 ft. before venturing south towards the pier. Another two frames were shot off for the record.

With a reserve of height I was able to work my way back north east until I was back in the Dunblane area. There was a very strong temptation now to belt directly for the club. However, ever cautious, I continued until I reached Auchterarder and was absolutely certain of getting home. I reached Portmoak 4 hrs. 36 mins. After take-off.

The 64,000 dollar question now was would the photographs be acceptable? Peter Kerrigan very kindly offered to develop the film there and then. After more anxious waiting he pronounced that I had pictures!

The next day, Richard Rozycki examined the film to ascertain that I was in the correct zone and declared that he was satisfied. The forms were duly filled in and that was that.

I must say that I feel a bit of an impostor, when I think of all the illustrious, dedicated, cross-country pilots who have actually covered the ground before me only to be foiled by cloud at the turning points.

In 1978, back on the ground, the volunteers were very busy - the clubhouse got a complete makeover with modernisation of the kitchen, bar and bedrooms. Bob McLean, who had been running the glider workshop, moved south to eventually form his new business "McLean Aviation", he was replaced at Portmoak by Bert Jarvis. The club fleet consisted of 2 x K8s, 2 x K-6s and a K13, and the private glider fleet was growing at a considerable rate. Roy Surtees resigned from CFI and was replaced by Andrew Wood. On the flying front, another successful Open Day was held in May but the Regional contest a few weeks later had to be abandoned due to poor weather. The editor of the *Portmoak Press* at the time – A. Shaw – managed to track down one George Lee who had now repeated his World Championship win of the previous year. The club magazine proudly claimed the "scoop".

> *"Before we left for the World Championships, I thought that the British Team were in with a good chance. We were a strong team: Bernard Fitchett, Steve White, John Delafield and myself."*
>
> *"We spent two weeks before the official practice week in France getting used to the conditions and generally unwinding so that we were in the right frame of mind for the competition. Unfortunately, John was not able to be there and he arrived straight for the competition. Later he had to withdraw on medical grounds. This was one big lesson that we learned: that you have to have time beforehand to prepare yourself for the hard work ahead."*
>
> *"Practice is terribly important. You must be totally at home in the air and used to the conditions that you are going to be flying in. I was a bit worried beforehand about navigation but I had one reasonable practice day when I did a 780k. This really boosted my confidence and I found it invaluable as a navigation exercise. It also gave me time to look at some turning points."*
>
> *"The weather was good by U.K. standards and it was very hot most of the time with the temperatures well up into the 80s. Most of the days were blue, especially at the beginning of the comp. Towards the end we had some good racing days. The tasks set were very large; they certainly believed in getting the most out of each soaring day."*

"It became a joke in the Open class that every day was a 500k day. Without doubt they did get conditions in France which were suitable for setting tasks of up to 600k and 700k."

"The tasks were set to maximise the soaring hours available so you had little choice in start time. You could not afford to hang about waiting for conditions to improve. Once it became even marginally soarable you had to be off. About two-thirds of the way through the competition the message finally got through to the organisers that they were over tasking the comp for the available weather conditions. It happened on a day when the start gate was not opened until 1:00 p.m. and there were 7¾ hours flying. No way could we see ourselves completing the task. A number of gliders got damaged that day and everybody landed out. After that the task setters pulled back a bit."

"I was not flying well at the start of the comps. We had a lot of blue days and they are not my favourite weather conditions. Also, I pushed a bit too hard in the early stages. Sometimes it worked. I was the only one to get back on one day but it was cancelled out later by having a low scoring day. You've got to be consistent. After a while I settled into the groove. There were a number of silly mistakes made from misreading the air mass, but most of them, when I analyse it now, were as a result of trying too hard. The World Championships call for immense concentration. You are working hard all the time. I did 90 hours flying in three weeks including the official practice week."

"One is bound to get keyed up before an event like this. You get butterflies, but as George Moffat always says 'they can work for you'. It is good to be slightly on edge. It gets you into the right mental state. Its no good being totally relaxed in the air or you would find your concentration slipping. During a race you are constantly monitoring what is going on and making decisions. I find it hard to relax in a race."

George Lee at Leuchars

"The last day was a super racing day. There was a two-minute gap between myself and the next person. When I landed I knew I had won and my crew came racing out with a bottle of champagne to celebrate on the spot. But I couldn't relax completely until the photos had been developed and checked. This took nearly four hours. When we knew that they were OK we all had a party with the German and Brazilian teams."

"A number of people have indicated that they thought it significant that three out of four members of the British team were professional pilots but I do not agree. It is true that powered flying speeds up your decision making capacity and you are used to being totally at home in the

air but I think that the crucial factors are determination and motivation to win."

Portmoak pilots were also hard at work chasing those elusive badges, but as we all know – when it's your day, it's your day. Mike Ward recalled one special flight the previous year for the autumn issue of *Portmoak Press*.

Three into one does go!

Flight no.115 and 116 on Monday October 2nd was the completion of my Bronze "C" flying tests with Mike Munday in the Bocian. Since I was on holiday for a fortnight, I decided to spend as much time flying as I could.

Flight no. 117 on Wednesday October 4th looked good for a five-hour duration flight and I had spent the previous night in the Bunkhouse so that I could make an early start if conditions were right. I awoke in the top bunk of room 6 at 7:00 am to people moving around outside and I remembered that our visitors from Lasham were here. Their motto certainly seems to me to be "The early bird catches the wave" so I dragged myself out of my sleeping bag and looked out at the weather. The sky was blue with a few wave clouds and the wind was a moderate North Westerly.

I got the K8 out of the hangar and did the D.I., organised my barograph, parachute and cushion, then I settled down to a hearty SGU breakfast (greasy eggs etc.). After breakfast I managed to get some help to move the K8 over to the aerotow strip and parked it behind the Nimbus 2 of Alan Purnell. By this time Mike Munday had the tug over and was ready to start the morning's aerotows and there was a whole row of "glass ships" behind me. I started to check that I had everything I would need in the next five hours and added a small transistor radio which Neil White had kindly loaned me, and my map, for good measure.

Getting ready I then remembered that five hours in the air would put a considerable strain on my bladder so I wandered to the edge of the aerotow strip as discreetly as I could. On returning to the K8 I was faced with all the Lasham pilots on their way to do the same. The comment from one of the pilots was "Now look what you've started" but my quick reply was "I thought these glass ships had toilets in them!"

By the time the tug returned from taking Alan Purnell to the hill, I was comfortably strapped into the K8 and doing my checks. Mike Munday came over to give me my briefing and when he saw my maps told me if I got enough height to go for my 50K. At this point, I must confess that I had not thought about doing my distance as I was more intent on doing the duration since I particularly wanted to get that part of the Silver C out of the way due to the fact that the K8 is not the most comfortable glider to sit in for five hours.

The glider was hooked on and off I went. I pulled off at 900ft and once I had checked that the hill was working did a low point to 750ft, the time was 08:59 a.m. and I settled down for the long flight. I soared Bishop hill to 2,500ft and pushed out towards Auchtermuchty where I found myself in steady lift and was at 6,800ft within 45 minutes of release. I realised that I had got my Silver height and then thought about my barograph, I had switched it on hadn't I? I couldn't hear it ticking because of the wind noise but I remembered that I had switched it on. I was beginning to get cold at this height, especially my hands, legs and ft so I decided to come down to a lower altitude and go back to the hill for a while in the hope that I would warm up. I was very glad that I had my transistor radio with me, it certainly took away a lot of the monotony and made me relax despite the cold.

Time Drags - The 3rd hour was the worst, I had not managed to get warmer since coming down to 2,500ft and to add to my problems it started to rain, so I pushed out towards St. Serfs Island and started to lose height so that I could plan my circuit and land. However, when I was down to 1200ft and about to head for my High Key point the rain stopped and after surveying the sky I realised that this was probably only a small shower and that it would not rain again. I proceeded back to the hill which I soared again to 2500ft.

My watch told me that I had been airborne for three hours and my aches and pains with sitting in the same position certainly confirmed this. I opened up the "Mother's Pride" which Betty Barr had presented to me before takeoff and was delighted to find cold hot dogs etc. After a quick demolition act on these, I remembered that I had chocolate in my anorak pocket but unfortunately it had melted so I had to scrape it out of the wrapper using my finger.

At the end of the 4th hour I was still very cold, my ft had no feeling in them and I was flying the glider using alternate hands so that I could sit on the other one to keep it warm (and massage my aches at the same time). I realised at this point that I would manage to last out the five hours so I decided to push out from the hill once more and try to contact the wave to make my last hour more interesting.

I headed towards St. Serfs Island and the vario reading was 3kts up. There seemed to be lift everywhere and within half an hour I was at 9100ft and completely above cloud. There were many gliders around, most of them above me. I had been flying the K8 at 35-40kt and from gaps in the cloud I could see that I was drifting towards Kelty.

On looking at my watch, I found I had been in the air for 4 hours 33 minutes and from this height it was time *to start my descent. I was about to open my airbrakes when I remembered Mike Munday's words "If you get the height, just go!". The lenticular which was giving me the lift seemed to run all the way to Tayport so I got the map on my knees and pointed the glider in the general direction of the Tay Road Bridge.*

At first the K8 did not seem to make much headway and I realised that its penetration was probably worse than I had expected so I lowered the nose and set my ASI on 100kt (still air VNE). Penetration at this speed was much better but the angle at which the glider flew was quite alarming! I passed over Auchtermuchty, Cupar was to my starboard and I was managing quite well to navigate using gaps in the cloud. The vario was showing between zero sink and two kt down and I had made up my mind that I would not fully commit myself until I had crossed the Tay. I changed course to the north so that I could go through a gap in the trailing edge of the cloud and start crossing the river directly above the road-bridge. I dropped the speed to 75kt as I expected to hit rotor and opened the airbrakes. The gap filled in slightly as I flew through it, but I was soon in clear sky with the clouds above me and I was looking directly at Dundee. The air was still again and I had not experienced any rotor. The altimeter showed 7000ft, my speed was back to 100kt and the vario showed two down.

I drifted down the Tay towards its estuary and set course for the North West of Arbroath which, according to my map, should take me directly over the airfield at Condor. At 14:01 p.m. I was overhead the airfield at 5600ft and I contemplated going further at this stage as I could probably have reached Montrose but I took into account the fact that I could not feel my ft, my reactions might not be as sharp as they should be for a field landing. I did some circling over Condor to assess the situation and plan my circuit. I could not see either of the wind-socks, which was probably due to my excitement, and I determined the wind direction from the drift in the turns. I touched down at 14:12 p.m. on the smooth grass and came to rest adjacent to the control tower. All was quiet except that wonderful ticking noise from the Barograph - it was like music!

I cannot express my excitement as I parked the glider and went to the control tower to announce my arrival. Looking out of the control tower window onto a completely deserted airfield except for a yellow K8 gave me a great feeling of satisfaction. On the journey to Arbroath, two of my favourite records came on the radio, namely "Whiter Shade of Pale" by Procol Harem and "I am Sailing" by Rod Stewart and I cannot think of any pop record which was more appropriate. It was later confirmed that I had flown for 5 hours 13 minutes from release, had gained 8350ft, and travelled 63 kilometres and landed out! I would like to thank sincerely all those who helped me achieve this rewarding flight, the instructors whom I have flown with for all their sound advice and encouragement, the treatment from the personnel at Condor and my retrieve crew.

Mike Ward

The early part of 1979 turned out to be wet and windy at Portmoak and it was not until late February that the wave conditions returned. Brian Scougall completed an exciting wave flight over the Firth of Forth and *Portmoak Press* published his story.

My First Cross-Country (Crossing the Firth of Forth)

Friday the 23rd February 1979 was a beautiful sunny day, in marked contrast to the weather of the previous few weeks. I arrived at the club about 10:30 a.m. and the first person I met was Mike Munday. I asked him to give me a briefing to fly and was surprised when he told me that someone was at 14,700ft in wave. At this point I decided that it would be an ideal day for a Silver C distance attempt. I remembered reading in John Lang's article that Arbroath was only "for the Smokies" so I decided to try a downwind flight to Dunbar. Mike gave me a briefing for the flight, saying that I could expect to lose up to 4000ft crossing the Forth.

By the time that I had D.I.'d the K6 and smoked the barograph it was 11 a.m. The gliders that had taken off before me had contacted the wave by taking a 3000ft. aero-tow to the north face of the Bishop. The ground wind was showing westerly about 10 kt and because of the 1% rule I decided to try to contact the wave from a winch launch to the hill.

I pulled off at 1,200ft and headed towards Bishop. It immediately became apparent that the upper wind was more northerly and that I would not have enough height to get around the corner of the Bishop to where the hill would be working, so I turned around and headed towards Benarty.

I reached the hill about 1,000ft. and although there was no wave cloud in evidence I suspected that the wave might be in phase with the hill due to the smooth nature of the lift which was giving about 2 kt on the vario.

By the time that I reached 2,500ft. my suspicions were confirmed and at this point I started to explore the area in order to find the best lift. There was still no lenticular cloud to mark the lift and I had to set up a "beat" using points of reference on the ground. At 5,500ft the lift petered out and I was trying to decide where to head for when I noticed a wave cloud forming over the hospital. I headed for one end of the cloud so that I would not fly through the worst area of sink. As I approached the cloud, the sink increased until I was flying at 90 kt with the vario showing "off the clock" down.

By the time I reached the front of the cloud I was down to 2,000ft where I spent an anxious five minutes in weak and intermittent lift before reaching the smooth air above. The wave over Benarty had been giving two kt up but I was now in a steady 8 kt up and the flying was much easier because the lenticular clouds showed where the lift was.

At 10,500ft I was still in 2 kt lift and beginning to feel very cold. I reckoned that I now had ample height to reach Dunbar, even allowing for areas of bad sink on the way. I flew out past the end of the wave in order to miss the worst sink before turning downwind.

I was now at 10,800ft and feeling very excited as I thought I had my silver distance in the bag. Although I was only flying at 40 kt in normal sink, I was covering the ground at a good rate and reached the coast at 9,500ft. I crossed between Kirkcaldy and Buckhaven aiming to reach the far side at Aberlady Bay, a distance of 12 miles. I was in normal sink for the first couple of miles and was about to get the camera out to take some pictures, when the sink rate started to increase steadily until the vario was showing 8 kt down at 50 kt. At this stage, I was not unduly worried and I put the speed up to 80 kt expecting to fly through the sink in a short time.

As the vario was now off the clock down and I tried slowing down to 50 kt every now and again to find out if the sink was still as bad, but even at this speed the vario was off the clock. The altimeter was unwinding at an alarming rate and by the time I was halfway across I was down to 5,000ft. At this stage I was beginning to have serious doubts as to whether I would reach the far side and as the altimeter unwound to 4,000ft I began picking ships to land beside. There were plenty of small ships about and I planned to land in front and to one side of *one (unfortunately there were no aircraft carriers about). Luckily the sink rate started to decrease and I reached Aberlady Bay with all of 2,300ft to spare.*

It was a great relief to be flying over "terra firma" again and as there seemed to be plenty of good fields ahead I decided to press on as far as possible. At Kingston I was down to 1000ft where I decided to land in a grass field which had a hayloft at the far end. This meant that I could pull the glider out of the wind on landing. Although East Fortune airfield was only about one mile away I remembered being told not to land there.

I started my circuit at 800ft well to one side of the field in order to give my self a long base leg so that I could sort out my height. This tactic seemed to work quite well as I got down without any problem.

I had just climbed out of the glider when I heard a terrific noise and on looking up saw a Vulcan bomber, which started to circle overhead at about 500ft. After a couple of circles however, he shot off into the distance. After parking the glider I set off towards the farmhouse which was about one mile away. I phoned the club for a retrieve and Mike Munday said that he would bring the tug down to tow me back.

During the aero-tow back to the club I felt very nervous crossing the Forth and was glad when we reached the far coast.

The distance flown was 42K and although I did not get my Silver Distance, the flight proved to be quite an experience for my first cross-country and I certainly will not forget it for a very long time.

Brian Scougall

The club magazine editor was very busy in 1979 and he even managed to track down Jim Woodley who had just completed his instructor's course. The language used in the story is drawn from an area in the East Coast of Scotland known as the "Kingdom of Fife", and can still be heard around Portmoak today – albeit from other aficionados.

An Instructors Course…

"It wisnae ma faut Billy."
C1. Does it mean anything to you? If not, this was the code for the first instructors' course at Lasham from 10th – 16th March 1979.
The week previous to the course seemed promising as Bill Scull had already convinced Hamish Wotherspoon and myself to take the Twin Astir down to Lasham for him as it had been stranded at Portmoak due to bad weather.
Thinking we couldn't possibly fail (the instructors' course) if we said yes, we said yes. The only problem was that on the Friday that we travelled down the weather was terrible so we couldn't take the glider with us after all. We eventually arrived at Lasham thinking "Bill's nae gonna be very pleased withoot his Astir." I think we were right – he wisnae.
There were three instructors taking the course – Bill Scull, Brian Spreckley and John Williamson. They were all very keen to fly, mind you they hadn't actually flown with any of us yet so it was understandable.
The first main problem arose when we were asked to rig the Super Falke. We found three main faults with it:
*1. A b***** thumb hole through the aileron.*
*2. A b******* outrigger wheel.*
3. A hole in the fabric at the rear end. (I told him that one folks, very polite wasn't I? Hamish).

*The second problem arose when it was time to start it. It wouldn't go. Hamish decided to tell Bill that he had a special way of starting it. Bill's comments were "Oh really, what is it then?" Hamish said "Ah well, you see it's rather epic, Big yin. What yae dae is yae gee the B***** a kick up the beak and gee the fan a burl and call it a big B******." We were then told to go for tea while they found a better way of going about it. Now came the tricky bit, we had to fly the Falke*

We went through our patter notes and exercises as best we could. I think they had to do all the landings. (We told them that we only did the take-offs because they were easier). Bill and Brian then decided to have a word about Hamish's patter. He said that he didn't know until doing the instructors' course that he was a compulsive swearer.

*Brian then looked very startled and said: "Oh it is going to be one of those weeks is it? It's either going to be B***** Shakespeare or Rabbie Burns." I explained that he shouldn't get too worked up as we were the best two that were send down first as I could speak English and also interpret for Hamish. Bill's reply was "Well that's a matter of opinion." Hamish and I both looked at each other took off our tammies and burst out laughing. We were then sent for more tea.*

*Later, we were invited out to an evening of choral music. Hamish declined by saying "What the B***** is that then? I don't think I have been to one lately, do they have any Bunny Girls there?" I quickly chipped in to recover the situation by saying "Why? Are you playing at it Bill?" He said "Certainly not, I'm a fan of Billy Connolly you know." We were then sent for more tea.*

The weather gradually worsened during the week and we left on the Friday evening to return home. The return journey took us fourteen hours. We would like to thank all those concerned who helped us on our instructors' course, and all club members for their help and advice – especially our CFI, Andrew Wood.

We have had great fun and enjoyment from our flying and hope to pass on this pleasure in some small way to others. By the way, the following is an extract from the patter notes for the effects of controls, which is not recommended for use on these courses:

Cawing the Handles …..

Now I'll show you how to burl the handles.

First the arsement pinge.

Come-a-hind me on the handle.

Glower owr the beak o' the bird and see the amount of ground in sicht betwix the beak o' the bird an' the Ben owr yonder.

It remains Ecksy Oxsy

This is the normal fleein' angle.

If yae pusch the handle forard, the beak o' the bird draps and taks up anither fleein' angle.

Now I'll richt the bird back tae its normal fleein' angle the noo.

Now yae gee it a burl big yin, you caw the handle.

Na'e whats the matter wi you then Big Yin, yer nae gonna be sicht the noo are yea?

Yer lookin' awfae peely-wally, ye'd better stick yer heed in this poke till we get the bird doon frae here richt awa.

P.S. Hamish is a Fifer.

Jim Woodley

Unfortunately the year was tinged with sadness as yet another obituary was printed in the club mag.

Thomas Arnott Moffatt

Tom Moffatt was killed in a light aircraft accident near Shoreham on March 11th 1979. Typically, at the time, he was helping out by ferrying the aircraft which crashed.

From the time he was an ATC cadet in Scotland during the war, Tom was fascinated with flying, starting in earnest by learning to glide in Germany with the RAFGSA. He was not satisfied by just flying: he required to know not only how, but also why, and why not. It is not surprising that he became involved in instructing, both with the ATC and with the various clubs with which he was connected over the years – he was a precise pilot and a demanding taskmaster, but more importantly he was a sympathetic and helpful instructor. He was not a clubroom pundit, but he was always willing to explain and justify his techniques to the most basic beginner – and they worked. He never forgot where his interest in flying was really kindled and perhaps his greatest pleasure was to encourage a similar interest in the hundreds of ATC cadets whom he sent solo over the years.

Tom was, however, much more than that – he was worker, helper, enthusiast and, above all, friend and companion to those he glided and flew with. There was almost no effort to which he would not go to help those around him, particularly when the going got sticky, and regardless of the fact that he had probably started work at the bakehouse at 4 a.m. the morning before appearing at the airfield.

We will not just remember Tom for that – he was an individual, a character, a personality. We will miss the wide grin below the glasses and moustache, whether in the two-seater, the tug or through the smoke in the bar. His death has left a gap which won't be filled. Never again will we see the Moffatt caravan near the clubhouse with two empty Glenmorangie by the step, and a small note "only one pint today please".

Our sympathy goes out to his wife and two daughters and all those whose hearts are heavy at his going.

R.D. Carswell

While gathering material for this book, I came upon a letter informing an early founding member of the SGU that he had been awarded an Honorary Lifetime Membership at the end of 1977. Andrew Thorburn had written to Johnny Gardner to thank him for all his work in the early days and wanted to assure Johnny that he was not forgotten. Johnny replied as follows:

Dear Andrew

Thank you for your letter of 24th October. With reference to your comments about my worry of being unknown, I am speedily approaching the 80s and therefore have nor am likely to have any further active interest in the SGU and care little whether I am remembered or not, within that sphere. In connection with anything of the kind, it takes years of effort to become widely known, but a very short time to be completely forgotten and when once I have 'passed on' it will matter not to me, so why worry now. You have done far far more for the SGU than I have, but when you demise, your efforts will suffer the same fate. I often wonder if the club will continue to develop beyond that stage, for as I see it, you still have to continue to be very active in its interest to keep things right. 'The Mill doesn't grind with waters that's passed', so lets hope there's a good spate to follow!

With regard to your request that I furnish you with such knowledge as I am able to recall of the past. I am approaching the dotage stage though I have not quite reached it yet. I am quite willing to do as you ask but it will probably be in the first person and I will leave you to select your want, and transcribe it into the third person.

I like and enjoy your 'Portmoak Press'. It's a fine production and a great step forward. I hope it will be possible for it to survive. I read it from cover to cover. Congratulations!

As a native of Scotland, I naturally love the country and everything about it. I love the hills, many of which I have climbed to the summit and rambled amidst. Particularly the Ochils and of course the Lomonds with their happy memories. Whether I will ever again see them, I know not. I have no homes there to which I have a personal claim, but there is an ever-open door in Alloa and a cousin in Paisley.

My health is the main drawback. I am still under the surveillance of St Thomas' Hospital here and am likely to be for some considerable time yet. I am due for an X-ray on Friday. What they hope to find in my lungs I know not, but I have been warned that I have to be very careful as I am subject to develop trouble very easily – make what you like of that. Strangely, they haven't stopped me from smoking even though they know that I smoke 40 Senior Service a day. Cancer wasn't the complaint, it's a virus infection they are keeping an eye on. I feel perfectly fit in myself, apart from a tendency to fall asleep every time I settle down in an arm chair. It's a bit of a dammed nuisance though when watching television. I so often fail to see the finish of a play.

I enjoy getting letters from my friends in Scotland and yours are always interesting. I am glad that you still enjoy good health.

Yours sincerely
Johnny

So, as you read this, and although you would never have known Johnny, you are helping to keep him "remembered" in the history of the SGU. Sadly, within a few weeks of writing this letter, Johnny was dead. Once again, Andrew found himself writing an obituary for the club magazine.

John (Johnny) William Gardner

It is likely that only a few of the ever changing membership of this club will be aware of the untiring efforts and dedication of Johnny Gardner to establish a national gliding site in Scotland.

Today, as we learn sadly of his death at the age of 79, it has to be made known that he was one of the pioneers from whom we inherited the successful establishment of the Scottish Gliding Union.

In the 1914-18 war, he served in the Gordon Highlanders, RNVR, RFC and the RAF.

In 1929-30 he was a founder members of the Stirling Gliding Club. In 1931 he attended a meeting of the Falkirk Gliding Club, at which an address was given by E.C. Gordon England, Chairman of the newly formed BGA. The purpose of the talk was to encourage the many small clubs to form a strong national body north of the border so that it could support the BGA in its claims for Government subsidy to encourage gliding.

Fired with new enthusiasm, Johnny became a founder member and secretary of the first amalgamation, called 'The Central Scotland Gliding Club'.

Little is known of the gliding done by that club, but egged on by his drive and newspaper articles (he was on the staff of the 'Alloa Journal'), another stage of amalgamation took place between the Edinburgh, Glasgow, Falkirk, Central Scotland, Kilmarnock, Crieff and Perth gliding clubs in 1934.

All of these clubs had ground to a halt due to constant breakage and the cost, in time and money, needed to repair the 'flying broomstick' type of primary trainers in use at that time.

Not only was he secretary to the new group but very much involved in rebuilding the broken machines collected from disbanded clubs. For two years, the organisation's meetings were held in Cranston's Tea Rooms in Glasgow, on possible hill sites or at the disused Stirling Ice Factory where he worked on the rebuilding of the damaged fleet. As he personally funded all the repair costs and could not be paid, he became what must be classified as the 'first glider fleet private owner'.

This state of affairs until the group, now named the SGU, became the owners of the machines which Johnny donated.

In 1935, having learned to glide at Sutton Bank, I had ideas of starting a club in Fife, so I visited Johnny at the Ice Factory in Stirling where I saw the extent of his work and enthusiasm. From then on we became friends, so much so that he advised me 'not to start another little club'

By 1936, the embryo SGU moved on to a piece of moorland on the Campsie Hills halfway between Lennoxtown and Fintry, and the Fife Gliding Club started near Kirkcaldy.

When the Fife club started soaring on the Bishop Hill in 1937, Johnny brought a group of his members to see the Falcon soaring there. Within a few hours, a new agreement with the Fife club was settled and he diverted all his energies to the latest amalgamation and the Campsie site was abandoned.

By 1938, the Fife club gave up its name and the SGU was at last registered as a limited company.

During the war years, Johnny acted as one of the caretaker committee while members joined the forces. During that time, he also served as an Admiralty Armament Supply Officer and, by the time gliding restarted in 1947, he was permanently resident in London.

For a number of years he acted as our representative on the BGA Council and its sub-committees, and then gradually restricted his gliding activities to an occasional summer visit to Portmoak to see old friends.

He was a prolific writer of reports, and those of us who had the good fortune to know him will always cherish the memory of his friendship and guidance during the SGU's formative years.

Andrew Thorburn

As the year moved on and pilots flew all over the country, Malcolm Shaw wrote himself into the history books by becoming the first pilot to declare and complete a 380 km. triangle in Scotland – other pilots had flown greater undeclared distances. Fortunately, Malcolm was happy to put pen to paper in response to a plea from the *Portmoak Press* editor for more material.

Lochs and Castles (380 kilometres around Scotland)

Instead of the usual 'how I did it', I thought it might be useful to reflect on some of the lessons that I learned on a flight in June.

It looked like a good, but certainly not an excellent, day with a 15 – 20 knot north westerly wind blowing and as I had 117 (ASW 15) to myself, I thought it worth declaring a target. At least it would give me something to work at during the flight.

Previously I had flown west as far as Crianlarich and north as far as Fordoun so, after glancing at the map, I picked Inveraray Castle and Aboyne. I did not measure it until later (380km). If I had, I might have chosen differently to give either 350km or 400km. Lesson 1 – flight planning is important.

Finding the first wave bar was easy. I followed a K8 out from the north-west face of Bishop Hill. He was doing better than anyone else, and following him took me to 10,000 ft. and up one bar to Balado. Lesson 2 –

never let pride stop you following a humble low performance glider.

The wave bars ran parallel to the Ochils and almost to Balloch where they began to line up more north-south. I topped up to 10,000 ft. again before jumping to Loch Long. Down to 8,000 ft., then back to 13,000 ft. we went – the best so far.

The cloud was much thicker now, and it was not obvious how to progress. I flew along Loch Long and then to Loch Goil, with almost no sink. Lesson 3 – follow the lochs.

There was no easy way across to Loch Fyne so, speed up to 100 kt, sink down to 6,000 ft. then back to only 7,000 ft.. Inveraray Castle stood out well from the eastern shore but the cloud sheet which stretched to cover it from the Atlantic made a photograph from behind impossible. Lesson 4 – don't choose a turn point on the upwind bank of a loch.

Coming back downwind was easy, although I would have preferred to have had more than 500 ft of cloud clearance. The Loch Long wave was just as good as before and I topped up here before moving on to the Trossachs.

I would have liked to have gone via Tyndrum but a large cloud sheet made this impractical. I picked up useful lift again at the bottom of Loch Lubnaig at about 7,000 ft. From now on, following the valleys (and clouds) it got better as I went north until, and without turning, I arrived at Loch Tay (11,000 ft.), then Pitlochry (17,000 ft. with 5 kt up on the vario at 90 kt).

The way to Aboyne was covered with a cloud sheet again (Lesson 3 – again).

I would have preferred to hang around and wait for improvement but it was obvious that the cloud was winning and at least I could still see a gap where

Aboyne ought to be, together with undulation in the cloud leading there, indicating the valleys below.

I was lucky. The cloud had a small hole over Balmoral Castle and stretching to the two small lochs near Dinnet. Aboyne airfield, however, was under cloud and there were no gliders to be seen. Lesson 5 – radio might be useful.

There was no point in hanging around. There was no wave and I still had 11,700 ft. The cloud stretched off to the edge of the Grampians and this was the quickest way out of trouble downwind to Kirriemuir. Fortunately there was wave here and in easy jumps, all the way home. Lesson 6 – get a complete weather forecast.

Flight time, six hours. Lesson 7 – You can only do this sort of flight in summer. No way could I spend six hours above 7,000 ft. in winter.

Malcolm Shaw

1979 almost ended in tragedy for one pilot. Bob Thomson, a commercial artist from Edinburgh, had taken up gliding in the middle of 1978. He recalled the story of his third solo flight for *Portmoak Press:*

Portmoak airfield lay under a frozen blanket on 31st December 1979. The time was 15:30 hours. Large sheets of solid ice were all around the launch-point and landing areas. Undaunted, we glider pilots took it in our stride when lesser mortals would have stayed at home.

My sixth flight of the day – and my third solo – now loomed up so I kept my 'chute on and helped push the K8 back to the launch point. Haste was all-important, as we wanted to get this one in before the light faded. A cable lay waiting and my small band of helpers were eager to assist me.

In no time at all I was strapped in. A few words from Jim Woodley, the instructor, then the canopy was closed and locked, checks completed, cable attached and signals given. Fascinated, I watched as the cable snaked tight, caught at an angle by a large piece of ice over to port. This suddenly detached itself and shot across the front of the K8. The cable jerked tight, the glider lurched forward as the nose reared up and my head jerked back against the headrest. Off we sped, rumbling and bumping along the ground in my effort to maintain some equilibrium.

After a longer than usual ground run, the K8 leapt into the air and started climbing, rotating into an alarmingly steep angle by 200ft. Speed rising, stick in forward position, I eased back, only to push it further forward as the angle became, to me, frighteningly steep. I was both apprehensive and puzzled by now, halfway up, near vertical and with the stick hard against the forward stop.

Was this just its natural mode? After all, I had observed the ability of the K8 to climb steeply and break cable in the hands of inexperienced pilots. My sum total was just two previous circuits on type.

The glider and myself attained a more natural attitude as we approached the top, and with a final check outside to ascertain my position, 1,250ft on the clock, I breathed again, put the nose down and pulled the release knob.

Oh no! Just two little words but I will never be sure if I said them out loud or not. Nobody need ever wonder how to tell a cable hang up. I knew it on the first pull. The second pull was instinctive, made all the more so by a surge of fear. Looking back, I was too frightened to panic. Everything went slowly after that. I remember screaming at the cable release as I pumped away at it, then coming around in a steep right hand turn fearing that the cable might foul the lower wing.

I lost the clear vision panel when I pushed it shut and it fell away clanking down the inside of the fuselage, hitting me on the shoulder. As if to torment me further, the elevator control jammed. I managed to free it with a swift to-and-fro movement on the stick. – a process to be repeated several times accompanied by seizures of panic.

After this initial turn, I levelled out and sat for a few moments looking out at the view, pausing and thinking some very personal thoughts of family and friends and the Hogmanay revelry which had been laid on at home that evening.

Brought back to reality by the elevator jamming again, I realised that I would have to try and circle the winch – so around I went again to the right. Sure enough, there was the winch, tiny and lonely but I could see no sign of the cable.

Straightening up, I flew on crosswind glancing continuously down at the winch. I was now over the ash runway and I decided, as I looked down at the deserted clubhouse to my left, to move up that way with whatever cable I had on board. As the elevator had not stuck for some seconds I plucked up courage and around I went. Straightening up on the clubhouse, the glider seemed to settle down a bit, with fewer jerks and tugs.

The idea of a further crosswind backtrack now seemed unnecessary, so I decided to try and land. I could see my circuit plainly laid out in front of me. I was on the downwind leg at about 500ft, there was my crosswind leg from the clubhouse to the ash strip, a nifty turn onto finals and a landing on the strip – remembering to aim between the two frozen puddles on either side. As I turned into wind my one remaining fear was that the elevator might jam again or the cable foul, as I knew that I must have been running short of play.

I watched the parked tug slip by under my port wing, I touched down spot on between the two ice pools. Main wheel and tailskid touched together, a smooth ground run, brakes fully open and the stick right back. The K8 stopped, stood poised for a few seconds then slowly dipped her starboard wing, with a gentle "humph" then all was quiet. It was one of the best landings I had ever made and certainly the most satisfying.

I opened the canopy and leaned over the side, puzzled to discover that the cable was not attached to the belly hook after all. Taking a breather before climbing out, I noticed the cars coming up the strip towards me. Then I went cold as I saw the drogue 'chute laid out neatly behind the glider with the cable stretching into the distance in a straight line. Only then did I realise that the cable had back released on the ground run at take-off and wound itself around the main-wheel axle.

I had been launched by the main-wheel, hence the steep angle of climb.

Back at the clubhouse, reports were written with special emphasis on the bashing that the controls had taken. Martin Grant took my statement and I signed it, being incapable of writing or drinking coffee, which I was spilling copiously from my shaking hand. After that, I seemed to remember buying the winch driver, who saved my life, a small whisky.

To conclude, we found the clear vision panel on the airfield and also a small tear in the canvas of the fuselage under the tailplane, where it could conceivably have come out after having temporarily jammed the elevator. I, for one, will be careful when closing a panel again.

Warning to ground handlers! At no time did it become obvious on the ground run that I had over-run the cable. So be warned, it worries me a little that it happens in a split second and if your attention is distracted …..! Wing tip holders, appreciate your responsibility here, and signallers too.

Whatever has happened to the good idea of the plastic tubing around the trace rope to keep it straight? Not lost I hope?

One more thing, I feel lucky to have had a switched-on winch driver who knew what to do – and did it, a good aircraft, a good briefing, an unflappable nature and the good sense to have listened to all my instructors in the past. The rest will be just fear, sweat, a certain amount of native skill and a strong desire to survive.

My special thanks go to the instructors of Portmoak who by their dedication, expertise and patience were responsible for this happy ending. I make special mention of the following instructors that I have flown with: Jim Wales, Jimmy Hempseed, Malcolm Shaw, Roy Surtees, Roy Howse, Mike Mundy, Valerie Peddie, George Peddie, Andrew Wood, Andy Penswick, Terry Slater, Jim Woodley, Martin Grant, Bob Lyndon. Also a special thanks to those instructors whom I have not flown with but who have passed on much good advice

Bob Thomson

The following item was written by Andrew Bain following his flight "sometime during the seventies":

This is a recollection from those far-off days when gliders were still only gliders and the Russians were still seen to be a considerable threat during the years of the Cold War.

I had reached the stage when I was beginning to be told that it was time that I tried for my Silver distance, and I was instructed – in the unsophisticated guidance of the times – to look out for a good south-west wind; to grab a club K6 by being early on the daily flying list, and to make straight for Arbroath. Well, the good sw wind never seemed to arrive when I was at Portmoak, but on one day in June a warm southerly did arrive, producing thermals on the south face of Bishop Hill, and off I went.

My luck and the thermals held until I came nearer to the east coast, when a sea breeze killed them off but, by then, I was in sight of Arbroath Airfield. In the peace and calm of still air I flew on, stupidly ignoring a large, freshly cut hay field by the side of the main road. I had been told to go to Arbroath – remember. What I had not been told was that the airfield was occupied by Marine Commandos and the Angus Gliding Club only had permission to use the site at weekends. So here I was, on a Wednesday, landing right in the middle of a sensitive military area.

One army truck and two soldiers later, I was inside the guardhouse where I tried to explain the reason for my unauthorised presence in the usual gliding terms: "50K, Portmoak to Arbroath, Silver distance and so on. The increasingly glazed eyes of the corporal in charge suggested that I was not helping him in producing an entry for his log that would satisfy his superiors. Then his face cleared, he had found the answer, and I gratefully accepted it as a way out.

So there it remains; a rather odd entry that records the unauthorised landing of a K6 from Portmoak in the middle of a Marine Commando depot – because of "engine failure".

Chapter 12
1980 – 1983
Over The Channel to France

1980 started off well at Portmoak. On the 18th of April, Dave Benton took his Nimbus-2 to 36,100 ft. in wave to the NW of Portmoak to claim the UK Absolute Altitude record and, with a gain of height of 33,600 ft., the British National Gain of Height record.

Back on the ground, discussions had begun with the local hang glider brigade over the sharing of airspace around Bishop Hill. As this relatively new sport was becoming more and more popular, there were ever-increasing numbers of hang gliders appearing above the west facing slopes of Bishop. After considerable discussion, a trial agreement was reached for a more controlled situation on the hill.

Andrew Wood, the CFI for the previous two years, announced that he was heading for America to take up an appointment in Minneapolis, and was replaced, as CFI, by Graham Smith. Another official to stand down in 1980 was treasurer Peter Copeland – he was replaced by John Hamilton. Bob Jones, later to become CFI in 2000, had a narrow escape at the end of August. Bob takes up the story:

In my logbook there is a brief entry dated 30 August 1980 which says:
"Spin from approximately 200ft to ground. P1 David Walker K13 written off. Cable break at 400ft. Completed recovery and started approach to the aerotow strip. P1 took control to land at launch point. Glider spun after final turn."
I had taken up gliding some years before at Lasham while at University but had stopped while I got myself established living and working in Glasgow. About 12 months before this incident I had joined the SGU and gone solo a few weeks later. On the day of the accident David Walker, a full cat

instructor, and I were planning to start work on my Bronze C. I had almost completed my first 50 solos.

I arrived at Portmoak for the weekend on the Friday night and had discussed my plans with David and he agreed to fly with me and see how things went. I didn't know at the time that although David was an experienced instructor he had done very little flying in the previous 12 months.

The following morning dawned with strong winds and heavy rain. Being keen, I put my name down for the morning ballot. I need to explain that in those days the ballot was considered the fairest way of setting out a flying list. Many people arrived early to start flying, but instead of simply putting your name on the list, we put our names into a ballot and the list was made in order of the names drawn. An unlucky draw could mean you didn't fly that day. I was fortunate, my name came out first and I was at the top of the flying list!

At about 10 am the rain stopped but there was still very a strong north wind. This can be a very turbulent wind direction due to the hills to the north of the airfield. The launch point was set up approximately where the south end of the new hangar is now. The winch was on the opposite side of the airfield on the northern boundary. This gave us a good into wind launch but the length of the winch run was short.

After a bit of a struggle in the strong wind we manhandled a K13 to the launch point. David and I strapped ourselves in. I knew it was going to be rough and I made my harness extra tight.

I had control of the glider and as the launch began and it was immediately obvious that the launch was going to be even rougher than I had imagined. At about 300 ft there was a huge gust and the airspeed increased dramatically. At this point I had a choice, either release the cable and take my chances with little altitude and the turbulence, or continue the launch. I chose to continue and raised the nose of the glider to try to reduce the speed (not recommended practice).

Perhaps not realising how high the airspeed was David grabbed the stick and pushed it forward. I think he created some slack in the cable because a few seconds later the rope jerked tight and there was a very loud bang. Even at that time I was a veteran of many failed launches and this was the loudest cable break I had ever heard. I thought at the time that the cable-hook must have been torn out of the glider! I was still flying the glider so I nosed down into a landing attitude. We were about 400 ft. I judged that we couldn't land ahead. Even with the strong headwind there just wasn't enough field left with the short north-south launch run.

In view of the conditions I decided the best thing to do was land with as few turns as possible. We were a little north of the farm track. I turned left up the north field planning to turn into wind as far as possible before landing. Just as I opened the airbrakes David shouted that he was taking control. He turned left again taking us back towards the launch point. As the glider went rapidly downwind the turbulence increased. I was monitoring the airspeed and had noticed that we were down to 46 Kt. As I was drawing breath to warn David about the speed the glider flicked over to the left in a fully developed spin at about 300 ft.

I knew that a crash was inevitable and that I was unlikely to survive. It was a grim moment and I could only hope that it wasn't going to hurt too much. The ground came spiralling upwards and I saw the people at the launch point staring transfixed. There was very little sensation of speed or g force. I saw a grey patch directly below. Instinctively I assumed the brace position best I could. I brought my fists up to protect my face and head, arms and elbows together to protect my body, and drew my ft back until they were touching the seat.

There was an enormous crunching impact. After a few stunned seconds I realised that I was still alive. I was under water and I could see the surface just a few inches above my head. My first reaction was annoyance; I really didn't want to drown! I didn't know if I was injured so I thought if I could raise my head by a few inches I could wait for help. I reached down and after a brief struggle with the buckle, which seemed to have been jammed by the impact, released the harness. Instead of cautiously raising my head, the large foam cushion I had been sitting on fired me out of the glider like an ejector seat. I'm not sure how long I had been underwater perhaps 20 to 30 seconds, but I'd been running out of air and that cushion made my escape much easier and may have saved my life. I found myself standing on the seat of the glider with my head and shoulders out of the water.

As I turned I found David in the seat behind. His head was above the water but he was immobile and for a second I thought he was dead. I reached under the water and released his harness. As I got his straps undone he started to move. I asked him if was OK and if he was able to get out of the glider and he told me he could. Thus reassured I climbed past him onto the wing root and sat on the fuselage with my legs either side. As I levered myself up the fuselage towards dry land I noticed

The K13 – trying to pretend it's a submarine.

blood dripping from my chin onto the top of the glider. I felt as though someone had hit me in the face with a cricket bat. By this time the people from the launch point had arrived and they helped us off the glider and I limped a few yards before being pushed to the ground. As I sat down the pain from my head and left leg found its way through my amazement that I was still alive. That's when I realised that our lives had been saved by a small pond just over the boundary fence to the west of where the new hangar is now. The glider had landed with one wing on the bank, and with the fuselage and other wing in the water. Until moments before, I had no idea the pond was even there.

It turned out that my injuries were minor cuts to the head caused by Perspex splinters from the canopy (the surgeon had to dig a couple of bits out), and a leg injury probably caused by impact with switches on the instrument panel. Fortunately no bones were broken.

After spending an interesting 24 hours at the Kirkcaldy Victoria I returned to Portmoak and the following day I flew with Ross Jones, our then full time tug pilot, in the Supercub. About a month later having recovered from my injuries and with help and encouragement from Ian Dandie and Simon MacIntosh I restarted flying solo again. It was another 6 months before I finally got my bronze C thanks to John Henry!

In the years that followed I have been privileged to become an instructor myself. I have enjoyed my flying and I've encouraged other people to enjoy our fantastic sport. I hope very much that this story doesn't put you off flying and perhaps you can learn a few useful lessons from it.

The technical brigade was hard at work over the summer and a new retrieve winch – using a Rover engine - was brought into service in August 1980. As if that wasn't enough, the new North aero-tow strip was also declared operational. First to make use of these new facilities was Jimmy Luke, who 'popped down to Doncaster' to claim his 300km.

September saw the SGU host a National Competition to help raise funds for the World Championship team. Two members of the team – Chris Garton & Chris Rollings – came to Portmoak to take part in the competition but Mr Rollings bit off more than he could chew – as reported in the Feb-Mar '81 issue of the *S&G*:

> *A Load of Bull*
>
> *"A Reluctant gliding correspondent" tells of a wager which doesn't make happy reading for vegetarians or anyone concerned about cholesterol.*
>
> *Landing in a field is bad enough. Landing in a field full of cows is worse. But the ultimate folly must be to land in a Scottish field, in a tasty Skylark, when that field is already occupied by a large brown and white bull who fancies a change of diet.*
>
> *Such was Chris Rollings' predicament during the Kitty Comp at Portmoak. Fortunately, glider pilots are not easily intimidated and Chris is no exception. Climbing boldly from the cockpit, he looked Angus straight in the eye and asked him politely to withdraw. Angus looked back inquiringly at this Sassenach Icarus and, undeterred, continued to nibble a wingtip. Delicious.*
>
> *What would have become of the SGU's aircraft had not the farmer turned up at this moment is difficult to say. Fortunately, farmer McTavish is a practical man. He assessed the situation at a glance, promised assistance and disappeared, only to return in the fullness of time (and several inches of aileron later) with a long stick from the end of which protruded a six-inch nail.*
>
> *Thus armed, and no doubt pondering the advances of modern technology in the field of cattle control, Chris continued to thwart Angus's attempts at sampling the tailplane pending the arrival of the cavalry. On reflection,*

Mike Carlton and the motley crew who arrived to rescue Chris do scant justice to the term cavalry – that brave body of men who slayed the Redskin, persuaded the Confederates to abandon UDI, and are forever galloping over the horizon at the last minute on BBC1 … I digress. Arrive they did, rescue Chris and the Skylark they did, and then occurred the bet which is the real subject of this interminable twaddle.

After the usual exchange of pleasantries between a glider-pilot-stuck-in-a-field-with-a-bull and a glider-pilot-turned-crew-on-the-right-side-of-the-fence-who-finds-comedy-in-the-situation, Mike and Chris got round to discussing Angus. Big brown and white Angus. Big edible Angus. "You couldn't eat a bull that size." "Bet I could." "Bet you couldn't." "Bet I could." "How long do you reckon it would take you?" "Eat the whole lot in less than a year." "Bet you couldn't." "Bet I could." "In less than a year? How about raw?" "Bet I could – in less than a year, and raw." "You're on." "How much?"

So there it was – the wager. Mike would buy Angus and Chris would eat him, raw, within a year. If Chris succeeded, Mike would pay £500 to the British Team Fund (a noble cause) and a further £500 to Chris (a less noble cause, probably with chronic indigestion). If Chris scoffed the lot in less than a year, then a sliding scale of payments designed to deter Mike from making other such bets in the future would come into force. If Chris failed to consume Angus within the year, he would pay £500 to the British Gliding Fund.

In due course, poor Angus, whose only crime was being in the wrong place at the wrong time, was butchered and his deep frozen remains brought to Booker in neat little parcels. With due pomp and ceremony, and not a little alcohol, at a party in the clubhouse on November 22, 1980, Chris ate his first plate of steak tartare and so began a task more

daunting, some would say, than that embarked upon by the unwitting Angus when he first bit that Skylark in a Scottish field.
There must be a moral there somewhere.

The trials of the cable retrieve winch were not going well, and by Easter 1981 it was agreed to scrap the system and start work on a "Cable Laying" winch. The club two-seater fleet, at the start of 1981, consisted of two T21s, two K13s and a Bocian. Amongst the ever growing stable of privately owned single seater gliders at Portmoak was Tom Docherty's Nimbus 2, and on June 16th he flew it to Cambridge, then on 16th August flew 617km to the Kent Gliding Club site at Challock.

The cable laying winch was soon completed and such was the improved launch rate that the club employed two professional winch drivers - Dennis Brown and Phil Morley – who provided seven day cover. Club members were so impressed with the cable-laying winch, that they ordered a second one!

The 11th October provided some interesting flights when a strong wave system set itself up over the site. A number of pilots were presented with an excellent photo opportunity when they looked down and saw Concorde flying at 7,000 ft starting its run in to a flypast at a local air show.

The year ended with the usual award ceremony; Brian Scougall was presented with the Club Championship cup and George Lee – by now a three times Open Class World Gliding Champion – was made an Honorary Life Member.

1982 started off well with Easter wave providing 20 badge claims for Gold or Diamond heights. No sooner had these epic flights been made when word came through that the C.A.A. were planning a new airway - to route aircraft between Edinburgh/Glasgow and Aberdeen – directly overhead Portmoak. The B.G.A. and SGU joined forces and, with the support of local M.P. Bill Walker, a Parliamentary lobby was planned.

Summer and Autumn flying was curtailed somewhat while the Mossmorran gas pipeline was laid under the ash strip, and all flying was by aerotow. This enforced lay off of the winch equipment was seen as an ideal opportunity to completely overhaul the winch equipment, ready for the following year.

1983 saw a refurbishment of the clubhouse bedrooms with new divan beds, comfy chairs, heating and carpets!

On the flying front, Jimmy Luke became the first pilot to gain all three Diamond badges from Portmoak. On his way to claim his Diamond distance, he flew in company with Andy Penswick and they both landed at Syerston to claim their badges on 27th June.

Tom Docherty was limbering up for greater things later in the year when he completed two 500 Km flights on consecutive days (26th & 27th June). In August, Tom completed 666 Km to fly from Lasham, across the Channel, to the south side of Paris. This epic flight was recorded in the *S&G* at the end of 1983:

Tom's Channel Crossing

The forecast at Lasham for Wednesday August 3rd promised good conditions for a longish flight although poorer conditions would affect that area north of Northampton. Alan Purnell was busy preparing for a 600 Km. triangle but found time to discuss conditions and the anticipated cloud base which by his quick, and as I found out later, accurate calculation would be of the order of 4000 ft. Not surprisingly my thoughts turned to that elusive prospect. A higher cloud base would be a distinct advantage for the Channel crossing. It made good sense to extend the track to Dover by going northwards round the London TMA. With the clag forecast at Northampton I declared Cambridge Airport which, if achieved, would take me conveniently on to the track previously followed in attempts from Portmoak.

I was in line for a launch about 10:30 a.m. with Alan Purnell and Chris Lovell already airborne and reporting weak but soarable conditions. The tug pilot was briefed and everything looked rosy. Too good to be true. Then followed two abortive launches. Well I never, that hadn't happened before!

Third time lucky, but to my dismay I was being launched by a different tug pilot. It is rarely very good when you don't get what you want! I was losing out on the launch height of 2000ft. with nothing in sight locally, so I burnt my boats, pressed on northwards and ended up using some low level smoke – what a start! Fortunately I scrambled out of that hole fairly quickly and was soon climbing back to launch height.

I skirted Booker and Dunstable both eagerly launching their morning queues. Conditions were firming up very nicely by now and I was anticipating seeing RAF Henlow which was hosting the Inter-Services Regionals. Startline chatter was remarkably different from the Lasham brand but equally noisy. A quick flick of the switch silenced all that and left me to concentrate on the much more welcome sound of the Cambridge vario. I passed Henlow which lay slightly south of my track and then through Biggleswade and Bassingbourn. Running quickly into the TP at Cambridge, this was to prove the best part of the entire flight – what a pity the pleasure of rounding a turn point is so often marred with a photographic fumble.

Now tracking 150° towards Chelmsford, conditions were not holding up just so well. I crossed the estuaries slightly farther east than my previous flight to Challock and benefited immensely in terms of confidence from the last experience. My wife Anne had pre-arranged with a member of the Kent club to listen out at Challock. My new radio was playing up in transmission but eventually, as I went over Challock, I was able to pass the message that I was heading for the coast and this was duly telephoned to Lasham. All thanks to my helper at Challock.

Between Folkestone and Dover cloud base was at varying lower levels with some sea air effect. This was disappointing to say the least. I entered cloud but was unable to make sufficient height above the ragged base around 4,000ft. asl. I was now obviously wasting valuable time. Eventually I headed back inland to a firmer based cumulus and succeeded in climbing to 5,300ft. and from there returned to the coast, avoiding the small amount of scraggy cu arriving at precisely 5,000ft.. It is difficult to describe the feeling at that moment. The air was crystal clear over the entire Channel. No visible prospect of any helpful lift and no prospect of adding that extra desirable 500ft. "Will I or won't I?" – a comment made by Justin Wills some years ago about having faith in your glider flashed through my mind. To hell with it – let's go! If I don't go now, I'll never go! All noble stuff.

With the crossing underway some minutes had passed and still the other side didn't seem any closer. I made the mistake of looking back over my shoulder. Those white cliffs were surprisingly close and the urge to turn back unbelievably strong. I resisted and settled down to a sedate glide in remarkably smooth air, my eyes shifting from ASI to vario – deliberately avoiding too many glances at the altimeter. I took the chance to look at the scene below. Plenty of shipping activity and movements in all directions but very little towards the French coast, where I speculated on the splash down area if all went wrong! Thoughts at mid Channel? Too late to turn back now.

I glanced at the altimeter now below 3,500ft. but holding remarkably well. Then all of a sudden we were making ground with a chance to look at the French coastline. I aimed to cross at that visible prominence just east of Cap Gris-Nez. I observed that the line of visible convection was well inland. I had used a bit more than half of the total height in the crossing and had to continue very carefully if I was to negotiate the on-shore clearance. The last thing would be to flop near the coast. Eventually a little chirp on the vario gently reminding me that it was still alive. I press on down to 1,400ft. asl. The patch-work of fields had an even symmetry of golden brown and rich green, quite unlike my usual gliding territory. We reached the slightly ragged cumulus formation and instantly had 2 kts. 2 kts of French thermal back into the fray, a few gentle turns to make sure it was for real and we gained a bit of height before pushing on for something better.

Quickly back to cloud base, which was surprisingly still only 4,000ft., I set the same 150° course aiming to skirt the Paris TMA on the east side with the line on the French half million map projected confidently to the river Seine through Troyes to Dijon and beyond! I was now trying to make up for lost time and abandoned the hassle of pinpointing those unpronounceable place names. Major rivers and straight line roads were to keep me right as I tried to hurry along. I crossed the river Somme to the east of unseen Amiens down through Roye, Noyon, Soissons with cloud base rising gradually.

A significant weather change lay ahead to the east of Paris TMA. The convection divided into formidable cloud streets spaced at considerable intervals casting deadly shadows over the intervening areas. Cloud base was now back up to the Cambridgeshire level of 5,000ft. and I was able to fly just below base. I could see the adjoining streets; the end of the one on the starboard side was in sight. The other massive street to the port side disappeared into a forbidding black sunless mass. I decided to stick to the one in the middle. Luckily this proved to be the one that went furthest. I was now more or less on a southerly heading and inevitably abandoned the route to Troyes.

Thoughts were beginning to turn to the aim of landing at an airfield if possible. Still high, I passed over an airfield with parachuting in progress, probably La Ferte-Gaucher. The end of the street in sight meant a glide over the Seine *towards Sens, then lots of flat areas by the river Yonne, but no airstrips that I could see. I continued to follow the river getting steadily lower. I hadn't thought that I would get this far down the river which now turned abruptly to the east round a hill.*

I had abandoned the map a little way back and now concentrated on an early landing. Joigny (I discovered the name later) was out of sight until I rounded the hill. The picture postcard setting of Joigny straddling the river and rising up the hillside was truly a sight for sore eyes. There just had to be an airfield here. I scanned along the flat areas at river level but nothing showed up. I lifted my eyes to the hill just above the township and could just make out a slender black line cut into the forest edge. It just had to be an airfield. I had enough height to fly over Joigny parallel to the strip. The approach was over the edge of the forest and I opted for a landing on the grass parallel to the tarmac runway. The time was 19:50 hrs (20:50 local time).

Joigny airfield sported a neat modern clubhouse and a hangar full of light aircraft. The bad news was that everyone, including the owner, had abandoned the place, put up the shutters and had gone off on holiday.

Shortly after parking the Nimbus, my one and only rescuer arrived having seen me gliding overhead. He turned out to be a construction foreman with enough English to deal with the situation. He whisked me off to the local gendarmerie (at my request) in the hope of a quick telephone call to Lasham. No chance! Oh – they were very helpful. Unfortunately my arrival had coincided with the report of a major road accident and a shooting! And boy do those Frenchmen go on!

Next day the magnificent aerotow retrieve was done by Ray Foot and Johnny Taylor with the Robin arriving exactly on time at 11:30 a.m. The retrieve was a lengthy four hour tow via the customs airfield at Troyes, le Touquet control and back across the Channel under lowish cloud and poor visibility to a customs landing at Lydd, eventually arriving back at Lasham before the light failed. The distance unfortunately fell short of my aim and totalled 666 km which means only one thing – if at first you don't succeed – Fly, Fly and Fly again!!!

Tom Docherty

Chapter 13
1984 – 1988
The Missing Years and an Historic Flight

Club records for 1984 are rather scant, and it was known that the club had been going through some financial difficulties at that time. New officials were appointed and a number of changes were implemented by the new Chairman – Z Goudie, and his Board.

One major concern – and for some members, the reason for some of those financial problems - was the recent imposition of an airway to be used to route commercial air traffic between Edinburgh and Glasgow to Aberdeen. Due to the restrictions imposed by this airway, visitor and membership numbers had deteriorated to such an extent that some SGU employees had to be laid off. The British altitude record, set in 1981 over the Grampian mountains was now in a "no go" area inside the airway. A working party was set up and they uncovered some interesting facts that the CAA had been "using" to justify the new airway. Apparently, the airway was based on an increased level of traffic at Aberdeen's Dyce airport. The working party, however, suggested that this increase included a large amount of Helicopter movements between the oil rigs in the North Sea – and this traffic did not use the new airway! As we will see, discussions with the CAA were to continue for the next twenty years and, although the airway is still there, there has been some move to accommodate glider pilots.

While all this was going on, the club still received popular press in the Sailplane & Gliding Magazine (S&G) when Wladyslaw (Richard) Rozycki published a chart showing the best years and months for wave flights. With the SGU and Portmoak showing numerous wave days and evidence of epic flights, the steady stream of badge hunters continued. Some members positively sought out publicity opportunities and this was rewarded when the STV "World of Sport" crew turned up to record a feature for their Saturday afternoon slot.

At this time the club's fleet consisted of 3 x K13s, 1 x Bocian, 3 x K8s and 1 x K6. Once again Tom Docherty caused a stir (this time of the green variety) when his brand new Nimbus 3 arrived on site.

Sadly the year produced some unwelcome publicity when Andy Penswick was killed in a tug accident. Once again, an obituary was required for the *S&G*.

Andy Penswick

It is with great sadness that we report the death of Robert (Andy) Penswick in a tug accident at Portmoak on October 25th 1985.

An extremely capable and experienced pilot, Andy's life centred on aviation. He was an RAF pilot, principally on Lightnings, and came to the SGU in 1980 on leaving the services where he had been very active in the RAFGSA. He is remembered as a popular member of Four Counties and admired for his enthusiasm in helping the younger pilots. While there, he organised several expeditions to the Borders GC at Milfield where he recognised their wave potential and eventually became a member, helping them search for an alternative site.

At Portmoak he was an instructor, BGA inspector and a source of knowledgeable and friendly advice with a nice blend of ability to organise, motivate and express his views.

As a pilot, Andy had a zest and flair for getting the most out of his flying. He flew a DG-200 and having gained all three Diamonds was exploring the possibility of achieving 750 km.

At the time of his death, Andy was deputy CFI and resident instructor at Portmoak. He was a man of considerable stature and achievements, popular and respected and his loss will be keenly felt by his many friends in the gliding world. It has been suggested that there should be a memorial to him and we are giving thought to the most appropriate way that this can be done.

Our heartfelt sympathy is extended to Andy's parents, Ralph and Chrissie Penswick.

Angus Napier

Later, the club did in fact come up with an appropriate memorial for Andy by way of the awarding of an annual Trophy – The Andy Penswick Trophy, *to be awarded for the longest flight in a club glider.*

Andy's parents gifted his DG-200 to the club. As this was an advanced glider and not appropriate for general club use, it was sold and a more suitable club aircraft (Janus C) was ordered.

Towards the end of 1984, there was a very welcome piece of news for one very special member of the SGU. Andrew Thorburn, now 74, and honorary president of the SGU, was awarded a diploma from the British Gliding Association for "…his immense contribution to the SGU during its first 50 years and as a single-minded ambassador to the whole of the gliding movement." During this fifty years, Andrew had amassed more than 4,000 hrs in the air.

Like the previous year, very little information has come to light about club activities during 1985. Although meetings and activities did take place, the records and minutes that have surfaced provide nothing of (historic) interest – it seems as if the operators of the club withdrew into themselves to concentrate on recovering the financial situation. Whatever they did, it seemed to have worked and the club started to turn the corner.

By 1986 the club was back on a financial keel and Z Goudie stood down from his role as Chairman, to be replaced by Stan Milne. Other movements included John Henry taking over as CFI from Hamish Wotherspoon and the resurrection of a "Buildings Team" – their first task being to fit new roller shutter doors on the hangar

On the flying front, Tony Shelton made history by being the first pilot to achieve a Diamond badge flight by staying within the confines of Scotland. His 500 km "triangle" flight went from Portmoak to Killin, then over to Edzell, down to Lismore Lighthouse (north of Oban) and back to Portmoak and he wrote about his historic flight for *S&G*:

Local Soaring – The 500km Way

The Scottish Summer of 1986 gave northern glider pilots few good days but the new 500km zig-zag prompted a couple of forays into the mountains. The first failed from lack of ground sightings (and navigator's nerve) west of Loch Lomond. The second from a rather foolish arrival overhead Killin with only one shot left in the camera. It became clear that my navigation had to be given a heavy rethink.

At Portmoak on Sunday 1st September, the wind at ground level was brisk and NNW, suggesting Lismore lighthouse, Edzell radio masts and Killin hotel might be the best 500km declaration. At 11:20 the winch lofted me in my Kestrel 22 to 1,200ft. where I discovered all the local air rushing vertically downwards towards Loch Leven. The wave must be good, I thought, abandoning

Bishop's bowl in favour of a 500ft. scrape along Vane towards Benarty.

An hour of rather difficult scratching took me to the top of a slow climb over Kinross to be rewarded with a vista of very wet wave covering my declared track to the west. Logical reasoning suggested abandoning the task; so I did. (However, read on.)

Having worked fairly hard at this first 12,000ft. there was an obligation to make something of the day. With 90kt indicated and the compass reading North, I pushed over the cloud tops to the next upwind wave trough to make a more accurate assessment of the conditions. I discovered: cloud base 5,000ft; cloud tops 10,000ft.; cumuli forming at 14,000ft; wind 350°/35kt at 10,000ft; wave length 7nm; mean lift 2.5kt (best 8Kt); wave alignment E to W and expected into wind height loss between waves 2,000ft at 90kts.

Cloud cover to the east didn't appear unmanageable. The Forth-Clyde valley was relatively open also, allowing Howard Fox to take a Diamond climb and Alistair Dodds to fly a very creditable 240km in the club K8. It also became clear that the wave pattern in the cloud tops was produced by a simple and unusually regular system with little interference from the weak secondary upper system.

These conditions are typical if wanting to seriously attempt a declared 300km triangle, but cloud cover to the north and west would inevitably make navigation difficult for anything ambitious. The stronger areas of lift didn't guarantee a gap in the cloud layer and the cover along the westerly track to Lismore appeared to be total.

A good day to practice a little navigation I thought as I pressed northwards to a confirmatory "fix" slot a couple of miles west of Aberfeldy.

(Note: Navigation over cloud can be a little daunting but given an accumulation of local knowledge and the use of

a stopwatch and simple chart work, it is possible to fly around with enough information to let down in a safe area when the wave system collapses. This sort of thing requires an apprenticeship and the underlying principle is if you are not amused, go home!)

Killin was a straight glide along the wave from Aberfeldy. With the ASI at 80kt and the compass reading West, I drove along the upwind face of the wave cloud, slowing down at the Ben Lawers gap to climb in 6kt to assess the possibilities. Cloud cover in a wave trough to the north of Killin looked thin so I pushed on.

The ground around the west end of Loch Tay and parts of the village of Killin were just visible and photographable. "Three six three, do you read? Please confirm that the new rules allow us to fly around a declared task backwards." The "affirmative" that I received set the task to "go" again.

The run across to the east was relatively uneventful, producing the long glide at 80kt, the compass pointing 060° and consuming height at a comfortable rate; 14,000ft over Killin, 10,500ft overhead Brechin. At this point it appeared that the task was off again as cloud cover to the north looked total, however as the wave was 7nm I slowly climbed to 11,000ft and pushed into wind over the cloud top into the next wave, where I sat for a while, gently winding upwards in the weak lift above what seemed to be total cloud cover.

The options were to descend, or give up and go home, so, with the necessary levers pulled for a descent through cloud, the Kestrel was rolled into a steep turn. Again luck was with me. Looking vertically down at the cloud, I was amazed to see, through the thin bottom of the trough, Edzell radar "golf-balls".

With two Turn Points in the camera and only 350km to go, I moved across the wave in a westerly direction to a lumpy cloud with its attendant area of stronger lift, there to take a climb and time off to work out the next step.

From 14,600ft, the wave could be seen as a regular pattern in the cloud tops, stretching away into the west as far as could be seen. The clear upper air reassuringly indicated at 15:11hrs that the existing wave system was set for the rest of the day.

With stopwatch in hand, note-pad strapped to right leg and the special ¾ million Touring Map of Scotland across my lap, I turned to 270° on the compass and trimmed the cruise speed to 85kt indicated. This course produced a nicely spaced set of ground sightings very close to the required track; Glen Clova, the A9 south of Killiecrankie, Tummel Bridge, a fleeting glimpse of Loch Tay to the south and a large gap showing Loch Ericht at its south-west end. The time at the west end of the Tummel Valley – 15:42 hrs.

The wave track I followed ran a few degrees to the north of the third leg of my task. This was all to the good, as the country below is not as lumpy as that further south, a fact that increased the confidence level in my backout and let-down planning.

From Loch Rannoch, the cloud cover, as far as could be seen to the west, appeared to be total. This generated something of a crisis and induced me to stop and climb after crossing Rannoch Moor above a very tenuous gap in the cloud. The estimated position at 16:00 hrs was the north end of Glen Etive at 13,000 ft.

At about this time the chatter between Connel and various light aircraft became very clear on 130.1, so the radio was used again to confirm that the clear skies were to be seen over the Firth of Lorn. With this gem of information, I was able to turn with some degree of confidence on to a 240° heading and drop downwind to the front of a large hump of cloud estimated to be 2nm north of Cruachan. A fast climb to 14,000 ft. gave a good view through a cloud gap of the south shoreline of Loch Etive.

This last fix allowed a confident flight over the remaining cloud into the relatively clear air over the north end of Lismore which gave me a fleeting view of my Turn Point at the south end of this long thin island.

Clouds to the south west and over the Sound of Mull were beautifully fashioned by the wave and it was possible without a great deal of difficulty to manoeuvre into the turning sector as the Lismore Light appeared from below a superb lenticular sitting over the south end of the island.

Having flown around and photographed the three Turn points, all that was left was to fly home, a relatively easy glide of 140km.

Taking time off to admire the cloud formations over the Firth of Lorn, I had great difficulty in restraining myself from consuming the remaining film, but having learned the hard way about film shortages, set out for home.

The track from Lismore ran east-west in clear air directly over Connel Bridge, and it was found possible to fly at an indicated 100kt while ascending at 4kt. Cloud cover again became total some 4nm west of Cruachan, from where, at 14,000ft. my JW Final Glide Calculator recommended 80kt, but as my genes are shot through with a survival factor, and the instrument gell-cell had powered the radio for the previous five hours, I compromised to crawl across the tops to the Ben Lawers gap before running downwind to clearer air to the east of Crieff.

The flight was not yet over. The not-flying-through-cloud syndrome, and the necessity to descend to below cloud base within reasonable gliding distance of Portmoak, forced a diversion to the north of Perth and a final zig-zag around cloud to find clear airspace and a let *down over Dunning. Arrival overhead Portmoak at 4,000ft was followed by a slow acclimatising let down to land at 17:50 and that final photograph.*

The culmination of all this was the usual (cliff hanging) bringing together of all the Official Observer evidence and to successfully claim the first ever 500km Diamond distance to be completed within the boundaries of Scotland. It was also the realisation of an ambition to complete all the Gold and Diamond legs in wave in Scotland.

Paul Copeland took over editorial duties for *Portmoak Press* and his opening issue contained some old stories about parachute care and articles from the early days at Portmoak. He had encountered the same problem as myself inasmuch as there was very little material available and, for a while, it was thought that pilots had forgotten how to write! In some cases, pilots were not even claiming their silverware at the end of the year – some didn't even know what was "up for grabs". In order to remedy this lack of enthusiasm, Paul produced an article describing the current silverware along with eligibility information. For completeness, I have replicated his article here:

The History of the SGU Silverware

The majority of SGU members are probably unaware of the history of the silverware which flashes across the scene at "Pot Parties", and then disappears from sight for another twelve months or so. For the past two years the "pots" have languished in boxes "somewhere in the office". And now we have unearthed them, polished them up and intend to show them as bait, to encourage enterprising cross country pilots to do better. There have been a few rollicking moments in the past, when they were subjected to hard treatment by celebrating glider men whose self-control had been swept away by the spirit of the occasion. The silver shows a few scars here and there, but considering the antiquity of the older ones, they have worn well, mainly because we admire them and what they represent. Their market value at present runs to many hundreds of pounds, but their intrinsic value is much more important to the SGU – recording as they do, the names of many of the people by whose efforts the club evolved. This is particularly true about the Silver Salver.

Taken in their order of arrival on the scene, here are a few notes about them:

The Alan Boyle Altitude Trophy

In the early thirties, when gliding first started in the UK, many clubs mushroomed all over the country, some in the most unsuitable of places. Among them was the Glasgow Gliding Club, which listed among its benefactors the Earl of Glasgow and his younger brother, the Hon Alan Boyle. The Glasgow club, like all others, withered away in 1933 and the remaining die-hards got together in 1934 and set up a working party to find a really suitable site from where ex members from the defunct clubs of Edinburgh, Stirling, Glasgow, Perth and Dundee could fly the primitive gliders they had salvaged from the wreckage of these clubs.

This was the first union of Scottish Gliding Clubs. Eventually they settled on a site near Fintry. There they built a tin shed to hold two dismantled gliders and a winch haulage system. Alan Boyle offered a Silver Cup for the best flight in each year. In 1936 this was won by Tommy Graham of Glasgow with a flight of 35 secs. Yes, just 35 seconds!

This feat, however, was never inscribed on the cup, which lay wrapped in tissue paper for nearly twenty years. This was due to the fact that after witnessing flights of up to three hours by the Fife Gliding Club at

Bishop Hill in 1937, negotiations for amalgamation with the Fife Club took place. This culminated in the registration of a limited company called the Scottish Gliding Union in 1938 with Alan Boyle as its President. In the meantime, the Boyle Cup lay hidden somewhere throughout the war years and it only re-appeared in 1955, nine years after the SGU had restarted at Balado Airfield near Kinross. By that time some of the earliest of our wave flights had been made so the Cup was offered for "The Best Gain of Height", suitably inscribed and nick-named the "Boyle Up Cup". In the post war years, Alan Boyle went abroad for some time and in 1947 retired from the SGU. He last visited us for our Jubilee Party in 1959

The Parker Cross-Country Trophy

Early in 1939, Robert Parker, the senior of three brothers who owned a group of clothing stores in Edinburgh and the Borders, joined the SGU at East Feal on Bishop Hill. At that time, Robert was also a member of the Edinburgh Flying Club at Macmerry Airfield where he flew "aeroplanes". On the resumption of gliding at Balado airfield after the war, Robert became Chairman of the Board of Directors and, during a period of expanding club activities, he provided the stability required when schemes ranging from the sublime to the ridiculous were offered by the eager-to-help brigade. When the club bought its first cross-country glider – a second-hand Olympia II – in 1951, he presented the Club with what became fondly known as the "Parker Span Pan" to encourage the advanced pilots. One of the five post-war members whose capital was used to restart the club, he made his final gesture to the SGU in 1960 by donating £500 to the Clubroom Building Fund. He had been warned of his serious heart weakness and unfortunately he died in a car accident from a heart attack just before the building of the new premises at Portmoak.

The Thorburn Service Salver

Twenty five years after the Union of those early Scottish Gliding Clubs, the SGU had moved from East Feal on Bishop Hill to Balado Airfield and finally settled on its own 50 acre strip at Portmoak. To mark this occasion, a celebration Dinner Dance was arranged to take place in the Bridgend Hotel, Kinross. Aware of the fact that the club now had two trophies to mark the skills of members pilotage, but no way of recording the names of those who had made great contributions in a variety of other ways, Andrew Thorburn presented the Salver to the club in order to record permanently the names of those who might be called "the back room boys" and who are often people unlikely to appear as winners of a flying trophy.

The Maclay Championship Trophy

When the club started searching around for ways and means to build the clubhouse, the architect, builder and price of £4,500 were all identified but the club funds available amounted to only £2,000, so a guarantor for a bank overdraft for the remaining money was required. The brewers "MacLay's of Alloa" were approached and one of their Directors, Fraser Shepherd, soon had available to the club a guarantee for £3,000 over a period of ten years. When then clubrooms were opened in 1961, Fraser presented the Maclay Trophy to be awarded annually for the best group of flights by a club member.

The Sutherland Out and Return Trophy.

The club attracted many wartime ex-RAF pilots and one of these, Charles Sutherland, an estate agent from Colinsburgh in East Fife joined the club. As well as flying gliders he did a great deal of aero-towing in the club Tiger Moths – quite a change from his wartime experiences of out and return flights flying Lysanders at night into France behind enemy lines. Charley did other things in style – one of these was to win a silver trophy for athletics at his old school. One day he brought that trophy to the club and offered it as an Out and Return trophy.

<u>The Thorburn Two-Seater Trophy</u>

The improvement in performance of two-seater gliders brought a headache when it came to sorting out claims so Andrew Thorburn presented the club with a new cup for the best performance in two-seaters – cross country or altitude.

<u>The Docherty Cross Country (Handicap) Trophy</u>

The advent of high performance "glass" gliders soon meant that club members flying wooden aircraft of a lesser performance didn't stand much chance of winning the Parker Trophy. Tom Docherty solved the problem by presenting a separate trophy to be won on handicap. The handicaps on the latest "glass" ships are very heavy, so the pilots of older machines stand a good chance of winning this one.

As we will see, other pots and shields would get added to the SGU trophy cabinet over the years.

By 1987 the club was well and truly back on its ft. Aircraft available to club members now included 2 x K13s, 2 x Ka8s, 2 Sport Vegas, 1 Bocian and another K13 in the process of a rebuild. Winter flying was available on Tuesdays and weekends with a full seven-day service resuming in time for the first summer courses at the end of March. One member, Lesley Freeman organised a flying evening for disabled people on May 19th. This proved to be a success and the seeds of another chapter of SGU history had been planted.

John Henry handed over his CFI duties to John Riley with Graham Smith as Deputy CFI and the resident tuggie job was taken up by Crawford Sneddon.

The cover of the October-November issue of *S&G* sported a full colour photograph of Peter Richardson flying a Sport Vega over Bishop Hill. The photo was taken by his father Mike while flying above him in another club aircraft – a Ka8b. It seemed that the SGU had turned the corner and was once again benefiting from some welcome publicity in that internationally famous gliding mag.

During the year, two more diamond heights were claimed (one to 21,000 ft.) and Colin McAlpine completed his Diamond Goal – sadly he had no photographic proof of his turn points as the camera he had borrowed had no film! At the end of year "do", Colin did pick up an award as the winner of the club ladder. Roddie McLean won the Silver Salver with other awards going to Peter Bower, Tony Shelton, Val & George Peddie and Paul Copeland. References were also made to Caroline Russell who made her first solo only a few days after her sixteenth birthday. Commiserations were offered to David Hatton who, after taking a slightly too high tow on a marginal day, missed his 50 km Silver distance by only a few metres.

The club continued to move forward and 1988 saw the introduction of monthly "Task Weekends". These were organised by John Galloway and provided regular "comps" for club members to hone their cross-country skills and in view of all this activity the BGA decided to hold one of their cross-country training courses at Portmoak in May that year. By the end of the summer, 19 entrants had taken part in these task weekends. Each competition day winner was awarded points and the eventual winners were John Galloway and Colin McAlpine in their Nimbus 2. Runner up, and leader of the club ladder, was Brian Scougall. Despite all this cross-country activity, Brian also took up the role of Tug Pilot for the year and John McFarlane from the Highland GC at Dallachy came down as resident course instructor for the season.

1988 also saw the arrival of the RAF with their summer Gliding School for ATC cadets. They stayed on site for one month and although the instructors remained throughout, the cadets were swapped out every week. As we shall see, this was the start of regular summer schools at Portmoak for the RAF and ATC.

Despite the numerous home made winches in sporadic use at the club, it was decided that a more reliable Bourne winch could now be afforded so an order was duly placed.

To mark the 50th anniversary of the founding of the SGU, Andrew Thorburn and Bill Lawson planted a tree outside the clubhouse. The tree is still there today, next to the crankshaft and plaque for "The Unknown Winch Driver" mentioned in Chapter 9.

Tom Docherty was up to his old tricks by "Popping down to Chatteris", claiming yet another epic flight to land near Cambridge. Mike Richardson, SGU Secretary at the time, put pen to paper for the *S&G* to report on a flight that he had at the end of the previous year.

> *Something Special*
> *An entry in the club log on Sunday 26th September caught my eye. – "easy 20,000 ft. again". This was from A. Pickles who was visiting from Lasham, with his Nimbus. This was the day that Colin McAlpine did his Diamond Goal with a borrowed camera with no film, two pilots flew Silver distance to Portmoak from Aboyne after gaining their Gold or Diamond heights – and this was the day that I had flown higher and farther, apart from my Silver distance, than I had before.*
>
> *The Forecast was for a north-westerly; at mid-morning it was one of those awkward winds, with enough north in it to make it difficult to get to the best part of Bishop Hill from a winch launch, yet not quite enough to get Benarty working. All launches but the last had gone to Bishop and had not soared. The K8 before me had gone to Benarty and had hung around for a while but was unhappy and came home.*

I got a good launch in the Olympia 460 and managed to stay on Benarty at between 1,400-1,600 ft. for about an hour before some thermals passing through could be used to get higher. At about 2,500 ft. I had enough to investigate a small wave which had appeared to the west of the motorway. I flew in lift all the way to it and beyond, slowly gaining height in what I assumed was the first bounce of air after crossing the Ochil hills. I was able to watch the car racing on the Knockhill circuit below and finally made 9,000 ft. over Dollar and then Ben Cleuch.

There was little temptation to try to go higher (my explanation for not being able to) – no barograph – so I headed back towards Loch Leven without losing much height despite my fast flying. Some more rising air was found over Kinross. Several gliders were high above. This time the temptation was too great and I soon found myself at 8,000 ft. over Dunning without really trying. Again, thoughts of going home were put aside when I was found by strong lift over Kinross and climbed around the clouds to 10,500 ft. With more exploration and skill, and oxygen, I might have got closer to Mr Pickles but the afternoon was wearing on so I landed after 4½ hours.

Two things continue to intrigue me. One is the frequent and rapid changes in cloud formation, from almost blue to very complex patterns of cloudiness – and not always the classic bars one reads about.

The other is the barrier which often seems to exist between struggling to maintain 1,500 ft. on the hill and the almost universally rising air 1,000-2,000 ft. higher. It seemed unkind to comment to the fellow member who came to help me after landing, and who had not "got away", that my biggest difficulty had been to get down to circuit height.

Mike Richardson

As 1988 drew to a close, the winter flying schedule of Tuesdays and Weekends kicked in and a request was sent to the BGA for more claim forms – such had been the demand for badge claims that year.

The Thorburn Service Salver was awarded to George Peddie with flying awards going to Richard Allcoat, Alan Bauld, Tom Docherty, Colin Hamilton, Tiny Irvine and Brian Scougal.

Chapter 14
1989 – 1990
Zig-Zag Across Scotland

1989 saw many changes to the operational side of the club. Peter Copeland resigned from his role as Director and Treasurer due to ill health (sadly Peter succumbed and died later in the year, and his family offered a new trophy to the club in his memory). His treasurer role was taken by John Ferguson. Stan Milne completed three years as Chairman and was replaced by Mike Richardson. Newcomers to the Board included Colin McAlpine (Secretary), Stan Perry and Paul Copeland. Following much discussion, the new Board agreed to issue a Catering Franchise – the first to take this on were Joe & Alma Nugent. The Board were pleased to note a marked improvement in the club finances and plans were put in place for a new office extension as well as new hangar lighting and guttering. Also agreed at the beginning of the year was another ATC camp and a whole month of BGA soaring courses for the autumn. Darren Powell was the club's tug pilot for the year and the new Bourne winch was delivered, albeit it remained un-operational due to early teething problems.

The club single-seater fleet was looking up too, with the arrival of an SZD Junior to replace the Sport Vega, and three Ka8s with another under repair.

Richard Allcoat took a Ka-6E to Sutton Bank via the Wallace Monument near Stirling on the way to completing his Gold Distance. One of the BGA courses was run by Chris Rollings and one of the pilots on his course went from Bronze badge to complete Gold with Diamond height in the same week!

Sadly, the year was marred by another accident on site. Darren Powell was flying the tug with Marcello De Felice, who was going to be the tug pilot for the following year. Their Super Cub crashed while in the circuit on the evening of August 24th killing both pilots.

At the end of year awards night, the following people picked up the silverware:

Thorburn Two-Seater Trophy – Val Peddie & Richard Hancock.
The Boyle Altitude Trophy – Ian Paterson.
Fastest 100km Triangle Trophy – John Galloway
Andy Penswick Trophy – Robert Milne
Peter Copeland Trophy – Colin Hamilton
Docherty Distance Trophy (handicapped) Richard Allcoat
Sutherland Out and Return Trophy – John Z Goudie
Maclay Championship Trophy – Brian Scougal
Thorburn Service Salver – Jim Burgess

1990 started slowly due to poor weather at Portmoak but it didn't stop the "officials" negotiating a 75% grant from the Scottish Sports Council for the purchase of a Piper Pawnee tug. The Bourne winch proved to be unreliable so a Supacat winch was ordered to replace it. Keith Buchan became the tuggie for the year and John Riley retired from his CFI role and was temporarily replaced by Brian Scougal. Anna Domonkos took on the role of course instructor and was the subject of an article in the "The Courier and Advertiser" later in the year, under the headline of "Hungarian Woman Seeks British Pilot's Licence":

A former teacher from Hungary is putting prospective glider pilots through their paces at Portmoak.

Anna Domonkos (29) is in Britain until September but she is hoping to get a commercial airline pilots job and stay on in Britain.

She arrived in April for a holiday to improve her English and was staying with a friend in Chester who is a keen glider pilot and knew the president of the Portmoak club and who just happened to be looking for an instructor – and Anna got the job.

In Hungary, she started off her flying career in gliders before getting a pilot's licence and finally, in March, a commercial pilot's licence.

Before Hungary's return to democracy the government subsidised sports flying so there are lots of pilots in the country. Most of them are unemployed however, as there is only one airline – Malev.

Anna has already applied to the Civil Aviation Authority to have her Hungarian commercial licence converted into a British one but with no success.

"I have to fly 50 hours in a twin-engine plane and pass all the exams again," said Anna.

Despite also being turned down by Britannia Airways as a trainee pilot and Highlands and Islands Airports as an air traffic controller, Anna still hopes to get a flying job. She is convinced she can pass if she can find an airline to sponsor her through the exams which are held at various centres around the country, causing expense for travelling which Anna cannot afford.

Married, with a son, Anna is missing her family although her husband has been out to visit her during the summer.

Anna is desperate to get a job in flying so that they can come to Britain to live but if not, then it would be back to teaching in Hungary and an end to her dreams of making a living from something she loves.

Research has failed to uncover any information as to whether Anna succeeded in picking up a pilot's job.

The first half of the year provided average soaring conditions and this culminated in the "Longest Day" when 141 hours were flown by 27 aircraft – at least one of which remained airborne from 04:00 to 18:35.

Despite "the nights drawing in", October 7th proved to be a "classic" day when Colin Hamilton completed his Diamond distance. On the same day Alan Purnell, visiting from Lasham with his Nimbus 3 completed an undeclared 951km. Alan takes up the story for *S&G*:

A 951km zig-zag-zig Across Scotland

I know you are aching to ask all sorts of questions, so here are the answers:
  a) *Because it was possible that day.*
  b) *Because I thought I had done only about 850Km.*
  c) *You cannot easily fit such a large task into Scotland.*
  d) *Each leg was different and had its own features to enjoy and problems to overcome.*
  e) *Half an hour after sunrise to 10 mins after sunset.*
  f) *A banana and a lump of cheese.*
  g) *Three bags.*
  h) *Lots of layers of warm woolly clothing and Damart lined boots.*

Saturday, October 6th, was atrocious, dreadful, gloomy, cats and dogs, miserable. It bucketed down all day and there were reports of flooding in Glasgow. At Portmoak the puddles were nearly large and deep enough to have white horses on them. Yet the forecast looked good for Sunday. An anticyclone SW of Ireland would give anticyclonic curvature to the isobars and north-westerlies – the best direction for good waves at Portmoak. But would the cloud and rain move away sufficiently to make it on for the Golds, Diamonds and cross-country.

I guessed - yes – and managed to persuade John and Sheila Hindmarsh and some of the other members of our Lasham contingent to stay on instead of rushing back south to go to work. Keith Buchan – the weekday Portmoak resident tug pilot – enthusiastically agreed to turn up at the crack of dawn so we could get early tows.

Sunday, October 7th, did indeed dawn clear – not that one could easily tell at 6:55 a.m. when it was still dark. A quick listen to the shipping forecast confirmed that the wind direction and strength would be suitable – yes, I know that the shipping forecast is 5:55 a.m., but who wants to be woken up that unearthly hour when modern technology allows it to be recorded. It was good to hear Graham Ross clumping down the corridor in the clubhouse as at least we could rig each other even if no-one else staggered out to the trailers. Another quick look out at this stage revealed some clouds scudding along from the north and an indication of a gentle westerly on the windsock, but no wave clouds. Well, so what, wave clouds are not always present on a good wave day and the gentle westerly could well indicate that we were in fact underneath the up bit of the wave.

We could not launch straight away because the ground moisture from the day before simply deposited itself on the canopies. I've had to pull off tow just before take-off speed when the canopy misted up on the outside and I didn't want to endure that trauma again now. Keith was ready with the tug before we were completely organised so I munched a banana and a lump of cheese in lieu of breakfast and piled in quantities of muesli bars and chopped up Marathons [Snickers] (have you tried eating frozen whole chocolate bars?) into the cockpit pockets. A litre of water was carefully stowed away where I could rest my arm on it to prevent it freezing – I didn't fancy a mouthful of ice crystals every time I took a swig.

Who was going first? There were no wave clouds, not much wind on the ground, and even that was from the wrong direction, and we could not be sure which piece of the hill was working properly. Because of the uncertainty, no-one objected to me offering to sample the conditions, so I elected to have a tow to near Glenfarg (a few miles north of the north face of the Bishop) – the theory being that if I did not contact the wave directly off tow I could fall back to the north face of Bishop and if that failed then on to the westerly face. I did not really doubt that there was a good wave there because the light westerly under an upper northerly was a sure sign that we were actually under the up.

So off I went at 8:10 a.m. and as we sailed majestically over the boundary fence the clouds magically organised themselves into a classic slot north of the north ridge. Keith knew exactly where to go so I was able to pull off at 3000ft in weak lift just behind the edge. I had a few tense moments as I pushed forward to beyond the edge, but I needn't have worried as the lift improved to the classic smooth strong stationary lift we predicted. I thanked Keith and called to the others that this was the place to be and set about optimising the climb.

I switched on the oxygen good and early as I was somewhat cold since the sun was not much above the horizon, whereupon at 12,000ft the lift petered out rather suddenly. Bemused, I cast about a bit but no go. I usually like to see how high the lift is going before setting off on a cross-country so this was a bit of a disappointment. And so was the view — cloud everywhere especially to the north (upwind) and the west — far too much for a safe cross-country.

But the east was clearer so I zipped along the edge to offshore at Leuchars (TP1) near St Andrews and came back along the same edge. By this time several others had been launched into the wave, but others who elected to go to the north face got stuck there in the turbulence of the down of the wave beating against the hill lift. Those who had a winch-launch to Benarty (the other hill that faced north) were also stuck until the wave moved back to be in phase.

By now it had opened up a little to the west so I continued along to Dollar (maintaining VMC!) where good lift was to be expected in the lee of the Ochils. Good lift prompted me to switch on the oxygen again, but disaster struck as I turned the on/off knob the wrong way and so I tightened it up so securely that no way could I turn it the correct way – calamity! I then realised that I was breathing rather too easily with the face mask on and discovered that the little metal gauze disk in the mask – used to mix the incoming oxygen and the outside air – had fallen out during my desperate efforts to apply extra force to the on/off knob. Double disaster!

Well, if I couldn't go up maybe I had better go along instead, so I started reassessing the cross-country prospects. It had begun to open up towards Crieff so I blasted through the down and weak up to the lee of Ben Lawers, losing about 3000ft. in the process. Yes, I know the theory says that one should cross waves at the weakest point to avoid too much height loss, but I get too impatient to do that very often, especially when one's mind is focussed on a really good looking lenticular dead ahead.

Being below oxygen height gave me the opportunity to try to turn the oxygen on again, but no such luck – all I managed to do was hurt my fingers and get out of breath. Believe it or not, Tony Mattin had exactly the same problem and had to descend and re-launch after rectifying the problem. He took a pair of pliers with him after that and I resolved to do the same myself next time. When Tony launched he got stuck on the north face in the down in his eagerness to get a reasonable low-point and had to use his engine to get forward into the wave.

Even with all this fiddling about, I was still going up at 14,000ft., so deciding that discretion was the better part of being anoxic I set off west along the now clearly marked wave bar. The west began to open up nicely and two beautiful lenticulars appeared to the south of me – one towards the Lake (yes – the only lake in Scotland) of Menteith and the other even further south towards Fintry. A dirty dive downwind at 120kts found 6kts lift over the leading edge, even at that speed. Six kt at 120 in a Nimbus 3 means off the clock at 40 with no water. I stopped only long enough to prove the point since the wind speed at this altitude appeared to be about 50kts – coincidentally confirmed by Roy Cross over the radio. Fifty knot winds are not suitable to hang about in so I zipped along at 120 (well within the flutter Vne at this height) towards the Lake of Menteith where it all fizzled out.

Looking west, the wave clouds were so broken up that it was difficult to determine where the lift was – so different from earlier when there was too much cloud – c'est la vie. Loch Lomond was enticingly close so I edged along in weak patchy lift and reduced sink to Balmaha pier (TP2) on the edge of the Loch before setting off back to where I thought the best lift was at the Lake of Menteith. Luckily the wave had not moved and I climbed rapidly up again. Meanwhile Colin Hamilton attempting a 500km in his Mosquito had been experiencing the same exceptional lift along the hills near Fintry on the more southerly track, and also met the poor broken up wave to the west.

The whole sky was opening up now, except to the north, which was disappointing as I have never achieved my ambition of soaring over Ben Nevis and along Loch Ness to Inverness, so there was nowhere else to go but the east coast. This part of the trip was uneventful past Crieff, north of Perth and across to Brechin. Montrose was hidden by cloud but there was a gap to the north, so I hopped along the coast to Inverbervie (TP3) which is a bit south of Stonehaven. I had met the cloud cover again here and could not see where the next wave was. I set off back to the west but with all the cloud about I got disoriented and fell into severe down in the Edzell area. The country-side is rather similar around here but I glimpsed Edzell under a cloud and set off to Loch Earn and Loch Katrine.

Again the wave was broken to the west so I turned again in the centre of Loch Lomond (TP4) just west of Ben Lomond. At this time Colin Hamilton was having trouble with his 3rd TP at the southern end of Loch Lomond and had to *make a dash for the wave near Fintry, which proceeded to disappear before his very eyes only to re-appear a few miles downwind. Brian Scougal sampled the same conditions on his 300km double dog-leg to the west. He landed for lunch, sold his glider to his prospective buyers and then did a 200km in the afternoon.*

I followed my inbound route back via Loch Earn to the lee of Ben Lawers keeping a careful eye on the cloud. Showers were being seen in the Portmoak area (and nearly downed Charlie Kovac) and I could see picturesque snow scenes on the hills below the clouds, so I kept a more southerly route past Perth and Dundee. Unfortunately there was a lot more cloud at Dundee and to the north, but there were fantastic lenticulars out to sea disappearing over the horizon towards Norway. I ventured just out to sea at Carnoustie (TP5) and came scuttling back across the Tay towards Newburgh as clouds began to build up again.

At this point Geoff Chaplin, a newcomer to Portmoak, pronounced himself lost. All he could see was a lake! With a large island in it. Since Loch Leven has five islands in it and Geoff reckoned he could see Brian Scougal who was near the Lake of Menteith, which has only one large island in it, we all jumped to the conclusion that Geoff was there. However, we need not have worried for before we needlessly advised him to set off 50 miles east, the clouds moved and he found himself at Portmoak after all! It just shows you how wrong you can be sometimes. It also shows how a lack of concentration can get you into trouble as I fell ignominiously into severe down while poring over my map as I tried to help Geoff.

A clear lenticular appeared in the Perth area but I had to "go for it" through the down. Halfway across the smooth backed cloud, while crossing the strongest sink with the vario off the clock, I spied a power plane coming straight towards me at my height and a mile or so dead ahead. It must have spotted me since it turned away to my right and dived away sinking rapidly. With all that down around I suspect he thought his engine was misbehaving. I often wonder what non-gliding power pilots think when they meet such conditions.

Anyway, I skimmed the feathery edge and was soon climbing at 10kts again at about 6000ft. I twice repeated the exercise to the north west of Perth and near Crieff, getting low each time, but then decided I was being a little silly getting low like that since the wave might not extend much below the cloudbase level.

I was getting a bit fed up causing myself grief so I resolved to be more careful and stay above 10,000ft. if at all possible. This policy paid off as the clouds began to disperse again and the better wave clouds were getting smaller and less obvious. It was remarkable how the sky could fill up with cloud and then empty again so rapidly. I chose a more northerly route to the east via Loch Katrine, past the northerly end of Loch Lomond to (the other) Ben Vorlich (TP6) before turning back, carefully taking each piece of lift as it presented itself until I was back in the Loch Earn area again. The clouds were getting even smaller now (except to the north still). It was almost like flying in the blue with lift appearing from nowhere. My nerve failed me at Blairgowrie (TP7).

I was at a loss as to what to do next as I tried to gauge how far I had actually been. That is not easy to measure across a folded map while trying to stay in a blue wave. I guessed I had covered about 700km, so in order to exceed 800km I resolved to return via Lochearnhead (TP8) at the western end of Loch Earn. The lift was still strong up to 13,000 or 14,000ft, but then died off rapidly. It was the feature of the day. The maximum altitude did gradually increase during the day but the increasing wind at altitude did not help. Tony Mattin was still trying to get a few extra hundred ft for his Diamond height but got frustrated with the day and landed too early with cold ft. But unbeknown to him *the upper wind was reducing and Diamond was on, as was demonstrated by John Hindmarsh who just managed to climb past the magic level.*

The trip to Lochearnhead and back was uneventful and I wandered about near Portmoak for half an hour gradually descending with a view to keeping the gel-coat in good condition before landing about 10mins after sunset at 18:20.

The IBM boys helped me de-rig in double quick time in the gathering gloom while getting their fingers cold in the dew depositing itself on the still cool wings. I rushed over to the clubhouse for a welcome cup of tea and came to the conclusion that I am not addicted to caffeine since it must have been about 24 hours since my last cuppa and I had not developed the shakes in the meantime.

After supper I measured the straight distance between the TPs (not counting the diversions) and found it to be 951km. The extra 49km would have been easy to achieve since 49km at 120kt in a 50kt tail-wind would have taken about 9mins, losing about 3,500ft. Such is life – if you don't plan ahead, you don't achieve.

Alan Purnell

The year ended on another high for the SGU with the handing over of the Scottish Sports Council funded Pawnee tug. The arrival of this unusual aircraft caused some interest in the local press. One headline read "Portmoak Gliding Centre Gets Lift" and the article went on to explain how the Scottish Sports Council contributed £26,000 of the £34,000 cost to import the former crop spraying aircraft from the USA and have it overhauled and converted by a King's Lynn company. Ever eager to make use of all publicity, the CFI – Brian Scougall – reported "The Pawnee has a 235 bhp Lycoming engine, and it has a 50% power advantage over our Cub tugs. It can make 700ft per minute while towing a glider – the Cub can only do 400ft per minute. With a release height of 2,000ft we can manage eight to nine launches per hour with the Pawnee. With this improved launching facility, we intend to go into all year round 7-days a week operation next year"

To help with this full-time operation, Roy Dalling from Long Mynd joined the club as the staff instructor/CFI. Awards were presented to Graham Smith (Thorburn Service Salver), Keith Buchan (Darren Powell Memorial Shield), Colin Hamilton & Alan Bauld (Thorburn Two-Seater Trophy) at the end of year social evening.

John Henry in the Piper Pawnee

Chapter 15
1991 – 1995
The Fire, the Flood and Some Sad News

Roy Dalling prepared for 1991 by taking on the dual role of CFI and resident instructor. Course plans were drawn up and Graham Niven started preparing for the new year as tug pilot in the immaculate Pawnee. Things were looking up and everyone was hoping for a bit of decent weather at the beginning of the year to get some early soaring in. The new Supacat winch was towed to the west end of the airfield on Thursday 14th February, cables were laid out and the first launches were completed just before lunch-time. The SGU was now in the envious position of having the newest launching facilities in the country – a new tug and a new winch! The weekend was the busiest of the year so far with pilots queuing up to test the new winch launch facilities and sample the impressive climb rates offered by the powerful Pawnee.

As the new week started, the weather deteriorated with heavy rain and high winds blowing across the open area of the airfield. Tuesday March 19th dawned dark for the SGU. A fire in the hangar, due to an electrical fault following the overnight wind and rain, completely destroyed four gliders: a club owned Ka-8, the Edinburgh University K-13, a syndicate T-21b and a syndicate T-49.

The long task of clearing up the hangar began and the club struggled to provide limited flying facilities over the following weekends.

The weather refused to pick up and this, coupled with a national recession, took its toll on the summer course attendance. The reducing visitor activity began to impact on the fragile finances of the club. As if that wasn't enough, the flat lands of the airfield quickly filled up with water following the heavy rain and the resulting puddles were so large that a number of geese and waders from the neighbouring Loch Leven RSPB site could be seen swimming across the flooded airfield. Even at weekends, club members were few and far between and the professional staff were left twiddling their thumbs.

During this enforced lull in activities, some club members used their time to set up an oxygen recharging facility in the hangar following the tidy-up operation after the fire, but the flying opportunities were few and far between.

As summer finally arrived, David Bruce managed to set up and run a successful cross-country course. Following comprehensive briefings, a number of pilots were aero-towed away from the site to fly various tasks on the way back to the airfield. During the week, five pilots completed their first field landings and three pilots completed their Silver Badges.

Recently married Mike and Mieke Heppenstall took over the catering franchise from Joe and Alma Nugent who had moved to East Fortune to run the café at the Festival of Flight Air Museum. At around this time, Irene Grala-Wojrezyk joined them on a work experience programme. By the end of the year, the Heppenstall's had moved on and Irene took over the catering franchise. The annual awards night that year was held in The Lomond Hotel where the following people picked up awards: Brian Scougall (Both club ladders), Dick Middleton, Richard Allcoat, Colin Hamilton, David MacFarlane, Graham Smith & Z Goudie.

By 1992, Irene had the new franchise under control and her parents, John and Sandra turned their attention to helping the new business in many ways. This assistance spilled over to SGU activities and the Grala family were to provide many hundreds of manhours around the clubhouse. Irene's fiancé, Steve Donald, also stepped into the breach when he took over as chef. Together, this family team built up the excellent catering and admin facilities at the club and were to become well known by everyone who visited the club during the following years.

Club records for early 1992 showed that more than 800 launches had been achieved during December and January, earning the club some very welcome income. One new club member preparing for his first flight on 12th Jan was Kevin Hook. As we will see later, Kevin was to become one of the club's top pilots and would be a regular winner of trophies and awards. Colin Hamilton took over the Deputy CFI role from Graham Smith and Roy Dalling flew with A.Laing to complete a 120km triangle in the club's ASK-13 on 5th February.

Sadly, while the ASK-13 was making its way back to Portmoak, news was reaching the club that Andrew Thorburn had passed away the previous day at the age of 81. Jim O'Donnell penned the following obituary for the *S&G*:

Andrew James Thorburn

Andrew, our president and a founder member of the Scottish Gliding Union in 1938, died on February 4th at the age of 81. A native of Kirkcaldy, he started his long gliding career in 1935 when he would travel every weekend to Sutton Bank. Somewhere around 1937 he thought it was time that Scotland came into the gliding world as a serious contender and he, along with a few other hardy souls, started flying from the top of Bishop Hill – a significant choice as it dominates Portmoak – and, on its lower slopes, he eventually built his retirement home.

After war service in the RAF, he returned to teaching his beloved art in Kirkcaldy and, in every spare moment, worked tirelessly in setting up the SGU. As its CFI, he supervised its immediate post-war activities at Balado Airfield. In 1956, when they had to leave Balado, Andrew was instrumental in acquiring a small strip of scrubby ground near the south-east corner of Loch Leven and then, through far-seeing business acumen and persistence, proceeded to add adjoining land to produce what became his pride and joy – the present Portmoak Airfield.

Andrew's enthusiasm and leadership rubbed off on all he came in contact with, and was always to be found where the work was dirtiest and heaviest. His flying was an example to everyone and, as an instructor and pilot, he did much to exploit and show the way flying should go at Portmoak.

Not for nothing will he be remembered as the father of the SGU – an accolade truly earned.

February wasn't finished yet – on 26th another well-known face at Portmoak passed away:

Frank Ireland
Frank died peacefully on February 26th. He and his late wife, Tibby, will best be remembered by older members as the couple who set up and developed the high standards of the then new clubhouse in 1961.
Frank, a master carpenter, turned his considerable skills to glider repairs and established our workshops, becoming a much respected senior inspector. After the couple gave up the club house, Frank ran the workshops until his retirement in 1975.
He will be remembered as cheerful, obliging and willing to help with any job large or small.

Colin Hamilton & Dave Hatton organised and ran a pre-bronze course for club members and, on 26th April, Colin put his coaching into practice by flying a 550km task in under 5 hours. Other club members taking advantage of the conditions that day included Richard Allcoat who flew to Sutton Bank via Edzell – this was a flight of 521km but Richard had been hoping to push further south for a 750km attempt. In addition, Peter Glennie, Ray Hill and David Bruce all completed their 300km Diamond Goal flights.

Back in 1986, the Scottish Gliding Association (SGA) was formed "to enable Scottish Gliding Clubs to work together for the benefit of the sport". This body had proved its success in a number of ways, the most beneficial of which – at that time - was the securing of financial backing to procure a very advanced two-seater cross-country training glider, the ASH-25. This 25 metre wing-span aircraft was to be shared between all gliding clubs in Scotland, and it made its first appearance at the Portmoak site at the club's open day on June 20th 1992. Great plans and epic flights were planned for this state-of-the-art aircraft and, as we shall see, many pilots from a number of Scottish clubs truly benefited from flying this wondrous machine.

The SGU ASH-25 being winch-launched. Note the lift-generated curvature of the 25 metre wing-span..

As the year progressed, the finances of the SGU became more and more strained and by the end of the year, with debts of £42,000 the club was almost bankrupt! Such a dire situation needed decisive action so one ASK-13 training glider was sold along with one of the Super Cub tugs. Chairman Trevor Murphy and Treasurer John Ferguson resigned and George Elliot stepped in as Chairman until an Extraordinary General Meeting, where Z Goudie took over the new Chairman's role and 13 Board members were elected. With the exception of the winch-driver, all paid staff were dismissed and Graham Smith took over as CFI from Roy Dalling when his stint came to an end. In recognition of Graham's contribution to the club, he was made an honorary member.

During the winter months, the club officials worked hard to put plans in place to help recover the financial situation.

Improvements for 1993 included a computerised accounting and flying-log system. The new financial recovery programme was declared to be "on target" at the AGM and the membership was invited to vote on some of the key elements. One such vote was to agree to sell the remaining Super Cub tug – leaving the Pawnee as the only tug in the fleet. Club officials had been negotiating with the RAF and the Air Cadets over a request to build a hangar and accommodation on site but this was discontinued when budget was removed from the Air Cadets. Ever keen to keep relationships alive, the SGU and the RAF entered into discussions for the use of part of the airfield for the Advanced Gliding School summer courses. These negotiations were successful and the relationship was to last for the foreseeable future. Most years from 1993 onwards, the RAF would bring a large fleet of gliders and motor-gliders, and impressive launch facilities, to the SGU. Here they set up their summer gliding schools where, each week, a new group of ATC cadets would learn how to make use of the soaring conditions offered at Portmoak.

Despite the difficulties experienced in 1993, by the end of the year, the SGU reported the following statistics:

Two-seaters: 4, single-seaters: 3, Privately Owned: 42, Tugs: 2
No. of launches 9034, of which 1174 were aerotows.
5683 hours were flown with over 10,500 declared kms covered.
Membership stood at 191 (flying) and 919 (temp. incl. visitors)

Following a frugal year, 1994 looked a lot brighter for the club and it was with a huge sigh of relief that the treasurer, Kevin Dillon, was able to report a satisfactory financial position at the AGM held in March. In addition to the very careful control of expenditure and the proactive revenue generation activities, the SGU was the recipient of a very welcome VAT refund of £40,000. At the AGM, the Board were given the go-ahead to order two brand-new ASK-21 two-seater training gliders. One of the ASK-13s was sold and a new enclosed trailer for the club single-seat SZD Junior was purchased.

On the flying front, Richard Allcoat carried the SGU flag to the Northern Regional competition where he won his class with his DG-300 Elan. September produced the early wave days of the season and the first to take advantage was Ian Trotter who flew to 22,000ft on 16th to claim his Diamond height. The very next day Kevin Hook, Mike Edwards and Mike Carruthers completed their 300km for their Diamond goals. Also worth noting was the epic flight of 50km flown by David McLellan to achieve his Silver distance – he was only 16!

By the end of the year, Eoin MacDonald, who had taken over the CFI role from Graham Smith at the beginning of the year, was in the envious position of having not one, but two brand new two-seaters at his and his instructors disposal. The new aircraft having been collected from the factory in October and November. The gliders were allocated the registrations of HPV and HPW and many a glider pilot, including the author, would make good use of these – ultimately flying their first solos in them.

By 1995, with the financial situation back on the straight and level, the club continued with the fleet expansion and modernisation. A second SZD Junior, with an oxygen system, was added at Easter and the Bocian, along with one of the Ka-8s, were sold. The club fleet now consisted of two ASK-21s, two SZD Juniors, one K-7/13, one Ka-8 and the Pawnee tug. A plan was put in place to purchase another new two-seater to replace the K-7/-13 the following year. The vehicle fleet was also being upgraded with the purchase of a custom built Land Rover tow-out vehicle. This had wide flotation tyres and was very "gentle" on the softer sections of the airfield. At around this time a new launch-point caravan was delivered and eager club-members soon had it fitted out with radio and an automated signalling system. The SGU was presenting a very professional face to the public and club-members alike and this was reflected in the steady increase in membership numbers.

Tony Spirling, from the Wolds Gliding Club, came to Portmoak to run the summer courses. Derek Aspey and Neil Goudie took the newest ASK-21 to 16,000ft and 300km flights were becoming common place in these fibre-glass ships. Alan Bauld and Graham Fraser flew a very fast "evening" flight in the other ASK-21. They launched at 7 p.m. and covered 120km out & return before coming back to land before 8 o'clock. Gerry Marshall gained his Silver height having re-soloed the previous year and he set out to find a suitable private, or syndicate, single-seater. He recorded his experience for the *S&G*:

One Owner, Never Thrashed
(Buying and syndicating a second-hand glider)
I re-soloed in July 1994 and completed my Bronze badge in October. During this time I had been weighing up the possibility of selling my BMW motorcycle to fund a share in a sailplane to give me more cross-country flying. Gliders and Sailplanes of the World by Michael Hardy (a book that needs updating) became my bedside companion as I identified club aircraft and I hunted through the adverts in S&G to see what was available.

Early on it is important to arrive at a figure you are comfortable with, because other costs will come along later. My maximum limit was set at £4,000 and I had to decide what I wanted to buy, how much I wanted to share the aircraft and could I afford the running costs?

I talked to people about aircraft, insurances and the benefits of wood construction versus glass. As you might imagine, there were pros and cons to be considered. It became clear that monthly insurance, maintenance and trailer parking would mean that, even after buying the glider, I would be faced with a monthly charge of £20 to £30.

The wood route could let me buy a Skylark III outright but I couldn't afford the monthly running costs and I was put off by tales of how much it costs to have bits re-covered. The rule appeared to be to buy the best you could afford.

Glass seemed the way to go and I would need at least three of us in the syndicate to make it viable from my end. Looking at price, running costs and performance I was heading for a Std Libelle, Std Cirrus or a Vega and then a Libelle 201b came up for sale on the club notice board.

I wasn't in a position to buy at that stage but when I met the owner, Tony Brown, I thought he would make a good syndicate partner. When I saw the machine, I knew that I wanted it. It was beautiful and, at £12,500, within my price range. Even better, it was at Portmoak, my club.

I needed another syndicate partner and would have to take my chance on the sale. It was then that I had the good fortune to be on the same course as Fred Joynes, an engineer, who was thinking along the same lines. I felt sure he would make an ideal third syndicate partner, with more experience than me.

As our club had four Libelles at the time, mainly owned by instructors, I was able to ask all about owning and maintaining one, and to familiarise with the strengths and weaknesses of the aircraft. A member then let me fly his aircraft and I was impressed with its performance. I was fortunate to have a range of similar aircraft on-site and could assess how they fared and what was considered the market value. This may not always be the case for a second-hand buyer, but definitely make sure you speak to at least one owner of the type of aircraft you would like to buy.

It is important at this stage not to be shy because it is legitimate to ask and important that you can verify what you hear as afterwards it could lead to potential costs and unwelcome friction. As my flying hours wouldn't allow a trial flight I had to ask every question I could think of.

Tony gave a full account of the glider – damage, repairs and access to the logbook, receipts and modification details. We checked the aircraft as thoroughly as we could and I certainly didn't feel disadvantaged not having an expert with us.

It had fair wear and tear in the places you would expect. There was minor gel-coat damage but only at an early and insignificant stage. The instruments were basic, but functional, and this was reflected in the price. The anticipated cost of updating them seemed reasonable. The glider was rigged and seemed delightfully straightforward. It had one-man tow-out gear and Tony offered to put in an EW barograph, oxygen mask and parachute as part of the deal.

The trailer only needed new protection underneath and some work on the wheel bearings, which seemed reasonable enough.

We settled on £12,000 with a third equal share to each member. I felt I had two excellent partners and hoped they felt the same.

While many syndicates run perfectly happily without an agreement, we decided to have a written one which covered the basics of ownership, use and upkeep. There is no substitute for goodwill and friendship but it is a safety net in case of problems and of benefit to each member.

An obvious advantage of having a share in a glider is that you can increase your flying-hours and experience. Even in poor conditions in July and August I managed 64hrs and will be aiming for 100hrs for the season. The rota system, giving priority days to each member works well.

Based on our annual estimate for insurance, trailer charges and maintenance, we put £30 a month into a syndicate account. This has given us a reasonable surplus to part finance some new avionics and Fred showed his worth by expertly refurbishing the panel to accommodate this new kit.

In starting out to buy a share in an aircraft, I found a wealth of experience out there only too willing to offer advice and give information. I might have been wiser to look at more alternatives but a preferred option was on the doorstep and the owner would be remaining in the syndicate and, for me, the aircraft was right.

I would encourage other pilots thinking of forming a syndicate to do so and enjoy the sport from a different perspective, soaking up the thrill of flying their own aircraft.

Know in advance what you are looking for in your price range and decide on who you would like in your syndicate. Monthly syndicate payments prevent the shock of big bills and struggling to find your share. Check with as many people as is reasonable. Look at it, touch it. If you like it, become a glider owner.

A new competition for Scottish Gliding Clubs – the Inter-Club League - had been set up and Portmoak members organised a number of task-weekends so that they could get in some much needed competition practice. As the season progressed, these eager competition pilots could be seen queuing up at the launch point most Saturday or Sundays mornings ready to set off on another task.

Following a relatively high turnover of winch drivers, former CFI, Hamish Wotherspoon took on the role and remained in charge of winching operations for a number of years. Hamish and his wife eventually lived in a caravan on site and he could be relied upon to have the winch set up and ready for the earliest of launches. When not launching, flying or maintaining gliders, Hamish would take out his other "toy", a big Cadillac, and enjoy a drive around Fife.

Chapter 16
1996 – 1999
Cadets, Walking on Air and the author takes up gliding

With the club firmly back on an even keel, the Board members started to look around for realistic, yet ambitious, plans for 1996. Ever aware of the need to recruit new members, a number of initiatives were considered. One such idea that met with approval was the Cadet Scheme which came under the auspices of two Full Category rated instructors – Bob Jones and Bob Petrie. The first cadet to join the scheme was Kenny Cowie. He had joined the club in 1994 when he was sixteen and although the club had agreed to subsidise his flying until he went solo, it had unwittingly stopped Kenny from progressing to solo as he didn't want to lose his subsidy. As a result of this, Bob presented a detailed charging scheme to the Board and offered to run the scheme himself.

The idea was to have a maximum of ten cadets participating at any one time and they would receive subsidised training and membership. The first year of operation saw six signed-up cadets and, thanks to some inventive marketing, the scheme was featured on Scottish TV's "Skoosh" programme and even attained a lunchtime news feature.

Later in the year, Bob Jones joined a group of club members on a visit to Husbands Bosworth to try out the English thermals. They were not disappointed as they met with excellent cross-country conditions where Bob and Frank Smith completed their Diamond goals. Another member, the up and coming Kevin Hook completed a 500km flight enabling him to complete all three Diamonds – not bad considering he only went solo four years earlier.

Club statistics show that flying membership stood at 234 with 723 temporary members at the beginning of 1996 and the cover of the April-May issue of the *S&G* sported an excellent photo of visitor Frank Birlston flying his Std Cirrus near Bishop Hill.

At around this time, Graham Lawrence brought a proposal to the SGU Board. He was keen to set up a project to provide gliding facilities for the spinally injured. His proposal was met with enthusiasm and "Walking on Air" was born. It took a lot of hard work by a few stalwarts for the project to move on but, as we will see later, this was to become an extremely successful and rewarding enterprise.

1996 was the year that I joined the club. Having flown as an ATC cadet back in the '60s I yearned to get back into gliding and it was almost 30 years later that, while driving on the motorway south of Kinross, I spotted a glider soaring the slopes of the hills near Loch Leven. I pulled off at the next exit and watched not one, but three gliders all working the lift on the north facing slope of Benarty Hill. As I watched from the car I saw that one was flying low and looked like it was going to land somewhere. I followed it along the road past the RSPB centre at Vane Farm and eventually I spotted the sign welcoming visitors to "The Scottish Gliding Union". I parked in the car park and went into the office where Irene told me about the facilities at the club, the membership costs, and invited me to look around. That first visit did the trick and within a couple of days I was back to join the club and sign up for a five-day course in May.

When I turned up for my course, I noticed that an excellent photographic display of the club history was being erected in the foyer. Peter Black had put a lot of effort into this exhibit and little did I know that I would become so involved with the club history in the years to come!

How did my course go? I completed 27 flights with durations ranging from ten minutes to one hour. My instructor was Tony Spirling and I learned such a lot in that week. I thoroughly enjoyed the whole thing and found the club members most welcoming and very friendly. Following that course I managed to continue my training and, after 38 flights at Portmoak, was finally sent on my own for my first solo on 1st August 1996. The rest, as they say, is history – but I will relate some of my stories in due course.

1996 called for yet another obituary for *S&G* from the SGU:

Wladyslaw "Richard" Rozycki
   Richard was one of our earliest members, having joined the SGU at Balado Airfield in 1947.

   Trained by the solo method, he attained his A and B certificates that year and gained his C from a bungee launch from Bishop Hill in 1948. He went on to become a member of the Kite-2, Skylark-2 and Olympia 463 syndicates, and was a director of the club from 1960 to 1962.

   Although he retired from active gliding in the mid-1960s, he retained a keen interest in the club and became a senior official observer. He set up his barograph calibration station in his cottage in the woods next to the airfield, and must have been responsible for the authentication of hundreds of claims over the years, handling each with unfailing courtesy, event those with the flimsiest of evidence.

   A chartered electrical engineer by profession, he became, in retirement, an authority on the natural life of the area. He was a keen bee-keeper and maintained a close interest in the weather, having set up a satellite receiving station in recent years.

   His loss will be keenly felt and we all extend our sympathy to his widow, Yvonne.

                                                            SBM

The summer months provided good flying opportunities for cadets and pundits alike. The first SGU cadet to solo, Kenny Cowie, gained his five hours and Silver height during a very successful Cadet Week. Dave Clempson (of the pundit brigade) flew his Open Cirrus around a 780Km course and Richard Allcoat flew with his dad in their DG-500 around a 500km task in 5hrs, averaging 130 kph. The following story of their flight was published in the *S&G* and brought some positive publicity and, consequently, started a mini "Gold Rush" of visitors seeking to secure their Gold badge claims from Portmoak:

We Took the High Road

The alarm clock rattled away and one eye opened to see a sky full of wave clearly marked and beckoning. Was it a glider pilot's dream or nightmare? Both eyes confirmed the best sky I have seen at Portmoak for some time. Panic set in because my son, Richard, and I had boxed our DG-500 (with winglets) due to forecasted gale-force winds, so now it meant rigging.

It was Tuesday, October 29th, and we were still rigging when we heard other members already at 10,000ft. At 10:25 a.m. we were going for it. A low point of 700ft on Bishop Hill, then at 9,000ft 15mns after take-off and still climbing at 10kt we were able to take stock of the conditions and get our breath back.

It was time now to dip our nose and jump a wave bar towards our first Turn Point at Edzell, 82km away. A clearly defined cloud street marked the way so, at 90kt airspeed in 2kt of lift, we sped along aiming to maintain between 8,000ft and 10,000ft. This level appeared to give us the strongest lift, but cloud tops were at 7,000ft where visibility of cloud formation ahead was obscured.

We were taking it in turns to operate our miniature video camera to give us something to view during the long winter evenings. Dundee moved behind on our right, then Forfar and Brechin with the Montrose Basin in the distance. We turned fast round Edzell into sun for the 159km leg to Helensborough, away on the other side of Scotland. Overhead Perth we were down to 7,000ft so slowed down in strong lift, then pushed forward again to fly at 100kts maintaining 10,00ft. With Stirling on our left. Lake of Menteith ahead, Callander and Loch Katrine, phew!, we were really scorching along. Good lift over Loch Lomond and *with only 11km to run to Gareloch, we got ready for more filming and a TP photo of Helensburgh.*

Our next leg to Aboyne, a distance of 166km with a 90° crosswind of 25-30kt, was fairly uneventful. Having covered 241km to Helensburgh in exactly 2hrs, we knew that a fast time was on, if only…

Outside temperature was about -20°C and we only had "in flight" Yorkie bars and orange juice for sustenance. Cloud street wave formations were breaking up now with ragged cumulus masking the wave systems. Jumping these ragged areas proved no problem by flying even faster through the sink and then slowly gaining height while flying fast in the subsequent good lift. A dusting of snow on Glen Shee told us that winter was approaching. Then a quick call on the radio to our pals at the Deeside Gliding Club and we were turning for home, 103km away.

Now grateful for the sunshine on our faces and an excess of 4,000ft on the C3 calculator, we high-tailed it back towards Portmoak. With Fife set out on our left, Dundee and the Tay below us and the Firth of Forth shimmering in the distance, a 100kt airspeed giving a groundspeed of 132kt, we were soon back home.

Having encountered very little sink between wave bars, we airbraked off our excess height over Loch Leven and landed back at Portmoak 3hrs 54mins after take-off. The average speed was 130km/h over 510km, flown between 8,000ft and 10,000ft.

We parked the glider, thawed out the ft and drank a welcome cup of coffee. Looking at the sky with lovely wave bars still evident and 2hrs 30mins of daylight left, should we have set the alarm earlier and declared 750km?

Our first attempt with the video camera was a great success giving us a 35min film of superb wave conditions.

This flight by Richard and Neville won them the BGA Frank Foster award for the fastest 500km flight.

The year ended on a particular high for myself. The world famous Derek Piggott had arrived at our club as guest speaker for the end of year "do". On the afternoon before the festivities, I was asked - as a very early solo pilot - if I would like to fly with him and show him the local landmarks! We flew for around half-an-hour and it was a most pleasurable experience and I couldn't believe who I was flying with.

In the evening Derek presented, amongst other things, the 1996 Scottish Inter-Club League to a very proud SGU team. All that hard work and preparation earlier in the year had indeed paid off.

During the winter months, Ian Dandie and Colin Golding, using much of Richard Rozycki's equipment, set up a new barograph calibration room in the central workshop and, at the beginning of 1997, this facility was officially certified by the BGA.

Eoin MacDonald handed over CFI duties to Vic Blaxill and then completed an Airfield Safeguarding document which was submitted to the local planning authorities. There was more officialdom afoot when the Civil Aviation Authority (CAA) withdrew permission for gliders to fly in class B and class D airspace without Air Traffic Control (ATC) clearance. Almost immediately, a work party was set up and negotiations with the National Air Traffic Services (NATS) at Prestwick commenced. Those negotiations were successful and a Letter Of Agreement was signed which allowed transit areas across airway Bravo 2 at weekends. One club member, Ken Moffat organised a visit to the CAA ATC Tower at Edinburgh airport later in the year and this helped increase awareness for both parties. Later in the year the good news was published in the *S&G*:

The new Letter of Agreement (LOA) allowing gliders to cross Airways B2 and B226 has been signed and will become effective from 18th June. Full details will be sent to all clubs, and pilots who are intending to fly across these airways or who may be attempting a flight to Scotland which may need to cross B2/B226 must have read this Agreement and signed the attached form to give to their CFI. The Scottish clubs will have copies of the Agreement and it will be part of their briefing to visiting pilots. It will be an annual requirement for pilots to read and sign as understanding the procedure.

The Scottish ATC authorities have been exceptionally helpful and the procedure is straightforward. As with Class D Airspace, pilots, when crossing the airway (Class A Airspace), will be in contact with an ATC controller.

Carr Withal
Chairman – BGA Airspace Committee

As is the case in many families, sons and daughters often follow their parents' interests and hobbies. The Goudie family were no different, Z Goudie (former Club Chairman) found sons Neil and Gavin quickly developing their gliding skills and showing their competitive streak. Neil penned the following item covering the UK Junior Championships for the *S&G* in early 1997:

Junior Championships, past, present and future – N. Goudie (Neil, who flies at the Scottish Gliding Union, went solo in 1990, flew in the 1995 Junior Championships and crewed for his brother Gavin last year. He has a Gold badge, a Diamond and 400hrs.)

The Junior Championships is fast becoming the most competitive event in the British soaring calendar, having developed from its conception in 1998. Since then some of its winners have become National Champions as well as members of the British Team at World and European events.

But this wasn't the first time junior pilots were introduced to competitive gliding. In the late 1970s British squad training was run for small groups by BGA national coaches helped by notable competition pilots. This encouraged the development of competition orientated pilots between the ages of 16 and 25. It became clear in the mid 1980s that the demand for squad training was exceeding available resources and so the Junior Championships was born.

For the first couple of years the results were fairly predictable even before the entry lists were posted! However, the early 1990s saw a drastic increase in the field and of the competitive spirit. Soon we had new names on the cup with some winners with only two or three years cross-country experience.

The 1995 competition was a real turning point in the standard of junior flying with exceptional weather producing speeds which would have graced any senior Championships. And the results from the Standard Class Nationals at Dunstable last summer have shown that junior pilots like Henry Rebbeck and Dave Allison are biting at the tails of some very experienced competitors. The presence of Justin Wills at the evening de-brief was beneficial and, along with a spirit of camaraderie between the pilots, led to an excellent week.

Last season the Mobil Junior Championships were, again, a huge success, aided not only by the organisation, sponsorship and the pilots and crews, but also by the home club committees who loaned club gliders to some of their younger pilots. Many, however, talked of the reluctance to allow club gliders to be taken away for ten days and the difficulty in hiring or borrowing equipment for competition flying.

Perhaps many clubs believe that losing a glider for a week would be a tremendous waste of income. But if these same clubs truly believe that gliding is to continue as a sport in Britain they must develop their young pilots' skills and not throw them to the side after their cadet schemes have been completed.

Gliding should not be limited to the fortunate few who have been brought up on a diet of Discus, LS-8 and ASW-24s, but to the large number of young pilots who use club gliders and whose skill is kept away from competition. At a competition forum at Lasham it was noted that clubs should make a strong effort to make gliders available for this and other competitions. Until clubs help their Silver badge cadets to get to the Junior Championships they may never realise the hidden talent that exists in their ranks. They may even have the next Lee, Wills, Spreckley or Davis and not even know it.

If you are a new Silver badge pilot, or expect to gain it by this summer, and are wanting to see what competition gliding is all about, and your 25th birthday was not before January 1st, ask the BGA for an entry form for the 1997 Junior Championships to be held at Bidford between August 25th and September 2nd.

The following year, both Neil and Gavin took part in the Junior Nationals at Lasham. Gavin scored 2881 points to finish 16th with Neil in 19th place with 2538 points.

During the year the Allcoats once again jumped into their DG-500 to notch-up a record-breaking flight – and the story of their flight appeared in the *S&G*:

Wave Goodbye to Scotland
SGU pilots Neville and Richard Allcoat (father and son) made Scottish gliding history on September 8th with the first 750km from Scotland, flying their DG-500 with winglets which also took on a speedy 500km last autumn.

Having just watched the video once again, it never ceases to amaze me how many things conspired to make September 8th a remarkable day. Our 750km diploma is in the bag, a first from Scotland, and we have a 45 minute video film of the flight.
Diary, Sunday, September 7th.
The BBC 1 forecast was for south-westerly gales to veer west at ground level by morning and to remain at 25kts, with

a maximum daytime temperature of 18°C and a rising pressure to 1013mb. This usually spells good wave as the winds veer with height, so I rang my boss and begged Monday off. So far, so good. At 7:15pm I phoned Dad, confirmed the forecast and made sure the batteries were charged and that he would be up with the lark.

Diary, Monday, September 8th, 09:00.

The forecast was correct and we met at Portmoak Airfield with wave already visible to the north-west. We uncovered our DG-500/20 metre winglets, loaded her up and were ready to launch at 09:50. Our declared task was Portmoak caravan site (PCS), Edzell (EDZ), Helensburgh pier (HEL), Aboyne clubhouse (ABO) and then free distance.

Declaration signed, photos taken, we winch launched at 09:52 to 1,500ft. Having climbed overhead Bishop Hill to 2,500ft we pushed west for a mile, contacting wave over Loch Leven. With 4kts of lift at 4,000ft, it was off the clock at 7,000ft. Climbing through 10,000ft with a wind strength of 45kts NW, we set off for EDZ, a distance of 75km. Progress was slow but the wave well formed and we turned EDZ after 75mins, heading for HEL 165km away.

The wave was set up parallel to the Grampian Mountains running 070°/250° but the wind was from WNW, giving a strong into wind component along the wave running west to the next turn point (TP). For over two hours we battled along the wave bars into wind towards HEL.

Cloud cover had increased from 3 to 7 octas from the east to the west coast, forcing us to climb to 12,000ft to see the few gaps ahead. The last visible gap to the west was fortunately just beyond Helensburgh and, having lost 4,000ft getting there, we were pleased to round the TP in lift, then head rapidly north-east towards ABO 170km away.

Now we had the advantage of a tailwind component along the wave and progressed quickly to ABO in clearer air and strong wave, maintaining 8,000ft to 11,000ft. We were careful to keep Callander on our right to avoid Glasgow airspace. Cloud cover was now reducing and we were able to stay between 7,000ft – 11,000ft, flying fast to ABO.

Round the TP we called Aboyne gliders to say hello. It was 02:30pm and at 10,000ft, Portmoak was easily within reach, but rather than flying very fast we decided to conserve height and arrive back at Portmoak as high as possible, hoping that we could get clearance from Scottish FIR to transit across Edinburgh towards Jedburgh and Rufforth.

The next problem was organising a retrieve from the Yorkshire area if we were heading south because with a 45kt tailwind we would not be coming back! Gavin Goudie was flying his Discus locally and valiantly volunteered to land, hitch up our trailer and head down the A1.

Scottish FIR could not get clearance from Edinburgh for us to transit overhead but suggested that we route east along the Fife coast to Buckhaven, cross the 12 miles of the Firth of Forth to North Berwick and report when clearing East Fortune airfield. This we complied with and NATS wished us a safe onward journey.

The wave was well formed over the Scottish borders so we made good progress at ground speeds often in excess of 120kts. Slight diversions east to avoid the Otterburn danger area then south-west to miss Newcastle airspace, we waved goodbye to Scotland.

John Ellis in his Nimbus 3t, flying from Sutton Bank, radioed to say hello and suggested the Pennine lee wave was very strong over Derwent reservoir and then to the south, so we headed towards him. Twenty minutes later he passed us, heading north at over 200kts closing speed, 8,000ft high still showing 4kts of lift.

With less than 200km to run to Rufforth and 10,000ft back on the altimeter, we could sit back, enjoy the evening sunshine and watch the Pennines and the Yorkshire moors roll by. By 6pm we were over York letting down from 5,000ft to a welcoming committee on Rufforth's 24 west runway.

Bob McLean helped us park our glider and his wife provided us with very welcome cups of tea – after all, one of their DGs had come home.

The crew arrived at 9pm and we were heading north by 9:45. After 8hrs 17mins flying a total of 770km and a 5hr drive home, we were back at Portmoak overjoyed, needing more than a little sleep but already planning the next adventure.

The Walking on Air committee, led by Graham Lawrence and Richard Hungerford was making excellent progress during 1997 and were awarded a Lottery Sport Fund grant towards a glider and facilities for wheelchair pilots. This, along with a donation from the Allied Dunbar Foundation and some local fund-raising raised £90,000 and the project was well and truly up and running.

On the flying front, Mike Carruthers and Tony Brown completed their Diamond heights and Ian Dandie completed his Diamond distance in Australia. A new member to the club also claimed his Diamond height that year – John Williams. As we will see later, John would become a key player in the future development of the club and would make some truly historic flights in the years to come.

As part of the airfield improvement plan agreed the previous year, work began in 1998 to lay a pipe along the old ditch that ran up the side of the farm road then the ditch was filled in and levelled. A 50 metre-wide strip to the north of the ash strip was also levelled. A near neighbour of the club, *Stewart Turf* of Grahamstone Farm, completed the grading and re-seeding of the area and it was agreed to ban all vehicular and aircraft movement over that section until the new grass had established itself. The club purchased a new Zetar tractor to help ensure the airfield grass was kept in good condition.

At that year's AGM, one item that came under discussion was the proposal to "re-badge" the site at Portmoak as "The Scottish Gliding Centre". The attendees voted in favour and from mid 1998 new road signs as well as advertising and promotional material sported the new image – although the company name would remain as The Scottish Gliding Union Ltd.

With the new image firmly in place, the club held an open day on 28th June to mark the 60th anniversary of Andrew Thorburn's first soaring flight from Bishop Hill. A group from the Vintage Glider Club attended and brought a Gull 1, an Olympia 2, a Ginn Kestrel, a Skylark 3 and a Swallow. Visitors flowed through the gate, the south field was brought into service as a car park with volunteer cadets directing traffic, and the event was deemed a PR success.

Two days earlier, Joe Fisher brought the newly converted Walking On Air K21 on site and this generated a great deal of interest at the open day. Earlier in the year Joe had spent six weeks at the Schleicher's factory designing and building the rudder circuit modifications which allowed hand controls to be operational from both seats in the K21. These modifications were to be adopted by other clubs looking to provide gliding for the disabled and, as we shall see later, Joe would be at the forefront of the ongoing development of the Walking On Air (WOA) project. One of the first things to be tackled that year was the rebuilding of the toilet block and a wheelchair access ramp into the clubhouse. This work was started just after the official launch of WOA on 30th August and was continued through the winter months.

On the flying front, another record was about to be claimed by an SGU member. This time, it was the turn of Chris Robinson. On the 12th October, he became the first member to gain his full Gold badge by flying all of the legs entirely in SGU club gliders. Other pilots claiming personal bests that year included Ken Moffat, George Ross, Steve Nutley, Adi Von-Gontard and Roddy Ferguson who all completed their Silver badges, and John Williams who flew 500km to claim his third Diamond.

Chris recalled the last leg of his Gold Badge for the club mag:

317k In a Club Junior (or 6hr 39m Without a Yaw String)

Well, so far so good, it's 06:30 on Monday (12/10/98) and I'm first on the flying list for a club Junior and I have a club barograph. Better than Saturday (but that's another story).

Having smoked my barograph I opened the hangar and started to fill the glider's oxygen cylinder. A couple of visitors appeared so I checked and filled their bottles first. Adi Von-Gontard has arrived and is second on the list and intends to fly the other club Junior. We fill "my" Junior - HRG, but there is a leak from the back of the regulator, which is buried deep in the instrument panel. Adi suggests that I take "his" Junior - FUS as he "only" wants gold height and doesn't need oxygen (Generous these Montana folk). So we extract FUS from the back of the hangar and fill it with oxygen. Have you ever known the aircraft you want to be at the front of the hangar?

Fred Joynes volunteered to DI the aircraft and get it to the launch point while I seek out an O.O. for my barograph and declaration. (There are nice folk in Lanark too). A quick call to my boss who had been on stand-by and so was agreeable to "A Wave Day Holiday".

Just after 11:00 I'm ready to launch, not bad - I've only been out of bed 6 hrs. I wonder if I'm too late for the "early" morning wave. During the launch I notice that the yaw string has caught in the edge of the sticky tape and is useless, it will stay there for the whole flight! At 1,200ft I pull-off and take a low point on the way to the north face of Bishop. At around 100kts with the mechanical vario still indicating 2kts up, I become suspicious. Operating the Climb/Cruise switch confirms that it is stuck in cruise mode and operating as an air mass vario. A pain but I can live with it. Up to 4,000ft at

West Lomond. I've checked the electric vario, it's rather optimistic and the total energy compensation of both instruments is poor. (Made a mental note to "fix" panel one way or the another – as Director for Gliders I arranged for new varios to be fitted to both Juniors). Now the Turn/Slip, although checked on the ground I always check it once airborne while turning. About 6 weeks ago I was suddenly caught in collapsing wave at 10,000ft and had to descend 6,000ft in cloud, this convinced me that an in-flight check is good practice and saves embarrassment with the laundry.

Now I'm up to 6,000ft and the wind has increased from 18kts at 1,200ft to 24kts and has veered from 300° to 310°. Things are looking good. I run along a wave bar tracking 030° out to the East of Perth. Now the problems start. It is Monday, so the airway to the West of Portmoak P600 is operational, but we have negotiated a crossing procedure. However, this involves contacting Scottish ATC by radio and hence requires an R/T Licence, which I do not have (Mental note: Get R/T Licence this Winter – got it, but it took until spring the following year). West of Perth the bottom of the airway is FL065 with a minimum altitude of 5,500ft. As QFE at Portmoak is 1000mb and Portmoak is 365ft amsl QNH is 1012mb. As flight levels are referenced to 1013.25mb it means that the base of the airway is just below 6,500ft as indicated on my altimeter. (All those sums for the Bronze paper weren't wasted). For safety I nominate 6,000ft as my maximum altitude, but to the South the base of the airway falls to FL060 and then to FL055, so I must be careful. Its also crucial to keep a good look out as power traffic often fly under the airway to use the beacons without incurring the cost of using the airway.

After sampling a few wave bars at altitudes ranging from 3,000 to 10,000ft I select one just North of Perth heading just South of Crieff. As the air is smooth I let down from 10,000 to 7,500ft using airbrakes and then accelerate to 110kts, weaving gently in and out of the wave to start the crossing at exactly 6,000ft in maximum lift. The general plan is to adjust my airspeed to maintain 6,000ft. Cruising between 60 and 70kts at around 5,500ft for 10 minutes and ¾ of the way across the wave bar begins to disappear. Time to change tactics, slow down, reach the end of the bar at just below 6,000ft and get as far North and West as possible.

Now there are two choices fall back to the bar behind or go forward. The bar behind would be further into the airway and could lead in to area where the bottom reaches down to 6,000ft or worse to 5,500ft. It should "guarantee" lift but with the chance that it may end before crossing the airway. The wave system can also become confused West of Stirling making a jump forward difficult (In September I was caught in a changing system near Fintry and landed-out at Kippen - Mental Note: Remember not to land at Blair Drummond Safari Park they have Lions).

I go North. The wind speed is 28kts, so subtract 10 and divide by 6 gives a wave bar spacing of about 3nm. The best glide speed (V_{ld}) for a Junior is 42kts, so add $^1/_3$ wind speed (V_{wind}) to give Speed to Fly (V_{stf}) of 51kts; I set this on the MacReady ring. Ignoring sinking air flying at this speed I would expect to lose a minimum of 1,500ft and take about 6 minutes to cross to the next bar. (In practice with sinking air I expect to lose double this height - 3,000ft).

I set off and as the sink increases I increase speed as indicated by the MacReady ring. If it gets above 90kts I won't make it. Half way across the wind speed has increased to 32kts and I expect to lose at least 3,500ft. I'm now in rotor and it's getting worse, 75kts just below max rough air, the vario wants 90kts, no can do. Down to 3,000ft at Crieff, press-on. I can see the field where I landed in February, perhaps the two fire engines, three police cars, an ambulance and that friendly local reporter would welcome my return - not if I can help it, press-on. 2,500ft very rough, but zero sink, 60kts then pull-up to 45kts in lift! Slowly at first then rapidly (8kts up) climbing to 10,000ft, one hour into the flight across the airway and in lift.

Sliding along the bar climbing beyond Comrie a pattern begins to emerge - wind 315° 37kts, bar spacing about 5nm aligned 220°/040°. At 12,000ft I can see the areas of weaker lift where the bars spread indicating where the sink is likely to be least between the bars.

Now well on track to Crianlarich the first turn point. Good strong lift South of Killin 6kts at 12,000ft. Something to drink and then onto oxygen. While contemplating the possibility of a diamond height I can see the river at Killin, where in July at 1,200ft, while preparing to land-out, two Tornadoes flew under me at 500ft and whizzed up the glen to the North. Around 15,000ft the lift falls off to zero and doesn't look like it will get any better, time to press-on to Crianlarich.

I'm in luck, Crianlarich is in a gap between the clouds and I press forward and take my TP photographs just before the bisector, but well in sector, jumping to the next bar all in one manoeuvre (2:20 elapsed).

Richard (Allcoat) said it was easy and I could do it, maybe he was right. I've flown several times with Richard when his father wasn't available in their beautiful DG-500 (Winglets) and benefited greatly from his advice on where to look for "green air" (i.e.: going up). Flying a Junior needs a lot more lift to keep it aloft than a DG-500, but the principles are the same. I've also done a lot of flying with Kevin Hook - one of my original instructors - particularly in the SSC ASH25. We flew (with Adi Von-Gontard) at the Bidford Regionals where we unfortunately learned the importance of good look out (we saw a fatal mid-air collision).
I do another look-out just to be sure.

Flying along a bar on the South side of Loch Tay I can see that the bars are aligned almost exactly along my desired track; so I shouldn't have to jump too many bars. Time to experiment, at what height is the best lift, how far out into the gap is the best lift, so how fast can I go? The answer is rather disappointing only 2-4kts up, with very little difference between 8,000 and 10,000ft tailing off to zero at 12,000ft. This means flying at 45kts along a bar so that I can gain to sufficient height (2,000ft) to jump to the next bar – it's going to be a long day.

Near Ben Lawers I pause and take a climb to 15,000ft. Toni Shelton advised that this is a hot spot for diamond height, but not today. (See postscript).

Just short of Pitlochry the system changes. Trying to find a way through I'm down to 6,000ft. I flew up this way with Alan Bauld in his Jodel in the Spring with snow on the ground; it's back again with a dusting on the tops. It will soon be Winter and there will be skiing, my other passion. No time for that now as I need some lift. Let's fall back and try that curved wall of cloud to the south. Mid-way there is a call from Portmoak – it's Ian Trotter asking if I'm OK. "I'm OK, but rather busy looking for lift" says I. "Good luck" says he and "right now please" thinks I. A little later and back at 12,000ft and a little less busy. I call back and advise that I'm OK, back on track but a front is beginning to show to the West. The lift here is weak and the wind has backed to 300° and fallen to 28kts.

I've found a big blue hole. Now the tactic is to get as much height as possible, nearly 15,000ft and tip-toe to the edge. Off to the right the Southern edge is nearly 20nm away. The bars over the far side seem to be setting-up more North/South. The wind is now 290° at 20kts. I jump. Not too bad at first, not much sink flying close to best glide (42kts) as there is a large tailwind component. There are two or three "sink holes" 6kts down, but I get across 18nm losing 6,000ft. Back to 10,000ft and jump a few bars North. I'm getting better at judging where the bars merge and the sink is weakest.

Well the GPS tells me that Abyone airfield is 3nm to the South West, but where is it? Come to think of it where is the village? To recap, I'm equipped with a smokie barograph and a camera, but nowhere to point it! Well I suppose any picture in sector is OK, but what should I photograph. Having consulted the map there are several readily identifiable landmarks, but the cloud is covering everything. I decide to head North East, but not too far, the Aberdeen CTA is at the East of Abyone village. From my map, Stavanger is in sector but my John Willie tells me I need 140,000ft for a final glide and I'm not sure how to say "I've landed my glider in your field" in Norwegian; maybe there is a better option, patience, so I wait. After 20 minutes of looking I can see the village through a small gap, camera on, turn, one shot - should be OK, second shot didn't go off - too quick film hadn't wound-on, continue to turn, another shot - it fired but maybe too far south. Try again, push North 80kts big pull-up Chandelle right keep the turn going, where is the gap - gone! One gap, one shot and that's all folks! (Another mental note: buy IGC logger/GPS as this photo stuff is too stressful – bought a GR1000, now I only have to worry about the batteries going flat!).

I feel cold. It's becoming overcast and I need to find somewhere to park in lift while I attend to a small personal matter. ("Small" it must be the cold. The Silver/Gold Endurance duration is set about right for my bladder - Elapsed time 5:00 hrs).

So I got round both TPs, if the photos are OK, so how do I get home. The direct track is through P600, not a good idea, particularly as the Northern end joins with Aberdeen CTA. Heading off SW I aim to track just to the West of Bravo-2. The wind has changed, at low level its almost due West and at 10,000ft 290° 20kts. The wave is breaking-up and the slots are closing; that is wrong they're not slots anymore rather rivulets at the bottom of a snowy valley (I told you I am a skier). I need to head West whenever I can and as the bars merge I turn West and speed-up. Its slow progress now as there is a small headwind component and the front is creeping forward from the West.

Near Dunkeld it gets better, proper bars, I take a picture and fly faster. Its after 17:00 and overcast. There is low cloud, it looks like weak wave has set-up in the valley between Perth and Crieff, just where I want to let down. I go further West and South, it's worse here. Back towards Methven letting down on the way using airbrakes and I run in with a 45 degree tail/cross wind. This cloud is a pest, the bottom is not far above the tops of the Ochil Hills, so I aim for Glenfarg at the end of a valley across the hills. These weak wave bars are strange in this light, soft and smooth almost vertical sheets like sails closely spaced on a clipper. Sliding down the face of one sheet increasing speed while maintaining height, pull-up Chandelle, dive round the end and jump the gap to slide down the next sheet the other way; zigzagging my way towards Glenfarg. To the East I can see Dundee (I landed-out there in February - my first time, you never forget your first time - so they say) and beyond Arbroath (100k out and return in March for Silver Distance, first leg of my cross-country diploma, plus Gold Height as a bonus).

I'm cold. Nearly at Dunning (landed-out here in August - sea breeze cut-off my return but soared for 2 hours up and down the valley before landing). Glenfarg reservoir and clear of the airway at last.

I suddenly realise I've been slicing along these bars at 80kts, I pull-up over the last bar and climb rapidly to 8,000ft. I think with 10nm to go a final glide is in order. I put the nose down, 100kts, Yeahaa.

Coming up on the left is Auchtermuchty (I landed out there in April returning from Forfar in thermal when the wave collapsed - too far East, should have pushed West further North). Bishop on the left, Loch Leven on the right, over the caravan site, camera on, pull-up, Chandelle, click, flash what was that! The default mode of my camera is auto which selects flash when in low light conditions; was it trying to tell me something?

Back over the Loch, secure my bits and pieces, one loop (well why not), open the brakes down to 2,000ft and then back onto the hill to re-calibrate my height judgement. Now a good circuit, wind 260° 10kts, call down wind, land in the South field and stop next to the tug hangar. Yes!

Down, but I think I need a crane to get out of the cockpit. As I open the canopy the yaw string blows free from the sticky tape to which it has been securely adhered for the whole flight - I give it its freedom.

Hamish Wotherspoon is first at the scene. Adi did get his Gold Height but could have gone higher with oxygen (Mental note: fix oxygen and buy Adi a beer or three).

Hamish offers his hand in congratulation, but has offered very much more by way of advice and encouragement in the past

Well its not been a bad year, my first as a cross-country pilot (my second in total). 300 launches, 250 hours and 2,500km mostly in the club Juniors, but also in K21, ASH25 and DG-500 learning the skills of cross-country flying from others.

I'm grateful to (all) those souls who collected me when I didn't quite make it back, and the tolerance and good humour of the farmers whose fields I visited (Rumours, largely spread by Graham Lawrence, that I am a honorary member of the Farmers Union are quite untrue, but justified).

Next year, (much to the relief of other club members, who have threatened to disable my alarm-clock) I hope to have a share in a glider, but at the time of writing (21st Oct) the wave season is not over and there is this 500k and if I get up early, get a glider, find a barograph on the right day it might just be possible...

Remember what Hamish used to say "It's all there to be learned boys" - so get out there and do it.

Construction work around the clubhouse continued into 1999 and the new year saw the opening of the rebuilt toilet block and wheelchair facilities.

The club fleet was also being upgraded that year when a new DG505 Orion was ordered. This aircraft had a 17m wingspan and had winglets to extend this to 20m. The single-seater fleet was augmented in February when the club took delivery of a used ASW19. This was short lived, however, when it was written-off in a landing accident in September that year, and was replaced by the French-built Centrair Pegase 101.

The Pawnee tug was out of service for three months during the spring due to difficulty in obtaining spares, so visitors and club members were limited to winch launching. By this time, the levelled and re-seeded strip to the north of the ash strip was put into service and the grounds-folk turned their attention to both sides of the farm road.

The Walking on Air group had good cause to celebrate, when David Nisbet flew his first solo on 2nd May and went into the history books as being the first Walking on Air student to go solo.

Another historic event took place on 9th August 1999. This time it was the Cadet group who came up with the goods. The following story was published in a number of newspapers across the country:

Like identical twins all over the world, Oliver and Roland Smith do almost everything together.

So when one decided the best way to celebrate their 16th birthday was to make a solo flight in a glider, the other was bound to agree. Now the pair have become the world's first identical twins to pilot a glider on the first day they were old enough to legally fly on their own.

The brothers trained for a year, making more than 80 flights accompanied by their instructors. Then, on their birthday, they each took to the air for five-minute solo flights at the Scottish Gliding Centre's Portmoak Airfield on the shores of Loch Leven.

Afterwards the twins said: "It is absolutely fantastic that we have been able to celebrate our birthday in this way."

Their instructor, Bob Jones, said: "Every pilot remembers their first solo flight and doing it on their 16th birthday is a very special achievement by Oliver and Roland.

Paying tribute to the dedication and determination of the two teenagers, from Bonnyrigg, he added: "They worked very hard for months to reach the standards necessary to go solo. Every instructor who flew with them was convinced they were fully capable and that it

Roland and Oliver Smith with instructors Mike Ward and Bob Jones

was just a matter of waiting for their birthday."

But their love of adventure does not end with flying . The boys, who attend Edinburgh's Stewarts Melville College, are both keen skiers and hold the Royal Yachting Association's highest certificate for dinghy sailing.

Back on the ground, the club officials became concerned about a planning request to build a house and equestrian centre adjacent to the North field. Representation was made to Perth & Kinross Council and the SGU awaited the outcome with bated breath.

The end of year award night was held at the clubhouse in 1999 and the following people picked up well deserved trophies:

Thorburn Two-Seater – Richard & Neville Allcoat
Boyle Altitude – Kevin Hook (23,325ft)
Marshall 100km Triangle – Kevin Hook (96kph)
Andy Penswick – Chris Robinson (318km)
Parker Distance – John Williams (510km)
Docherty Handicapped Distance – John Williams
Sutherland Out & Return – John Williams (270km)
Lomond – Z. Goudie (208km)
Maclay Championship – Kevin Hook
Peter Copeland – Richard & Neville Allcoat
Hot Wings – John Galloway
Nick Wales – David Nesbitt/A.Wilson
Lucky White Heather – E.Wilson
Darren Powell – Vic Blaxill
Silver Salver – Jim Proven

As the millennium drew to a close, the success of the Cadet scheme was acknowledged with the following youngsters completing their first solos:

Kenny Cowie, Kit McLean, Ross McIntyre, Richard Mortimer, Alastair Wilson, Alan Ramsay, Roland Smith, Oliver Smith, Ronald Finch and Raymond Roberts

Chapter 17
2000
A New Millennium

The year 2000 started with southerly winds and blustery showers. These conditions seemed to remain for a long time and the few die-hards who ventured to Portmoak in the early weeks of the year had to make do with the turbulent conditions that these weather patterns produced. On one such day at the end of January, the outgoing CFI, Vic Blaxill, briefed me for a solo flight in one of the club Juniors, and I flew for an hour or so over the south facing cliffs on Bishop Hill. When I landed, Vic came over and, after the "how did you get on?" questions, casually asked "Have you thought about joining the Board of Directors?" I hadn't, but over a coffee in the clubhouse I decided that it might be interesting and agreed to be nominated. And so it was, at the March AGM of that year, I was elected as a board member of the SGU, and was allocated the "gentle" responsibility for member communications. The rest of the board for 2000 consisted of:

Alan Bauld	Chairman, with responsibility for winch & equipment
Brian Cole-Hamilton	Vice-Chairman, with responsibility for buildings & property
Jim Provan	Secretary
Alisdair Stewart	Treasurer
Bob Jones	Chief Flying Instructor
Chris Robinson	Safety and Glider Fleet
Joe Fisher	Tug and Walking On Air
Fred Joynes	Publicity
Neil McAulay	Cadets
Eoin MacDonald	Airfield and Duty Rosters

Statistics available at the start of the year show that the club had five two-seaters, four single-seaters, one tug and 55 privately owned gliders. The launch rate for the previous year was an impressive 10,089 launches, 725 of which were aerotows. Full membership stood at 217, eleven of whom were female members.

As Vic Blaxill stood down from his CFI role and planned to migrate south, he was presented with a special award for his distinguished services to the club.

Another famous face hanging up his gloves in 2000 was Hamish Wotherspoon. Hamish had been CFI for many years and latterly he and his wife took up summer residency in a large static caravan on site. From here, Hamish was able to fulfil his latest job of Chief Winch Driver and many a pilot setting out for an early morning badge attempt had cause to be grateful for Hamish's willingness to launch them within a hour of dawn. *"Aye, I can get yeh intae the sky, boys, but efter that, you're on your own"*.

By this time, a number of the cadets who had soloed in the previous years were stepping up to attempt bronze and silver badges. One such cadet was (Red) Raymond Roberts and he takes up the story of his silver badge duration leg:

I had spent the last week staying at Portmoak in the good old Cadet Caravan whose heater had just broken down. As I lay there one night, with mild hypothermia setting in, I decided that sometime this visit, I would go for silver duration - the five hours. The weather had been forecast as a strong westerly with occasional showers, good enough for a five hours attempt. I spent two solid hours getting to grips with the EW Barograph, reading the manual and trying to figure out what it actually did. I cracked the EW problem, bought some Kit-Kats and juice and found some warm gloves and a hat. I now had an assortment of essentials that I could just pick up and take, should I suddenly find a chance to do the duration flight.

From the very start I knew that Wednesday would be a disaster. I had overslept as a result from staying up the night before. It was almost 2:00 p.m. before I managed to get K8

(CTZ) on line and ready, only just enough time to fit five hours in before last landing at 19:00. I was tired and irritated at the amount of time it had taken me to get ready. Foolishly I took off anyway despite my condition (the obvious symptoms that I would not last five hours in that state). Thirty-four minutes later I was landing in a rather crowded North Field after having been flushed out of the sky. It had been a frustrating day but I had learned many lessons and tomorrow I would make full use of these experiences.

I had gone to bed early on the Wednesday night and woke up early feeling ready to go. I had put the K8 into the hangar last so that it was first to come out and get DI'd. I put my collection of essentials in the cockpit and dragged the K8 on to line. The wind was a light westerly and the Discus and DG pilots were waiting for the wind to increase but I thought that it would be sufficient enough to keep me and the K8 up, so I thought I'd give it a go. Ten minutes after that decision I had reached my first goal - sitting in the K8 with everything ready to go; EW barograph flashing, food and drink, sufficient pee bags and me ready to go, focused on the upcoming task with no nagging worries of "did I do that" or "should I....." etc. I urge all future duration attempts to try and get to this stage, it makes life so much easier. I had a good launch to 1400ft and headed for Bishop.

As it turned out, only part of the bowl worked and I had to do constant s-turns in it just to stay airborne until the wind picked up. Unfortunately when it did pick up, I could tell from the drift that it had gone near Northerly. I had to try to get to West Lomond or else I would have to land. Fortunately, it did work and I got up to 1800 ft without much problem. The first problem that I came across was the fact that my backside was killing me and I'd only been up for an hour. I know a K8 isn't exactly comfortable but I could hardly feel my poor backside and no matter which way I sat, the throbbing got worse. The problem was quite literally a pain in the a***! I had to put up with it though and forced my mind to accept the gruelling pain inflicted upon me. Thermals popped up now and again and I used the height at the top of these thermals to let the aircraft gain lots of height and then slowly float down away from West Lomond. This gave me 5 minutes or so where I could use minimum effort to fly and thus conserve energy and not get too tired. The sky kept changing and with it the conditions. It was interesting to observe these changes over a longish period of time while in the air.

Three and a half hours into the task, I noticed some medium strength showers approaching from the North West. I would have to land if I didn't do something sensible. I resolved the situation by gaining as much height as possible from a thermal that had thoughtfully developed near me. I dived through what I thought was the weakest part of the shower, back towards the ridge. I arrived on a reluctantly working north face of West Lomond having lost 1500+ ft! I will now never underestimate the power of water on the wings. Little problems like these plus small challenges like making something of a very small wave bar that would often appear in different places, made the flight quite interesting and I found that 30 or 45 minutes had passed virtually unnoticed.

The time came an hour after drinking my Irn Bru when that marvelous call of nature came. This was another new experience. The advantage I had on that day was that I was sitting relatively upright in the k8. The major disadvantage I had was that the pee bag had a leak. While drying my face with a pair of gloves I vowed to foresee these problems in the future! The time spent from then until the five hours mark was spent pushing out, losing height whilst trying to find wave and then returning to the ridge and topping up with height. Radio calls from the ground enquiring my whereabouts were hampered by the fact that I could not transmit. I was staying up for longer in the hope of getting silver height but I couldn't tell anyone. I over flew Portmoak *waggling the wings of CTZ as vigorously as I could. The yaw string was doing a windscreen wiper impression but hopefully those on the ground would know I was safe. Unknown to me, Tiny Irving in his Discus had thoughtfully radioed the apparently frantic people on the ground letting them know I was safe.*

After half an hour more of failed attempts at contacting wave, I realised I was making mistakes and decided that silver height just had to wait for another day. I touched down in the south field 6 hours and 2 minutes after setting off. Someone kindly towed the glider away for me as I dragged my numb and aching body over to the clubhouse for an eagerly awaited cup of hot tea. I recounted my flight, and my tips for a five-hour attempt:

-Take along plenty of food and drink - dehydration can set in surprisingly quickly.

-Don't set off too tired - ideally get a good night's sleep the night before.

-Choose an aircraft that you are comfortable in - comfort is everything.

-Don't attempt the 5 hours in scratchy conditions - You will not last! Ideally, a good westerly with little traffic on the ridge.

-Test out your pee bags with some water over a sink – very important!!!

- Set out early in the day if possible and get everything ready the day before.

-Take a barograph for evidence.

-Make sure no one wants the aircraft so that you don't get called down half way. Good Luck!

As my duties on the board became more clear, I decided to resurrect the club magazine - *Portmoak Press* - to assist with membership communications. After about three or four months in the preparation stage, my first issue of *Portmoak Press* (Vol2K) hit the streets in October 2000. This issue had over

300 copies printed and *Portmoak Press* was on its way once again.

Walking On Air was also enjoying some welcome publicity. Following the successful modifications to the ASK21 by Joe Fisher, news soon got around that there was an excellent facility for disabled pilots at Portmoak. Various day-visits from the spinal injuries units at Edinburgh and Glasgow helped rehabilitate a number of their patients and a few went on to become permanent members of the club and experience the joys and excitement of gliding. Of course, no organisation can operate without a willing band of volunteers, and WOA was no different. One such volunteer was Les Ladomery. He produced an article, originally written in his native Hungarian, then translated to Dutch for "Termiek" magazine, then into English for the first issue of *Portmoak Press*:

> *Most people believe that gliding is only for the able-bodied and that people who have become wheelchair-bound through a terrible misfortune are not able to fly, except as passengers. Nothing is further from the truth, as I discovered at the Scottish Gliding Centre. Let me tell you about it.*
>
> *Having worked and lived in a number of countries, I finally retired in Scotland with my family. As someone keen on flying, the first thing I did was to look for a gliding club. I found one in an excellent location near Loch Leven, 25 miles north of Edinburgh. A large field which lies under two hills offering westerly, northerly and southerly faces ideal for hill soaring. In addition the Grampian Mountain range some sixty miles north west, produces excellent waves which can carry gliders aloft to thousands of ft. Thermals also abound during the warmer months. The Scottish Gliding Centre (SGC) is under first class management by people dedicated to the sport. Little wonder that the SGC has many and frequent visitors from other clubs.*
>
> *At the SGC, I was made immediately welcome. The members were very helpful and friendly and accepted me, a*

Hungarian born Australian, without reservation. I have found Scottish people to be kind and considerate. Not surprisingly, in 1998 the Scottish Gliding Union (principal Club and owner of the SGC) founded a charity aimed at making gliding available to the disabled. The charity is called Walking on Air, a voluntary organisation run by its own members and dedicated to making gliding available to disabled persons, not just as an "experience" through joy flights, but as regular pilot training on the same footing as able-bodied persons. The stated aims of Walking on Air are: to introduce as many disabled people as possible to the joys of unpowered-flight; to train disabled people to fly solo and to gain all available badges and licences recognised by the British Gliding Association (BGA), including training as instructors both for disabled and able-bodied persons; to bring cross-country gliding over the spectacular scenery of Scotland to the widest possible audience; to introduce disabled people to the thrills of aerobatic flight; to aid disabled pilots in the purchase, modification and operation of their own single-seater gliders and to promote gliding as a sport accessible to all.

Walking on Air operates a modern two-seater fibre-glass ASK21 glider, adapted by the manufacturer Alexander Schleicher to be entirely hand-controlled. Joe Fisher, an instructor pilot at the SGC, designed the modification. A lever placed next to the airbrake replaces the rudder pedals, while the airbrake is arranged in such a way that it can be locked in several positions, allowing the left hand to return to operating the rudder. The adaptations have been approved by the BGA and, in part, by the German LBA. These slight modifications still allow the normal foot-operated rudder pedals to be connected for pilots with normal leg movement, or isolated from the system for pilots who cannot use their legs or who suffer from muscular spasm of the legs. The re-conversion only takes a few minutes. At the time of writing this article, one disabled pilot, David Nisbet, is flying solo and is preparing himself for the BGA bronze 'C' badge. Another, Alistair Murray, is very near to going solo. Others are making good progress. "Gliding is a friendly and welcoming sport, each flight an exhilarating experience" say Alistair and David. "Unlike with other sports for the disabled, once you are strapped into the cockpit of a glider you can fly or compete on an equal basis with able-bodied pilots. While soaring over the countryside, we forget that we are wheelchair-bound, we feel serene and free. It is a wonderful experience which we recommend to all disabled and able-bodied people alike".

Walking on Air is organising several holiday gliding courses during this year and next. These courses are open to any disabled person, who has a working knowledge of English and has adequate use of his or her arms and hands. The Clubhouse is fully accessible by wheelchair and offers meals and refreshments. Accommodation is available with separate showers and toilets, all wheelchair friendly. Disabled persons from The Netherlands and from other countries are welcome to join the courses, to have individual training or just come and see us glide and have a gliding experience. You can find out about costs and other details by telephoning, e-mailing or visiting Walking on Air's website. I hope that, if you are disabled, you will find the work of the Scottish Gliding Centre an inspiration to learn to fly in unpowered aircraft. Gliding Clubs the world over may also wish, like the Scots and to my knowledge the Germans and the Americans, to set up voluntary organisations to help our disabled friends who would like to join us among the birds in silent flight, free to walk on air.

Edinburgh University Gliding Club (EUGC) was also growing in popularity at Portmoak. After a successful freshers' week publicity campaign, scores of students arrived at the site and the EUGC gliders and instructors were fully occupied conducting trial flights. Their bright yellow painted fleet consisted of an ASK13 two-seater and a single-seat ASK8. This K8 displayed an interesting piece of artwork on the rudder – a cartoon dog wearing goggles and a scarf – and was affectionately known as "Snoopy".

Much needed maintenance work on the winch was completed during September but, due to some excellent planning and hard work by the winch drivers, downtime was kept to two and a half days. This was no mean feat especially when the operation included, amongst other things, the removal of both drum assemblies – each weighing over 500lbs.

One recent addition to the winch-driving team was Pete Benbow and he wrote the following article for *Portmoak Press*:

How I become a Winch man.
Having reached forty years of age I decided to take a year's sabbatical. I was debating what to do over the forthcoming year, should I make a serious attempt on the Munros, perhaps return to sailing, maybe re-solo after 22 years absence from gliding. My wife forced the matter by arranging for me to take a trial flight at Portmoak. Trial membership and a week's course quickly followed.

Shortly after joining the club, during an afternoon gliding session whilst waiting for a flight I was asked to 'run cables'. Being a novice I was unaware that running cables is similar to having a contagious disease; it is an easy job to pick up but once caught, you are put into a form of quarantine as your erstwhile chums melt away from you so as to avoid the chore. I watched from the white mobile as my fickle friends deserted me for their lunch. During the next few hours of waiting by the winch for a set of cables to become available I chatted to the incumbent winch driver. We mulled over the design and build of the winch. We covered the foibles of winch driving. We discussed pole-bending and non-pole-bending pilots. We wafted through the vagaries of the weather. We touched on the matter of a vacancy having arising for a part time winch driver. I was younger and more foolish then, intoxicated by the glamour of a winch drivers' work, I applied for the job. Several weeks later I found myself sitting alone in the winch cab in a blustery cross wind on a Saturday morning contemplating hurling a human being in a fabric covered bag of sticks several hundred metres into the sky. It was then that I realised how it must have felt to awaken with a hangover in the rat infested bilge of a Man-o'-war with the dread realisation that the new pals you were drinking with last night were in fact a press gang. Still, it is good work if you can get it. And now for the serious bit ....

How to save a winch drivers eye-sight (and sense of humour).

Requesting a launch from the winch driver and signalling the launch is a simple task. It consists of a radio call to indicate what is to be launched and on which cable. Followed by a lamp signaling the 'take-up-slack' and 'all-out' or 'stop-signals'. Alas! There is a human tendency to add complexity and confusion to even the simplest tasks.

When you are operating the radio at the launch point to request the launch of a glider on a specific cable, consider the content of the radio call that you are making. There is a correct way to do this, which is to make the call "Winch, Base, <Glider type>, <Which Cable>". The winch driver will respond with "<Glider type>, <Which Cable>". Always make your request in ONE transmission. It couldn't be simpler. Consider the timing of the radio call that you are making. It is best to make the call after the cable has been attached to the glider and the glider's wings are level. (It is inadvisable to make the call before the cable is attached as there is the possibility of a mistake leading to a cable becoming live whilst it is being handled.) Once the winch driver has *confirmed his receipt of your request he has to focus on your signal lamp whilst awaiting your next signal. If the interval between the radio call and the "take-up-slack" signal is protracted it can place quite a strain on the drivers eyes and sense of humour (particularly if staring into a declining sun).*

A prolonged delay combined with a forgetful driver may cause confusion over which cable/glider combination is being used. Bear in mind that it only takes the driver three or four seconds to start the winch engine, engage the requested drum and start taking up slack. If after making the launch request a delay occurs then, please, inform the driver that a delay is expected (perhaps consider abandoning the launch and re-starting from the initial radio request).

Keen to get as many stories as possible for *Portmoak Press*, I convinced one older member to tell me about his early experiences in gliding at the SGU. Jim Burgess and I sat down with a cuppa in the clubhouse and I scribbled my notes as best I could. Little did I know that Jim's story would spawn the idea to write this book. The story appeared in the magazine under the heading of "Stories from Yesteryear":

On the first day with my editor hat on, while seeking out stories in the clubhouse, Jim Burgess came over and relayed some interesting stories about the early days of the gliding club. For instance, he told me that the early club mag was called Uplift and was first issued in 1958. The editor, in those days was Denis Bryce. "But he drowned in the loch" said Jim. Not, as I assumed, by diving a glider into the loch. "He was a bit of a joker." recalled Jim. "I was up at the winch end and Denis came up with a couple of his pals. He took off his jacket and threw it on the ground. 'Come on Jim, we're going for a swim' he said. But I couldn't swim so I left them to it. Anyway, Denis got into difficulties and everyone thought he was fooling around, but he wasn't and he drowned."
What about the early days?, I asked.

"When we were based at Balado," said Jim. "we had thirty members. As a new member, I had to pay two guineas joining fee and the annual subscription was £3. I remember joining a holiday course in 1952. There were eight of us on the course, and the instructor was Tom Davidson. It cost £14, was for seven days flying and included full board at the Kirklands hotel in Kinross. There were three of us to a room and we slept on Z-beds."

"What about the flying?" I asked.

"Well," said Jim. "I got a passenger flight in a T21 first. It had an open cockpit and it was all over quite quickly. The real training started when I got into the SG38. This was the School Glider no. 38 and was brought over from Germany after the war. We did low, medium and high 'hops'. They fixed a length of square section timber onto the leading edge of the wings to reduce the amount of lift and I was told to tuck my trousers into my socks and turn my flat-cap back to front. The winch cable was connected and I was off for my first low-hop, or ground slide. I only got a couple of ft off the ground and could only practice small lateral movements. I remember at the time thinking that this was just like a 'witch flying a broomstick'. The lump of wood was taken off and I tried medium hops and, finally, my first high hop. This was to about 250ft and I had to land ahead – no instruments, and no turning! Anyway, this enabled me to claim my 'A' badge. My 'B' badge was achieved in the Kirby Cadet by proving that I could do a left and right circuit. The first 'real' glider was the Tutor – it had an altimeter and an Air Speed Indicator!"

I asked Jim how he travelled to the club.

"I used to get the bus from Dundee, change to another bus in Perth and then walk to Balado from Kinross. One day, I missed the last bus back and George Whyte flew me, in his Piper Cub, to a field at his brother's farm just outside Dundee. I didn't drive because I failed my driving test back then."

As a last comment, Jim told me about the time "they" raised the cost of a high tea from 3/6 to 5/6 (for you youngsters out there, 3/6 was three shillings and six pence, about 17p today). The club members protested by boycotting the canteen and eating their sandwiches in the car park!

One aspiring contributor to *Portmoak Press*, for whatever reason, chose to remain anonymous and offered up the following story under the pseudonym of "Slarty Bartfast":

 <u>Man bites dog</u>
   A man biting a dog doesn't make much of a gliding story but it does seem to our intrepid reporter that the following incident has a similar smack of poetic justice.
   Rumour has it that an incident along these lines occurred recently when an instructor, who may wish to remain relatively anonymous, was handed the opportunity of demonstrating a premature launch failure of the winching variety with a very, very, early trainee pilot on board. So far, nothing very unusual in the tale, but it appears that it was the said trainee pilot who occasioned the premature failure of launch by pulling "the bung" with no prior warning and certainly not by arrangement. Our intrepid reporter has been assured that this was indeed a totally unplanned incident and that it succeeded in immediately grabbing the instructor's full attention. As the instructor involved said during his subsequent interview with the Portmoak Press's roving reporters "always expect the unexpected". The pupil was apparently considerably taken aback by the sequence of events which followed his pulling of the bung. From our reporter's short discussion with him it would appear unlikely that he will repeat these actions in the immediate future. The sharp bang as the cable released and the following sequence of events leading to his safe arrival on the ground appear to have left a notable impression on him, although he had for many years watched practice cable breaks from the

ground. Fortunately he appears to wish to continue with gliding although I did not ask him if he was looking forward to cable break practice later in his career.

This tale is not told to embarrass any of the people involved but to serve as a reminder to us all of how quickly circumstances can change, not necessarily by our own hand. As mentioned earlier in this item "Anonymous", the instructor, uses the phrase "always expect the unexpected" and has amply demonstrated that he was ready when it happened to him, how ready are you?

The annual Christmas party was held at the clubhouse and awards were collected by the following people:

Richard Allcoat & Colin Hamilton (Thorburn Two-Seater).
Kevin Hook (Boyle Altitude).
Tony Brown & George Turnbull (Andy Penswick).
John Williams & Kevin Hook (Parker Distance) – joint winners.
John Williams (Docherty Handicapped Distance).
John Williams (Sutherland Out & Return).
Z. Goudie (Lomond Triangle).
Kevin Hook (Maclay Championship).
Steve Nutley (Peter Copeland).
John Galloway (Hot Wings).
Andrew Bates (Nick Wales).
Joe Fisher (Darren Powell).
Chris Robinson (Silver Salver).

That intrepid reporter, Slarty Bartfast was at the awards evening and he penned the following item for *Portmoak Press*:

As myself and Mrs. Bartfast were both unable to avoid this year's "bit of a do", in the form of the club's annual dinner and presentations, we have recorded our thoughts and observations on this memorable event.

It all seemed to begin sedately enough but, to our relief, things began to liven up half way through the meal when members' skills at origami were put on display. We are pleased to be able to report that design and construction of various flying machines was varied and demonstrated a generally high level of skill. However, flying accuracy and ability to strike the assigned target were sadly lacking. We have recorded a précis of the opinions of our fellow diners as to possible causes: -

Drink, Age, Presence of spouse, Inebriation, Quality of paper available, Lack of drink, Lack of presence of spouse, presence of someone else's spouse.

One of our members, who has dined at her majesty's pleasure many the time and oft, displayed notable skills in design and construction but even his efforts were outclassed for accuracy and predictability of trajectory by the daud-o-breid (lump of bread) bomb. Joe the Fish has declared that classes in paper dart construction (with and without payload) and in determination of flight path will be held in the club bar on Friday nights prior to next year's bash. Possible practice targets, culled from apparent targets are; designated recipient, recipient's trifle, low cut ladies dresses and half-cut ladies. Although professional entertainment was "laid on", our own David was persuaded to demonstrate his yodelling and remained stoic throughout. All present owe a vote of thanks to the cadets for their show.

Throughout the evening Steve, Irene, John, Sandra and their helpers put in a whole lot of effort and put up with a fair bit of banter and nonsense. Thanks to all of them the rest of us had a super evening.

Prizes were then presented and our congratulations go to all who received an award. "Stack em high" Hook did very well indeed and Neil Irving bore receipt of the "nae luck award" very well.

The evening drew to a close, the attendees went home and the drinking classes arrived.

Chapter 18
2001 – 2002
Puddle Paddlers, a BGA Diploma and the Storms

Portmoak weather at the beginning of 2001 was wetter than ever and the airfield had more puddles than grass. John Henry, as adventurous as ever, was seen paddling his canoe across one particularly large puddle. When he made landfall at the other side, he declared that the club should change its name to the Scottish Puddle Paddlers Union!

Three Edinburgh University pundits were keen to try out their newly acquired syndicate glider but the poor weather meant they would have to be patient. The January issue of the new *Portmoak Press* revealed their story:

Pigs will Fly
Guy, Andrew and Tim have had a moment of madness and broken into the big, scary world of glider ownership. After a few random conversations in pubs we decided that buying was the way to go. Barely a month later we are the proud owners of SZD-30 Pirat, Charlie Bravo November, BGA no. 1413, which will henceforth be known as Piglet. The name was chosen in honour of the small Winnie the Pooh character who told us to do it.

Piglet is a lovely example of late 60's Polish agricultural engineering (she is very strong but looks like a tractor). She will be getting acclimatised to the cold Scottish climate very soon. Many thanks to Colin Golding for inspecting her for us and to Andrew's parents for towing her up to Portmoak.

Some SGU members did manage to get into the air during that long winter and an intrepid *Portmoak Press* reporter was on hand to witness some strange goings-on:

A Short Tale

Well, not quite, as this is more a tale of two of our vertically challenged members. As you know from my last article I don't name the individuals involved, but the tale goes something like this.

Towards the end of a bad day with no flying due to rain squalls the weather cleared late in the afternoon and aircraft were dragged out of the hangar as quickly as possible to make the most of the remaining couple of hours of daylight. What a delight it was to watch enthusiastic members pulling out the two-seaters and D.I.'ing them, but alas due to the way the east side of the hangar had been packed the Juniors and the club K8 were far from readily accessible. Nothing if not resourceful and fair desperate to fly, one of our shorter members of a Bronze hue with a predilection towards Cap 413, collared a Full Cat and obtained his gracious consent to accompany him in the DG505.

The battery and parachutes were put into the DG505, it was DI'd, and taken to the launch point. Although anxious to get off, there had been no rushing and so both gentlemen were settled and relaxed as the aircraft was brought on line and pre-flight checks completed. Canopies were closed, a brake check made and the cable was clipped on and take up slack was called. However, before "all out" could be given the Bronze Boy called a halt and pulled the bung due to canopy misting. Canopies were cleared and at the second attempt the launch went ahead successfully, the wheel was popped up and they got on with the flight.

The flight went well, but as another member (a vertically challenged provider of ethnic dress), wanted a wee shot before it got dark the decision was made to return to the field. Ah, how things can change! The aviators got to high key point alright, the Bronze Boy in the front thought "time to pop the wheel down" (that so-and-so in the back hasn't said a cheep about it just like all the other instructors) and the trouble started. You see the short arms didn't seem to get the undercarriage lever forwards firmly enough to be sure that it had locked and there had not been the comforting sound of the over centre lock going home. The situation was briefly discussed and the Ayrshire Cat in the back had a go at lowering the wheel with the same result. Prolonged discussion was now out of the question as finals were being turned and the decision was made to land with the undercarriage "down" as the lever appeared to be fully forwards and the handle was vertical, however the possibility of it collapsing on arrival was duly noted. The landing was held off as long as possible and the wheel stayed down. Both aviators were grateful not to have the difficulty of getting the aircraft back to the hangar and having to face Chris Robinson with the undercarriage doors in a poly bag.

After the incident both of the guys involved believed that the problem was due the shortness of their arms which prevented them from pushing the undercarriage lever firmly enough and but nevertheless they reported the incident. Since then there has been repeat of the situation and a cursory examination of the undercarriage revealed no obvious fault. At the time of writing, Joe Fisher's decision is that further investigation is required and that the undercarriage should not be retracted in the mean time. Time moves on and this information may be out of date by time of publication so check before you fly the DG505.

Like the Cat says "always expect the unexpected"

One day in early January, a small band of fierce sheep had found their way onto the South field and a merry group of faithful members could be seen "rounding them up". At first, they split into pairs (the members – not the sheep!) and ran this way and that. The sheep didn't look too perturbed and coincidently ambled back to their field through a convenient gap in the fence. As our satisfied troop made their way back to the club-house, the "ring-leader" sheep could be seen keekin' between the trailers and as soon as the coast was clear led the rest of them back onto the South field. The troops trooped back and this time made loud noises of the sheep-scaring kind. Ah, this did the trick – the sheep ran all the way home. Or did they? Of course not, they simply used the far trailer as a low-level turning point and were back munching our grass faster than ever. The third attempt involved the use of a car, as well as the determined group. It all looked good fun but as usual, the sheep returned to finish their lunch.

Enter Adi Von-Gontard and his dog "Max". Adi had found Max at the local dog pound and had picked him as a pet. It wasn't until later that he found out that this "rescue" dog was a highly trained, albeit out of work, sheepdog. Over the months, Adi even purchased a few sheep of his own so that Max could keep his hand/paw in. What followed on the airfield was like something out of "One man and his Dog" (Sorry Adi, this is one of those BBC2 programmes we used to watch in the UK – Ed). Max, who a couple of minutes ago was just an eager pet dog, suddenly turned into an efficient sheep-rounding-up pet dog. This was poetry in motion, yes – even better than the ASH25 in a tight thermal turn! As soon as the sheep saw Max, they knew this was the real thing – not a bunch of daft old folk. The boss-sheep immediately led the flock back to their field and they haven't been seen since. Well done Adi, but especially well done Max.

As the weather improved and SGU pundits began to plan cross-country flights, the whole country encountered a Foot and Mouth epidemic. Ever keen to support the farming community, the club declared a ban on all forms of cross-country flying in line with the BGA recommendations - to remove the risk of landing in, and contaminating, farmers' fields.

Another non-flying activity which had been causing concern for SGU officials over the last year or so was the challenge to the planning permission for the erection of a house at the equestrian centre at the east edge of the north field. The latest position was reported in the local press:

Airfield saga comes to an end

The long running saga over the plan to build a house near the runway at Portmoak Airfield looks to be over.

The Scottish Gliding Union has been contesting the plan on safety grounds for almost two years and at a meeting of Perth and Kinross Development Control Committee on Wednesday, councillors finally agreed with the Gliding Club.

Four years ago, permission was granted for the establishment of an equestrian centre near the airfield, despite opposition from the Gliding Club.

They argued then that horse riding and gliding were incompatible but the plans were passed and then the proprietors of the equestrian centre asked for consent to build a house near the runway.

After protracted negotiations, the committee agreed what they considered to be a compromise by giving planning permission for a house tied in with a section 75 agreement restricting equestrian activities below gliding flight paths.

The proprietors declined this and instead appealed to the Scottish Executive over a previous refusal of planning approval but having lost that appeal in December, they turned to the council asking for a resurrection of the original planning application which had been approved subject to conditions.

This request was put to the committee on Wednesday but after discussion they decided to withdraw the compromise offer and refuse the application.

The refusal was made on four grounds. Firstly the house was prejudicial to public safety because of its close proximity to gliding activities; and secondly the house would be a development within an area of great landscape value that had not been justified on the basis of operational need.

In addition, the house was contrary to the council's housing in the countryside policy and the erection of a new building would be detrimental to the visual amenities of the area.

As summer approached, ace reporter, Slarty Bartfast was once again on hand to observe the goings on at one of the weekly courses:

Dumped

Once upon a time, well the other week, there was a course for Ab Initios at dear old downtown Portmoak. A nice experienced full (have I misspelled that) cat was in the process of instructing a well on the way to solo gentleman. So far it had been an uneventful flight, the winch launch had gone well under the control of Ab who on completion of the launch had made an acceptable turn south towards Benarty and Cemetery Ridge to try to take advantage of the light Northerly wind. The flight was uneventful in the late afternoon with the Cat having a wee rest in the back (was it a cat nap I wonder) where he couldn't be seen although he was making usual sort noises that Cats do when there is an Ab Initio in the front. After a short while it was obvious that the wind wasn't playing the game and that no hill lift of any significance was to be had. As usual the game was played out by sailing gaily up and down the beat until height was getting short for getting back home comfortably. The Cat said nothing as he was probably playing the old game of wait and see. Would Ab realise in time and turn back now with just enough height to make a full circuit? Would Ab leave it a bit late and cut in part way down the downwind leg? Would Ab blow it altogether and not notice the slow loss of height with the inevitable comment coming from the back at the last moment.

Just at this moment fate dealt its hand and the glider flew into a weak thermal. "Ah"! said the Cat "that was a thermal", by way of a passing comment, similar to "isn't that an awfully pretty young lady running for that bus, I do hope that she doesn't get a black eye". Ab interpreted this as "get stuck into the thermal" as by this time he was getting awfully conscious of the size of the electricity pylons and so he cranked the glider over to the best of his ability. The fates are indeed cruel and poor old Ab not being too sure as to which wing had lifted had a fifty-fifty chance of being right, but of course he wasn't. Instead of the copious quantities of lift he was hoping for to rescue the situation he found sink – BIG TIME. The sudden turning of the aircraft took the Cat somewhat by surprise and by the time he had gathered his wits and made the clarion call of "I have control" it was all too late to get back to the airfield. A field was duly selected and a successful landing made.

Tea was a little late that night as the Cat and the course members dismantled the glider, packed it into its box and returned it to the airfield.

Like the Deputy Big Cat says, "always expect the unexpected".

My own gliding was progressing at a reasonable pace, I had gained my Bronze C and was now working towards my Silver badge. The first of the three tasks achieved was the 5 hour duration leg and, as editor of the club mag, I felt obliged to write about it:

I had been away in England all week and had checked Friday's forecast from more than twenty sources (TV, radio, Internet etc.). I was hoping to attempt my five hours on the Friday, but the early forecasts were not too convincing. This was the middle of May and the whole country had just experienced the hottest weekend of the year, with an area of high pressure sitting slap bang in the middle. I was hoping for at least some wind, preferably from the west, so that I could get a good start off Bishop Hill. Anyway, I was still unconvinced as I drove up through Cumbria towards Scotland on Thursday afternoon. Just south of Carlisle, I remembered that the BBC Radio Scotland "Forecast for climbers and sailors" had been moved from the 18:56 slot to 17:56. I quickly retuned my car radio and heard some very promising news. Tomorrow (18th May) was going to be affected by an area of low pressure in the North of Scotland and the area between the River Tay and River Forth would have a Westerly wind with some sunshine in the afternoon. That was it, decision made, and tomorrow I would attempt my Silver duration.

I was first to arrive, around 8 o'clock, and put my name on the flying list. I wanted one of the Juniors for this epic flight. Next, I signed out one of the club's EW barographs (regular readers will remember my Silver height flight – without a barograph!).

A couple of course members had just ordered their breakfast so I knew that I couldn't expect any help from them for at least half-an-hour. OK, get the keys for the hangar and at least get the launch-caravan and trucks moved out, or so I thought!

I unlocked the padlocks and managed to open three of the four roller doors. The fourth one decided to throw its chain off the sprocket, with the door half open. Not a good start, but undaunted I used the framework behind the white mobile (4x4) to climb up and repair the chain. Once inside the hangar, I checked the service board to see what aircraft were available. My favourite Junior (FUS) was U/S due to a broken cable release, but at least the other one was serviceable. Next problem, where was it? It was in the middle, behind a Falke and a K13 – so they would need to be moved. While waiting for help, I decided to get batteries and a parachute. As I put the batteries in place I noticed a hole in the instrument panel where the audio vario would normally go. Oh well, it would be novel to try this without an audio.

After a lot of pushing and pulling, the Junior was finally on line, having been duly D.I.'d. As I declared my intentions to Bob Petrie and received a briefing (watch out for some *showers coming through before lunch-time, and make sure your launch time gets logged accurately), I could see a couple of club members looking rather depressed that I was planning to take the Junior away for so long. Sorry people, but sometimes a man's go to do what a man's go to do.*

I stowed my maps, barograph, water, sandwiches, pee bags etc. and launched at 10:35.

The first hour or so was spent in hill lift off the face of Bishop. I couldn't get much higher that 2000ft but didn't really miss the audio vario. The second hour was more interesting. I could see showers coming in from the West and had to dodge around them as they approached Bishop Hill. Fortunately they seemed to skirt past to the South, over the airfield, but at one time I was convinced that I would have to abandon my attempt if the weather looked like closing in. The third hour saw a complete change in the weather, now we had sunshine and obvious thermals popping up to the West. This was much better, I pushed out towards the motorway and was soon experimenting with the thermals – I even switched on the T&S to see how accurately I could fly "on the ball". I regularly took on water and food, and regularly got rid of water too. I checked my navigation from my maps, I looked at various fields to "select" appropriate ones – only practising, you understand, as I was now at 4000ft and having a great time. During the last couple of hours, other gliders sniffed around and occasionally we shared thermals. One single-seat pilot flew past with his retractable undercarriage still down. I couldn't resist a radio call to tell him. Sorry, but I was only jealous that my wheel was of the fixed type. I hope he remembered to put it down again for his landing.

I even tried practising my turn-point aiming. Wow! It's not as easy as it looks, and I probably lost too much height trying to get my wing to point at the crossroads at Glenfarg. All good stuff, with plenty of height to play with. I took one more thermal and drifted back towards the airfield. I was hoping to get a Silver height but after almost five hours, I was more than satisfied with my flight.

I called the launch caravan to confirm my launch time, the current time, and my time in the air (well, you've got to be sure about these things, don't you), and finally touched down at 15:42 – after 5hrs 7mins.

I had a very comfortable flight, and I'm pleased to say that I think I was well prepared for this one – both mentally and physically. What's next? The other two legs, of course.

Activities back at the club became focussed on the refurbishment of the front office and the procurement of a portacabin to house the accounts department and the flight briefing room.

On a sadder note, news came through that Hamish Wotherspoon had died following a battle with cancer. A memorial plaque was fitted to the door of the winch as a mark of respect for this greatly missed pilot, instructor, CFI and winch driver.

As mentioned earlier in this book, it is often common for offspring to follow their parents footsteps into occupations or hobbies. Airline pilot and intrepid glider pilot Keith Buchan's daughter Sarah was no exception. She had cause to celebrate her 16th birthday, and she put pen to paper for the club mag:

Going Solo - at last!
The 9th of July 2001, the start of Cadet week and the finishing touches to the training card being signed off - hopefully! The weekdays passed amazingly quickly and, before I knew it, Friday had arrived. The only exercise I'd done was spinning, so, on the Friday evening, Neil McAulay (bravely) got in the back of the K21 to do cable-breaks with me. Four or five "breaks" later and my card was complete.

So, the 24th of July arrived and this was it, my sixteenth birthday and the day (I hoped) I'd go solo. Dad made me get up extra early to ensure I caught an instructor and a glider first thing - to get it over and done with. Gliders all out and ready, in true Portmoak style, and everyone goes for breakfast! "Great" I think, "a chance to psyche myself up." Not a chance, as I soon discovered.

Sitting, chatting away, I spy Ian Dandie appear. In he comes and says, "Right! Let's go, there's your glider sitting waiting." Totally taken aback I go, get into the glider and off we go for a check-flight. Once back at the launch point, Ian takes his parachute out of the glider and claims that I am going on my own "because you've scared me enough!" So, not having a chance to work myself up, here I was, getting the cable attached. Wings level, and dad watching from the launch-point, "All out." was called and off I went. At the top, the cable left me on my own… "Right, let's go." I thought, and as normal I went off and soared the hill for 20 minutes. "Fine" I thought as I landed and dad came to tow me back. Then Ian said that I should only have done a circuit! Oops, sorry Ian. I was chuffed as it had turned out and I was smiling non-stop for the rest of the day.

So, the hard work from me and the greying instructors (you know who you are!), and the money from dad, had finally paid off. I'd done it, and loved every minute.

Sarah's flying progressed and, in no time at all…

The epic (well!) Junior Flight

The day had come when Bob Petrie told me that I'd done enough solos in the K21 and I was now a Junior pilot. "Oh God!" I thought, the stories I had heard about what could happen when flying this single-seater had terrified me!

So, bravely I got in and got my bearings (and briefing) before going on-line.

"All out" was yet again called and I went up, at least I went up for the first 600ft or so, then I hit the wind-shear! The speed jumped from 60 kt up towards 80 in a flash and as I was pulling back, the cable broke. As taught, I put the nose down, recovered and landed safely. Flustered and taken by surprise, I got towed back to the launch-point and told to go again. I didn't want to go again so, one week later, when the conditions were better I jumped in and soared for 20 minutes, loving every minute of it. The hill was scratchy so I decided to go back and let someone else have a flight. The Junior is a lovely glider (now that I have had a whole flight). You'll be lucky to get me out of it! Fly it while you still have the chance.

Recipients of the annual awards at the end of 2001 included:
B.Scougall & E.Crosbie (Thorburn Two-Seater)
K.Hook (Boyle Altitude – 20,864ft)
C.Robinson (Andy Penswick)
K.Hook (Parker Distance)
K.Hook (Docherty Handicap Distance)
J.Williams (Sutherland Out & Return)
J.Williams (Maclay Championship)
K.Hook (Peter Copland)
J.Williams (Hot Wings)
C.Robinson (Darren Powell)
A.Gordon (Silver Salver)

By the time the January 2002 issue of *Portmoak Press* was ready for publication the circulation had increased to more than 300 SGU members via e-mail, and to every BGA registered club in the UK. A small number of paper copies were printed and left in the clubhouse for non-electronic users and archive copies were available from the club web-site.

That first issue of 2002 proudly acknowledged a prestigious award for an old stalwart of the club – Jim O'Donnell.

BGA Diploma

Jim O'Donnell is well known in gliding circles. He started his career at the SGU's site at Balado in 1954 where he earned his instructor's rating from Ann Welch in 1958. As a dedicated member, he was largely instrumental in effecting our move to Portmoak in the late 1950s and was heavily involved in the major construction of hangars, roads and bridges.

He has served the club as CFI and as Chairman and was for many years the mainstay of our instructor team. In addition, he served as an ATC civilian instructor from 1960 to 1970, latterly as an A1 category instructor.

In recent years he has almost single-handedly acted as instructor and mentor to our Tuesday club whose membership is of mainly older but none-the-less enthusiastic pilots who make themselves available for instruction mid week.

A recent hospitalisation however has brought to our attention the fact that Jim must be coming to the end of his distinguished gliding career. Although now in his seventies, even after this upset, Jim shows little intention of easing off and continues his efforts to assist the club and gliding in general by his example and dedication as an instructor and patriarchal club member.

Well done Jim, and on behalf of everyone at the SGU, past and present, thank you.

As that first issue of the year was being read, Portmoak – and many other parts of the UK – were subjected to relentless storms. The situation at Portmoak warranted a damage report from the treasurer, Kevin Hook.

Storm damage reports
The storms on Monday 28th January have caused substantial damage to the club's buildings, although fortunately no damage

has been incurred by our flying facilities (except for a waterlogged pitch!).

The clubhouse roof has been badly damaged, forcing us to move all of the furniture from the clubroom. In addition, water damage has forced the temporary closure of the kitchen and the briefing room.

At the time of writing, I anticipate the following dates for return to normal:

1. *Limited kitchen service should resume on Saturday 2nd February*
2. *Limited seating and dining space will become available in the clubroom during the week commencing Monday 4th February*
3. *The briefing room should return to normal during the week commencing Monday 4th February*
4. *Renovation of the clubroom ceiling, followed by complete re-decorating will take place during the week commencing Monday 11th February*
5. *"Normality" should resume during the week commencing Monday 18th February.*

The following summary details the most significant damage to the buildings. Given the age and condition of many of our buildings, we must assume that many of our losses will turn out to be uninsured.

SGU Buildings

Tug Fuel Store - Nil

Tug Hangar – Nil

Glider Hangar - Several of the top corrugated sheets are lifted and bent but not separated. Require straightening and re bolting to prevent further damage in future storms. Repairs to commence week beginning Monday 4th February.

Briefing Room - Felt torn from roof in two places. Minor repairs required.

Clubroom - Felt and insulation completely blown away from main clubroom area (10m x 8m). Tarpaulins in place to minimise further water damage. Quote for re-felting and tarring received. Insurers have given verbal go ahead. Awaiting suitable weather to start work.

Anemometer, radio aerial, TV aerial and kitchen extractor fan all blown down and require repairs/replacement.

Roof space to be inspected by David Hyde for lasting water damage once roof repair has been completed.

Main clubroom - ceiling and kitchen ceiling damaged by water penetration. Awaiting repair quotation from Steve Back.

Main clubroom contents removed to other locations and undamaged.

Main clubroom walls mildly stained by water. Redecoration to be undertaken before repositioning furniture.

Fence - A large section of fence adjacent to the entrance road has been blown down. Ian Meacham will re-erect this when time permits.

Portacabin - Some roofing felt has been peeled away. Minor repairs required.

Workshops - Boarding protecting sliding door mechanisms has blown away. Minor repairs required.

Zenair Hangar - Doors blown from mountings. No permanent damage.

Jim Wales Hangar - Ridge panels displaced. Minor repairs required.

Jodel Hangar - Minor damage to South facing wall. Down pipe displaced at North wall.

Toilet Block – Nil

Farmhouse - Nil

Blister Hangar - Window in west facing wall blown in. No action required.

Then the bad weather continued…

Storm Damage on 28th January 2002 - Update

Following a further week of wet weather, repairs to the clubroom roof have not progressed at all. The tools are on site, and the contractor is ready to pounce when we get a forecast of dry weather. We will not be starting work until the weather is right; the repair needs to be of a quality that will last as long as the building remains in use.

The revised schedule for repairs is now as follows:

1. *Seal clubroom roof with a single layer of felt as soon as weather permits.*
2. *Complete repair with two further layers of felt whenever weather permits.*
3. *Assuming that the roof is made watertight in time, the clubroom ceiling is to be taken down on the evening of Sunday 24th February to allow the roof space to dry.*
4. *Ceiling to be replaced on 4th to 5th March*
5. *Redecorating and replacement of electrical fittings to be completed 6th, 7th, 8th March*
6. *There will be no catering during the 12 days from 25th February to 8th March, whilst the clubroom is in turmoil.*
7. *Kitchen ceiling to be patched during week commencing 25th February*
8. *Permanent repairs to the kitchen ceiling to be completed during November.*
9. *Briefing room roof to be repaired as second priority to clubroom roof, when weather permits.*

On the flying front, Peter Clayton had to make an unscheduled landing late the previous year and, after an appropriate amount of time to reflect on his antics, felt that other pilots might benefit from his experiences:

> <u>How not to do your first land out.</u>
> *It was a reasonable day, all the launch point experts said that Benarty should be working, so after a good launch in FUS I turned left and quickly found a thermal over Findatie Farm before I even got to Benarty – great! Sadly the thermal only went up to 1,400 ft, but that seemed to be a safe height to go onto the North face of Benarty to get the lift that the pundits promised. Over*

Vane Farm and on over the cliffs – funny, no lift. Never mind, let's go a little further along – still only zero sink. Mmmmm. At the West End of the ridge turn back east to track back towards Portmoak – still plenty of height. Funny, in sink now……. (strange that you can get zero sink going one way on the ridge and bad sink the other way!). Never mind, as the wind is NNW there must be lift in the NorthWest-facing bowl over Vane Farm. No there isn't!! Now down below the level of the ridge over Vane Farm, so too low to turn back to land out next to the Loch, especially as I didn't check out suitable fields when I flew past them, so have to fly round the ridge East towards Portmoak – still in sink. Low over the road, and then over Findatie Farm, at least now seem to be out of the bad sink but still going down. Now low flying cross wind, can't land in the fields as there are cattle and power lines everywhere. Too low to turn left towards Portmoak to land in the South field – trees too high. S**t. Now very low, over the road and over the field growing lawn South of the drain. Must keep speed up. Gently turn left more or less into wind, fly low over the drain, land into low corn crop in field. Phew!! Relief!! Radio to report landing out and let heart rate drop towards normal from stratospheric level.

Walked back to launch point to report details. Some small consolation to hear that two other pilots got caught in the same unexpected sink on Benarty – but they got back! Neil Watt volunteers to come to find the farm whose field I have landed in. Eventually find that it is Kirkness Farm on the Ballingry road. Find farmer, very helpful, gets his wide wheelbase tractor out to tow the glider out of his field with minimum damage to crop, but says that he will charge £100 to cover his time and damage to crop. Seems a lot but farmer not prepared to negotiate and I think that we should not upset a local farmer – especially as he is being helpful - but suggest that he makes a claim on our insurance. He says that if we insist on this he will claim more in view of the hassle involved. Go back to SGU, get trailer and retrieve crew. De-rig FUS and tow short distance back to club.

They say that you learn from your mistakes. I hope that I have learnt something from my catalogue of errors. Here are a few lessons for a start, most of them of course obvious:

- *Do NOT always assume that you will manage to scratch back to Portmoak somehow. (I think that one of the problems of the early training is that you always expect to get back and therefore do not consider adequately the possibility that you might not. The worse scenario is when you are in a marginal case rather than an obvious land out situation where you – should – realise that you have no choice).*

- *ALWAYS keep an eye out for suitable/possible landing out fields. If there is any doubt that you will not get back do not fly away from suitable fields that you have identified.*

- *Give yourself plenty of time (and height) to land in the identified field. Do not put yourself under more pressure than necessary and whatever you do don't put yourself in the position where you are faced with ever decreasing options as height is lost before choosing your land out field.*

- *Do not put off doing your cross country training and field selection after the point where you are beginning to gain confidence and to venture a little distance away from Portmoak – you may need these skills sooner than you expect!*

- *Personally I think it would be a good idea to make a point of landing out on purpose as part of the cross country training – surely much better to make this important step in training in a controlled way than by*

being in a forced, possibly (probably!) very stressful situation.
I hope the above little comedy of errors may prove to be of use to others that may find themselves in a similar situation.

In 2002, the areas adjacent to the farm road were levelled and re-seeded and before long the club was able to provide a launch-line for north and north-west winds, without obstructing the landing area in the south field. In my relatively short time at the club I have been able to observe the shifting of the contours of the field and this remains as a constant reminder that our airfield lies very close to the water table that is Loch Leven. No sooner have you worked out where the bumps and hollows are than they change position and a new one waits to bite the unwary pilot just as they start to round-out.

One pilot who fared well during the year was Bill Grieve. He had gone to Feshie Bridge, the home of the Cairngorm Gliding Club:

Feshie to Banff 11th May 2002
I released from the tug about 1400ft and began climbing the southern ridge Ben Mhor. Over the crest you come upon the spectacular cliff face which falls down into Loch Einich. I couldn't help but be in awe of the panorama which unfolded below me with beautiful names like "Strath Spey", Aviemore, and Loch Garten where the Ospreys flew with such grace. Hunched in the cockpit of my K8, I set off north, crabbing into a westerly wind and began to relax as I found lift. As I proceeded towards Loch Garten, I was caught in a heavy snow shower which hit me without warning. I couldn't believe it! Below, the whole countryside was basking in sunshine and I was being plastered in snow! I had no choice but to stick the nose down and push through it. East of the Cromdale Hills I attempted to head west

towards Easterton, but in a K8 it was like hitting an invisible wall. This convinced me that Easterton wasn't important. Staying in the air and getting my 50K was, so I continued to crab my way north dodging several showers of sleet and occasional rotor which rocked the K8 around a bit and certainly concentrated the mind. My heart rate must have been going up and down like a yo-yo. Below, the landscape began to change as the mountains gave way to the large coastal plain of Banffshire.

I could relax now, as there were plenty of landing sites and my hopes soared as I could just make out the coastline taking shape as the sun shimmered on the Moray Firth. I thought about making one last attempt to head west for Easterton but the beguiling beauty of the Banffshire coastline with its long sandy beaches and picturesque fishing villages drew me northwards over the plain. I followed a river which reached the sea under a stone arched bridge at Macduff. With the wind at my back, I cut my speed to a minimum and gently sauntered along the coastline above the beach. Ahead I could see a small thumb of land jutting out into the sea creating a small cove. "That'll do for me" I thought and began to look for a suitable field. There was all the usual stuff with crops or animals, but just behind the spit of land was an empty grass field – perfect! I checked it out and concentrated on my landing. Once again my luck held, soft lush 4 inch high grass.

I sat in the cockpit with the euphoric feeling and gave a great sigh of relief. I looked around at the scenery and spotted a young boy (I later found out his name was Cameron) driving across the field towards me in a small quad bike. He was followed by his father, Stuart, then some way behind his mother. As she caught up with them she declared that she had phoned the emergency services. We phoned back to cancel but, alas, it was too late for the long suffering Grampian Police force. Two squad cars arrived on the scene as I was having a coffee in the farmhouse. They took their disappointment at not finding a mangled body in the wreckage well, and left with good grace. I was given a guided tour of the farm and discovered that Stuart and his family were the only breeders in Scotland of "Suffolk Punch" – a beautiful chestnut horse used in bygone days to pull the dray carts from the breweries. In the last two days, three foals had been born – one that very morning and I watched it suckling from its mother.

Stuart told me that I was welcome to use his fields anytime I liked. The excellent hospitality of Stuart and his family will remain in my mind long after I've forgotten about the flight. It really was a pleasure to land in his field.

Footnote: When I arrived back at Portmoak from the Feshie expedition it was about 10 o'clock at night and quite dark. Douglas Tait came lurking out of the darkness to congratulate me and said "When did you last eat?" inviting me into his caravan for an excellent fry-up. Thanks Doug, it was really appreciated.

Matt Stickland recalled his early forays into gliding and old reliable, *Portmoak Press*, shared the story with its readership towards the end of 2002.

A Long Day's Journey Into Flight

Round out, hold her off, hold her off, stick right back, a gentle kick in the seat of the pants as the glider touches down, brake to a stop and that's it. The first solo complete, only three years and five days since my first glider flight. As I sit with the canopy up, my mind runs back over the past three years and the highs and the lows of learning to fly.

I have been interested in aircraft for as long as I can remember. Probably started by my dad taking me to air shows at Biggin Hill as a boy. The visit to the RAF recruiting office at 17 to enquire about pilot training - only to be informed that poor sight, colour blindness and hay fever were not good attributes in a budding fighter pilot. A degree in Aeronautical Engineering, a stint as a wind tunnel engineer with British Aerospace, a PhD in Fluid Mechanics and finally teaching Mechanical and Aeronautical Engineering. But somehow I had never thought about learning to fly. That was until 1998.

For some reason, in the spring of 1998 I suddenly had the urge to fly! I'd had a couple of flights in light aircraft with friends and was somewhat disappointed that, once up in the air, all you did was fly around a little and then land. Not much more than taking the car for an aimless Sunday afternoon spin. It was also far too expensive to be given serious thought. However, gliding might be a reasonable alternative. But where to fly? The easiest way to find out was on the web. I found the BGA site and the club directory – lots of clubs all over the country. But which one? Here a little lateral thinking came into play. I discussed taking a gliding course with my wife and agreed that we could combine it with a weeks visit to her parents down in Yorkshire. A check on the web sites and a couple of calls later, I was booked on a week's course at Rufforth in September.

Arriving on the airfield on Monday morning it was a beautiful autumn day with light mist slowly being burnt off by the rising sun. There were five others on the course and we were soon all hard at work getting the gliders out; a K7M and a K13. In retrospect old, rudimentary gliders but to my untrained eye sleek soaring machines. The first two days of the course were made up of two aero tows, two motor glider flights and two winch launches. But, by the end of my second day I was now able to at least fly straight and level, carry out a co-ordinated turn with the airspeed under control. The rest of the week was spent on winch launches and by the end of the week I was capable, with a little prompting, of completing a launch, circuit and landing. To say I was pleased was an understatement and considering a day was lost to rain, I had learned a lot in just one week.

The course had been well thought out. The initial aerotows were a gentle introduction to gliding so I wasn't faced with the excitement of a winch launch from first flight. The use of the motor glider over the first couple of days had been a great help as it allowed me to get used to handling an aircraft and planning a circuit whilst not worrying about finding lift to extend the flight. However, once the course had ended it was the start of autumn, back to work and the start of term. My gliding career would have to wait until next year.

Now that I had tasted the pleasures of gliding, I was ready for more. Again a look at the BGA web site and I found the SGU. A quick phone call and I was booked on a course in May '99. I arranged to stay in the clubhouse and arrived ready and raring to go on the Monday morning. Five on the course and with just one instructor, Frank Smith, flying was extremely limited. Fortunately, however, Ian Trotter volunteered to help out, so flying increased.

The benefits of the ridge (Bishop Hill) in extending flight times and allowing the student lots of stick time on each flight was a great bonus when compared to the short flights down at Rufforth. By the end of Thursday I had my first practice cable break. Again the weather intervened and the last day was lost to bad weather. I had progressed by leaps and bounds and I was committed to continue learning to fly. However, with two young daughters creating havoc at home I could not spare the time to travel the hour and half from Ayrshire to Portmoak on a regular basis so my flying was put on hold for the time being. I was convinced that, with my limited spare time, learning on a course was the only way forward.

After two years lay off I was ready to start again. I booked on to a course in June and waited impatiently. Would all that I had learned so long ago be forgotten? As soon as I was strapped into the K21 (HPW) it all seemed so familiar. I explained my previous flying experience to George Ross in the back and he seemed willing to let me take it on the first launch. I was somewhat surprised to find that I controlled the launch reasonably well. The day was calm and so it was almost straight into the circuit. A couple of tips and prompts from George and we were back safely on the ground. I had not forgotten that much after all. Monday was spent on circuits and I was soon back in the groove and confident in my flying. However, from Tuesday the wind picked up and it became rather bumpy on the approach. It was remarkable how difficult I found it to correct my flying for the new conditions and I took a step backwards. But the ridge was now working well and I got on with the usual handling exercises. By the Thursday I was starting launch failure exercises again. Friday, the brake pads on the winch needed replacing so I was limited to a flight in the motor glider and practice circuits. I was close to solo but another layoff would see me back to square one. I was determined to go solo this year so, after a quick chat with Debbie, the prospective gliding widow (hopefully not in the literal sense), I rang up to get on the next available course.

I was fortunate to get the last place on the last course of the year! George was again the instructor and it was a reassuringly familiar voice in the back seat as I set off on my first launch of the week. Monday started with strong blustery winds from the east, so it was circuits all day. I found speed control difficult on the final approach, but George assured me that this was OK and that I should worry more about planning the circuit and getting in position for the final approach rather than worrying about landing. Tuesday still had strong easterly winds but they were steady and my approach and landings started to improve again. The prompts from the back seat "watch your speed", "keep the nose down", became fewer and fewer. The occasional landing was even fully held off. Wednesday was wet in the morning but calm with a light easterly wind. After an early lunch we hauled HPW out and set off for an afternoon's flying. After David and Douglas, my colleagues on the course, had had four flights each it was my turn. On the first flight there was a series of simulated cable breaks flown at altitude followed by a high speed pass and pull up into a simulated low cable break. A demo of an awkward height break, followed by me flying the high break and awkward height break. Both were flown by turning 360° to land back near the threshold. I now had the feeling that solo was not far off. Back to the launch point and George climbed back in "One more circuit to see how you get on". This sounded reasonable, but I asked if there were to be any more launch failure practice. I was assured that there was not, so I carried out the pre flight checks and settled into the launch. Established in the climb 60kts indicated. But then the speed began to bleed off. Put the nose down to increase speed but still the speed kept bleeding off! Speed down to 50kts and the nose still going down. Two pulls on the yellow knob and keep the nose firmly down to pick up 60kts before turning downwind. "What did you pull off for" from the back seat once we were down and stopped. "Winch power failure!" I replied, pleased that I had not been caught out.

The glider was pushed back to the launch point and I was invited to get back in. Whilst strapping in I noticed that George was doing up the straps from the side of the cockpit and I thought this is it - "Off you go then. Keep it simple and enjoy it". Well this was it, after just over three years, the moment of truth. I carried out my pre-flight checks as usual, reassured by their familiarity. I ran through eventualities, playing out the various possible launch failures in my mind. "Take up slack." Surprisingly I was not nervous, just apprehensive. I knew that I had been trained well and George would not have let me go if he did not have confidence in me. The canopy was beginning to mist but that had happened before and it usually cleared just after the start of the launch, once air started flowing through the ventilator. I also had the clear view panel open slightly so it shouldn't be a problem. "All out" and I was off. HPW picked up speed quickly and gently lifted off. I eased back into the climb and watched the speed rise, 45kts, 50kts 60kts BANG, what the….. Nose down firmly, establish 60kts, two pulls on the yellow knob. Awkward height - make a decision. Looks like room to land ahead – go for it. Full airbrake, keep the 60kts indicated don't let the nose creep up. Round out, hold her off, hold her off, gentle kick and she's down. Full wheel brake, keep the wings level, steer a straight line. Slowly to a halt with a couple of hundred metres to spare. Sitting there I wondered whether I had done anything wrong. But when the retrieve crew arrived I was relieved and pleased to learn that it was a real cable break. Could have happened to anyone at any time. It just happened to break on my first solo! As we pulled HPW back to the launch point I ran through the events in my mind. I was amazed at how automatic my response was and how well prepared I was for this unlikely event. Once we were back at the launch point we had a laugh about what happened.

Then I was strapped back in and off on my second solo, which lasted a little longer than my first but was definitely not as memorable.

So, three years, and 68 flights later I have the pleasure of being a solo glider pilot. Have I come to any conclusions about what I have learned? Could I have achieved the same end but easier or quicker? For me, taking courses was ideal. I do not have the time, or the patience, to sit around on a Saturday or Sunday waiting for a flight. I enjoy flying and when I am on the airfield I want to get as much airtime as possible. I should not have allowed so much time to elapse between each course but circumstances dictated otherwise.

All of the instructors I have had have been excellent. They have different styles, which some students may not be able to accommodate. But, if you don't like your instructor - change. If you are not progressing with one instructor, try another. The difference in style may make all the difference. When you find one that you like, stick with that instructor if at all possible. There is nothing more confusing than being told different things by different instructors. No matter how much they try to standardise, they still tell you different things.

Never get downhearted if you get something wrong, just try and get it right next time, but not at the expense of the rest of your flying. Don't worry if you can't land the damn thing. If your flying is fine and your circuit well planned the rest will follow. Flying in a thermal is hard to do well, so don't worry if you can't. If you can keep it in 4kts up on a weak day but can't execute a circuit and land safely you are not going to go solo. So forget the thermals and sort out the important things first. But most of all, enjoy your flying.

I must express my thanks to all at Portmoak. Irene and Steve for making all my visits so comfortable, Frank and Ian for getting me half way there and specifically to

George who has that remarkable ability to remain calm as you try to kill him on a daily basis and will stay patiently quiet or gently prompt you as you try and get yourself out of another mess of your own making. Because it is only when you can see the mistakes that you make and rectify them yourself that you realise that you can actually fly. Then the mistakes become fewer and fewer and your flying becomes more natural until it is almost second nature. When you are not concentrating on just flying the aircraft everything is much more relaxed and straightforward. As for flying solo, it's great - but I miss having someone to chat to.

Finally I must thank Prof. Boyle and Prof. Gray for funding my flying at Portmoak. I must confess that there has been a hidden agenda to my learning to fly which, if the editor permits, I will tell you more about at a later date.

Perhaps reminded by the storms at the beginning of the year that the club hangar was well over 50 years old and was beginning to show signs of wear and tear, the SGU Board invited feedback on their proposal for a new purpose-build hangar. The design was very adventurous with a battery store and heated parachute store at one end and aircraft along both sides facing outwards. Each glider would have its own set of sliding doors which meant that members would only need to remove the aircraft they would be flying. Previously, in the old hangar, it was not uncommon to shift four or five aircraft before you could remove the one you were looking for. This old method often stopped many prospective flying activities if a suitable team of helpers could not be found, and many pilots gave up on the day as it was too difficult to drag everything out first. This had an effect on club income and some gliders at the back of the hangar didn't fly for months on end. This new hangar design would remove the "last in – first out" scenario and it was anticipated that a higher utilisation of the club fleet would be achieved. Private owners who had been keeping their gliders in their trailers when not rigged for flying were also offered space in the new hangar so that they could leave their aircraft rigged all year, safe in the knowledge that they would not need to struggle with rigging aids when they wanted to fly. All in all, a futuristic vision for private owners and club members alike. The options for the new hangar would be discussed at the Information Meeting scheduled for the start of 2003.

The Scottish Gliding Association's ASH25 was allocated to Portmoak at the end of the year and the author took the opportunity for a short flight:

ASH25 to the Wallace Monument (& back)

It wasn't a great day. In fact no-one was flying. The course people were in the briefing room and the windsock was showing Westerly with a bit of South, and quite blustery at that. Bishop Hill would be working but there would also be some turbulence downwind of Benarty. I had been passing the club and popped in on the off-chance of a quick flight, so I was disappointed when I saw that "the toys" were not out. The SGA ASH25 was rigged and staked out just inside the trailer park and I was very keen for a cross-country (in advance of my Silver Distance attempt - any time soon). Bob Petrie was keen to go as my P1 but was suffering from a head cold ("by doze is blogged"). As we watched the clouds scudding by and looked forlornly towards the ASH, another opportunity presented itself. Colin Hamilton arrived to do some work on his glider but was quickly tempted by the prospects of a "wee hurl" in the ASH25. We gathered the maps, drinking water and a couple of Mars Bars and prepared the ASH. Nothing declared, we launched and sauntered in the lift in front of Bishop. After a couple of beats, Colin suggested we set off up-wind towards a couple of likely looking clouds. They provided 2-3 kt and we slowly progressed upwind. Colin pointed out the good clouds and I attempted to circle under them. I tried to milk every last drop out of each thermal but Colin reminded me that we needed to push on while we could still see the next source of lift, and not spend too much time drifting down-wind. With 25 metres of wing, and flaps, the ASH "can boldly go...and get back again!" Although I was studying the map, I was aware that the GPS was telling us what height we needed to be at to get back. We pushed West and had a grandstand view of the racers practising at Knockhill. Before long we were past the Wallace Monument - about 30K out. I thought we looked low and Colin took over to take a weak climb to "top us up". The GPS said we were now at final glide height so we turned East and dolphined our way home. Speeding up and slowing down at the appropriate places, with associated flap movements, we quickly arrived back over the site with plenty of height in hand. We landed about two hours after we set off and covered about 60K. Not an epic flight by pundit standards but extremely useful in terms of navigation, use of flaps, a 25metre "hot ship", and preparing the way to shake off the shackles of being tied to Bishop Hill. Thanks Colin!

At the end of year, the silverware was distributed to the pundits who had flown hard and worked hard over the previous twelve months:
Thorburn Two-Seater (J.&D. Williams)
Boyle Altitude Trophy (K.Hook – 22,900ft)
Marshall 100K Triangle (D.Thompson)
Andy Penswick (C.Robinson)
Parker Distance (D.Clempson)
Docherty Handicap Distance (D.Clempson)
Sutherland Out & Return (D.Clempson)
Lomond (D.Thompson)
Maclay Championship (K.Hook)
Peter Copeland Trophy (K.Hook)
Hot Wings (K.Hook), Junior (G.Hall), Nick Wales (A.Bates)
Darren Powell (I.Trotter), Service Salver (J.Fisher)

Chapter 19
2003-2005
The club throws open its doors

The year started off with a well attended information meeting on 4th January. The clubhouse was filled to capacity when the Chairman, Brian Cole-Hamilton, welcomed the members, and reviewed the progress which had been made towards the goals set out in the five-year plan (1998 to 2002). Most major objectives had been achieved, except that membership had risen by only 10% instead of the planned 40%, and that a replacement clubhouse was now not considered financially possible in the foreseeable future. He indicated that a new long term plan, to cover the next ten years, was under development, and would be presented at the end of the year.

Key elements of the new plan included the replacement of the winch in 2005/2006, the appointment of a full-time instructor, and the early provision of a new hangar, which was becoming urgent due to the deterioration of the existing building and the uneconomical cost of repairs.

On the subject of the new hangar, Kevin Hook explained the logic behind the location and design of the new building - plans for which had been on display in the clubhouse for the previous few months. The design concept would allow the removal of any glider from the hangar without moving any other one, and it was hoped that the utilisation of club aircraft would thus be significantly improved as well as the reduction the incidence of hangar damage. Kevin also reported that the take-up of spaces by private owners had been good, enabling the construction to be increase to the maximum possible size of 20 bays. The cost of the entire project was estimated at £120K, of which the SGU contribution would be £70K. The general concept of the project was favourably received, but various members expressed concern about the proposed tensioned fabric doors, on grounds of durability, security and resistance to vandalism. Other members objected to the plan to demolish the old hangar, and urged its retention. The Chairman confirmed that all comments and criticisms made at the meeting would be considered by the Board. This was indeed considered at the following evening's Board meeting and the hangar project was given the go-ahead, albeit with steel sliding doors rather than the fabric design. As the Information Meeting came to an end, the chairman thanked Bob Jones for his stint as CFI and the reins were handed over to Neil McAulay, with George Ross as Deputy CFI.

Following a plea for stories for the club magazine - club instructor Frank Smith offered up some of his recollections:

A Different Sort Of Eventuality!

Most glider pilots tend to think of eventualities in terms of cable-breaks, winch failures or rope breaks. I can assure you that there are many others to consider! From forgetting essential pins at rigging and having your wings flap more than they should, to having loose objects in the cockpit float around your ears after performing negative g manoeuvres. Cases of unlocked canopies flying open are commonplace, and ground loops at the start of the launch, or stalling halfway up, are all designed to catch the unwary. I daresay that most of you could add to the list. Let me relate a couple of incidents that have occurred during my flying days that you might find amusing, or even instructional. I apologise to those readers who may already have endured the same fate - just pass on to the next article.

A few seasons ago I was flying our syndicate Vega on aerotow. There I was, blissfully following Darren in the tug, under a beautiful sky, when a bumble bee flew into the cockpit through the DV panel and alighted on my leg. It was the biggest B I've ever seen! The combination of tug and glider was perhaps around 600ft. "Always keep your eyes on the tug," makes good sense - except if you have a huge (I swear it was growing in size!) beastie crawling towards important parts of your anatomy, then you can be forgiven for casting your glance somewhere else. It's amazing what can pass through one's head at such times. Thoughts of an agonising sting, followed by partial or full paralysis or even loss of consciousness were considerations which flashed through my brain.

I must admit that for a few vital seconds my concentration was fatally distracted. So much so, that when I looked up there was no tug to be seen! It wasn't above me so it must be below, and so it proved. I was miles out of position, high, potentially in an extremely dangerous position, especially for the tug pilot. Recovering as quick as I could, the rest of the tow was uneventful. The bee was trapped with a duster and dispatched at height somewhere over Kinnesswood.

After landing, I went to see Darren and apologised profusely. He just laughed when I told him the story and said that he thought something must have been wrong. He had every right to have ditched me, especially at that height.

Moving on to last year. Again on aerotow, same glider but this time being tugged out from Sutton Bank towards the wave lying to the west of the airfield. We'd reached 1500ft with some way to go to reach release point in front of the wave bar, when I hear this buzzing noise. My first impression is that it is coming from outside, but it's not. Slowly coming into my peripheral vision and crawling up my right leg is this monstrous queen wasp probably packed with millions of youngsters. My experience of yesteryear, which should have provided me with the ability to cope, failed miserably as I panicked, looked away from the tug and went screaming out of position. Luckily this time the glider had descended into a low, but very low, tow position. Grabbing a cloth from the pocket I managed to squash the wasp and it fell down the side. Zooming back up to normal position, I quickly radioed the tug and told him the story. He politely asked if all was well and we proceeded. A little later we had some more chat and I asked him to drop me in the most suitable spot to contact the wave.

So we drone on a wee bit longer and higher. Then the tuggie comes on the radio and asks "Can you hack it from here?", which all coincided with a very angry, and very much alive, wasp reappearing on my trouser leg. Keeping my head I managed to release the rope and the tug dived away for another punter. As he circled down he called up to say that I still had my wheel down. Bloody Hell!, I've got this killer beast roaming around the cockpit and he's worried about my undercarriage!

As I tried to dispatch the wasp for a second time, I idly notice that in spite of events the glider is gaining height quite rapidly. It's at times like these that you realise how vulnerable you are. Tightly strapped in, you can't move your legs very much and certainly can't see your lower parts. Another swipe at the wasp and finally it appears to be dead and as I pass through 5000ft I gratefully push the offending insect out.

So, what lessons can we learn from all this nonsense. Well, first of all make sure that you are not taking up any unwanted passengers - in the case of the wasp, I think it may have already been aboard. Fly with the DV panel shut, at least until release of cable or rope. Perhaps be trimmed neutral, or nose down.

It all may sound very funny, but the consequences could have been anything but. Certainly the rapidity of departure from normal tow position can be alarming if total concentration isn't given to one's flying. I like to get a buzz out of my flying, but not if there's a sting in the tail.

Behind the scenes, Neil Irving, John Williams, Bob Jones, Glenn Douglas (SGA), Roger Coote, Bruce Cooper and Carr Withall (all BGA) had all been working on behalf of the club to address the latest airspace developments. The five areas affecting the SGU were the Edinburgh CTR, the Scottish TMA,

Airway P600, Airway B226 and the Glenrothes ATZ. As part of the new airways crossing procedures, SGU members were asked to complete a crossing form every time they crossed class D airspace.

An early 2003 issue of *Portmoak Press* included a report by Matt Stickland:

> *Strathclyde University Flight Test Course 2002*
> *I have been very fortunate that the Heads of the Department of Mechanical Engineering at the University of Strathclyde have always been very keen to promote CPD (Continuing Professional Development) for their staff. However, I was a little surprised when my suggestion that learning to fly would improve my teaching of flight mechanics and aerodynamics was well received. It was with their support that I finally flew solo at Portmoak in 2001 and took the wealth of knowledge that I gained from learning to fly into the lecture room where it now adds a new dimension to the classes I teach. My tortuous route to solo was recounted in "A long Days Journey into Flight", Portmoak Press, Jan 2002.*
> *During my flight training, towards the end when I could fly and talk at the same time, I had a number of conversations with George Ross, in the back. We discussed how our students might benefit from flight experience in a K21 at Portmoak. At that time I was in the process of implementing a new course, Aero-Mechanical Engineering, which was to be accredited as an Aeronautical Engineering degree by the Royal Aeronautical Society. Part of the accreditation requirement for this degree was some form of flight experience and flight test. There are currently 20 Aero Eng courses in the UK and over 75% of these have their flight test/experience provided by the Flight Test*

Laboratory at Cranfield University. The course they provide consists of a number of flights in an instrumented Jetstream with the students in the rear taking data from LCD displays in the back of the seat in front. I participated in this course as an undergraduate back in the 80s and thought then, as now, that there was considerable scope for improvement and the time in the air could be better spent.

Strathclyde University is extremely active in the ERASMUS and SOCRATES schemes and has exchanged a large number of students with universities in Germany. During these exchanges my attention has been drawn to the excellent work, on sailplane design and manufacture, carried out by the AKAFliegs, (Academic Flying groups). These groups are voluntary and membership is not a prerequisite of the German Aeronautical Engineering degrees. However their influence may been seen in the fact that the sailplane manufacture industry in Germany is the world leader with 90% of the sailplanes designed and built there. They also provide a focus for undergraduate and postgraduate project work. The success of the AKAFliegs and the possibility that the simplicity of a sailplane would lend itself to analysis made the development of a course, based around sailplanes, an attractive proposition.

I discussed my ideas with George Ross and Kevin Hook and, as they were both very supportive, I approached the board to see if the SGU would help. The board agreed to let me run a trial course so I buckled down to write a syllabus.

The Syllabus is loosely based around the types of testing undertaken in the Cranfield Jetstream. However, the limited flight instruments available in the K21s restricted the test possibilities. But, even with these limitations, a comprehensive course was developed.

The trial course was run at the beginning of September 2002, over three days, with four of our fourth year Mechanical Engineering with Aeronautics students as guinea pigs.

Day 1

We arrived early on Monday morning and, after a quick coffee were given a safety briefing by John Northern as one of the holiday courses was running in parallel on the site. This covered general airfield safety and how to handle the aircraft. When this was complete we proceeded to the hangar and extracted the aircraft we were to use for the day. At the aircraft the students were instructed in: Fitting of Parachute, Use of Parachute, Protection of canopy (wind, misuse of DV panel), Harness and quick release, Canopy release handle, Adjustment of rudder pedals, Cable hooks, Cable release, Flight Instruments, Flight controls, Check for ballast requirements.

This pre-flight briefing was so that, when the instructor and tug pilot (George Ross and Ian Dandie) arrived, we could commence flying straight away.

The Weather on the first day of the course was ideal for test flying, zero cloud and zero wind, a flat calm day, so a decision was made to start flying as soon as possible in case flying conditions changed over the next couple of days. The aircraft was towed to the launch point and the flying, aero tows to 4000', commenced.

Flight 1: Demonstration of aircraft controls,

The purpose of the first flight was to demonstrate the aircraft controls and instruments to the student and get them used to flying the aircraft before the more rigorous exercises commenced. The effects of deflecting the rudder, elevator, ailerons and trimmer were demonstrated and then the students were allowed to fly the aircraft; attempting to control heading, airspeed and co-ordinated turns. They were also introduced to the effect of reducing the airspeed too much – the stall. Each flight lasted about 30 minutes as some attempts at soaring were made.

Flight 2: The stall

The second flight's purpose was to investigate the stall and stall recovery.

Mushing stall – the aircraft speed was allowed to reduce gradually and the indications of the stall; buffet, increased rate of sink, reduction in aileron effectiveness and decrease in wind noise were demonstrated. The changing effect of the rudder as the stall was approached (as the rudder is deflected the aircraft rolls) was demonstrated. The possibility of a wing dropping at the stall creating the possibility of a spin was also discussed.

Steep stall – from level flight the aircraft was pulled into a steep climb and the speed allowed to decay. When the aircraft now stalls the low airspeed causes the tailplane and elevator to lose their effectiveness and the nose drops. As the nose drops the elevator is still ineffective and this was demonstrated.

Accelerated stall – to show that the aircraft can stall at any speed, the aircraft was established in a 2g, 60°, banked turn and the speed reduced until the stall was approached.

Flight data – During the flight the students recorded the indicated air speed (IAS) at which the aircraft stalled in level flight and the airspeed at which the aircraft stalled in the 2g turn. If the load factor was not exactly 2 they recorded the actual g for post flight analysis

By the end of day one we had carried out all of the introduction flights and two students had investigated the stall. Ideally the students should have calculated the stall speeds pre-flight but it was considered that the flying program should be flexible to accommodate possible changes in the weather.

I took a dual flight at the end of day one to check my calculations for flight 4 which indicated that the phugoid oscillation was divergent! I thought this unlikely but thought I had better check that this was not the case – plus I would get a flight in as watching everyone else fly was getting me down. I was surprised to find that, with the cg forward, the phugoids stick fixed and stick free were neutrally stable and my calculations were not too far out!

Day 2

Up bright and early and into the briefing room at 9 o'clock to do some sums. The pilots would arrive at 11:30 to start flying at midday so there was a lot of work to be done.

Task1: the students calculated the gross mass of their aircraft and, given the wing area from the a/c handbook and the C_L-vs-α plots for the wing sections calculated the IAS for the stall of the aircraft in straight and level flight and the 2g turn. This data was then compared to the actual values from the flights of the previous day. The calculations produced a result within 1kt (typically 37kts) of the stall speed for the aircraft in level flight and within about 5kts of the measured stall in the 2g turn. Post flight they recalculated the accelerated stall speed for the actual g they pulled and got better results

Task 2: The students were asked to calculate the drag coefficient of the aircraft;

$C_D = C_{D_o} + kC_L^2$, *where C_{D_o} is the parasite drag and k is the induced drag coefficient. Working from very limited information and using analytical and empirical equations and ESDU data sheets. the students calculated these values.*

Typically the drag coefficient was estimated as

$C_D = 0.0096 + 0.0208C_L^2$

Using an ESDU data sheet the effect of deploying the airbrakes was also calculated as;

$$C_D = 0.0241 + 0.0208C_L^2$$

Note that the effect on increasing the induced drag coefficient was assumed to be negligible and was ignored. With this data the following parameters were calculated (the values are typical of those calculated);

IAS for minimum sink rate (max endurance) 40kts
Minimum sink rate 120 ft/min
IAS for minimum glide angle (max range) 52 kts
Sink rate 60kts full airbrake 350 ft/min
It was noted that the sink rate with full airbrake was low but, as we could flight test, we could find out whether or not the result was valid.

Flying started again at midday with the last two "stall flights" followed by the performance flights.

Flight 3: Aircraft performance,
The aircraft was towed to 4000' and then flown at a number of constant airspeeds. At these airspeeds the IAS and rate of sink were recorded. With the ideal flight conditions it was possible to record up to four different IAS and VSI readings. The airbrakes were then fully deployed and rate of sink and IAS recorded for two airspeeds. It was found that the VSI went off scale (>1000 ft/min) at airspeeds above 60 kts and 900 ft/min recorded at 60 kts – indicating that something was wrong with the theoretical estimate! On completion of the a/c performance flights, two dynamic stability flights were completed as the Met forecast for Wednesday was not favourable for the afternoon.

Day 3
The poor forecast for the afternoon caused us to start flying early and, after some difficulty getting the tug started we started flying about 11 o'clock with the weather beginning to close in. The final flight was to investigate the dynamic stability of the aircraft.

Flight 4: Static and Dynamic Stability,
The students had demonstrated the short period oscillation, the spiral divergence, and the phugoid oscillation. The aircraft was then placed into four phugoid oscillations with initial conditions of 60kts IAS 10° and 30° pitch angle stick fixed and stick free. During each phugoid the student recorded the maximum and minimum IAS and made a subjective assessment of whether or not the oscillation was damped. At the end of the flight, if there was sufficient height the student had the opportunity to request either more instruction in the handling of the aircraft or aerobatics (most chose aerobatics).

Because the course was not compulsory for these students and they had volunteered for the course. I rewarded those who requested with a 15-minute flight, off the winch, to experience some ridge soaring.

By 1:00 am on day three all flying was complete and we retired to the briefing room for some post flight analysis and a debrief on the course in general.

The performance flight data was analysed and the data produced was, typically;

Drag coefficient C_{Do}=0.016, k=0.0018

IAS min sink 41 kts

Minimum sink rate 110 ft/minute

Analysis of Schleicher's own polar gives C_{Do}=0.011, k=0.0.021

The data for the airbrake were significantly in error because the ESDU data sheet only calculates the drag increment for a single airbrake – we have two. I'll need to correct that for the next course and include the effect of change in the lift distribution.

When all the performance analysis was complete there was just time to have a debrief about the flying and a discussion about the course.

Conclusion

The course met, if not surpassed, all expectations. The students found the course to be an educational experience as well as a lot of fun. The flying and theoretical work complemented each other and reinforced the students' knowledge of flight mechanics and aerodynamics.

The cost per student was below what we would expect to pay Cranfield for an equivalent course (please don't tell Kevin or the board).

It was also decided that the course should be run for Aero-Mech students at the end of their second year. During their 3rd year they have the large design project and by the end of the third year the educational value is reduced.

The course still requires development in a number of ways:

The instruments used were the standard flight instruments within the aircraft and their state of calibration was unknown. The VSI is not a very accurate instrument to determine rate of sink. Recording the time to descend 100ft is probably a better method. The use of electronic barometers to record altitude during the performance and dynamic stability flight should be investigated as well as GPS. Also, the possibility of measuring elevator position so that the a/c neutral point can be determined needs to be investigated.

The theoretical work should be carried out pre-course as the time available on site was limited and it would be better to utilise this time for post rather than pre flight analysis.

The performance measurement became rather repetitive as each aircraft was tested several times. It might be preferable, for the performance estimation, to use the DG505 which has removable wing-tips, and therefore the aspect ratio can be varied and the effect of AR on induced drag investigated. Also the variable centre of gravity in the DG could be used during the dynamic stability flights.

Aeronautical Engineering is an extremely popular course and the numbers of students that we would like to put through the course could be quite high. If I can get my hours up I would love to get up to instructor standard so that I can help out in the air as well as on the ground. But, until then, we rely on the goodwill of the club to provide instructors and tug pilots. Care needs to be exercised in the way that the course is integrated into the running of the SGC so that it does not interfere with club members flying. Experience from the trial course shows that, as we only use aero-tow, we do not interfere with flying off the winch and, because the tug is available, the holiday course and club members have easy access to the tug. The Board and the U of S are currently discussing how we can develop this course to the advantage of both the SGU and the U of S.

I have also found that the gliding club could offer a wealth of possibilities for undergraduate projects. I currently have a fourth year student modelling the wind flows over Bishop Hill with computational fluid dynamics. This should indicate the regions of best lift for different wind speeds and direction. When this is complete he will then look at the flows off Benarty in a south-westerly to see how the wind flow over the airfield is affected by the curlover and, hopefully, show the problems that could be encountered during launch and landing. I would like to put his results into Portmoak Press (I've already allocated the space Ed.) and on the web towards the middle of next year. I would also like the student to fly the ridge to see if his results are correct. So if there is a willing volunteer out there please let me know.

There are tremendous benefits to both the SGU and U of S if we can work together. For us the academic value is undeniable. For the club it will provide a useful income

stream, increase the utilisation of the tug, create good publicity and introduce a large number of aviation-minded people to the possibility of gliding as a hobby.
None of this would have been possible without the hard work and enthusiasm of Ian Dandie, Kevin Hook and George Ross – Thanks.

As the spring of 2003 came to an end the club prepared for the summer courses, a full-time instructor was selected for the season. Tragically, the week before the courses were due to start, the new instructor - Martin Moss – was killed when he and Dick Rukin were involved in a motor glider launching accident at their home club in the north of England.

Andy Sandison from Cambridgeshire and SGU's own Neil Irving jumped into the breach to provide instruction for the summer season and the courses got under way.

Summer 2003 also saw the final leg of the Scottish Inter-Club League take place at Portmoak. John Williams provided an update for *Portmoak Press:*

SGU Wins 2003 Scottish Inter Club League

After a year or two in the doldrums we are firmly back on the map after winning this year's Inter Club League. After securing a small lead over Fulmar at Easterton four weeks ago (much thanks to Dave Thompson winning two classes on the last day) it was all to play for on our home territory last weekend.

We had visiting teams from Angus, Cairngorm, Deeside, Fulmar and Highland – all we needed was the weather to make a great competition weekend….. Well we did have weather, but not the kind we'd have ordered, more the kind to frustrate the competitors as well as Mike Carruthers in his capacity as Competition Director and Kevin Hook in his as Task Setter and Scorer. Still, a competition it was and compete we did, even the retrieve crews got plenty of action as a result.

Despite lots of heavily overcast skies and plenty of heavy showers, all classes launched on the Saturday. Highlights of the day were Duncan McKay winning the novice class for Deeside in an Oly 2 – landing in the same field as a rather different vintage LS7 – and Neil Irving landing his Astir beyond Dollar to win the Intermediate Class for us and extend our overall lead.

Sunday dawned a little brighter with less heavy showers and after it had cycled a few times, all classes were launched and headed off more in hope than expectation into a leaden sky with obvious heavy rain just east of track at Perth. In the end John Williams managed to surprise himself by getting around Methven, Blairgowrie, and Dunning to complete the task and win the Pundit Class while Dave Thompson found a field (or at least a grass covered slope!) north of Perth to take 3rd in the Novice Class.

That did it – we'd won by some 7 points from Deeside in 2nd and Highland in 3rd.

A huge thank you to the SGU Team of Competing Pilots John Ferguson, Gavin Goudie, Kevin Hook, Neil Irving, Dave Thompson and John Williams, and to all those who helped deal with a huge workload when we did the organising, in particular to Mike Carruthers, Kevin Hook, Ian Trotter and Steve and Irene.

At the end of summer, Andy Sandison headed back to the warmer weather in the south of England and he penned a letter to *Portmoak Press*:

To all club members and the visitors I flew with, a short note thanking you for making my summer such a memorable period. Full-time instructing is something that I had not seriously considered before, but I can recommend the experience to anyone who is lucky enough to get the time off, in my case between jobs - between careers, in fact.

A special word of thanks must go to Irene, Steve, Sandra and John for making me feel at home. Their hospitality in the clubhouse was second to none and it was really appreciated.

I found the whole experience very rewarding, the people friendly and helpful, and though it was quite hard work at times, overall I felt that I was more on a paid holiday than doing a job, and I was very sorry to have to leave. I also got my diamond height, which was one of my aims, though the weather made me wait a while for it. Apologies to all those who I did not manage to say "goodbye" to before I left... it was all a bit manic towards the end of my contract, not helped much by my silly attempt to fly through a "wee dyke" (A Scottish stone wall, not the other sort!). You'll be glad to know that my trusty Vega "890" is repairable, and will fly again next year.

Since coming down south I have been pitched headlong into my new teaching job, and the signs are that I have made an excellent move: the kids are friendly, the work interesting, and almost everything is free! I will also be getting outrageously long holidays, so I will be up at Portmoak before long, you can be sure of that, and I look forward to seeing you all again. In the meantime, fly safely, and remember, don't do what I do, do what I say!

Other summer activities of 2003 included the test flying of the BGA Scheibe SF25c – Rotax Falke and tug-master John Graham Smith produced a report for the membership:

The SGU had requested that the British Gliding Association Motor Falke visit the club during the week of 14th to 19th July 2003. The purpose of the visit was to evaluate its use as a Glider Tug and also consider what benefits it might display over the Syndicate Falke 2000 when used for field landing and navigation exercises.

While the aircraft was available over the weekend, glider towing was only undertaken on Saturday 19th as the weather situation necessitated the return of the aircraft to Bicester on the Sunday. The weather on the Saturday started off with a 10knot easterly. The first tow was undertaken with a Junior and appeared impressive with the ground run of both glider and Falke being similar, which might have been expected, to that of the Pawnee.

Subsequent tows were undertaken with the ASK21 and DG505, these being equally impressive in the shortness of the ground runs. It was, however, noted that the Falke tended to become airborne either at the same time as, or slightly before, the two-seater gliders.

The writer took the opportunity to sit in on one of the tows with the Junior and observed both climb rate and descend technique. The start of the tow necessitated lifting the Falke from the runway as early as possible so that the drag could be minimised and the combination allowed to accelerate to a comfortable towing speed. The Falke then climbed at a reasonable 3 to 4 kt. On release, the technique was to partly throttle back the Falke and then select full spoiler, at the same time gradually increasing the speed to some 80 to 90 kt. The throttle was then closed with the descent rate being in excess of full deflection on the VSI. The landings were undertaken with power as required. The BGA Falke was fitted with an electrical constant-speed propeller – this was malfunctioning during the test and, on the flight observed by the writer, the engine was slightly over-revving. Although a fixed-pitch propeller is available, this was considered not to provide as good an acceleration or climb rate as either of the constant speed units due to its slightly coarser pitch.

Towing continued throughout the day. It was evident that the ground runs became longer as the wind strength dropped and that the clearance above the equestrian centre fences was not particularly impressive, especially with the DG505 in tow. The wind then changed direction, due to thermal activity, and was slightly off the rear-quarter of the aircraft prior to an attempted tow with the DG505. Although the Falke became airborne after an extended ground run, the tow was abandoned by the glider pilots as they were unable to unstick the DG505. No further towing was undertaken after this aborted take-off.

The writer spent some time in conversation with Dave Bullock in order to obtain further information on his experience of towing from Bicester, as well as under wetter conditions than were apparent on the day of the evaluation. It transpired that when the conditions were noticeably wet at Bicester, it had proved necessary for wing tip holders to pull forward on both tips of a K13 in order to get the combination started. As the writer has been at Bicester under similar conditions, it is his opinion that the glider and Falke would not have sunk as deeply into the ground as might be likely at Portmoak. The grass at Bicester also tends to be kept much shorter during the winter months. Both would contribute to a better performance at Bicester than might be likely at Portmoak.

Although no field landing or navigation work was undertaken, sufficient information was gleaned from both discussion and monitoring of the flying of the Falke to form an opinion on its performance, relative to the Falke 2000 in these roles. The performance of the Falke 2000 at Portmoak under the wet conditions when it was first flown from this site was also taken into consideration in arriving at the following conclusions:

Advantages

Burns fuel at a rate of 12-14 litres per hour. It is therefore far more frugal than the Pawnee when undertaking glider tows.

Can be operated on Mogas, hence probably also a cost saving.

Turn around times for local tows are similar to those obtained from the Pawnee, due to the much faster descent possible with the water-cooled heads on the Rotax engine.

Towing of solo gliders is possible with two persons in the Falke. This would permit both training and checking of tow pilots.

The Falke would also be available for field landing, navigation, and other gliding exercises such as circuits, approaches, aerotow rope breaks etc.

Possibly lower maintenance costs than for the Pawnee (although, see Items for Further Debate).

Capable of towing up to dual gliders such as the DG505, although this would require favourable ground/weather conditions. (see Items for Further Debate).

Offers a noticeably higher climb-out rate than the Falke 2000. This makes the climb out from practice field landings safer, and also permits the possible use of fields that might not otherwise be considered suitable due to terrain avoidance considerations. This would also aid in managing faster turn rounds when teaching glider circuits, as the Rotax Falke would climb to the required height in a considerably shorter time.

Disadvantages

Requires that pilots have SLMG or TMG class ratings — could be short term problem for established tow pilots due to lack of experience in this type of aircraft, as well as differences training for constant speed propeller.

The constant speed propeller is stated to provide a better performance than the fixed pitch unit. Would therefore probably be necessary at Portmoak. As electrical unit appears to be problematic, this would necessitate use of a hydraulic unit with associated complexity and higher maintenance requirements.

Does not appear to be suitable for heavier two-seaters when the ground is wet or soggy, or in light or nil wind conditions. The combination of both would render towing impractical at Portmoak.

If used in addition to the Pawnee, the Rotax could be operated on Avgas but this requires a stricter maintenance schedule. Use of Mogas, as recommended, would require a separate storage and dispensing system.

Rotax engine is still subject to increases in TBO and lifetime is uncertain. Lycoming, although "old technology", is a known item.

Availability could be a problem if the Falke is also required for gliding or NPPL work. This is likely to be on those days when the Falke would be most required for an additional tug as it would be on non hill-soaring days, or during periods of high pressure when soaring is unlikely.

The propeller clearance on the Rotax Falke is low. If the aircraft were inadvertently landed in some of the rougher areas of the airfield, this might result in a propeller strike, with costly results. The Pawnee is much better able to cope with the rough areas and hence would not be as likely to have to wait for aircraft to be cleared from the smooth landing areas.

Items worthy of further debate

Ability to cope with high winds and/or crosswinds. This is an area that has not been explored. In light of experience with the Falke 2000, it is unlikely that the Rotax Falke would be suitable for use in a crosswind component of more than 10 kt. It would also be unlikely to be suitable for use during periods of strong turbulence as the longer time required for initial acceleration of the combination would render it vulnerable to gusts etc.

Would there be sufficient "other use" of the Falke to render it value for money? Considering the high cost of a new motor glider, would there be sufficient interest from club members for gliding exercises in this aircraft? If it were to be also used for NPPL training, this would then raise the question of its availability for towing or glider exercises.

While a new aircraft is likely to cost in excess of £60,000, another route could be available. As in a recent article in S&G, it is possible to purchase a second-hand Falke and have it refurbished and re-engined by Scheibe. It is believed that this route could result in an aircraft suitable for towing but at approximately two-thirds of the cost of a new one.

The syndicate Falke 2000 has been found to require a high throttle setting when attempting to start taxying when the ground is fairly wet and soft underfoot. When one considers the effect of a glider also sinking into the airfield in these conditions, the writer would express some concern about the ability of the Rotax Falke to operate (as a tug) under these circumstances.

Although maintenance costs would initially appear to be likely to be lower the question of maintenance of the constant speed propeller requires to be taken into consideration. The likely life of the Rotax engine is still to be determined, hence this is currently another unknown factor.

In this document, the writer has attempted to highlight the basic advantages, and disadvantages, of the Rotax Falke. What is clear is that this motor glider could certainly not cope with the range of gliders and weather/ground conditions that the Pawnee is capable *of operating under. It would certainly provide a back-up tug under suitable conditions and subject to the availability of adequately trained pilots. One point that has not been raised is the necessity to lift both glider and tug from the ground as quickly as possible to permit the combination to accelerate. This would require re-teaching of the aerotow take-off technique as it differs from the standard "roll the glider on its main wheel until it lifts off of its own accord" method used behind the Pawnee. Glider and tug pilots would also have to be able to readily adapt to the different take-off techniques dependant on the tug in use.*

There may well be other relevant points that will require discussion and further investigation. This, however, is a matter for the consideration of the Board, should they wish to pursue this matter further.

By the end of 2003, tug master Graham Smith had taken on the role of full-time instructor and was able to provide training five days a week. All of this was explained at the end of year Information Meeting. Around sixty members attended and a number of topics were covered, all around the strategy for the next ten years. The background to the club, coming up to 70 years old, was highlighted and the sterling efforts of members during those previous 70 years was acknowledged. Progress against the last plan was discussed, as were the plans for the years ahead. During the discussion around winches, a couple of interesting slides on "vintage" Portmoak winches were shown. An animated "artist's impression" of the new hangar was shown and progress discussed. The session ended with a plea for members to offer their assistance to help with the prep work ahead of the construction of the hangar.

The next topic up for consideration was the suggestion for an open day in July 2004. The reason for the open day was to celebrate the club's 70th anniversary, and a number of options were discussed. Although the first meeting of gliding enthusiasts was in 1934, the true amalgamation of the clubs, and therefore the creation of the "Union" did not take place until 1937 so there was some debate as to the validity of the 70th anniversary. Nevertheless, it was agreed that the principle was sound and the event could coincide with the opening of the new hangar.

As the first issue of *Portmoak Press* for 2004 was being finalised, John Guy submitted an item for consideration:

A Tale of Two Flights

What's special about that, you may ask? Nothing really. But of the two wave flights I've done, there is rather a large gap! Thirty seven years to be precise.

If you look in my log book you will notice that I did no flying from 1967 to 2001. I am not the only one. Those of us who have been in the same boat, we all seem to put it down to the same things: demanding jobs with long hours, demanding children, huge mortgages, unsympathetic bank managers and wives.

But now I'm retired, the children have been pushed out of the nest; the mortgage has been paid off and I'm getting under my wife's ft. Yippee.

In the old days, training was rapid and not very thorough. I shudder to think now of what we got away with.

I became a member at Portmoak in 1965 (having done my basic training at Lasham), I was checked out in a T21 by Tom Davidson and John Henry, then sent solo in the club Tutor. This was the nearest thing to a flying brick that I had ever met. I never even made it to Bishop Hill, in the eight times that I flew it.

Then I graduated to the club Slingsby Swallow. A sort of squared off K8, which did not have a brilliant performance but was fun to fly. The air brakes were *huge and very effective. The first wave flight was in the Swallow on 29th. March 1966.*

Tom Davidson showed me how to smoke the barograph and sealed it for me. It was 3.45 p.m., and the wave looked good. I had never been in wave before but I was told I would be OK.

The tug, a tiger moth, towed me west over the loch to 3,000ft. I felt the surge so thought this must be it and released. I was not mistaken and went up like a lift. With the wind speed about the same as the cruising speed of the glider, I just had to point North West and sit there. Within about forty minutes I was at 11,250ft. There was slide film in the camera so I snapped the view to the west, breathtaking.

I was still going up but I had no oxygen, I was getting cold and most importantly, the gaps in the lenticular bars had filled in, so I had no way of knowing where I was. Common sense prevailed. I opened those huge air brakes and stuffed the nose down. I trimmed it to fly virtually hands off as I punched a hole in the cloud. Fortunately, it was a relatively thin layer and I broke through at 4,000ft, directly over Portmoak. What a relief. I relaxed and took some snaps of the airfield, but they came out rather dark.

Back on South Field, the only landing strip then, I was greeted by Tom, who signed my barograph.

My silver "C" gain of height was accepted and the certificate is still valid and carefully filed away.

Having been away from gliding for so long I quite rightly had to start from the beginning again. Things had changed a lot from those far off days. The gliders are faster and heavier and the training is far more thorough. I had forgotten everything. It took three weekly courses and a lot of mid-week training to get me off solo again. I blamed two things, the weather which had been appalling for the previous two summers and the fact that

I could not master speed control. Eoin MacDonald came to my rescue on the Bronze 'C' course. I was not flying with reference to the horizon; I had been chasing the ASI round the dial. After that was put right, progress has been back on course.

Having re-soloed this May I have been working hard to re-do my bronze 'C' to bring myself up to date with the theory as well as the practice of gliding. The new booking system for training flights has been a boon this year; eliminating the waiting around which I regard as the curse of gliding training.

I caught Neil Irving and said, 'There are still a few things on my Bronze C red card that I need to do, are you free next Tuesday?'

'OK', he said, 'but the forecast is for a hurricane. We can always go to the briefing room and sort out your navigation theory'

Tuesday, 7th October 2003, wind north west 15-20 kt, 4/10ths cloud, in the form of lenticulars from north east to south west, as far as the eye could see. Cloud base 4000ft.

'It took me ages to get into that stuff this morning' said Neil. Always the optimist. 'We'll try for Montrose this afternoon'.

We got out the DG505, put the tips on and DI'd it and by one- thirty we were at the launch point and doing checks. Eventualities out of the way, I said brightly, 'Benarty first?'

'No', he said, 'It takes ages to get into the wave from there; we'll try for the north face of Bishop'. 1,400ft. on the launch, a smart turn to the right and we were off towards West Lomond at sixty kt.

'I have control', said the voice from behind, as I foundered around in sink. We closed up on the ridge and found a little lift in the bowl. A few short beats and

we had enough height to make it round the corner to the north face.

At 1,500ft we ventured a short way away from the ridge to try and nibble at the wave. It was very elusive and patchy at first. Sudden bursts of 10 up, but they were not sustained and it was rather turbulent.

'Try circling in the strong lift when you find it again.' said Neil. It worked! We clawed our way up to cloud level and inched forward in the 40 knot wind. Then suddenly we were in the real stuff at 4,000ft. The turbulence died away and, with a little gentle probing forward, the vario needles hit the stops and stayed there. We started climbing in earnest. The needle of the altimeter wound round steadily. It was very easy to drift back over the wave bar if you were not careful. Positioning the glider in the best lift required quite a lot of concentration in the strong wind.

'We need at least 10,000ft. to jump in front of the next bar north,' said Neil.

It was not long before the altimeter obliged. So, with a bearing of north - north west, I pushed the stick forward and trimmed for 100 kt and we were off.

'Aim for that small saddle in the wave bar, we must stay above cloud.' I did as I was bid. It was like a six mile landing approach. My eye was fixed on the saddle. Were we going to clear it? Was it moving up the canopy, which meant that we were undershooting or was it moving down? It did not move relative to that fixed point on the canopy. We were going to do it. But only just. We lost 4,000ft. in six miles at one hundred kt.

'Let's hope we find lift on the other side of the bar!' There are some people who fill you with confidence! Of course we found lift!

We entered a corridor about five miles wide, bounded on both sides by strong lenticular bars that extended well out to sea, and there in the middle of the *corridor, on the coast was Montrose, waiting for us. I thought, there is nothing to stop us now. Don't hang about, cold was creeping into our toes, so I pushed the stick forward. 100 kt on the ASI and the varios were still showing two kt up! I could not believe it. What a ship the DG is, a Rolls Royce of Gliders.*

I remembered that I had a camera in the boot of the car. What a relief, Neil has brought his logger so our epic flight can be recorded for posterity after all.

We turned Montrose at over 10,000ft and on the way home reached 12,000ft. I looked at my finger nails, they looked dark grey. I'm suffering from anoxia, help! Then I remembered I was wearing Raybans. On lifting them up, my nails became a healthy pink. What a relief! I was a bit worried about Neil though, he seemed to be enjoying the flight despite my sloppy flying. Is this one of the effects of anoxia?

It would have been great to have had oxygen and found the top of the wave, but we had achieved enough for one day, so set course for home.

Jumping back to the bar we had first climbed in was a piece of cake. Found Bishop and some heavy sink to help us get down. Ran into an air pocket just as Neil was taking a swig from his bottle. Result, lemonade all over the inside of his canopy!

'I want a nice tight circuit, don't get caught out by these strong conditions,' said Neil wiping his canopy.

Carefully does it, plenty of speed on the approach. Nicely lined up on south field, plenty of airbrake as I'm high. Clearing the fence at the right height. Watch the speed, 65 kt.

Wind gradient! Damn! Worse than I expected!

'I have control!' comes the voice from the back. Airbrakes are closed and we float to a soft touchdown. I've just learnt the most important lesson of the day, which I will not forget.

Nor will I forget the best flight I have ever had, thanks Neil.

At the end of the year, *Portmoak Press* reported that "Old Joe" had died after a short illness:

Joe Gadzinski, also known as Joe the Pole, or Joe the Winch, was a well-known face around Portmoak for many a year. Visitors to the SGU will remember him sitting quietly with his bowl of soup or cup of tea, looking out at the airfield. In 1978, Joe was our professional winch driver and he had many epic flights in his Cumulus, and his rebuilt Lspatz. He will be greatly missed, and the clubhouse seems empty without him.

The year ended with the usual awards night and trophies were presented to the following:
B.Scougall & J.Galloway (Thorburn Two-Seater)
K.Hook (Boyle Altitude Trophy)
J.Williams (Marshall 100km Triangle)
T.Brown & G.Fraser (Andy Penswick)
J.Williams (Parker Distance – 753Km)
J.Williams (Docherty Handicapped Distance)
J.Williams (Sutherland Out & Return)
J. Williams (Lomond)
J.Williams (Maclay Championship)
B.Scougall (Peter Copeland)
J.Williams (Hot Wings)
J.Williams (Height Gain Ladder)
S.Derwin (Nick Wales)
C.Guthrie (Darren Powell)
C.Hamilton (Instructor's Quaich)

As can be seen from the awards list, John Williams was sweeping the boards. Not content with simply flying, he joined the Board and was immediately promoted to chairman as Brian

Cole-Hamilton stood down, following his three year stint, at the March 2005 AGM. Brian had been instrumental in driving ahead with the new hangar and by the time the AGM was underway, foundations had been dug and steel work was arriving on site.

Work on the hangar progressed steadily through the spring of 2005 and the publicity department produced press reports and invitations to the forthcoming 70th anniversary and open day, which became a two-day event on 10th & 11th July. New Chairman John Williams summed up the event for *Portmoak Press*:

> *On Saturday we entertained and flew our National, European, and Local political representatives as well as a number of ex-members. These included legendary pilots like Roy Surtees, James Allan, Andrew Wood, Bob McBain, Bob Smith and Geoff Berry. We were particularly pleased when Geoff agreed to "Cut the Tape" for the official opening of the new hangar. This was especially fitting, as Geoff had been involved in the building of the original hangar way back in 1957. The politicians learned a lot and seemed to enjoy their flying, and they went away with a new level of understanding of our sport, which can only be a good thing for us all.*

Geoff Berry Cutting the tape at the official opening of the hangar, watched by Mike Barnacle, John Purvis, Martin O'Neill and Chairman, John Williams.

> *Some of the ex-members cast considerable doubt on our thinking on "currency" – after two minutes handling an*

unfamiliar aircraft after a twenty five year break and they looked like getting their names back on those club-trophies yet again!

We had good press coverage with reporters from The Scotsman and the Perth and Kinross group on the day and they produced some excellent articles for us during the following week.

In the evening we saw a busy clubhouse, a packed bar, a ceilidh and an excellent buffet. Rab's Lake of Menteith trout catching prowess and Steven's cooking seem to be a very fine combination.

Sunday saw a continuous stream of members' spouses, friends and children being flown with the tug and three two-seaters in non-stop operation all day. No less than 37 aero-tows were done – something of a recent record I think. Did anyone spot the 2050 CFI among those P2s just tall enough to see out of the rear seat of a K21?

All of this took an enormous amount of organisation, time, effort, and dedication from an awful lot of individuals. All deserve our heartfelt thanks, and should feel very proud of the part they played in marking this piece of club history in such an enjoyable and successful way.

A number of the dignitaries who flew at the weekend were fortunate enough to fly over the "T in the Park" music festival at Balado but I suspect few of them knew of the link between the SGU and the old Balado airfield.

Another link with the past had come to an end, news had reached the club that Betty Barr had died. Betty and her husband, Charlie, had been the club stewardess and steward at the opening of the clubhouse at Portmoak. After Charlie died, Betty continued to operate the catering facilities for several years until she was involved in a car accident.

One Portmoak Pilot decided to try his hand further afield in search of his elusive 50K Silver Distance. Peter Clayton set off on an epic trip to South Africa. *Portmoak Press* relayed his story:

South African Soaring Safari

It all began on a wet day at Portmoak last October (an all too frequent occurrence!). To pass the time I was looking at the notice board in the clubhouse and saw a poster with a photo captioned "13,000 ft and climbing at 8kt". Now that didn't sound like Portmoak! I read on, to see the other attractions advertised by Dick Bradley's Winter Performance Camp at Bloemfontein in South Africa. All of which looked great, especially when compared with the rain outside. I looked at Dick's web site that evening and then e-mailed him. In due course an LS4 was booked for the second and third weeks in February – right at the end of their season. I trawled the web to find a way of getting to Bloemfontein and booked a 6am KLM flight from Edinburgh to Johannesburg via Amsterdam (great views of the Sahara on the way) and a hire car for the easy drive 400km drive to Bloemfontein on good, almost empty, roads.

What a change from Scotland in the winter! Blue skies, 35°c temperature and SUN! I found the Gliding Club from the directions on the web site. It seemed empty in the early afternoon, then I found Reb Rebbert packing gliders from the UK into the container to return home. All the "local" gliders were away on the day's task. Dick's Soaring Safari operation uses his ASH25, Ventus, LS6 and LS4 (as well as the gliders from the UK in the main season). They use the facilities of the Bloemfontein Gliding Club at New Tempe airfield, which is part power - using hard runways as well as the grass runways used by gliders.

As the afternoon progressed, gliders began to return and Dick briefed me on the local airspace, flying conditions, radio routines, etc. Interesting to hear that because of the high altitude (ground level is 4,500') TAS is significantly higher than IAS. One key briefing item was "brown fields are good, green fields are bad" for landing out – due to the hidden presence of hard termite mounds in the green fields. The large ploughed "brown" fields are excellent for landing out, as the soil is very fine and gliders stop quickly.

After briefing I was introduced to the LS4 and its Cambridge navigation instrumentation (GPS is very helpful in the flat countryside). When setting the instruments, I tried in vain to zero the altimeter only to be told that they "won't wind back that far" and have to be set at 4,500' – the true height. No check-flight in a two-seater but briefed to be careful of the dust cloud behind the Cessna tug and the hard bumpy ground on take off. Once in the air it was clear why gliding in South Africa is so good – the air was very unstable and the tow to 2,000 ft pretty vigorous, similar to Feshie on a good day. Off tow and have a good look around to try to register the landmarks, identify the edges of the airspace and get used to the LS4. Lovely glider, similar to the Pegase but nicer, and more forgiving. Lots of strong lift and equally strong sink. Great!

Every morning Dick gives a weather briefing at 10am, following which each pilot is set a task for the day. At the end of the day, the loggers are downloaded onto "See You" software and a full debriefing given. This was very useful as I was given a lot of advice about the need for tight turns in thermals, not to waste time in weak thermals, speeds to fly, etc., etc.

On my third day I was tasked to fly to Dealesville and return for silver distance. This was the first time I had attempted a "real" cross-country in a glider so it was quite a thrill to fly away from "home". The Cambridge system gave a clear indication of the course to follow; distance to go, etc., and I arrived over the tiny town at almost 10,000' (5,500' AGL) I returned to New Tempe, then flew around the area to enjoy the fabulous flying conditions.

The conditions the next day were not so good, with warning of thunderstorms. I was tasked to go to Dealesville *again, but half way there was faced with the storm and attempted to fly round it. After an hour I was forced to give up and land out. I found a nice-looking brown field near a farmhouse and landed. After phoning New Tempe, who asked for my detailed GPS latitude and longitude (mobile phones seem to work everywhere in South Africa), I left the glider and went to find the farmhouse. The farmer was away but when I got back to the glider there were farm workers there who were very helpful. One of them spoke some English and offered to get a tractor to tow the glider out of the field. In the end the retrieve crew were able to get the 4-wheel drive and trailer to the edge of the field and we de-rigged and carried the parts to the trailer. If we had tried to drive onto the field we would have been bogged down in the fine soil. Because the farms are huge by our standards and the good roads few and far between, it helps to land near a road or retrieves can be difficult. The GPS co-ordinates are very useful to the retrieve crew.*

The next day promised to be much better and I was tasked to fly out and return to Andersfield, a total of 165km. The conditions were amazing by my standards with 10 up thermals and a cloud base of 13,500' – most of the flight was between 10,000' and 13,000' and I arrived back over the start point at just over 10,000'! In those conditions it was quite easy and it would have been easy to repeat the task. Oxygen is fitted in all the gliders but as the ground level is 4,500' and one soon acclimatises, it is suggested that it is not necessary below 13,500'.

The following day was not so good, with a 20% chance of thunderstorms, but I was tasked to fly a declared 305km triangle to Hoopstad, Hertzogville and return to attempt a gold and diamond goal distance claim. It seemed a huge distance for me to attempt but the previous day had given me more confidence – misplaced as it turned out! The first leg to Hoopstad was 155km and was not too difficult until some 25km from the turn point when it all seemed blue over Hoopstad in the distance. There was a promising looking cumulus about 20km to the East between the turn points so I went towards that. As I approached the cloud, I was about 3,000' AGL, and as I went under the cloud the sink rate went up until it was off the bottom of the clock at 10+ down! Finally when I was down to 1,500', and my nerve was about to give in, I hit the lift – bliss! The lift was equally off the clock and I climbed to cloud base at 10,000' – a great experience as I started the climb thermalling tightly over a farmhouse, which then got smaller as I climbed almost over the same spot! After that I flew to the first turn point, then backtracked under the same thermal to get to the second turnpoint at Hertzogville. I found another good thermal over the town which took me back to 11,000', then turned for the 118km leg back to the start point to complete the task. At first all went well, but with 60km to go the sky in front went almost completely blue (I later learnt that a thunderstorm had gone through and soaked the ground). I tried to final glide from 5,000' AGL but about 20km from New Tempe it was clear that I wasn't going to make it and I selected a field near to a farmhouse. However I misjudged the height, turned finals too high, landed too far into the field and had to ground loop and slide sideways into the fence at the edge of the field. Again a phone call to New Tempe telling them I had landed out, with the bad news that I had damaged the undercarriage and the underside of the fuselage on the stones at the edge of the field. During debriefing after the retrieve the view was that part of the problem was probably that, in spite of drinking all of the water in my 2 litre Camelback, I was dehydrated in the hot dry air after a flight of over 5 hours and my judgement suffered. In future I must get a bigger Camelback and drink as much water as possible before take off. So much for gold distance and diamond goal hopes!

The silver lining was that shortly after I landed a 4-wheel drive came across the field driven by the Afrikaans farmer and his wife to check that I was all right. They took me back to their farm to wait for the retrieve and could not have been friendlier. We all sat in the shade of a tree in the garden drinking home made ginger beer and eating peeled prickly pear from the garden (tastes like kiwi fruit, but nicer). The next day I went back with suitable gifts to thank them and spent most of the afternoon there. I was invited to come and stay next year and to bring my wife with me this time! Wonderful people with whom I hope to keep in touch.

After this the weather began to change, with thunderstorms and torrential rain. There were big floods in Bloemfontein with water up to car bonnets. The other visiting pilots did fly but had several land outs. I had a flight in the front seat of the ASH25 with Dick, who showed me just how easy it was (for him!) to fly cross-country even in poor conditions. It would probably have been a good idea to have had such a flight at the beginning of my visit.

Bloemfontein is the capital of the Orange Free State but has little of great interest to visitors except the museum and the botanical gardens. The atmosphere at the Gliding Club is very relaxed with an honesty system for drinks from the bar, snacks, etc., which are all very reasonable. Four nights a week an evening meal or barbecue is prepared at the clubhouse and on the other evenings most visitors go out to a restaurant in Bloemfontein. Everybody is very friendly and I never felt threatened anywhere during my visit – not at all the violent image that one can get of South Africa in the media here. A great place to visit – especially during the Scottish winter!

On my return I sent off my silver distance claim to the BGA and waited for the reply. After a month I spoke to Basil Fairston who told me that he was not happy that the claim had not been signed by a BGA official observer.

Apparently other (much more exalted) claims were also held up. Eventually the problem was solved by the Soaring Society of South Africa officially appointing Dick Bradley as their international claims officer entitled to authorise BGA claims in South Africa and four months after my claim flight I received my silver certificate.

The trip was well worth while and very enjoyable. I didn't get gold or diamond distance and even the silver caused problems, but I learnt a lot and, in spite of that unfortunate field landing, gained a lot of confidence and experience. I cannot recommend Soaring Safaris highly enough.

By the end of the summer, the new hangar had been completed, commissioned and was full of aircraft. Everyone was pleased with the outcome and the club proudly showed visitors around the new aircraft store. John Williams continued to test the boundaries of his skill and endurance to gain the BGA 750K Diploma. Official Observer (OO), Kevin Hook, updated the membership via the club mag:

My congratulations go to John Williams on completion of his 750km diploma on Thursday, 23rd September – and all done within Scotland. As the OO processing his flight, I can confirm that everything is in order and we await ratification of his flight by the BGA.

Not only did John achieve his long held ambition, but he actually soared for almost 850km at 100kph including the legs to and from his remote start/finish at Bridge of Cally. It was an incredible triumph of determination on a day which had the rest of us struggling. He crossed to the Isle of Mull twice (I can tell you from personal experience that this is not a pleasant place to be grovelling at 3500ft) and found his way through the barely intelligible mass of seven and three quarter octas over the centre of the country. He made steady progress, leaving his only mistake until half way down the final leg - a mistake that reduced his task speed to "only" 102kph.

Congratulations John - time to start running wave cross country courses for the rest of us.

Portmoak Press also printed detailed instructions on the operation of the new hangar. These included the use of the sliding doors, locking mechanisms, parachute store, battery store and general housekeeping of the hangar and surrounding ground.

Chapter 20
2006 – 2007
Epic Flights – Old and New

Towards the end of 2005, a few intrepid SGU members had agreed to ferry an old open cockpit T21 from Strathaven to Portmoak so that Strathaven and SGU members could keep the old bird flying. On a cold December, John Henry and Joe Fisher wrapped themselves up, strapped themselves in and John O'Donnell towed them home to Portmoak behind the Pawnee. John Guy produced an excellent DVD of this historic flight and the "World Premier" was held at the end of year "bash".

A very proud Walking on Air group met with spontaneous applause when news of their achievements during the year was presented that evening:

Walking on Air
The Royal Aero Club (RAeC) Certificate of Merit was awarded to our very own Walking on Air at a ceremony held at the National Army Museum in Chelsea on 3rd February. Joe Fisher, Rab Mitchell, David Tuttle and Irene Donald accepted the award on behalf of WOA. HRH the Duke of York presented the award and was seen chatting to the group after the ceremony. Don't know (yet) what Rab was saying but it caused HRH to laugh and smile about something!

A certain *Portmoak Press* reporter, Slarty Bartfast, also attended that annual event and his rantings were published in the first issue of 2006:

It was a wild Saturday night at the club on January 8th - and that was just the leg from the car park to the inside of the clubhouse! Despite some peoples' worries, the power (and the roof) stayed on and a good night developed. The place was full to overflowing and Steve, Irene and the team managed to somehow deliver an excellent dinner (after reminding a few of us what we'd once ordered and long since forgotten) to the packed tables.

Then began a wee experiment - a combination of a bit of home entertainment and a well-kent guest speaker. John Guy's talents as a Hollywood producer soon became evident with a DVD of "The flight of the T21" - compiled on that cold December day when an intrepid trio of Jim O'Donnell (Pawnee), Joe Fisher and John Henry (alfresco at the cold end of the aerotow rope). Great fun to watch. After that John Williams introduced our guest speaker, none other than Mike Bird, with an "Address to the Platypus". Mike did us proud, somehow managing to entertain the pilots and normal people alike with a mixture of wit, wisdom and his vast experience. Things like "there are two ways to increase cross country performance, span and talent - and the good news is that you can buy span!". It's astonishing how quickly twenty minutes disappears when you get the opportunity to listen to someone like this.

John Williams was obviously paying attention to Platt (Mike Bird) and exercised his right to reply to all those doubters and accusers through the pages of *Portmoak Press following his recent 500km flight at an average of 150km/h in his LS8:*

Fancy a quick one?
Some are accusing me of getting old and past it, listening to Plat about TINSFOS and even resorting to battery driven aids.... so maybe it's time to pass on a few pointers about how-to-do-it before all gets forgotten. As in many things it's worth putting lots of time and effort into the pre-stages to make the main event that bit special. On the 14th of September last year, it took more than three hours getting ready to start – once started

there was no stopping right through to an unstoppably fast finish. So much so that everything since has been almost an anti-climax.

Entry is everything

There are days when things are going so well that just a bit of extra pull on the wire and before you know it you're straight in – at other times it needs such a delicate touch – gliding gently over every curved feature for as long as it takes. All I can suggest is to coax your machine for every available inch and sooner or later something will move in the air or the earth and you'll start to sense a gentle but quickening rise – a great feeling.

Keep it up

There is nothing so disappointing as falling out after all that careful effort. If you feel things starting to slip – move position a little and watch carefully to see if things are better – just turning a few degrees to one side or the other can make all the difference to staying up.

Getting the task done

Don't get high. It may feel good but your performance will suffer and no-one will be impressed by a slow finish. Also don't turn around unless you're confident you won't fall out as a result – it can happen to even the most skilful in a matter of moments. When forced to turn (e.g. if your height demands it – or at the vital turns between legs) you must really pay attention – hitting the sink during such a critical maneuver is disastrous and may take hours and hours to retrieve. Then when you're absolutely sure that the finish is close just let rip – push as hard as you can – so long as you weren't really high earlier there is really nothing to lose. Afterwards If it's been a really special performance you'll need to unwind. Batteries have to be re-charged and maybe covers replaced while you think back on those delightful waves. You may want to boast to others (from near the top of a ladder is a great place.) You can even use uras if you like that sort of thing. But remember that even if you feel tired now – you may have a chance to do it all again at first light tomorrow. So it's off early to bed .....

If you are still unclear about what John is talking about, read on, this was the S&G version:

Fancy a Quick One? (another version)

In November 2004, I'd flown a fast 500km despite losing a chunk of time (and nearly some more important things!) by falling into cloud at Linn of Dee. The forecast for September last year had been looking promising for several days with a moderate north-westerly flow due across Scotland. So I put the LS8 (Z7) into 15 metre mode, added four barrels of water and declared the same task – a remote start and finish at COM (Comrie, suitably clear of the P600 airway) via HEU (Heugh Head, just north of Aboyne), LVE (Loch Venacher, near Callander) and MOS (Mossat, north of HEU).

The winch launch was fine but after an hour and a half I hadn't even reached 2,500ft – never mind a wave system or a start sector. That took an additional two hours, with an initial wave climb followed by almost falling out again in a very unstable, shifting wave "system"

More than once the thought of landing back at Portmoak for warmth and lunch came to mind – but each time the thought seemed to generate another knot of lift and eventually the start sector came into view.

Without much confidence I pushed off along the first leg and, despite fairly scruffy looking lines of cumulus, found that I could climb on track while maintaining decent speed to arrive at HEU 109km away in 44 mins for 147km/h.

The second leg worked out okay after I jumped to a wave bar just south of Loch Tay that led in and out of a cloudy LVE for 137km/h.

Jumping further to windward on leg three seemed to be a mistake with a need to jump downwind again to reach MOS – but at least I'd the mistake (and the terrors) of falling into cloud at Linn of Dee, as I had the previous time. To my surprise, leg three had been the fastest yet at 173km/h, though I was down to 5,500ft at the turn and had to put in a few beats to climb enough to reach Loch Muick, which looked as though it would work well.

I couldn't resist a call to Aboyne to tell Roy Wilson of my progress – he'd finished a fast 500km two hours earlier in the same tricky conditions that I'd been struggling in before starting. It seemed that the 150km/h task might just be possible.

The rest of the leg became a blur – trying to remember when I'd started, work out how many feet of the allowable 1,000 metre height loss I'd use, and what speed in knots I'd have to maintain to cover the remaining kilometers...With brain hurting I decided to just fly flat out – put the Artificial Horizon on and blast through any cloud that got in the way – and who cares if I land out after the finish? Nearly did just that and took an age to scrape back into lift at 3,000ft to make it home after all. Rushed to download the trace – and was delighted to discover that I'd done it – by the slightest of margins – 504.8km at an average speed of 150.1km/h.

So here are a few of my personal thoughts on how to achieve high speeds in wave:

Weather and Tasks

Just as with thermals, you need both the right day and the right task. The biggest recent breakthrough has been the ready availability of good satellite images. Looking at them each day helps to build up a picture of how wave systems are likely to set up in a particular area. It's even possible to overlay the satpic onto task planning software before selecting the task. Then launch and be pleasantly surprised to find that the same wave bars have hardly moved when you get there! For maximum speed, just set the task along the energy lines and avoid both into-wind and down-wind jumps. Wave systems often align with terrain as well as wind and therefore bend through significant angles. These can be used to advantage – although on the Scottish East Coast they can rather disconcertingly take you out to sea before refracting back into the turn point near Stonehaven.

Wing Loading

There are two balances to be struck. Firstly if you fly with water ballast will you risk being embarrassed by the freezing level and won't be able to climb high to get across an area of poor lift or 8 octas. Secondly it's wonderful to have maximum wing loading to blast along strong wave bars – but the higher sink rate can be a real pain when desperately trying to get established in wave in the first place.

Operating Height and Maximum Lift

On a given day the best lift can be really close to the wave bar – on another it can be at least half way to the next bar up-wind. I don't understand how or why this happens – but it certainly pays to explore a bit each day. With height there's another trade off to consider. Imagine that the clouds are no more than normal ridges and treat them that way. So maximum speed is often at or below ridge (cloud) height. Unfortunately from here you can't be sure about the shape (or existence) of the clouds and gaps further on track. Climbing high can give you more of a satellite view and a chance to understand what lies ahead. So it's best to fly fast and low when confident about what's ahead, ease back and climb en-route when you're not. Don't ever turn or stop unless things ahead look horrible.

Imaginary Lines

Often the skill lies in "joining the dots" of disorganised clumps of cloud to invent a wave bar that really ought to exist – sometimes the ones that aren't there work better than the "real" ones!

Pythagoras and Speed

Understand the vectors. To fly along a wave bar you need to maintain an into wind component equal to the wind speed. On a day with 40kts winds at flying height and at 40kts airspeed you can only "park". Fly at 50 and you progress along the bar at 31kts, at 60 its 45kts, at 70 it's 58kts. To achieve 150kph along the leg you need to fly at shade over 90kts. A well-ballasted LS8 will do that and maintain height if it stays in lift of only 3kts or so.

Reverse McCready theory?

To stay in the height band with the strongest lift I sometimes find myself speeding up in the best lift and slowing down again the weaker stuff. This is far from what we've all learnt in thermal flying. Some of the classical theory still holds though – assess the climb rates available a few miles ahead and set your speed so that you reach it in a position to best use it.

Learning and Motivation

These two more things that have really helped us raise speeds in recent years. A big thank-you to John Bridge for setting up the National Ladder website. Not only does the importance of speed to scoring become clear but we can see just what those other pilots have been up to – their traces speak more loudly than any "howidunnit" I've ever heard. And so more thanks goes to Kevin Hook at Portmoak and Roy Wilson and Jack Stephen at Aboyne for continually cranking up the competitive stakes – long may it continue! Hopefully I can continue to up the ante - I wonder if the Antares electric motor really will be quiet enough to evade the logger's noise detector - and will someone recharge my batteries on the way round?

John's reference to the "Antares" was in anticipation of the imminent delivery of his new self-launch electric powered glider. This "first in the UK" machine would open up a whole new world of gliding possibilities for John and he and Kevin Hook would soon be vying for ladder points and end of year trophies.

When John first visited the Antares factory in Germany, his non-flying partner, Wendy MacPhedran, took advantage of the offer of a trip to Germany, and the S&G published her thoughts and observations:

Another view of Antares

I knew nothing of Axel Lange or his Antares motorglider when my partner, John Williams, unexpectedly asked me: "How would you like to fly to Germany so I can sit in a specially fitted large cockpit in a newly conceived electric motorglider? Oh, and fly out Monday and be back Tuesday night?" I tried to be enthusiastic but, try as I might, this was tough. I silently expected the highlight of the trip to be standing around for eight hours in a dirty, boring, smelly old Nissen hut of a factory with people who spoke a language I didn't understand (quite apart from the fact that the spoke German and I did not).

Being the supportive partner I like to think I am, my initial revulsion gradually evolved into reluctance – and then I realised that Zweibrucken was close enough to Trier to allow a visit. I determined that I could withstand hour after hour of knee/hip pain standing on concrete floors in an all-male environment if this was followed by a delicious dinner in an open-air four-star restaurant on the streets of Trier. Fine wine, gentle breezes, flower boxes on every window, children playing in a small city park across the street. Yes, I could do this. So my conditions were set – excellent food, fine wine, luxurious hotels, ancient history, and perhaps some shopping for things you can't get anywhere near Portmoak.

On approach into Frankfurt's Hahn Airport, I was struck by the thought that it was probably an ex-World War Two airfield, much like those near Portmoak. I felt slightly disturbed as we left, wondering how many young men drove on these very roads 60 or more years ago to jump into airplanes that bombed Scotland, and how many were now lying at the bottom of the Channel or the North Sea. I shook off the discomfort and tried to enjoy the countryside during our two hour drive. As we approached Lange's factory at Zweibrucken Airport (complete with WW2 Nissen huts) the same uncomfortable feeling – of closeness to past conflicts – surfaced. Another irony was that we left Scotland as the G8 summit was starting at Gleneagles; I hoped politicians would work to avoid asking young men to kill each other in beautiful places like this. Of course, the whole reason we went to Germany during the G8 was that airspace restrictions around Portmoak were getting in the way of gliding and John knew he wouldn't get "the big flight" in. I feel big relief when we have a few days in a row that are obviously not "the flying day of the year". His continual studying of weather charts and webcams somewhat abated, and the pressure was off both of us.

This was the part of the trip that I anticipated having to "grin and bear it". I was glad that I had worn old, dark clothes so the grime and smell of the greasy old hangar/factory would not ruin any favourite clothing.

We pulled up outside a modern new building. Nice, but perhaps a bit too slick to be friendly. We walked in the front door and saw that the security door to the inner rooms was propped open with a wedge of wood. OK, so people are relaxed here – trusting, even. I started to LIKE this place. No nasty smells, clean floors, fresh air and lots of light. It might not be as bad as I expected.

We were met and welcomed by Ola Roer Thorsen. First glance put his age at about 16, but I quickly realised that he was in his 20s, even if he still had an "aw, shucks" face and demeanour. Ola was wearing a blue t-shirt and khaki cotton pants, and interacted with us in the same casual way pilots meet pilots on airfields. We walked from the office building to the factory. Imagine my surprise when I opened the door into a large, airy and bright room filled with large pieces of aircraft, wing moulds, all sorts of cutting machines, and relaxed (mostly) young men in jeans and t-shirts going about their work. They were friendly and openly smiling at me! It was very clear that they were enjoying their work. In fact, it looked as though everyone liked working here. I began to wonder who it was that created this work environment. Why was everyone so happy? Why was Ola so relaxed and able to be himself instead of trying to impress us? Why did the finish guys touch the partly constructed sailplanes with what was almost tenderness? What's going on? This felt more like an artist's studio than a factory.

I have to admit that I got bored listening to John and Ola discuss the relative merits of one type of epoxy compared with another and about how the cockpit absorbed impact so that the pilot didn't have to. I wanted to know more about these people; how their experience of giving birth to these aircraft resulted in a more reliable, enjoyable glider.

As we stood looking at the crumple-able nose cone, a pleasant-looking man came over and shook our hands and said hello. He didn't seem to speak English so I just smiled and nodded, as you do.

Ola took us to where our test aircraft was being rigged. The view was stunning – a big-sky perspective of cumulus clouds with slightly greying bottoms, just like the kind John likes (actually, I like them tightly rounded and pink – J). As Ola and John were putting one of the wings on the plane, I took one look at the size and obvious weight of it and realised that, should we take one of these beauties home, there was no way I was going to be able to lift that and keep it steadied as John positioned it. Then the counter-balance rigging device emerged (comes as standard equipment) – it somehow twists and turns through every axis in an almost effortless way. This device was my friend! Even I could manage that.

We drove to lunch with the same pleasant man we had met in the factory. Ola walked us into the cafeteria-style eatery and we sat at a booth with schnitzel and fleischolanzl. The place was chosen because "it has decent food at sensible prices". Again, I liked the style. The pleasant man smiled and listened as we exchanged questions and answers about Antares and gliding in the UK and Germany. I didn't realise until later that he was the owner/founder, Axel Lange. Okay, so I have a preference for the non-fussy and an aversion for people who try to charm me with extravagancies but these people were genuine. And if I was right, it was Axel who set the tone and chose his partners to reflect his own values. Who is this guy?

After a very conscientious briefing by Ola, John was ready to fly. It was at this point that I realised one should not make assumptions about age and/or someone's skill based on the freckles on their face. Ola was brilliant – absolutely amazing. He knew this aircraft inside out and upside down. John turned on the engine and taxied to the runway. It sounded like a large room-fan, a rhythmic "swoosh" with no hint of that harsh two-stroke racket. The winglets perched delicately at the end of the elegant, long, sinuous wings. It's easy even for a layman to imagine how this contributes to silky, responsive handling.

Once John was airborne, I set my sights on finding Axel. My curiosity was at a peak – how did this unassuming man bring together such a strong team and enable them to work so well together? How did this engineer-by-trade accumulate the management skills to create a team capable of building the glider of the future? I found him in his office and when I asked him why he started this project he told me that when he first thought of Antares back in 1996, he felt "this was my chance to do the right thing". He was familiar with the idiosyncrasies of two-stroke engines and he dreamed of reliable, almost silent, high performance engines. He knew he'd need partner specialists to create a design that was inspirational – the embodiment of the future of gliding. Not being a man who does things by half, he went to Loek Boermans to design the wings and an F1 engineer to design the crash-proof cockpit. By this time I was hooked. If Axel has asked me to work for him I would have signed up immediately. He has what many quiet leaders posses – dignity, genuineness, and uncompromising passion to create something beautiful. I asked him why so many pilots were buying his plane, since it was clear that his "good idea" had taken shape and the production line was at full capacity. "Some buy for the silkiness of the flight," he said, "Some for the sophistication of the engine, but most buy because the glider is smart."

I noticed John returning so went outside. As we unstrapped John, the guys asked him how it went. It wasn't necessarily the fact that John was smiling as they opened the canopy, it was the depth of that smile. It came from his *toes. This was a happy man and I realised that a sale was imminent.*

The word that John used for the experience was "exquisite!" and for those who know John, he uses big words like that very rarely, and always selectively. I wondered whether or not there would be big-sell pressure tactics at this point. I shouldn't have worried. These men make these planes because they love them, because it's the right thing to do, and because they can. The closest they got to trying to sell this state-of-the-art flying machine to us was a quiet question: "So what do you think?"

Purists may not approve of engines in gliders, and those who do may not trust batteries in place of good-old-fashioned petrol motors. No one at Lange Flugzeugbau is going to try to twist your arm to buy one. However, I adore my pilot-partner and want to spend another 40 years with him. I trust these men and their glider, and if buying this Antares puts a smile on John's broad face each time he flies and brings him home safely, nothing will stop us having one!

Towards the end of March, one of the winch drivers – Steve Boston – became suspicious that the winch engine had become noisier than usual. The local Deutz agent was contacted and he visited the site. He confirmed that there was a problem with the engine's bottom-end and recommended that winching stopped immediately.

The engine was removed and Dave Clempson and Sant Cervantes took it to Hindles (The Deutz agents) in Cumbernauld for a full investigation, arriving as the workshops opened at 08:00 on the Monday morning.

Meanwhile, back at Portmoak, the cost of aerotow launches up to 1500ft were reduced to £13 for club members and day-to-day flying was maintained.

By 08:10 on the Monday, the Deutz service engineer had promised that the engine would be stripped and examined, and that we would have the results by the Tuesday afternoon or Wednesday morning. Unfortunately they did not fulfil this promise and it needed Douglas Tait's visit on site to encourage them in their work. They removed the sump and could find nothing wrong so promptly declared that a replacement engine was needed. Further negotiations resulted in the engine being taken away to Duncan Rogers in Glasgow. Here there was a better outcome, they stripped the engine and spotted the problem and even offered the club the use of a temporary engine until the original was repaired. Thanks to sterling efforts by a handful of SGU members and employees winching was able to recommence at the weekend, just five days after the original shut-down.

One old and bold gliding pilot was considering hanging up his flying gear and the following article from John Whitfield appeared in *Portmoak Press* towards the end of 2006:

The Final Flight?

I'm finding it increasingly hard to make time to fly but the forecast is good so I leave work and arrive at Portmoak to locate the Pilatus tied down in the South Field.

The DI shows that the tyres require inflation but otherwise all is OK and by mid-morning I've winch launched and I'm working some punchy, broken thermals on the north face of West Lomond.

After about 30 minutes I establish that the best lift is to the south of Auchermuchty but repeated attempts fail to make contact with any wave lift in front of what is obviously a wave induced cloud with a base of around 4,000ft.

As I fly under the cloud to about half a mile down wind of the leading edge, the lift becomes a steady +5 knots so, with the T&S wound up, I turn north, increase the airspeed to 60 knots to ensure a northerly track and climb steadily up through the cloud for a few minutes until I fly into clear air again at about 6,000ft in +6 knots.

Climbing steadily past the cloud tops at 9,000ft, I continue a normal wave climb to 14,000ft on oxygen, find a weak point in the wave then head north towards the next likely looking area of lift.

I re-establish in 4 knots at about 11,000ft and tracking steadily southwest with occasional glimpses of the A9 I continue climbing to 16,000 ft well to the north east of Dunblane.

I have now been flying for more than one and a half hours and although, unusually, the cold is not too bad, I am minded to check my supply of comfort bags – none!

More importantly, 16,000ft allows a good overview of the cloud tops 7,000ft below and although I still have a very oblique view of the Kincardine Bridge through a small gap away to the south east, it is obvious that to the east any gaps are now becoming few and far between. Heading back towards the general direction of Portmoak I ignore any lift and set my speed to 70 knots. When I confirm Auchterarder over to the west I am at 12,000ft and it is now time to dump some height doing what the Pilatus was built for.

A few loops, Spins and stall turns (not very crisp as the Pilatus has a small rudder which seems rather ineffectual at this altitude), then back onto a heading for home.

I settle down on the T&S and compass as the cloud tops come up to meet me at about 9,000ft. Patience is the name of the game – and trying to relax as much as possible.

After a time, which seems like forever, and with about 7,000ft on the altimeter, I catch sight of the ground giving me a reassuring positional check.

I select half airbrake, trim for 70 knots and estimate that I have a further 3,000ft to lose before seeing the ground again. At about 6,000ft it starts to rain but it doesn't last long and with a bit over 4,000ft on the altimeter, I catch some glimpses of the ground – and then Loch Leven ahead.

I lose height over the loch in an enjoyable manner, check the circuit etc., lower the undercarriage, trim to approach speed and complete a leisurely circuit, turning finals into the South Field where the Pilatus rolls gently to a halt and I lower the port wing onto the ground. I push the glider a few yards and tie it down. I don't think I'll be flying again.

Two years previously, the club had purchased a relatively new French single-seater – the Pegasse 101. This aircraft had a reasonable performance with retractable undercarriage and was very popular with a small band of pilots, the author included. Unfortunately, the vast majority of SGU single-seater pilots who were limited to flying club aircraft were not so comfortable with this less-forgiving aircraft and for many weeks, it languished in the hangar without generating much income for the club. Towards the end of 2006, a decision was made to replace this glider with a more suitable single-seater. An ex-service Discus B was located and arrangements made for delivery to the club at the beginning of 2007.

As 2006 came to an end, more changes to the controlled airspace around Portmoak were being finalised and a small band of hard working club members and officials prepared to hold a full briefing in the new year. The main effect of these new changes would mean a ban on all glider flying higher than FL195 except in specially designated high level gliding areas. Other activities towards the end of the year included some detailed testing of a new form of glider-friendly (low energy) anti-collision equipment.

The annual awards night took place in December and the clubhouse was once again filled to capacity with an excellent evening being had by one and all. The following people stepped up to the front to proudly accept their awards:

The Thorburn Two Seater Trophy
For the longest (handicapped distance) flight in any Two Seater
Winners:- Santiago Servantes and Valerie Alexander in the Scottish Gliding Association's ASH 25.

The Boyle Altitude Trophy
For the greatest gain of height.
Winner: Tony Brown in DG202 (14,790ft)

The Marshall 100 Km Triangle Trophy
For the fastest (handicapped speed) 100 km triangle (but less than 125 km).
Winner: Kevin Hook in DG400 (78km/h)

The Andy Penswick Trophy
For the longest (handicapped distance) flight in a club glider,
Winners: John Williams and Vic Leitch in DG505 (184km)

The Parker Distance Trophy
For the longest distance flight originating from Portmoak. Not handicapped.
Winner: Kevin Hook in his DG400/17 (747km)

The Docherty Handicapped Distance Trophy
For the longest (handicapped distance) flight originating from Portmoak.
Winner: Kevin Hook in his DG400/17 (754km)

The Sutherland Out and Return Trophy
For the farthest (handicapped distance) turnpoint achieved from Portmoak for a flight originating and ending at Portmoak.
Winner: Dave Clempson in his DG200 (596km)

The Lomond Trophy
For the longest triangular flight achieved from Portmoak subject to the 28% rule.
Winner: John Williams in his Antares 20E (390km)

The Maclay Championship Trophy
For the winner of the Open ladder competition.
Winner: Kevin Hook

<u>The Peter Copeland Trophy</u>
For the winner of the Weekend ladder competition.
Winner: Kevin Hook
<u>The "Hot Wings" Trophy</u>
For the winner of the "Hot Wings" ladder competition.
Winner: Z Goudie
<u>The Height Gain Ladder Trophy</u>
For the winner of the Height Gain Ladder Competition
Winner: Kevin Hook
<u>The Darren Powell Shield</u>
For service to the club during the year.
Winner: Charles Guthrie
<u>*The Nick Wales Trophy*</u>
For the "most improved pilot".
Winner: Garry Simpson
<u>*Instructors Quaich*</u>
Most popular instructor.
Winner: John Riley
<u>*Service Salver*</u>
For outstanding service to the club.
Winner: Dave Clempson

In many ways, 2007 proved to be a continuation of the constant strive for epic flights from Portmoak. Of course all flights are different but each "first" is an epic for someone. One such pilot searching for the final leg of his Silver Badge was Craig Chatburn. *Portmoak Press* recorded Craig's epic 50km cross-country flight:

> *Well it's been a long time coming, 2 1/2 years to be exact since my Silver height and duration.*
> *I arrived at Portmoak on a day when the Blipmaps promised a good thermal day in the middle of Scotland. A cold front had just gone through and a new airmass was upon us, there was a threat of sea breeze fronts on both coasts later.*

I was down as second pilot to have a flight in the ASH with Sant, but as he said there was only a window for one good training flight that day, would I like a hand to rig my own glider? I thought about it, I had only had a few flights this year between the K8, T21, K21 and Falke so not very current, and thought it would be good to get a bit of soaring & thermal and landing practice in my shared Std Jantar 3 (HUB) so we set about rigging it.

Then I thought I should set a task and after some advice from Sant, John D, John W and of course Kevin, the task was set so that either way if I reached any of my chosen turning points I should have Silver in the bag.

The task set was PCS-LOM-CAD-DRU-PCS, giving me quite a few options to get a silver leg, on hindsight Lake of Menteith and Callander are both too close, if in sector for CAD I was also in sector for LOM. The reason in my mind was that if I struggled to reach Stirling then I had the choice of two valleys to attempt the best path.

So, plans made, logger and GPS checked and wired - off to the launch point with the sky still not looking promising, took a launch around 11:30 with small thermals starting. Off we went, great start, due to poor launch technique and it being my first flight in the Glider for 6 months, 750ft at the top of the wire, got to the hill at 600ft only to be met by the ASH coming my way also at 600ft, chicken - me - yes, turned and after an abbreviated circuit came in too fast at 65 kts. Although current to fly, not very current if you see from that circuit, long float, long walk back to the launch point. Now in a queue at the launch point, Hang Gliders were launching about 400ft below the top of the Bishop and gain height just about 200 ft above the tops, thermals were kicking off and we stopped for lunch!

So, now I'm 6ᵗʰ in the queue, I help to launch other gliders, watching where they go. A K21 goes up the wire and straight into thermal over the Loch Edge. A Ventus and a pair or Cirrus turn left for a thermal, Then a Cirrus and the Ventus land again. Now it's my turn, I head for the Bishop bowl as no other gliders are on the hill, and the Hang Gliders have stopped for a rest on the top. I had a better launch this time 1200 feet (I later hear that the weak link went at the top of the launch) so I arrive at Bishop around 1000 feet. After a couple of S turns, I'm climbing in a thermal from the bowl up to 4400ft still QFE. This is easy I thought, so I set off on track for LOM, along a broken cloud street, stopping too often to get back up close to cloudbase. All the way to Dollar on that street then a big blue gap to Stirling. I tried a few times to go further west but realised I was on the wrong side off the Ochils and got caught in the curlover, I only got to within a mile of Alva so I headed back to Dollar, climbed as far as I could around 3400ft. I saw that a nice into-wind street had formed right over the Ochils from Dollar. I thought long and hard about using it but with terrain clearance and nowhere to go if it all went wrong so I turned back for Balado.

At Balado my next thought was to climb and cross Glenfarg and head up the north side of the Ochils. Each time I tried after climbing to around 4000ft, I was washed out in the lee of the Ochils. Hmmm...plan B - get a good climb head for Perth and try up the middle of the Earn valley. Perth was good, a nice climb to 5300ft, I was watching the traffic from Scone, very busy, so rather than go that way I headed for Callander, a few km down track and was again faced with a big blue gap. I dialled CAD into the GPS, 50ish km to go into wind, tried Drumshade 40ish km, so I turned round and thought downwind would now be the best option. On track for DRU there was just blue sky, but further south a nice cloud street, so I followed this, again taking too many climbs. This ran out around 8km from DRU, at 2900ft, I was well within final glide so for the first time in 3 hours I felt good.

Have you ever tried to spot Drumshade from the air? Without the GPS I don't think I would have seen it! All around is a great valley full of fields though. I turned DRU and headed home, now around 1600ft over Glamis Castle. A nice thermal to 2400ft, headed for masts 5km south of Glamis and took a climb but only back to 2200ft. What to do now? What if the logger wasn't working? What if......, so I turned round and headed back to Drumshade where nice thermals were working to around 2000ft, I had a great time playing in the sky for 30 minutes then it was time to land. No windsock at Drumshade when they are not operating (weekdays) but a nice field to land in. Circuit and landing were fine but needed to be careful when taxi-ing off line as there are a few rabbit holes.

Now, with no retrieve crew organised in advance, I called the clubhouse. Thanks to Irene once again, as she organised a retrieve. While I was waiting taking the wing-tape off etc., Rodger, a member of Angus and SGU turned up, we had a chat then off to his place for a cuppa – a fine cuppa it was too. Just as I left his house, Gary arrived to retrieve me back to Portmoak. We loaded the glider into the trailer in around 40 minutes - not bad when disorganised like me. We were about to drive off when I thought I'd have a last walk round as something was niggling me. I found the tail-plane propped against the side of the trailer – oops! So, with many thanks to Gary for the retrieve we got back and parked the trailer around 9pm. Was I really in the air for nearly 4 hours to do a 50k silver distance? Wow!

Portmoak Press was also the recipient of a large brown envelope containing the latest writings from that long time contributor – Slarty Blartfast. This time he had been spying on cats!

Cats' Tales
Day 1

Once upon a time, there was a Full Cat who was a good cat and stayed by his own fireside during the week, and at his adopted one at the weekend in Perthshire. He purred and frolicked with his mates who came to see him, and others of his kind, at the weekends. However, as the spring, and then the summer, came round he had a mind to wander, although he remained close to his adopted fireside at the weekends. He wandered into deepest Ayrshire to have a bit of fun with some long established pals who stayed in the area and some say he nearly strayed into recently revised forbidden territory close to Maybole. Happily, he managed to avoid trouble but decided to move his midweek dalliances to a different part of the world, Krinkly Bottom, where the milk was said to be creamier. He licked his paws and set off late one Wednesday afternoon for the destination of his heart's desire. On arrival, he was given a truly feline welcome by the local kindred cats, but wisely declined a saucer of milk until after the evening's fun. What shall we do tonight purred his pals and the Full Cat pushed his head up and felt the force of the wind on his whiskers. 'Goodness me' he declared, or words to that effect, 'that appears to be a noticeable cross wind'. As an impartial observer on the occasion, the wind didn't seem to be in the least angry, but it was definitely strong.

It had been a long hard day and poor old Slarty had been working with Kindred Spirit that day at his Ice Cream factory and had persuaded him to come along for the evening frolics at Krinkly Bottom. Kindred Spirit hadn't been too keen to come along as he had had a heavy sales date that day and was wearing a posh new pair of trousers accompanied by a swanky pair of shoes that he declared had 'cost a bloody fortune'. However, Slarty managed to prevail on the basis that it would relax him. Bad mistake. Never listen to Slarty.

The Full Cat found a paper aeroplane in a big shed and decided to have a go on the basis that a wee flight in it might just be the Cat's pyjamas. Looking around for a fellow conspirator, he persuaded the farmer's sheepdog 'Collie' to get in along with him. The non-participating felines gathered round and wound up the elastic band, good and tight. Off the two aviators went. The elastic band worked wondrously well with a good take off that indicated that the wind wasn't totally across the path of departure.

What fun it all was whizzing hither and thither in the bright blue yonder, or more accurately the steel grey yonder. But, 'nae man can tether time nor tide' the time to come home had arrived and the Full Cat pointed the paper aeroplane back towards the point of departure. Things didn't quite go according to plan. The origami, after coming round into wind(ish) to get back on the ground at an appropriate point didn't quite gel as intended so, 'if at first you don't succeed' etc. The tap was opened up to perform a go around but sadly the elastic band spluttered and stopped. Potential energy at this point was of the order of 100 to 150 feet and the kinetic energy appeared to be enough to keep it flying, but not an awful lot more. By a nice bit of flying the Full Cat gained as much height as he could, swung the paper aeroplane downwind in a path parallel to the runway although now sadly over the farmer's adjacent fields and certainly not the airfield. The soil in the area is gooey and deep and the fields in the area are fairly small and fenced. Add that to now proceeding downwind into a setting sun and you will see that neither the Full Cat nor 'Collie' was at ease. After some anxiety the dynamic duo arrived back on terra not so firma and managed to avoid the fences running at right angles to the flight path. On arrival and the cessation of all movement, they disembarked without further conversation, examined the paper aeroplane and congratulated each other.

Due to lie of the land, the spectator cats did not see the arrival of the paper aeroplane and feared for the worst and although they knew that at least one of dynamic duo had nine lives they didn't know how many he had already used up. They dashed out to see how things had faired for their pals and the CFI (Chief Feline Inspector), being of substantial build and not too quick on his paws jumped into his 4 X 4 and proceeded across Krinkly Bottom airfield towards the landing spot. Sadly, halfway there it got a bit bogged down in their own wet soil and had to be abandoned. Kindred Spirit having viewed the fun standing on a nice dry piece of ground sprung into action and ran across to the estimated point of arrival quickly finding that he was ploughing through the mud regardless of posh breeks and the swanky shoes. At one point, he was observed to be hopping about on one foot then he knelt down with one knee of the posh breeks in the mud and stuck his arm down about 6 inches into the mud to pull out one of the swanky shoes. He then scooped out as much mud as he could quickly manage, put the shoe back on his foot and started running again. In the meantime P3 had rushed out to help but having foreknowledge of the airfield (his dad having been the CFI at one point) wasn't so rash and managed to avoid running into the worst of the mud (no sense of fun). Others ran across and arrived breathing heavily to look down to see that both of the aviators were alive and well with the aircraft the right way up and not standing on its nose. The aircraft was examined, within the confines of its predicament and no significant damage observed. The problem now facing the assembly was to get the aircraft back to its nice, comfortable hangar that night without inflicting further damage.

The cats pushed and pulled, and managed to release the aeroplane from the mud then pointed it at the fence where they had established the best crossing point was. Sadly best available was far from ideal in that although it was fairly easy to remove sufficient fence posts, flatten the barbed wire and push the aeroplane across the drop in level immediately beyond the fence and into the airfield was daunting. Necessity is the mother of invention and old pallets, planks, and any other filling materials to hand were brought into play. With Herculean effort, the aircraft was finally back in the airfield and the fence visually returned to its original condition. Sadly, the airfield's own bog now lay between the aircraft and the hangar. Nae bother to us said the local cats we'll just get our wee tractor down, tie a rope to the aeroplane and have it out of here in no time. Time had slipped by and it was now starting to get dark. The tractor was started up without any difficulty, driven part way down the runway and then turned off into the boggy area. It ploughed through the reeds and mud without significant difficulty and everyone sighed with relief when it was roped up to the aeroplane and started off slowly and steadily towards the higher firmer ground. At first, all went well until about halfway to solid ground the tractor's engine began to cough and splutter until the inevitable happened and it stopped. A diagnosis of the problem was quickly reached in that the tractor had run out of diesel. The local cats quickly confirmed that the only fuel station in the area was now closed for the night but they might have a wee drop of diesel to hand. The diesel was located and brought down to the tractor, poured into the tank, the fuel system bled and the tractor eventually restarted, although it wasn't running too well. The by now inevitable happened and in pitch darkness the tractor gave up with the aircraft still some distance from firm ground, where the tired helpers might just be able to start pushing it back to the hangar. Slarty's (t)rusty old Peugeot 106 was now brought into play in an atmosphere of desperation. With over 190,000 miles on the clock it was an experienced vehicle that knew what it was about. It was driven across the solid ground and pointed towards the stranded aircraft. A substantial rope was attached and the wee car requested to do its best. The smell of the clutch was pretty powerful but the Peugeot did its duty that night and pulled the aircraft back to the hangar. Everyone had had more than enough so we wrapped up and went home.

Now, Kindred Spirit lives in block of modern flats with written rules like 'don't hang your washing over the balconies' and unwritten rules like 'don't enter the building with dirty shoes' and 'remain well dressed at all times'. Kindred Spirit failed to meet any of these criteria as he stepped out of his car under cover of darkness. Only one thing for it, off with the shoes and trousers and make a dash for the lift hoping not to meet anyone. For the first time that night Kindred Spirit's luck held and he got into his flat unseen. Modern flats are not designed to cope with the mud in the volume that Kindred Spirit had brought home nor are there facilities for dealing with mud-filled shoes. Buy him a pint of beer sometime and he will no doubt regale you with his version of the evening and subsequent events from his point of view. Worth every penny.

Slarty got home just after one in the morning, couldn't be bothered eating anything and went off to his bed for a good 5 hours sleep. He wasn't the only one that night.

Day 2

P3, Slarty and Kindred Spirit thought that it was effectively all over bar the bit of tidying up that the Krinkly Bottomers could manage at their leisure, so they stayed at home. The Full Cat was made of sterner stuff and turned up the next evening to help. Diesel had been obtained, put into the tractor; the fuel system bled and the tractor spluttered into life to drag itself clear of the mire into which it had noticeably descended overnight. So they drove it across to help liberate the CFI's 4X4. A rope was attached with the tractor on as solid ground as could be managed. My sources tell me that failure wasn't marginal and was in fact quite a spectacular non-happening. The Krinkly Bottomers then put their heads together and came up with the idea of using the club glider winch to pull out the 4X4 after they had dug at least some of the mud away from the 4X4 to release some of the suction. After all, the winch was designed to winch wasn't it and it had a nice big Jaguar engine to ensure that it did the business. The winch was brought out and carefully positioned to reduce the length of cable in use but remain on solid ground with care taken to minimise the risk of the winch being dragged forwards rather than the 4X4 being dragged out. The winch was started and warmed up. The winch revved up, the 4X4 revved up, slack was taken up, the all out given and plenty of wellie applied to both devices. It is said that you could have heard the noises accompanying the disintegration of the winch half shaft in the next county. The 4X4 remained wholly unmoved and the residents of Krinkly Bottom village expanded their vocabulary.

The airfield cats now had: -

a) an abandoned vehicle that they were unable to move at the side of their runway

b) a winch that was inoperable for the foreseeable future

c) an SLMG that had a wee job or two to be carried out before it was going anywhere

d) darkness all around them, again.

Day 3

The Chief Feline Inspector (Krinkly Bottom Division) had a few favours to call in and brought in the heavy squad, in the form of a local farmer with an awfully big tractor with impressively large tyres. A bit more digging around the 4X4 was done and this time it was dragged free of the glutinous mud. Rumour has it that the 4X4 was never the same again and that the owner got shot of it soon afterwards.

Conclusions

Troubles don't always come in threes. They can be significantly more prolific.

I wouldn't have missed the fun for all the tea in China and am sorry that I didn't make it on days 2 and 3.

The Krinkly Bottom squad dealt with the series of problems and own goals by keeping on rising to every challenge thrown at them. I take my hat off to them.

Sadly, Krinkly Bottom closed as a gliding site shortly afterwards but the refugees continue to show their resilience within gliding.

All of the foregoing may just have been a dream after eating too much cheese. If you can't identify any or all of the characters in this tale then buy me a beer and I'll try to remember.

Another item in the post bag was a letter from the President of Edinburgh University Gliding Club, David Reitter:

Alain Chainey Award

Peter Williams, the longest-standing member of Edinburgh University Gliding Club (EUGC), has received the 2007 Alain Chainey award for outstanding contributions to university sports in recognition of his service to the club spanning several decades. Next year, the EUGC is celebrating its 50th anniversary and for more most of this time, Pete Williams has been member, supporter, valedictorian, instructor, maintenance expert, fundraiser, string- puller and honorary president of the club.

It was in the mid 1960's when Pete came up from London to work as deputy director and later director of the department that is now called Computing Services. Their offices were located in KB and behind Buccleuch Place, where there is now nothing but sheds and a Beetle garage, where Edinburgh's very first computer was housed. EUGC members still joke about whether the first computer really predated Pete, or the other way round.

In the early years, 1970, Pete took a hiking trip up to the Cairngorms, where he stayed at a youth hostel in Kingussie. Another chap staying there was Ken Stewart. Ken was the national coach of the British Gliding Association and he invited Pete to come along for his first glider flight. Much better than hill-walking, said Ken, and Pete agreed. Pete learned to glide at Feshiebridge, the same Highland gliding site that the Gliding Club goes to every now and then.

Pete soon became a gliding instructor. Instructors are accomplished pilots with many hundreds of hours of flying experience. For about two decades, Pete passed on his skills and taught new students to fly. In the genealogy of the club, Pete is basically the great-grandfather of the current generation - it goes like this: Pete taught JP. JP eventually became an instructor an taught Andy, and for a couple of years now, Andy has been teaching the current members.

So, in flying terms, there's a little bit of Pete in every one of us. Among Pete's other students was Kate Byrne. Having met in 1979 in the Gliding Club, they eventually got married. After a hiatus of a few years in the 80's, both came back to the club and now, Kate instructs for the club just like Pete used to.

Pete has always been a practical person. Most people outside the world of aviation would never think of taking an aircraft apart or inspecting its mechanics. Pete loves aircraft and has been at the centre of our glider maintenance for decades now. He is a sought-after source of knowledge at the 300-odd member club at Portmoak and at the university's Gliding Club.

It takes a lot to keep an aircraft flying over the course of 30 years. Gliders are elegant machines; they're rugged and can take hard landings. When they fall out of the sky and recover, they take enormous G-forces in various directions. But gliders are also delicate: handle it in the wrong places when you push one across the airfield, and you'll damage it. Once a year, gliders are thoroughly inspected for wear. Small punctures in the wings and fuselage need to be fixed, various hinges greased and instruments calibrated. It's a science, and know-how is key. We trust our lives in the technical expertise, and in this case, in Pete's expertise. And in a way, every time we fly our aircraft, there's a little bit of Pete keeping us in the air.

It is about three years ago when what was then our main training aircraft showed deterioration in the wooden structure that forms the wings. We had to take it out of service. Former university offices behind Buccleuch place, now turned into a shed, became the operating theatre for the glider's wings. In what we think was about 140 hours of work, Pete and some other club members took the wings apart and refurbished them. The big yellow glider flew again and has been used to train many new pilots since. Pete's friendship and long-standing support of his club are invaluable to the other members. The concrete help we have been getting in keeping the aircraft flying is worth gold to us: we could simply not afford to keep the aircraft if it wasn't for Pete.

University clubs are always in flux. Members come and go. Some of our oldest members have managed to fly with the club since their undergrad years and now drag on their PhD's, but their service pales compared to the time Pete has been with the club. When membership figures went down in the late nineties, Pete and Kate stuck around and kept the club alive. Members like Pete and Kate are those that you would wish every club.

When summer comes around, Pete and Kate can be seen at the national competition for pilots in university gliding clubs, the Inter-Uni Task Week, and of course their car happily tows one of the several gliders we take to the *"comp", all the way around the country. When a pilot has to put down the glider in some farmer's field, an hour later he can be sure that his crew will turn up to pick him up. Invariably, that was Pete at so many occasions. They'd take off the wings and carefully stow them in a trailer. As it happens, one of our trailers was designed and built by Pete.*

The Alain Chainey award is aimed at those people external to the University and its Sports Clubs, who selflessly give up their time to help the Clubs within the Sports Union, Clubs which without their contributions would not be able to function in the way that they do.

The Award is given in honour of Alan Chainey, who, whilst a member of the University infrastructure has always been happy to give up his time and work outside his remit, assisting individual Clubs, primarily the Men's Football and Golf Clubs, in numerous ways and with no extra reward for over 30 years.

I, supported by the current committee and certainly by dozens of active and former members of Edinburgh University Gliding Club, would like to congratulate our member, mentor and friend Peter Williams for the 2007 Alain Chainey Award.

It is fitting that the last "story" in this book is an absolute first and a truly historic, epic, flight. The Scottish Gliding Union has witnessed many magnificent men (and women) in their flying machines over the previous seventy years and, in some cases, has been instrumental in creating those magnificent pilots whose stories have been relayed in the pages of this book. This last story explains how John Williams flew up and down Scotland in his new Antares to claim a total distance of 1,200km and a prestigious European Award. John takes up the story for S&G:

1,200km in Scottish Wave

For a few years now, we've been exploring the potential of Scottish wave to go further and faster than before.

After Richard and Neville Allcoat extended the last leg of a "Portmoak milk-run" 500km flight to finish at Rufforth for 750km in their DG-500 in 1997 there have been more recent wave 750kms (Jack Steven, Roy Wilson, Kevin Hook and myself).

A little bit of competitive spirit, great gliders, better weather information (especially satpics) and airspace that's getting more difficult but still usable have given us a priceless opportunity to do things that have never been done before. Is there any other sport where old f**ts in their fifties can open up new records?

Trying to fit big tasks into Scotland has driven us to explore new territory. The far west of Mull at Bunessan did that for 750km tasks in northerly wave, but the country just isn't wide enough to fit in legs of more than 250km that are needed for a four-leg 1,000km. The only option was to use the full length of the country and go all the way to the north coast. Studying westerly wave patterns suggested that Cape Wrath was usually too cloudy to be a good turn point and John O'Groats too far from upwind hills – so the village of Tongue (TOG) with its prominent causeway part way between the two fitted the bill well.

When it turned out to be possible to reach it last October we sensed the possibility of a double out-and-return on the right day when daylight hours were longer. Colin Hamilton proposed new waypoints at Achnabourin (ACN – east and a fraction north of Tongue, now the most northerly on the UK turn-point list) and Glenfarg (GFG – just north of Portmoak) deliberately designed so that GFG-TOG-Loch Venachar (LVE)-ANB-GFG came out at 1003km.

During the first few days of April 2007 we watched as a big lozenge-shaped anticyclone built over central England, *leaving a freshening westerly over Scotland on Easter Sunday. With the newly created waypoints and that task so recently thought out, there could only be one declaration to make.*

A self-launch at 07:15hrs led straight into weak wave near Glenfarg (GFG). Not a classic sky, but enough wisps and gaps to encourage a start at 07:29 and to tiptoe towards the mountains. I'd mentally adjusted to it being a long day – maybe I'd need to stop and climb high to cross difficult clouded-over areas – although the forecast had also hinted at a weak front approaching later in the day, so maybe speed would matter too.

At Pitlochry it was evident that just to the west of track it was almost eight octas, while to the east it was blue. The workable energy line was right up the edge of the Class F advisory route between Glasgow and Inverness, so I did what the AIP recommends and informed Scottish of my presence in that area. Having a transponder helped. What didn't help was my asking if I should stay on ATC frequency and getting an "affirm" as a reply. There ended almost all the useful sharing of soaring info between gliders for nearly the whole day – a mistake I don't intend to repeat.

As I approached Feshiebridge I could begin to see stacked upper system lenticulars in the distance – a long way off but enough to create hope that conditions near Tongue might be good if I could get across the Great Glen. A well-defined gap just south of Inverness provided 10,000ft; and by Lairg there was a smile on my face from being gently sucked up into the first layers of that upper system. The lenticulars arched themselves along the contours of Loch Shin and led steadily beyond Tongue – justifying an overshoot of the turn point by some 15km to get into sector without leaving the lift.

A panorama of the wild coastline and wonderfully turbulent seascape off an aptly named Cape Wrath from

12,000ft was the bonus. Not the quickest first leg at 97km/h – but it was still only five past ten.

Thoughts now turned to the problem of getting to Loch Venachar, some 250km to the south. That would demand pushing to the south-west, but in that direction lay ever-increasing cloud cover. Thin veils of upper system moisture helped the decision-making by revealing a line that took me to 15,000ft over the Cromarty Firth, high enough to cross an amorphous bank of medium cloud which was obscuring Loch Ness and eventually (after losing 5,000ft) reach the next visible gaps near Dalwhinnie, where the lost height was restored.

With very few visible gaps it was time to throttle back, preserve height and make ground upwind. A ramped area of cloud north of Crianlarich helped me stay in the clear long enough to dive downwind, clip the Loch Venachar sector and get back to a promising energy line at Loch Tay at 7,800ft. This was the first 500km done in a little over four hours. No shortage of daylight then, but where was that forecast frontal feature?

I had a steady run north to Inverness with ATC apparently now getting used to my meanderings up the advisory route and I became almost immune to the regular R/T activity. I did take heed though when a power pilot called to inform ATC that the turbulence and mountain wave influence seemed stronger than forecast. I couldn't resist replying that I was at that moment climbing above the Black Isle at more than 1,100ft per minute. That climb was really well-placed and worth reaching 16,000ft in, as the view ahead looked most uncertain.

For the next 100km or so, it seemed like progress really slowed. Energy lines became much less distinct, headwind increased and cloud seemed to be forming in front of me faster than I could penetrate even with 95kts on the ASI. Yet again, I yielded to the curse of "upwinditis" and almost turned Tongue again before turning downwind through heavy sink to cut the Achnabourin sector, where mercifully there was still a gap to show an exit route to the south. I'd just made it ahead of that little insignificant line on the forecast chart – in reality, a nasty mass of building cloud cover – I think that even half an hour later the task might have been impossible; 750kms done in just over six hours and a good-looking sky on track. Maybe my luck was in. Beyond (and out over) the Moray Firth there were beautifully developed upper-system lenticulars – Easterton and Aboyne pilots should be revelling in those. Heading for the same Black Isle hotspot I'd used going north, I found 5kts to 17,500ft. Then Bruce Cooper came on frequency to tell ATC that he was crossing the advisory and I was bemused to hear them warn him of another glider at FL170 near Inverness – it is really weird to be talked about in the third person and not feel at liberty to pass on useful gliding info direct – oh, to be back on a real gliding frequency. With a tailwind component and plenty of height it took me only 32 minutes to get from Inverness to Perth, a distance of some 130km. At least the speed cameras on the A9 don't point upwards…

After 7hrs 36mins the declared task was done, and that last blast had brought the average speed up to 132km/h. It was still just after 3pm local time and Bishop Hill was working – should I land?

I tried to remember how much further south I'd have to go to extend Russell Cheetham's UK three-turnpoint distance record – was it about 20km? If so, Edinburgh airspace was in the way. Still, I would regret it forever if I didn't give it a go – there aren't many times in life when an opportunity like this one presents itself. So I climbed on the ridge at Bishop Hill – found a bit of weak wave and turned downwind towards the Firth of Forth – the wide part, but clear of the TMA. Even if I had to land out near the south coast of the estuary that ought to be enough to claim the distance record. Then a pleasant surprise: there was usable wave out over the sea from 4,500ft – no excuses for turning back then. Berwickshire had faint lines of lift and much cloud – so how far should I continue? Conflicting voices swapped places every minute in a tired and adrenaline-doped brain. Keep going – you could maybe reach Sutton Bank for 1,250km. Stop right now – you only need to nick one tiny piece of airspace and you'll blow the whole flight – haven't you done enough – and isn't your North of England half-mill map still in the car?

In the end I compromised, calculating that Jedburgh should be just through the 1,100km mark. I still had a chance of soaring home and that would leave the whole flight in Scotland. Somehow that seemed like the right thing to do.

The return home needed work to find energy lines – all seemed to be weakening and wanting to cut straight through the TMA – but, with some relief, I re-crossed the Forth and punched through some strong turbulence to land back at Portmoak after some ten and a half hours in the air and more than 1,200km of soaring flight.

It was a Hell of a day. Not the very best wave day, I think, but outstanding for me because I got lucky when I needed it and never had to wait for lift until I desperately needed it. I've never been able to say that about a long flight before – maybe some day it can happen again when I have more maps, a toothbrush and a cross-border visa with me.

That flight of John's was to earn him a prestigious European award – the OLC – organised by the German flying magazine "Aerokurier". Until that flight, previous winners had flown along the large continental countries with their large land masses. For the first time, the award-winning flight was conducted in the UK and, in particular, within the confines of Scotland.

The year had produced numerous epic flights for SGU members and visitors alike and three members proudly stepped up to collect their national awards at the BGA event, which was held at the Hellidon Lakes Hotel & Country Club near Daventry, at the beginning of 2008:

Santiago Cervantes
Rex Pilcher Trophy - first Diamond Distance of the year.
Kevin Hook
L DuGarde Peach Trophy – winner of the National Weekend Ladder
Manio Cup – for the fastest handicapped 300km.
De Haviland Trophy – for the greatest gain of height.
John Williams
BGA 1000km Trophy – for the fastest flight over 1,000km.
Wakefield Trophy – for the longest handicapped distance.
Enigma Trophy – winner of the Open National Ladder.
FAI 1,000km Diploma

Kevin Hook (left) and John Williams with their hoard
of trophies awarded for their efforts during 2007.

To be continued…

Gliding Certificates and Badges

The following information is an extract from the BGA publication - *Laws and Rules for Gliding Pilots* (sixteenth edition) and is aimed at helping the reader understand the requirements of various gliding badges and certificates.

"A" Badge
One solo circuit in a glider or motor glider in unpowered flight after the launch, followed by a satisfactory landing. An appropriate level of knowledge of rules of the air and local airspace restrictions must be demonstrated to the supervising instructor at the time of the first solo flight.

"B" Badge
A soaring flight of at least five minutes, at or above the previous lowest point after launch, followed by a satisfactory landing.

"Bronze (C)" Badge
A minimum of 50 solo flights or 10 hours in a glider with the following elements:
- Two soaring flights, each of 30 minutes duration, if launched by winch, car or bungee or each of 60 minutes after release from aerotow at a height not exceeding 2,000ft.
- A minimum of three flights in a dual controlled glider with a Full Rated Instructor who will be satisfied during the BGA Bronze Badge General Skills Test that the candidate has the ability to operate the glider within its limitations, complete all manoeuvres with smoothness and accuracy, exercise good judgement and airmanship, maintain effective lookout, and maintain control of the glider at all times…
- Two field landings into a field or, if a suitable field is not adjacent to the club site, into a marked area of the airfield.

The altimeter should be covered or the millibar scale offset for this practice…

- The candidate must pass the BGA Bronze Badge Theoretical Knowledge Test.

Cross-Country Endorsement

The requirements for this certificate are:

- Two soaring flights, one of at least one hour and one of at least two hours…
- …the ability select or reject fields as to their suitability for landing…
- …the ability to plan a triangle task of at least 100km… and to navigate to the satisfaction of the full rated instructor…

Silver (C) Badge

- A duration flight of not less than 5 hours from release to landing.
- A distance flight of not less than 50km…
- A height gain of at least 1,000 metres…

Gold Badge

- A duration flight of not less than 5 hours from release to landing.
- A distance flight of not less than 300km…
- A height gain of at least 3,000 metres…

Diamonds

- A pre-declared Goal Flight of not less than 300km…
- A distance flight of not less than 500km…
- A gain of height of not less than 5,000 metres…

Abbreviations

AGM	Annual General Meeting
Amsl	Above mean sea-level
ASI	Air speed indicator
ASL	Above sea level
Ass Cat	Assistant Categorised Instructor
ATC	Air Training Corps
BAC	British Aeroplane Company
BGA	British Gliding Association
bhp	Brake horse-power
BI	Basic Instructor
CFI	Chief Flying Instructor
DI	Daily Inspection
E	East
Eon	Elliots of Newbury
FGC	Fifeshire Gliding Club
Flt.Lt	Flight Lieutenant
fps	Feet per second
Full Cat	Fully Categorised Instructor
GC	Gliding Club
Km	Kilometres
kt	Knots (Nautical Miles per hour)
N	North
NE	North East
NW	North West
O/R	Out and Return
O/S	Ordnance Survey
RAeC	Royal Aero Club
RFD	Reg Dagnall Design
S	South
S&G	Sailplane & Glider
SE	South East
SGU	Scottish Gliding Union
SW	South West
TA	Territorial Army
TP	Turn point
uras	Ref to a web-based glider pilot network
Vne	Velocity never exceed
W	West

There are numerous references throughout the book to Turn Points (T/Ps) and, to give the reader an idea of the geographical locations of these, the following pages contain a list of all Scottish Turn Points and a few from Northern England.

Turnpoint	Latitude	Longitude	Code
Aberchirder	57 33.512 N	2 37.802 W	ABR
Aberfeldy	56 37.270 N	3 52.428 W	ABF
Aberfoyle	56 10.717 N	4 23.070 W	ABL
Abington	55 30.146 N	3 41.788 W	ABI
Aboyne	57 4.515 N	2 50.571 W	ABO
Aboyne Bridge	57 4.213 N	2 47.239 W	AB1
Aboyne Dinnet	57 4.301 N	2 53.397 W	ABD
Achnabourin	58 29.280 N	4 12.768 W	CAN
Achnasheen	57 34.694 N	5 4.810 W	ACH
Airdrie Southwest	55 50.472 N	4 1.473 W	ASW
Alford	57 14.272 N	2 43.527 W	AFD
Aln Bridge	55 24.323 N	1 51.793 W	ALB
Alnwick Moor SW	55 20.991 N	1 50.779 W	ALM
Alston	54 48.576 N	2 26.547 W	ALO
Altnaharra	58 17.210 N	4 26.578 W	AHA
Alva	56 9.166 N	3 47.916 W	ALV
Alyth	56 36.992 N	3 12.707 W	ALY
Amulree	56 30.612 N	3 47.301 W	AMU
Appleby	54 35.272 N	2 29.940 W	APP
Arbroath	56 34.851 N	2 36.909 W	ARB
Ardrishaig Lighthouse	56 0.738 N	5 26.646 W	ARL
Ardvasar	57 3.883 N	5 53.615 W	ARD
Aspatria	54 45.549 N	3 19.904 W	ASP
Auldgirth	55 9.549 N	3 42.466 W	AUL
Backwater Reservoir	56 43.018 N	3 13.312 W	BAC
Balado	56 12.581 N	3 27.702 W	BDO
Balfron	56 5.024 N	4 22.149 W	BAF
Ballachulish Bridge	56 41.283 N	5 10.928 W	BAB

Turnpoint	Latitude	Longitude	Code
Ballater	57 2.821 N	3 2.183 W	BTR
Ballinluig	56 38.952 N	3 40.317 W	BLG
Balloch	56 0.486 N	4 35.443 W	BLH
Balmaha	56 5.020 N	4 32.922 W	BMA
Banchory	57 2.841 N	2 30.042 W	BCY
Banchory East	57 3.201 N	2 27.337 W	BCE
Banchory West	57 3.495 N	2 33.385 W	BAW
Banff	57 39.774 N	2 30.781 W	BFF
Barrhill	55 6.094 N	4 45.806 W	BAH
Bassenthwaite Lake NE	54 40.429 N	3 11.957 W	BTE
Bassenthwaite Lake NW	54 40.094 N	3 14.692 W	BTH
Beadnell Harbour	55 32.996 N	1 37.604 W	BDN
Beattock	55 17.739 N	3 26.658 W	BET
Beauly	57 28.563 N	4 27.748 W	BUY
Bellingham	55 8.584 N	2 15.718 W	BEL
Bentpath	55 12.102 N	3 5.006 W	BEN
Berwick W	55 45.397 N	2 2.481 W	BER
Biggar	55 36.871 N	3 32.323 W	BGA
Blair Atholl	56 46.283 N	3 51.433 W	BLR
Blairgowrie	56 35.520 N	3 20.086 W	BGR
Blanchland	54 50.824 N	2 3.240 W	BLN
Braemar East	57 0.199 N	3 20.582 W	BMR
Braemar Stadium	57 0.298 N	3 24.360 W	BRS
Brampton	54 56.253 N	2 41.737 W	BRP
Brechin	56 43.412 N	2 38.872 W	BCN
Bridge of Avon	57 24.336 N	3 21.674 W	BOA
Bridge of Cally	56 38.806 N	3 24.204 W	BOC
Bridge of Gaur	56 40.688 N	4 26.909 W	BOG
Brora	58 0.707 N	3 51.202 W	BRR
Brough	54 31.485 N	2 19.113 W	BRH
Bunessan Pier	56 19.163 N	6 14.902 W	BSS
Buttermere	54 32.460 N	3 16.601 W	BTT
Cairnwell	56 52.784 N	3 25.259 W	CAI
Callander	56 14.576 N	4 13.045 W	CAD

Turnpoint	Latitude	Longitude	Code
Canonbie	55 4.794 N	2 56.932 W	CAO
Carlisle	54 53.709 N	2 53.210 W	CLL
Carrbridge	57 17.027 N	3 48.966 W	CBR
Carron	57 27.263 N	3 17.652 W	CRR
Carter Bar	55 21.346 N	2 29.062 W	CBA
Castle Carrock Dam	54 53.250 N	2 42.743 W	CCK
Charlestown NE	57 29.467 N	3 11.674 W	CTN
Charlestown of Aberlour	57 28.222 N	3 13.915 W	COA
Charterhall Field	55 42.438 N	2 22.634 W	CHR
Chollerford Bridge	55 1.760 N	2 7.629 W	CFB
Clova	56 50.506 N	3 6.415 W	CLO
Clunas	57 29.401 N	3 53.955 W	CLU
Cockermouth	54 38.931 N	3 20.542 W	CMO
Coldingham	55 53.137 N	2 9.466 W	COH
Coldstream	55 39.236 N	2 14.492 W	COD
Colt Crag Reservoir	55 5.832 N	2 7.087 W	COT
Comrie	56 22.418 N	3 59.237 W	COM
Connel	56 27.294 N	5 23.461 W	CNL
Corgarf	57 9.775 N	3 14.054 W	CGF
Corran Lighthouse	56 43.245 N	5 14.547 W	CLT
Coupar Angus	56 32.721 N	3 16.054 W	COU
Crask Bridge	58 11.092 N	4 30.700 W	CSK
Crathie Bridge	57 2.373 N	3 13.067 W	CTH
Creagan Bridge	56 32.839 N	5 17.473 W	CBG
Crianlarich	56 23.429 N	4 37.115 W	CRI
Crieff	56 21.983 N	3 51.122 W	CFF
Crinan	56 5.499 N	5 33.311 W	CRN
Crocketford	55 2.158 N	3 49.738 W	COF
Cupar	56 19.159 N	3 0.723 W	CUP
Currock Hill	54 56.065 N	1 50.456 W	CUR
Dallachy	57 39.437 N	3 3.958 W	DAL
Dallas	57 33.562 N	3 27.714 W	DLS
Dalmally	56 24.050 N	4 59.011 W	DAM
Dalston	54 50.873 N	2 58.848 W	DLT

Turnpoint	Latitude	Longitude	Code
Dalwhinnie	56 55.655 N	4 14.922 W	DWI
Derwent	54 51.622 N	1 57.344 W	DER
Dingwall	57 35.889 N	4 25.271 W	DIN
Dollar	56 9.727 N	3 40.599 W	DOL
Doune	56 11.206 N	4 3.684 W	DOU
Droma Bridge	57 45.162 N	5 0.737 W	DRB
Drumshade	56 38.547 N	3 1.613 W	DRU
Dufftown	57 26.643 N	3 6.954 W	DUF
Dumfries	55 5.158 N	3 36.638 W	DUM
Dunblane	56 11.164 N	3 57.958 W	DBN
Dundee	56 28.896 N	3 1.157 W	DDE
Dunkeld	56 33.823 N	3 35.130 W	DKD
Dunning	56 18.770 N	3 35.214 W	DNG
Dunoon	55 56.811 N	4 55.294 W	DNN
Duns	55 46.737 N	2 20.717 W	DUS
Easterton	57 35.226 N	3 18.497 W	EAS
Eastgate	54 44.639 N	2 4.509 W	EAT
Edzell	56 48.739 N	2 36.291 W	EDZ
Ennerdale Water W	54 31.470 N	3 24.627 W	EWW
Falgunzeon	54 56.584 N	3 44.445 W	FAL
Falkirk West	56 0.168 N	3 55.003 W	FAW
Fearnan	56 34.438 N	4 5.034 W	FEA
Ferness	57 29.659 N	3 44.247 W	FER
Feshie Airstrip	57 6.113 N	3 53.504 W	FE1
Feshie Descent Point	57 6.884 N	3 56.020 W	FE3
Feshie S	57 0.003 N	3 52.551 W	FE5
Feshie Start N	57 9.422 N	3 51.470 W	FE2
Feshie Watersports	57 7.003 N	3 55.273 W	FE4
Feshiebridge	57 6.100 N	3 53.671 W	FES
Fettercairn	56 51.093 N	2 34.499 W	FET
Finavon	56 42.318 N	2 49.643 W	FIN
Fordoun	56 52.182 N	2 24.742 W	FOD
Forfar	56 38.757 N	2 54.016 W	FFR
Fort Augustus	57 8.761 N	4 40.525 W	FOA

Turnpoint	Latitude	Longitude	Code
Fort William	56 49.566 N	5 5.207 W	FTW
Fort William NE	56 52.561 N	5 2.933 W	FNE
Fraserburgh	57 41.518 N	1 59.697 W	FBG
Freuchie	56 14.016 N	3 9.356 W	FRE
Gairlochy	56 55.028 N	4 59.249 W	GLY
Galashiels	55 36.207 N	2 46.803 W	GAA
Gallowfauld	56 32.907 N	2 56.356 W	GAL
Garten	57 14.898 N	3 45.152 W	GAR
Garve	57 36.890 N	4 41.362 W	GVE
Glen Dee Bridge	56 58.583 N	3 36.931 W	GDB
Glen Falloch	56 20.417 N	4 43.230 W	GFL
Glendevon	56 13.849 N	3 39.172 W	GLE
Gleneagles	56 16.966 N	3 45.064 W	GLN
Glenfarg Reservoir E	56 16.884 N	3 26.376 W	GFG
Glenfiddich Lodge	57 22.921 N	3 8.487 W	GFD
Glenforsa	56 30.921 N	5 54.903 W	GLF
Glenlatterach Dam N	57 33.713 N	3 20.880 W	GLT
Grains	54 34.908 N	2 12.391 W	GNS
Grantown	57 19.295 N	3 36.374 W	GTN
Grantown NE	57 20.483 N	3 33.215 W	GNE
Grantown S	57 15.891 N	3 39.479 W	GTS
Grantown SW	57 18.213 N	3 40.031 W	GWS
Gretna Services	55 0.594 N	3 5.268 W	GES
Haddington	55 57.644 N	2 47.416 W	HDD
Haltwistle	54 57.948 N	2 27.109 W	HWL
Hawick	55 26.114 N	2 45.153 W	HAK
Haydon Bridge	54 58.407 N	2 14.761 W	HBR
Helensburgh	56 0.085 N	4 44.242 W	HEL
Helmsdale	58 6.987 N	3 39.030 W	HDL
Heugh Head	57 11.821 N	3 1.055 W	HEU
Hexham	54 59.038 N	2 7.489 W	HEX
Huntly	57 26.481 N	2 47.707 W	HTY
Inchkinloch	58 21.858 N	4 23.874 W	INK
Insch	57 20.267 N	2 37.087 W	INC

Turnpoint	Latitude	Longitude	Code
Inverary	56 13.913 N	5 4.438 W	INV
Inverness	57 28.910 N	4 11.555 W	INS
Inverness East	57 28.681 N	4 3.755 W	INE
Inverness SE	57 25.110 N	4 8.061 W	ISE
Invershin	57 55.435 N	4 24.052 W	IVS
Jedburgh	55 30.345 N	2 34.338 W	JED
Keith	57 33.088 N	2 57.265 W	KTH
Kelso	55 35.706 N	2 26.000 W	KEL
Kempock Point	55 57.750 N	4 49.028 W	KEM
Kenmore	56 35.139 N	4 0.119 W	KMR
Keswick	54 36.572 N	3 8.481 W	KEK
Kielder Castle	55 13.994 N	2 35.263 W	KCA
Kielder Reservoir	55 10.705 N	2 27.621 W	KIE
Kilcreggan	55 59.066 N	4 49.230 W	KIL
Killin	56 27.766 N	4 19.190 W	KLN
Kinbrace	58 15.538 N	3 56.465 W	KIB
Kinclaven	56 31.590 N	3 22.083 W	KIC
Kincraig	57 7.564 N	3 55.580 W	KCG
Kingussie	57 4.689 N	4 3.153 W	KIG
Kinlochewe	57 36.269 N	5 18.215 W	KWE
Kinloss	57 38.950 N	3 33.722 W	KLS
Kippen	56 7.599 N	4 10.249 W	KIP
Kirkby Stephen Station	54 27.325 N	2 22.162 W	KST
Kirkharle	55 8.223 N	1 58.088 W	KIK
Kirkmichael	56 43.202 N	3 30.005 W	KML
Kirriemuir	56 40.433 N	3 0.401 W	KRM
Kyleakin	57 16.347 N	5 44.694 W	KYL
Laggan Bridge	57 1.122 N	4 17.021 W	LBR
Laggan Dam	56 53.379 N	4 40.408 W	LDM
Lairg	58 1.450 N	4 24.099 W	LAI
Lake of Menteith	56 10.466 N	4 18.105 W	LOM
Lanark	55 40.554 N	3 48.097 W	LRK
Lanchester	54 49.311 N	1 42.956 W	LCH
Latheron	58 17.014 N	3 22.029 W	LAT

Turnpoint	Latitude	Longitude	Code
Lattrig	54 36.844 N	3 6.949 W	LAR
Lauder	55 42.896 N	2 44.377 W	LAD
Ledmore	58 3.995 N	4 58.344 W	LMR
Lindores	56 20.313 N	3 11.566 W	LDR
Linn of Dee	56 59.293 N	3 32.735 W	LOD
Lismore	56 27.332 N	5 36.460 W	LIS
Loch Bradan East	55 15.159 N	4 27.768 W	LBE
Loch Eil West	56 51.559 N	5 20.987 W	LEL
Loch Errochty East	56 45.874 N	4 6.306 W	LER
Loch Gairloch SE	57 41.629 N	5 39.412 W	LOG
Loch Garry N	56 49.394 N	4 13.504 W	LGN
Loch Kinord	57 5.046 N	2 55.493 W	LOK
Loch Laggan NE	56 58.500 N	4 24.295 W	LGG
Loch Lochy NE	57 2.661 N	4 48.227 W	LOL
Loch Lomond Tarbet	56 12.211 N	4 42.657 W	LLT
Loch Morlich	57 10.061 N	3 42.135 W	LMO
Loch Moy	57 22.932 N	4 2.234 W	LMY
Loch Muick	56 55.656 N	3 11.458 W	LMU
Loch Mullardoch East	57 20.445 N	4 56.752 W	LMD
Loch Quoich East	57 4.284 N	5 11.023 W	LOQ
Loch Seilich N	56 58.046 N	4 2.195 W	LSN
Loch Venachar	56 13.713 N	4 15.706 W	LVE
Lochailort	56 52.680 N	5 39.983 W	LOA
Lochbuie	56 21.354 N	5 52.365 W	LBU
Lochearnhead	56 23.132 N	4 17.226 W	LEA
Lochgilphead	56 2.257 N	5 26.489 W	LGI
Lochgoilhead	56 10.487 N	4 54.195 W	LGO
Lochindorb Castle	57 24.352 N	3 42.507 W	LDB
Lochmaben	55 7.733 N	3 26.484 W	LMB
Lockerbie	55 7.131 N	3 21.702 W	LOC
Longtown	55 0.624 N	2 58.485 W	LTN
Low Lorton	54 37.127 N	3 18.904 W	LWL
Luncarty	56 26.855 N	3 28.347 W	LUN
Lussa Loch S	55 29.840 N	5 37.725 W	LUS

Turnpoint	Latitude	Longitude	Code
Maryport NE	54 43.234 N	3 28.901 W	MNE
Melmerby	54 43.818 N	2 35.952 W	MLM
Methven	56 24.958 N	3 34.868 W	MVN
Milfield	55 35.335 N	2 5.377 W	MIL
Milton	57 20.317 N	4 30.825 W	MLT
Mingary Pier	56 41.307 N	6 5.629 W	MIG
Mintlaw	57 31.509 N	2 0.089 W	MIN
Montrose	56 42.785 N	2 28.325 W	MTR
Moota Hill	54 42.820 N	3 19.022 W	MTH
Morpeth	55 11.449 N	1 42.922 W	MOP
Mossat	57 15.801 N	2 52.172 W	MOS
Moy Lodge	56 54.991 N	4 33.750 W	MOY
Muir of Ord	57 31.024 N	4 27.603 W	MOO
Murton	54 35.554 N	2 25.190 W	MUT
New Cumnock	55 24.070 N	4 10.970 W	NEC
New Deer	57 30.654 N	2 11.596 W	NED
New Galloway	55 4.872 N	4 7.891 W	NEG
Newmill	55 23.083 N	2 51.753 W	NEM
Norham Bridge	55 43.139 N	2 10.549 W	NBR
Oban Airfield	56 27.911 N	5 23.984 W	OBA
Oban Station	56 24.728 N	5 28.458 W	OBN
Ousby E	54 42.351 N	2 34.758 W	OUS
Oxton	55 46.275 N	2 47.282 W	OXT
Peebles	55 39.075 N	3 11.565 W	PEE
Penrith	54 39.191 N	2 45.612 W	PEI
Penrith East	54 40.088 N	2 41.712 W	PIE
Penwhirn Reservoir	54 59.023 N	4 55.506 W	PWN
Perth	56 22.797 N	3 24.527 W	PTH
Pitlochry	56 41.964 N	3 44.429 W	PLY
Pitsligo	57 35.290 N	2 11.289 W	PGO
Port Appin	56 33.277 N	5 24.621 W	PPP
Portmoak Caravan Site	56 11.558 N	3 19.957 W	PCS
Portmoak Clubhouse	56 11.328 N	3 19.311 W	POR
Potarch Bridge	57 3.905 N	2 38.932 W	POA

Turnpoint	Latitude	Longitude	Code
Powburn	55 26.881 N	1 54.544 W	POW
Rannoch Station	56 41.153 N	4 34.601 W	RAN
Rattray Head	57 36.616 N	1 48.994 W	RHD
Rhossdhu House	56 4.234 N	4 37.989 W	RHO
Rhynie	57 19.923 N	2 50.027 W	RNI
Rosneath	56 0.338 N	4 47.629 W	RSN
Rosthwaite	54 31.549 N	3 8.962 W	RTH
Rothbury	55 18.600 N	1 54.610 W	RBY
Rothes	57 31.890 N	3 12.505 W	ROH
Rothes NE	57 33.065 N	3 8.444 W	ROE
Rothesay	55 50.253 N	5 3.255 W	RSY
Roybridge	56 53.443 N	4 50.462 W	RBR
Selset Reservoir	54 35.362 N	2 7.649 W	SEL
Silloth	54 51.618 N	3 23.085 W	SLL
Skelling Farm	54 41.876 N	2 35.002 W	SKF
Smailholm Tower	55 36.256 N	2 34.559 W	SMA
Spean Bridge	56 53.582 N	4 55.202 W	SPE
Spey Dam	57 0.670 N	4 20.186 W	SPD
Spinningdale Bridge	57 52.623 N	4 14.190 W	SPN
Spittal of Glenshee	56 48.742 N	3 27.455 W	SPL
St Boswells	55 33.967 N	2 38.872 W	STB
St Fillans	56 23.489 N	4 6.253 W	STF
St Mary's Loch	55 29.541 N	3 12.283 W	SML
Stirling	56 8.314 N	3 55.070 W	STI
Stirling Northwest	56 8.070 N	3 58.273 W	SIW
Stirling South	56 4.651 N	3 55.216 W	SIS
Strachan	57 1.226 N	2 32.195 W	STR
Strathaven	55 40.521 N	4 3.869 W	SVN
Strathcarron	57 25.341 N	5 25.736 W	SCN
Strontian	56 41.755 N	5 34.281 W	SRN
Syre Bridge	58 22.288 N	4 13.919 W	SYB
Tarbert	55 51.935 N	5 23.829 W	TAR
Tarfside	56 54.368 N	2 50.155 W	TFS
Tarland	57 7.809 N	2 51.171 W	TAD

Turnpoint	Latitude	Longitude	Code
Teviothead	55 20.522 N	2 56.144 W	TEV
Thornhill	55 14.418 N	3 46.648 W	THN
Thornton	56 9.777 N	3 8.273 W	THO
Tindale	54 55.852 N	2 36.075 W	TDL
Todhead	56 53.015 N	2 12.917 W	THD
Tomatin	57 20.160 N	3 58.910 W	TIN
Tomintoul	57 15.182 N	3 22.360 W	TOM
Tongue	58 28.565 N	4 25.061 W	TOG
Troutbeck	54 38.176 N	2 56.941 W	TBK
Tulla Loch East	56 33.290 N	4 44.944 W	TUL
Tulla Loch West	56 32.384 N	4 48.812 W	TUW
Tummel Bridge	56 42.472 N	4 1.410 W	TUM
Turriff	57 31.998 N	2 27.686 W	TRF
Ullapool	57 54.275 N	5 9.624 W	UPL
Ullswater	54 36.677 N	2 49.931 W	ULL
Warcop	54 31.832 N	2 23.909 W	WAR
Wast Water E	54 27.409 N	3 15.870 W	WWE
Wast Water W	54 25.297 N	3 20.697 W	WWW
Waterbeck	55 5.117 N	3 11.096 W	WAB
West Lomond Hill	56 14.730 N	3 17.811 W	WLD
Whiteadder Reservoir	55 52.164 N	2 34.035 W	WHR
Wick West	58 28.281 N	3 18.073 W	WIK
Wigton	54 49.762 N	3 9.852 W	WGT
Wooler	55 32.862 N	2 0.721 W	WOO
Wooler East	55 31.907 N	1 50.084 W	WOL